CAMBRIDGE GREEK AND LATIN CLASSICS
IMPERIAL LIBRARY

GENERAL EDITORS
PROFESSOR E. J. KENNEY
Peterhouse, Cambridge
AND
PROFESSOR P. E. EASTERLING
University College London

APULEIUS

CUPID & PSYCHE

EDITED BY

E. J. KENNEY

*Emeritus Kennedy Professor of Latin
in the University of Cambridge*

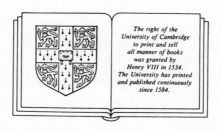

The right of the
University of Cambridge
to print and sell
all manner of books
was granted by
Henry VIII in 1534.
The University has printed
and published continuously
since 1584.

CAMBRIDGE UNIVERSITY PRESS

CAMBRIDGE

NEW YORK   PORT CHESTER

MELBOURNE   SYDNEY

Published by the Press Syndicate of the University of Cambridge
The Pitt Building, Trumpington Street, Cambridge CB2 1RP
40 West 20th Street, New York, NY 10011, USA
10 Stamford Road, Oakleigh, Melbourne 3166, Australia

First published 1990

Printed in Great Britain at the University Press, Cambridge

British Library cataloguing in publication data

Apuleius, Lucius
Cupid & Psyche. – (Cambridge Greek and Latin Classics:
Imperial Library).
I. Title   II. Kenney, E. J. (Edward John)
873.01

Library of Congress cataloguing in publication data applied for

ISBN 0 521 26038 8 hardback
ISBN 0 521 27813 9 paperback

BT

CONTENTS

Frontispiece   Amor and Psyche by Pierre Paul Prud'hon. British Museum, London. Reproduced by courtesy of the Trustees

Preface		*page* vii
Abbreviations and references		ix
Introduction		1
1	*The author*	1
2	*The book*	2
3	*The 'message' of the* Metamorphoses	6
4	*The story of Cupid and Psyche*	12
	(*a*) *Significance*	12
	(*b*) *Sources and models*	17
	(*c*) *Narrative voices*	22
	(*d*) *The conduct of the story*	24
	(*e*) *A note on allegory*	27
5	*Style and language*	28
6	*The text*	38

APVLEI METAMORPHOSEON LIBRI IV 28 – VI 24: text and facing translation	39

Commentary		116
Works cited by short title		226
Indexes		238
1	*Latin words*	238
2	*General*	240

PREFACE

This edition was commissioned in 1983, but its *origo initialis* is to be sought in lectures delivered as long ago as 1979. Ten years indeed is none too long for the task of writing a commentary on *Cupid & Psyche*. As I have repeatedly read and brooded over this short text, I have been made ever more keenly aware both of its richness and subtlety and of the impossibility of doing it anything like justice except at inordinate length and expenditure of time. From the first of these extravagances I am saved by the limitations imposed on this series; from the second by a cherished and comforting slogan of the late Sir Moses Finley: 'If it's more right than wrong, let it go.' Here then it goes, hoping that the condition in that sentence will seem to competent critics to have been met.

In that event, a proper proportion of the credit must go to those friends and colleagues who have of their kindness contributed information and constructive criticism. The Introduction and Commentary have been read in draft by Professor Easterling and Dr R. L. Hunter; and the Translation by Professor Easterling. To their comments and suggestions I owe substantial improvements of both matter and presentation. I must also thank for helpful advice Professor W. S. Allen, Professor W. G. Arnott, Dr A. M. Bowie, Professor M. F. Burnyeat and Dr Paula James. Dr Klaus Kruse of the *Thesaurus Linguae Latinae* has dealt patiently and comprehensively with my enquiries about Apuleius' vocabulary. I am greatly obliged to Professor W. S. Watt for his generous permission to print a number of unpublished conjectures on the text. The debt which I owe to Mrs Hazel Dunn for typing the text and (twice) reducing the Commentary to order is one which can be appreciated to the full only by the other Fellows of Peterhouse who have made similar trial of her professional skill and unfailing good humour.

J. Arthur Hanson's edition of the *Metamorphoses* in the Loeb Classical Library (2 vols, Cambridge, Mass. and London, 1989) came into my hands only after this book had gone to press. Having consulted it I have amended my translation in a handful of places and added a sentence to the Commentary.

January 1990   E. J. K.

As these pages pass through the press, I take the opportunity of re-cording my gratitude to Susan Moore for her expert and tactful sub-editing, to Roland Mayer for his care and vigilance in reading the proofs, and to Pauline Hire and Nancy-Jane Thompson for their encouragement and advice at all stages of the book's history.

April 1990   E.J.K.

ABBREVIATIONS AND REFERENCES

ANRW   (edd.) H. Temporini–W. Haase, *Aufstieg und Niedergang der römischen Welt*. Berlin–New York 1972– .

CHCL   (edd.) P. E. Easterling–E. J. Kenney, *The Cambridge History of Classical Literature*. I *Greek literature* 1985; II *Latin literature* 1982. Cambridge.

CIL   *Corpus Inscriptionum Latinarum*. Berlin 1863– .

GLK   (ed.) H. Keil, *Grammatici Latini*. 8 vols. Leipzig 1857–70, repr. 1961.

GP   (edd.) A. S. F. Gow–D. L. Page, *The Greek Anthology. The Garland of Philip and some contemporary epigrams*. 2 vols. Cambridge 1968.

HE   (edd.) A. S. F. Gow–D. L. Page, *The Greek Anthology. Hellenistic epigrams*. 2 vols. Cambridge 1965.

H–S   J. B. Hofmann–A. Szantyr, *Lateinische Syntax und Stilistik*. Munich 1965.

K–S   R. Kühner–C. Stegmann, *Ausführliche Grammatik der lateinischen Sprache*. 3. Auflage ed. A. Thierfelder. 2 vols. Leverkusen 1955.

LIMC   *Lexicon iconographicum mythologiae classicae*. Zurich–Munich 1981– .

LSJ   H. G. Liddell–R. Scott, *A Greek–English lexicon*. New edn H. S. Jones. 2 vols. Oxford 1940 and repr.

N–H   R. G. M. Nisbet–Margaret Hubbard, *A commentary on Horace: Odes Book I* 1970; *Book II* 1978. Oxford.

N–W   F. Neue–C. Wagener, *Formenlehre der lateinischen Sprache*. 3. Auflage. 4 vols. Leipzig–Berlin 1892–1905.

OCD[2]   (edd.) N. G. L. Hammond–H. H. Scullard, *The Oxford Classical Dictionary*. 2nd edn. Oxford 1970.

OLD   (ed.) P. G. W. Glare, *Oxford Latin Dictionary*. Oxford 1982.

Roby   H. J. Roby, *A grammar of the Latin language from Plautus to Suetonius*. Part II *Syntax*. London 1896.

TLL   *Thesaurus Linguae Latinae*. Munich 1900– .

TRF   (ed.) O. Ribbeck, *Tragicorum Romanorum fragmenta*. 3rd edn. Leipzig 1897.

References to the text of the *Metamorphoses* are by book, chapter and section as in Robertson's edition.

In the Commentary certain words are distinguished according to their degree of rarity:

* = first attested in Apuleius
† = attested only in Apuleius
‡ = *hapax legomenon*.

See also list of Works cited by short title, below pp. 226–37.

INTRODUCTION

1. THE AUTHOR

The principal sources for the life of Apuleius are his own works.[1] We do not know his other names; the *praenomen* Lucius given him in late MSS is due to inference from his apparent self-identification with the hero of his novel. He was born about A.D. 125 at Madaura in North Africa; identification of his birthplace is also due to inference from the *Metamorphoses* (11.27.9), but is almost certainly correct. In the *Apology* he merely describes it as *splendidissima colonia* (24, p. 28.19 Helm), but Augustine evidently found in his MS of *Met.* the same ascription of the work to 'Apuleius Platonicus Madaurensis' as in our oldest extant MS, F (*Civ. Dei* 8.14). His family was prosperous and could afford to send him for his education first to Carthage and then to Athens. His travels took him to Samos, into Phrygia, and to Rome, where he practised as a rhetorician.[2] On his way home he was detained by illness at Oea in Tripoli, where he met and married, at the instance of one of her sons, whom he had known at Rome, a wealthy widow, Pudentilla. The marriage was unwelcome to interested parties among the bride's relatives, who prosecuted A. on various charges, principally one of gaining Pudentilla's affections by magic. That magic was a subject of absorbing interest to him is evident from *Met.*; and though he was easily able to dispose of these particular accusations, his reputation as a wizard was established by the time of St Augustine and persisted into the Middle Ages and after.[3]

The brilliant rebuttal of the case against him in his *Apology* demonstrates both his learning and the literary and rhetorical gifts which had made him famous in Oea and which on his subsequent return to Carthage earned him a statue and a prestigious priesthood.

---

[1] See e.g. Schanz–Hosius–Krüger 100–2, Butler–Owen vii–xix, Walsh (1970) 248–51. For a lively account of the historical background to A.'s life see Haight ch. 1 'The age of the Antonines' (3–23).

[2] For how long is unclear. The final episodes of *Met.* take place at Rome, but though 'Lucius' is identified with A. himself at 11.27.9 (see below, p. 5), biographical inferences are hazardous: cf. Butler–Owen x–xii.

[3] Schanz–Hosius–Krüger 135, Haight 90–110.

It has been plausibly suggested that A.'s first language was Punic, the native African tongue.[4] It is a tempting speculation, for if it is true that 'an acquired language, when used by a virtuoso, tends to be more richly treated'[5] – a proposition borne out in our own literature by, for instance, Joseph Conrad and Vladimir Nabokov – the extraordinary richness and exuberance of the great novel from which our story is taken may indeed be a manifestation of 'African' Latinity, though not in the usual sense of this now generally discredited term.[6] From the *Florida*, a collection of excerpts from his speeches, it appears that he was active as a public figure at Carthage in the 160s, but there is no evidence for the date of his death.

2. THE BOOK

The *Metamorphoses* or *Golden Ass* was almost certainly written later than the *Apology*, to which Venus' remarks about country weddings sound uncommonly like an authorial reference (Commentary, 6.9.6n.), but there is little solid evidence for more precise dating.[7] The former title is that given the book in the MSS, the latter that expressly stated by Augustine to have been given it by the author: *Apuleius in libris, quos asini aurei titulo inscripsit* (*Civ. Dei* 18.18). 'The story of a splendid ass' (for this sense of *aureus* see *OLD* s.v. 5) seems less pointed than 'Transformations', with its inescapable reminiscence of Ovid's *Metamorphoses*.[8] The world of A.'s novel is every bit as uncertain and labile as the Heraclitean flux of the Ovidian universe: '... the essence of *The Golden Ass* is that no event or character in it can be trusted to remain what it may at first seem to be. Nothing that is said – even by the narrator – can be taken at face value.'[9] It is a work in eleven books, a number which is a literary curiosity in itself. From Ennius onwards the book – that is, the amount of text contained in a

[4] Gwynn Griffiths (1975) 59–60.
[5] Ibid. 64.
[6] See below, p. 28 n. 122.
[7] Schanz–Hosius–Krüger 103, Walsh (1970) 248–51, Gwynn Griffiths (1975) 7–14; cf. Comm. 6.4.4–5n.
[8] For A.'s debts to Ovid see further below, pp. 5, 7, 19, 23, 28–30.
[9] Tatum (1979) 21; cf. id. (1972) 310–13. On the title of the Greek original see below, p. 8.

papyrus *uolumen* –[10] was consciously treated by the Latin poets and many prose writers as a literary unit forming an integral part of larger symmetrical and balanced structures. Epic seems to favour schemes based on multiples of three: examples are Ennius' *Annales* (18 = 6 × 3),[11] Lucretius' *De rerum natura* (6 = 3 × 2),[12] and Virgil's *Aeneid* (12 = 6 × 2).[13] Within individual *libelli* the Augustan poets cultivated structures based on multiples of five: examples are Virgil's *Eclogues*, Horace's *Satires* I and *Epistles* I, Tibullus I (all 10) and, most elaborately, Ovid's *Amores* (3 books: 15 + 20 + 15 = 50 elegies). Of the extant Greek novelists Heliodorus (10) and Xenophon (5)[14] conform to the second pattern; Chariton and Achilles Tatius (8) and Longus (4) are at any rate in even numbers.[15]

A. can hardly have been unaware of or indifferent to such an anomaly. Close study of *Met.* shows him to have been self-consciously attentive to the whole range of traditional literary artifice. It seems more likely that the unusual structure is designed to draw attention to the special status of the 'extra' book, in which the story, as will be seen, takes an unexpected turn that has occasioned much debate.[16] This is not to say that Book XI was tacked on to the novel as an afterthought; the allegorical and symbolic organization of the whole composition is too well contrived and closely integrated for that.[17]

[10] *CHCL* II (= *The early Republic* (1983)) 15–16, 18.

[11] Skutsch (1985) 5–6.

[12] Kenney (1971) 12–13.

[13] Camps 51–60; cf. Statius' *Thebaid* and (as originally planned) Lucan's *De bello civili*. As it stands Silius' *Punica* is in 17 books, but it has been plausibly suggested that the intended number was 18, to correspond with Ennius' *Annales*.

[14] What we now have is an abridgement. According to the Suda the work was originally in ten books.

[15] It may or may not be significant that the Byzantine travesty of Achilles Tatius, *Hysmine and Hysminus*, is in eleven books. Other late examples of this number are Rufinus' translation and continuation of Eusebius' *Historia ecclesiastica* and Venantius Fortunatus' *Cain* (Heine 37 and n. 126); St Augustine's *Confessions* are in 13 books (ibid. n. 127).

[16] An imperfect analogy is perhaps to be found in the first book of Propertius, with 20 love-elegies + 2 *sphragis*-poems; cf. Skutsch (1963).

[17] For Pythagorean–Platonic explanations of the number eleven see Heller 332–9, Tatum (1982) 1101–2.

The story is told as a first-person narrative by one Lucius.[18] When it opens he is on the last stage of a journey to Hypata in Thessaly, the home of his mother's family, through which he is connected with the philosopher Plutarch. We soon learn that he is indiscreet, credulous, and inordinately curious about magic – hence his journey, since Thessaly was popularly thought of as the land of witchcraft. Books I–III recount his adventures at Hypata, which end by his being turned by mistake into a donkey. At this moment, before steps can be taken to turn him back into human shape by finding him roses to eat, there occurs one of the many violent and apparently unmotivated peripeties on which the plot of the novel hinges. A gang of robbers bursts into the house where he is staying, plunders it, and carries him off with the rest of the booty.[19] Brigandage is indeed prominent in the plots of the Greek romances; but the part played by this and other varieties of lawlessness in what purports to be a realistic contemporary setting is striking and perhaps at first surprising.[20] However, A. was not a social historian; his book is no more to be read as a documentary report on the actual state of Roman civilization than is *Tom Jones* on Fielding's England. What follows in Books IV–X is a portrayal of moral chaos, with Lucius adrift in it. 'The themes of adultery and revenge, and the effect of *fortuna* on other people's lives, are examined in ever greater depth and with a continually worsening cast of characters.'[21]

This then is the setting in which we follow Lucius, now the plaything of Fortune,[22] through a series of adventures in which he more than once comes face to face with death and undergoes much suffering. They end when he manages to escape from a climactically degrading predicament to spend the night on the sea-shore at Cenchreae, the port of Corinth. The interval between his transformation and his escape has been a year, and spring has come again,

[18] On the technical implications and possible pitfalls of this device see van der Paardt 78–9.

[19] 3.28.1 *nec mora, cum* ..., a recurrent formula: Comm. 5.6.1n.

[20] See Millar, esp. 71–2, 74–5. For banditry as part of the provincial way of life in early Imperial Asia Minor see Hopwood.

[21] Tatum (1969) 515. Cf. Heine 35–6 and below, pp. 10–11.

[22] On the role of Fortune in the novel see the articles of Fry and Roccavini and cf. Comm. 5.5.2n.

bringing roses with it. Now, in Book XI, the goddess Isis appears to Lucius in answer to his prayers and promises him relief, which is duly forthcoming. The first fifteen chapters of that book contain the most elevated writing in the novel; the sequel is curiously prosaic. This relates Lucius' final transformation – a literary one, into Apuleius himself[23] – and his subsequent further progress in Isiac–Osiriac observance. The account is detailed and circumstantial, and the work ends, with the narrator happily enrolled as a shaven-headed member of a college of priests 'founded in the time of Sulla' (11.30.5), on what to most readers must come as a distinct note of anticlimax.

The main narrative of Books I–X is interspersed with stories told by or about various characters encountered by Lucius on his travels.[24] The longest of these inserted tales, occurring near the middle[25] of the main part of the novel, is the story of Cupid and Psyche. It does not occupy a book or books to itself, but straddles the divisions between Books IV, V and VI in the manner of the complexes of episodes in Ovid's *Metamorphoses*;[26] and, as in Ovid, these divisions are used to mark important stages in the action and to focus attention on the contrasting situations of the heroine at each juncture.[27]

---

[23] This occurs with breathtaking insouciance in the report of a dream in which Osiris has referred to the new proselyte as *Madaurensem ... admodum pauperem* (11.27.9). The passage has occasioned vigorous controversy and several attempts have been made to emend the text, but there is no solid reason to question the obvious implication: that the experiences of 'Lucius' are to be read as, in some sense, autobiographical. Cf. above, n. 2.

[24] On these 'Milesian' insertions see below, p. 7.

[25] For the importance of centrality as an organizing principle in Latin poetry see Kenney (1971) 13 and n. 2, Fowler (A.) 62–5. A.'s evident awareness of his poetic predecessors, esp. Virgil and Ovid, might be expected to embrace this aspect of their art. But cf. also Anderson 82, noting that A. 'has positioned his myth of Love and Soul in the centre, like the myths of Soul in the *Phaedrus* and Love in the *Symposium*'.

[26] As noted by Scobie (1973) 72.

[27] 5.1.1 *Psyche ... suaue recubans, tanta mentis perturbatione sedata, dulce conquieuit* ~ 6.1.1 *interea Psyche uariis iactabatur discursibus, dies noctesque mariti uestigationibus intenta et ... inquieta animi.* Similarly Books VI, VII, VIII and IX all break off 'on a note of suspense with ... Lucius involved in a dangerous situation' (Scobie (1978a) 50).

3. THE 'MESSAGE' OF THE *METAMORPHOSES*

It is generally, though not unanimously,[28] agreed that there is a good
deal more to *Met.* than the preceding summary would indicate and
that A. intended to convey in it some kind of allegorical message. His
introductory chapter does not immediately point the reader in this
direction:[29]

> At ego tibi sermone isto Milesio uarias fabulas conseram
> auresque tuas beniuolas lepido susurro permulceam, modo si
> papyrum Aegyptiam argutia Nilotici calami inscriptam non
> spreueris inspicere, figuras fortunasque hominum in alias
> imagines conuersas et in se rursum mutuo nexu refectas ut
> mireris. exordior. 'quis ille?' paucis accipe. Hymettos Attica
> et Isthmos Ephyraea et Taenaros Spartiatica, glebae felices
> aeternum libris felicioribus conditae, mea uetus prosapia est;
> ibi linguam Atthidem primis pueritiae stipendiis merui. mox
> in urbe Latia aduena studiorum Quiritium indigenam ser-
> monem aerumnabili labore nullo magistro praeeunte aggressus
> excolui. en ecce praefamur ueniam, siquid exotici ac forensis
> sermonis rudis locutor offendero. iam haec equidem ipsa uocis
> immutatio desultoriae scientiae stilo quem accessimus respondet.
> fabulam Graecanicam incipimus. lector, intende: laetaberis.
>
> (1.1)

> Now, in this Milesian discourse I propose to string together
> various stories for you and to soothe your well-disposed ears with
> an agreeable murmur – always providing you are not too proud

---

[28] The weightiest dissentient voice is that of Perry, who regards *Met.* as 'a
story dramatically told at length for its own sake as entertainment, not as
information or for the purpose of illustrating something else' (248; cf. 371
n. 107). Cf. Scobie (1969) 30–1, Heine 33–5, Sandy (1978) 124–9, Scobie
(1973) 64–83, Heiserman 145–66, esp. 162 'a comic novel that is not
governed by any formulable religious or moral idea'. Further bibliography at
MacKay 480 n. 1. It is interesting that no scholar could apparently be found
by Hijmans–van der Paardt (qq. v. vii) to defend the 'separatist' position.

[29] It is impossible to explore here all the problems raised by this much-
discussed passage. See e.g. Reitzenstein 48–55 = 124–30, 66–73 = 140–7,
Smith 514–20, Scobie (1973) 65–8, Wright (C. S.), Scobie (1975) *ad loc.*,
Mason (1978) 1–2, Scotti, Harrauer, Lausdei 232–7, Winkler 180–203.

to look at Egyptian paper written on with the acuteness of a reed from the Nile – to make you marvel at men's shapes and fortunes changed to other appearances and then changed back again.[30] Let me begin. 'But who is this fellow?' Briefly: Attic Hymettus, the Isthmus of Corinth, and Spartan Taenarus, happy lands immortalized in yet happier books, these are my ancient ancestry. It was there that I served my novitiate in arms to the language of Athens. Then, coming to Rome, by painful labour with no teacher to show me the way I tackled and mastered the native tongue of Roman scholarship. Thus I excuse myself in advance if, as an unpractised speaker of a strange language, that of the courts, I give offence. As a matter of fact this very linguistic change is appropriate to the kind of writing I have undertaken here – this art of changing horses at the gallop. It is a Grecian story that I now begin. Your attention, reader: you will be pleased.

On the face of it what is promised here is entertainment (*lepido* . . . *susurro, ut mireris, laetaberis*)[31] and a parade of literary *tours de force*.[32] The elaborate apologia for the shortcomings of the writer's training and equipment for his task is a rhetorical commonplace not to be taken at face value. What nowhere appears is any hint of instruction or edification; indeed the promise to string together stories 'in a Milesian discourse' strongly implies the reverse. Aristides of Miletus (fl. *c.* 100 B.C.) was the author of a collection of stories, the *Milesiaca*, which were translated into Latin by Sisenna early in the first century B.C.[33] Their unimproving character is illustrated by the story that copies found in the baggage of Roman officers after the defeat of Crassus in

[30] For the Ovidian resonances in this sentence see Scotti 43–55.

[31] The word *lepidus* recurs to describe several of the stories inserted in the novel, not least *Cupid & Psyche*: 1.2.6, 1.20.5, 2.20.7, 4.27.8, 9.4.4; cf. 9.14.1 *fabulam . . . bonam prae ceteris* (Fredouille 23 n. 4). For the pleasure to be got from reading about other people's haps and mishaps cf. Cicero's famous letter to Lucceius (*Ad fam.* 5.12.4): *nihil est . . . aptius ad delectationem lectoris quam temporum uarietates fortunaeque uicissitudines.*

[32] The *desultor*'s act was to leap from horse to horse in full gallop. For the stylistic implications of the phrase *desultoriae scientiae* see e.g. Walsh (1970) 64–5, Smith 517–19, Scobie (1973) 67–8, (1975) *ad loc.*

[33] On A., Aristides and Sisenna see Reitzenstein 48–73 = 124–47.

53 B.C. afforded the Parthians material for unflattering deductions
about the moral fibre of the Roman army (Plutarch, *Crassus* 32).
Many of the inserted stories in *Met.* are precisely of this kind, repre-
sentatives of a traditional genre as old as the art of story-telling, the
locker-room anecdote, represented in later literature by such collections as Poggio's *Facetiae* or Balzac's *Contes drolatiques*.[34] Similar insertions are a feature of Petronius' *Satyricon*.[35]

The narrative framework into which these stories are incorporated
is announced in the last sentence of the prologue as a 'Grecian' story,
fabula Graecanica.[36] This story was not of A.'s own devising. Transmitted among the works of the Greek satirist Lucian (fl. *c.* A.D. 165)
is a piece entitled Λούκιος ἢ Ὄνος, *Lucius or The Ass*. This tells
in the first person the story of one Lucius who is changed into a
donkey by the same sort of mischance as befell A.'s hero and after
various adventures manages to change himself back again: in short a
briefer version of *Met.* without *Cupid & Psyche* or any of the other
inserted stories.[37] We also learn from the *Bibliotheca* of the Greek
scholar Photius (*c.* A.D. 850) that there once existed a book, distinct
from the Lucianic Ὄνος, which he describes as Λουκίου
Πατρέως Μεταμορφώσεως λόγοι διάφοροι, *Various tales of Metamorphosis by Lucius of Patrae*. It is generally accepted that A.'s book is
an adaptation, and the Lucianic Ὄνος an abridgement, of this
lost work. On such subsidiary questions as whether the 'Milesian'
stories in A. also figured in his model or whether he introduced them
himself (possibly taking a leaf from Petronius' book), debate continues.[38] Given their cardinal role in underpinning the central
allegory of *Met.* (see below), it seems most likely that they were an

---

[34] For the extraction and retelling of these stories by Boccaccio and others
after the rediscovery of *Met.* by Zanobi da Strada see Haight 111–15, Scobie
(1978*b*).

[35] Cf. Walsh (1978) 19–21.

[36] Cf. Varro, *L.L.* 10.70–1, distinguishing between *Graecus* 'Greek' and
Graecanicus 'of Greek origin'; but it is possible that A. chose the word simply as
a slightly recherché synonym for *Graeca*.

[37] See the useful comparative schema at Walsh (1970) 147.

[38] On this and on other matters of dispute, such as the length of the original
and the authorship of the Ὄνος ascribed by the MSS to Lucian see e.g. van
Thiel (summary at Walsh (1974)), Mason (1978) 1–4, Scobie (1978*a*) 43–6.
On A.'s relationship to Petronius see Scobie (1969) 101–4, Walsh (1978).

Apuleian innovation. That he found the story of Cupid and Psyche in his sources in anything like its present form is, for reasons which will become clear, scarcely conceivable.[39]

The only other hint of A.'s intentions offered by the prologue is the curious insistence on things Egyptian in the description of the work as *papyrum Aegyptiam argutia Nilotici calami inscriptam*, 'Egyptian paper written on with the acuteness of a reed from the Nile'. This has been plausibly taken as a hint of the ultimate source of the ass-story: in Egyptian cult the ass, as symbolic of the evil Seth and Typhon, was the enemy of Isis.[40] In that case, *argutia* must be read as referring to content as well as style: the story itself is 'clever', its import to be grasped fully only by readers who are themselves *arguti*.[41] Such readers may be alerted by these apparently anodyne phrases to the possibility that there will be more in what follows than at first sight meets the eye.

Many critics have felt that A. goes on to make it uncommonly easy for even the *doctus lector* to overlook any such deeper significance as may be here hinted at.[42] Though much enriched and complicated by the inserted tales, the basic plot of *Met.* – echoed, as will be argued, by the plot of *Cupid & Psyche* – is essentially identical to that of the surviving Greek romances and the *Satyricon*: lovers separated and reunited.[43] The narrative is varied and eventful, replete with sex, magic, violence, and robust (often black) humour. The style is vivid, highly-coloured and arresting, appealing alike to the reader uncritically in search of enjoyment and to the scholar who is equipped to

[39] Cf. Walsh (1970) 197, Gwynn Griffiths (1978) 145.

[40] Gwynn Griffiths (1975) 24–6, (1978) 145–6, Tatum (1979) 43–7. The quest is taken further afield by e.g. Scobie (1975) 38–41, Anderson 198–210.

[41] See *OLD* s.v. 6a and cf. e.g. Hor. *A.P.* 364 *iudicis argutum ... acumen*.

[42] Cf. e.g. Sandy (1978) 124–9.

[43] Kenney (1990) 197. The point is obvious for *Cupid & Psyche*, rather more complex for Lucius, whose metamorphosis and subsequent adventures may be read as symbolizing his spiritual separation from an understanding of the true nature of love; cf. Walsh (1970) 174–5, Fredouille 28. For a useful conspectus of the basic plot of the romances and the changes rung on it by the individual novelists see Hägg ch. 2 'The ideal Greek novel' (5–80), with interesting illustrations. For detailed similarities between *Cupid & Psyche* and the romances see Comm. *passim*.

identify and appreciate the allusions to and motifs borrowed from
A.'s literary predecessors, especially the Latin poets.[44] A. never
bores.[45] The reader who simply allows himself to be swept onwards
by the swift current of his narrative and the kaleidoscopic sequence of
Lucius' adventures is thus all the more disconcerted to find, on
arriving at Book XI, that the resolution of the hero's plight is apparently attended with serious philosophical and religious implications.[46] It is not merely Lucius' body but his soul which, by the grace
of Isis, is released from bondage into a higher service in which,
paradoxically, the only true freedom is to be found. 'His transformation into an ass . . . is a metaphor for the fallen state of unredeemed
man.'[47] The casual reference by 'Lucius' to the family connexion with
Plutarch (1.2.1) suddenly takes on retrospective significance: he has,
belatedly and by the hard way, proved himself worthy of the philosophical heritage which his earlier conduct disgraced.

Careful reading of A.'s text shows that this revelation has been
sedulously prepared: '. . . the reader who can put down the book still
satisfied by the artless description of the first chapter has ignored the
patterning of anecdotes and adventures which culminate in the
dramatic climax of religious conversion to Isis'.[48] Especially significant are the words of the priest to Lucius after his retransformation:

> Multis et uariis exanclatis laboribus magnisque Fortunae
> tempestatibus et maximis actus procellis ad portum Quietis et
> aram Misericordiae tandem, Luci, uenisti. nec tibi natales
> ac ne dignitas quidem uel ipsa qua flores usquam doctrina
> profuit, sed lubrico uirentis aetatulae ad seruiles delapsus
> uoluptates curiositatis improsperae sinistrum praemium
> reportasti.   (11.15.1)

Having endured many and various sufferings and having been
tossed by the fierce tempests and stormy winds of Fortune, at

[44] Helm (1914), Herrmann 14–24, Walsh (1970) 53–66, Mason (1978)
7–12 (Greek authors), Comm. *passim*.

[45] At least until 'Lucius' enters the light of common day at 11.17. After
that the going gets decidedly heavy.

[46] '. . . comme si les aventures de *Tom Jones* s'achevaient sur la conclusion
du *Pilgrim's Progress*' (Fredouille 8).

[47] Heller 332.

[48] Walsh (1970) 142; cf. Sandy (1978) 129–37.

last, Lucius, you have come to the harbour of Peace and the altar of Pity. Your birth and rank and learning were of no avail to you, but through youthful instability you sank to servile pleasures and earned the bitter reward of an ill-starred curiosity.

The second sentence of this speech is a succinct summary of Books I–III of *Met.* and of the events leading to Lucius' metamorphosis. His downfall and his many ordeals were the result of his degrading sensual infatuation with the slave-girl Photis and of the debased curiosity which led him to pry into magic instead of devoting himself to the liberal studies and beneficent mysteries for which his upbringing had qualified him. Read or reread in the light of the priest's words, every incident and every story in Books I–III is revealing of Lucius' obdurate perseverance in the wrong path.[49] An especially striking case, deserving mention here since it is echoed in *Cupid & Psyche* (Comm. 5.2.3n.), is the episode in which Lucius is warned against inopportune curiosity by coming across a group of statuary depicting Actaeon spying on Diana, a warning which is then reinforced both implicitly and explicitly by his kinswoman Byrrhena.[50] This and several other such hints[51] were clearly meant to guide the alert reader to an understanding of the deeper meaning of the novel as the drama of a soul lost and saved.

[49] Tatum (1969), Walsh (1970) 176–80, Sandy (1972–3), Scobie (1978a) 50–2, van der Paardt 80–4. It must, however, be admitted that the stories in Books VI–X, after *Cupid & Psyche*, cannot so easily be related to the theme of Lucius' fall and redemption. To pursue this subject in detail would take us too far afield, but it is worth pointing out that there is no question of authorial inadvertence here. Lucius' failure to draw any conclusions relevant to himself from the moral chaos in which he finds himself is so glaring that A. must have expected the reader to notice it. Indeed, in the celebrated scene in the mill (9.12–13) he seems to go out of his way to underline the point (cf. Penwill 69, Heine 31, Scobie (1978a) 53). Cf. below, p. 14.

[50] 2.4–5; cf. esp. 2.4.10 *lapidis Actaeon simulacrum* curioso optutu *in deam proiectus iam in ceruum ferinus*; 2.5.1 *'tua sunt' ait Byrrhena 'cuncta quae uides'*, 2.6.1 *at ego curiosus alioquin* etc. Cf. e.g. Wlosok 73–4, Walsh (1970) 178, Tatum (1979) 38–9.

[51] Even Photis warns Lucius that by involving himself with her he may get more than he bargains for: *'heus tu, scholastice' ait 'dulce et amarum carpis. caue ne nimia mellis dulcedine diutinam bilis amaritudinem contrahas.'* On the face of it this is no more than the age-old paradox of Love as bittersweet, Ἔρως γλυκύπικρος (Comm. 4.31.1n.); in the sequel it is only too accurate a prophecy. The *inremunerabile beneficium* which Lucius begs of Photis in the

4. THE STORY OF CUPID AND PSYCHE[52]

(a) Significance

That this longest and most elaborate of all the inserted stories in *Met.*
has a special significance for the allegorical interpretation of the novel
as a whole is accepted by most recent critics.[53] The main arguments
for this view may be summarized as follows.

(i) The insetting of 'a story within a story . . . designed to illuminate
the larger whole'[54] was a technique used by Greek poets from Homer
onwards but particularly cultivated by the Alexandrians. It was
bound to be familiar to any educated writer, especially from the
famous example in Catullus' *Peleus and Thetis*. A. shows himself

---

shape of the magic ointment which is to change him into a bird (3.22.5) is
eventually granted to him in the shape of contemplation of the divine image of
Isis (11.24.5). This cannot possibly be passed off as coincidence: *inremunerabilis*
is attested nowhere else in Latin. (Fredouille (11) notes the correspondence
but curiously fails to appreciate its significance; cf. ibid. 14 on Psyche's prayer
to Juno (6.4.1–3) and Lucius' to Isis (11.2).) Even the reminiscence of Photis
in the description of Isis' hair (2.9.7 ∼ 11.3.4) may well be deliberate: 'the
suggestion of Fotis' beauty being present in the august deity indicates that
Lucius' earlier misconceived attraction has been sublimated and transferred to
a meaningful object – to the goddess who can benefit Lucius rather than lead
him to disaster' (Smith 529). Cf. Sandy (1978) 136 on Photis as 'a kind of
priestess'; and on the implications of her name de Smet 617–19: '[it] does not
accidentally consist of two syllables, ending on -is . . . she is the direct opposite
of Isis, the truth and the inner light' (619), '. . . the encounters of the "I" with
the servant-girl are the anti-pole of his encounters with Isis' (623).

[52] At this point the reader who does not already know the story will find it
useful to refer to the translation before proceeding.

[53] See e.g. Nethercut, Schlam (1968), Tatum (1969) 508–14, (1979),
Walsh (1970), Scobie (1978a) 53, van der Paardt 81, Gwynn Griffiths (1978)
145–51. The length and positioning of *Cupid & Psyche*, if nothing else, rules
out any idea (Fredouille 27) that it relates only to its immediate setting, the
story of Charite. 'The removal of the tale of Cupid & Psyche from the centre of
the work would leave the romance broken-backed' (Scobie (1978a) 48). It
is true (Fredouille 26–7) that the Platonic emphases of *Cupid & Psyche* are
not reflected in the Isiac episodes, but this is less a matter of 'un autre type
d'expérience spirituelle possible' than the use of a different style of imagery to
express the same idea, the progress of the soul towards a mystical union.
Stabryła's reading of the story in structural terms as 'a metaphor of
Charite's career' (271) similarly underplays its role in the novel.

[54] Walsh (1970) 190.

throughout *Cupid & Psyche* so deeply conversant with the Alexandrian literary tradition, both as known to him directly and as mediated through his Latin models, that it is inconceivable that he could have employed the technique without intending it to carry its full charge.[55] It is, that is to say, inherently unlikely on purely literary-historical grounds that the story can have been meant to be read as autonomous entertainment.

(ii) The story is related in Lucius' hearing by a drunken old woman, who tells it to Charite, prisoner of the gang of bandits, to take her mind off her troubles and who introduces it with the words *sed ego te narrationibus lepidis anilibusque fabulis protinus auocabo* (4.27.8). This clearly echoes the prologue to the novel itself[56] and can only be meant to suggest an analogy between the effects to be expected in each case: just as Lucius will not grasp that these *narrationes lepidae* are relevant to his own situation until after he has been saved by Isis, so the reader of *Met.* will not realize that instruction lurks beneath the promised *lepidus susurrus* until he reaches the same place in his reading as Lucius in the story.[57] Even those who do not fully take this ironic point should still deduce that what follows may have more than immediate relevance.

(iii) There are notable similarities between Lucius and Psyche as hero and heroine of their respective stories. Both are of distinguished origins, which avail them nothing, Lucius a member of the Roman

---

[55] Kenney (1990) 197. Cf. the interesting remarks of Dickens (quoted by Scobie (1978a) 48) on 'making the introduced story [of Miss Wade in *Little Dorrit*] so fit into surroundings impossible of separation from the main story, as to make the blood of the book circulate through both' – as distinct from the inserted stories in (e.g.) *Pickwick*. Dickens evidently thought the idea a new one.

[56] Winkler 53, hedging however on the question of A.'s intentions.

[57] Cf. Comm. 6.8.4n. In effect, therefore, the prologue and its reprise at 4.27.8 constitute an implicit challenge to the reader who fancies himself as *doctus*. How many such have passed the test with first-class honours is anybody's guess. But A. plays fair: the manner in which *Cupid & Psyche* is introduced, together with the implications of the story itself and its length and placing in *Met.*, fly signals which are as clear as they well could be without being so explicit as to be, in a literary point of view, pointless. *Lucius'* failure to grasp the point cannot be used to discount its allegorical significance (Heiserman 159); cf. Wlosok 70.

provincial noblesse,[58] Psyche a princess. Each is exposed to the assaults of a malignant Fortune (identified in Psyche's case with Venus: Comm. 5.5.2n.) in a hostile or uncaring world. Both are saved in the end by the *undeserved* intervention of divine grace. This last point should perhaps be emphasized, since Psyche at all events might be thought to have earned her salvation by the successful performance of the tasks set her by Venus. Here however some reservations are in order. In the first place, her invariable reaction on being confronted with each successive trial is despair, and in each case it is only the power of Cupid that sees her through. Moreover, when she falls at her last hurdle, it is through her own act, motivated by the identical combination of *curiositas* and *simplicitas* that has been her undoing from the start. Her rescue by Cupid is occasioned by *his* desire to be reunited with her. She cannot therefore really be said to have deserved her salvation, except in so far as she never ceases to yearn for Love. In that sense she has, however imperfectly, followed Pan's advice (Comm. 5.25.6n.). Nor can she be said to have 'matured' through her experiences[59] or to have grown 'from a condition of uncertainty to a state of enlightenment'[60] – her last state before the final rescue is as uncertain as her first. Similarly with Lucius. There is no suggestion that he is reformed by his experiences or that he has learned anything from them: this is not a case of πάθει μάθος.[61] As a donkey he indulges as far as he is able the same lusts that brought about his downfall – and this *after* he has heard the story of Psyche.[62] In both his case and Psyche's what calls down the 'divine grace'[63] of Isis and Love respectively is the helpless *need* of the seeker for salvation rather than his or her deserts or convictions.[64]

---

[58] For the possible implications of Lucius' distinction see Mason (1983).

[59] Rambaux 204–6.

[60] Hooker 34.

[61] Cf. Aristotle, fr. 15 Rose 'initiates are not required to learn but only to undergo' (παθεῖν καὶ διατεθῆναι), cit. Burkert 69 n. 13 (but see his qualifications ibid.).

[62] Cf. above, p. 11 n. 49, on *Met.* 9.12–13; Smith 522, Sandy (1978) 126–30. This point is missed by Penwill 50–1, objecting that the story is artistically pointless if read as 'a restatement of the novel's main theme'. Lucius' unawareness that this is *de se fabula* is an ironical reproach to the reader who fails to take the same point.

[63] Tatum (1979) 57.

[64] ' "Faith" and "salvation" in votive religions do not imply "conversion",

(iv) In both stories the theme of *improspera curiositas* is central. The theme was clearly introduced by A. to motivate the novel and to link the stories together.[65]

(v) Both human protagonists obstinately persist in the path to ruin, blind and deaf to repeated warnings, direct in Psyche's case, indirect for the most part in Lucius' – as befits a highly educated young man trained to appreciate literary nuances.[66]

(vi) Both submit to a goddess and are required to undergo ordeals which lead to a final state of union, in Psyche's case with Love, in Lucius' case (mystically) with Isis, who among other things is Venus Caelestis (cf. below, (vii)). As part of their ordeals each undergoes a kind of death in the course of a descent to the Underworld, physical in Psyche's case, symbolic in Lucius'.[67] The outcome of both unions is *uoluptas*, Pleasure.[68]

(vii) The divine protagonists of both stories shade, so to say, into one another. Venus appears in Book XI as one of the guises of Isis,

even if they presuppose a change in orientation when an individual turns to the god' (Burkert 14; cf. ibid. 17). Lucius' trials should not be seen as a part of his Isiac initiation, which begins only when his eyes have been opened to his errors by Isis' priest. '... "the History of a wicked life" plays no part whatsoever in the temperamental preparation of Lucius for conversion' (Sandy (1978) 127; cf. ibid. 129). Neither his nor Psyche's *simplicitas* can possibly be accounted to them for virtue, as suggested by Tatum: '[they] deserve the protection they finally receive because neither can learn to be evil' ((1969) 512). This is not borne out by the references to Psyche's *simplicitas* at 5.11.5 and (more particularly) 5.15.4; and Cupid's address to her as *simplicissima Psyche* (5.24.3) is, in the context, clearly reproachful. On the similarities between Psyche and Lucius see also Gianotti 36–7. For an interpretation of the story in terms of Isiac initiation see Merkelbach.

[65] Wlosok 75–6, Sandy (1972) 180.

[66] Cf. MacKay 477, noting the proverbial stubbornness of the ass; 'the real fault of Psyche ... is disobedience'.

[67] 11.21.6–7 ... *et inferum claustra et salutis tutelam in deae manu posita, ipsamque traditionem* [initiation] *ad instar uoluntariae mortis et precariae salutis celebrari* ..., 11.23.7 *accessi confinium mortis et calcato Proserpinae limine per omnia uectus elementa remeaui, deos inferos et deos superos accessi coram et adoraui de proxumo* [precisely as Psyche had done]. Cf. Sandy (1978) 129, Gwynn Griffiths (1978) 150; and on the journey as initiation Burkert 92–3.

[68] Psyche: 6.24.4 and n. Lucius: 11.24.5 *inexplicabili uoluptate simulacri diuini perfruebar*; and cf. the last words of the whole novel, *gaudens obibam*. Cf. Tatum (1969) 513–14, Walsh (1970) 192 and n. 5, Gwynn Griffiths (1978) 155–8, Kenney (1990) 196.

who is also identified with both *Fortuna* and *Prouidentia*;[69] and the
opening words of her initial outburst are re-echoed by Isis in her great
epiphany in Book XI.[70]

(viii) Finally, and most obviously, the name Psyche is Greek for
'soul', ψυχή. The point is more than once emphasized by A. through
word-plays with *anima, spiritus*, etc.[71] As will be noted presently, the
identification of the protagonists in the 'mysterious husband' story as
Cupid (Love) and Psyche (the Soul) is due to A. himself, and it
strains credulity to maintain that he did not intend the names to carry
their full – which in A.'s case inevitably means neo-Platonic – implications. It was crystal-clear to Fulgentius in the fifth century, as it
would have been to any educated ancient reader, that this was the
case, and he duly interpreted the story as a religious myth. Many of
the details of his interpretation[72] will hardly command assent, but
his instinct that the story only makes sense as allegory is sound, and
he would have been astonished by the blindness of some modern
scholars to its obvious character as 'an Odyssey of the human soul'.[73]
What Housman observed of the scholiasts on Lucan holds good in
this connexion also: '[They] were not well equipped in the matter of
brains for understanding him, but they possessed another organ: they
understood him with the marrow of their bones, which was the same
stuff as his.'[74] Perhaps it is enough to ask the simple questions posed

---

[69] See Comm. 4.31.4, 5.5.2, 5.9.2; 5.3.1nn.; 3.22.5 (Lucius to Photis)
'*ac iam perfice ut meae Veneri Cupido pinnatus adsistam tibi*', 11.2.1 '*Regina caeli, siue
tu Ceres alma . . . seu tu caelestis Venus*'. On the problems posed by the merging
identities of the gods in *Met.* see Gwynn Griffiths (1978) 145ff., esp. 150:
'there is no rigid pattern of correspondence' – a point generally valid of the
allegory of *Met.* (cf. Kenney (1990) 187, 197–8).

[70] 4.30.1 ~ 11.5.1: 'an explicit indication of identity' (Gwynn Griffiths
(1978) 151).

[71] See Comm. 5.6.7, 5.6.9, 5.13.4nn.; Tatum (1969) 509–10, Kenney
(1990) 182–3. On A.'s preoccupation with 'significant names' see Hijmans.

[72] Conveniently summarized by Walsh (1970) 218–19. For other
attempts at allegorization see Friedländer 18–19.

[73] Grimal (1963) 19. *Contra* e.g. Purser xliv; but that an allegory is differently explained by each interpreter does not prove that it cannot really be
an allegory.

[74] Edn of Lucan (Oxford 1926) vi. Fulgentius, a Christian, was of course
attuned to allegory as he would have encountered it in Biblical exegesis and
such works as Prudentius' *Psychomachia*. Allegorical interpretation, however,

by Elizabeth Haight: 'Is this the eternal story of Love and the Soul? If not, why are Venus' servants named Anxiety and Sorrow? Why is her enemy dubbed Sobriety, and why is the child of Love and the Soul called Joy?'[75]

(b) Sources and models

The cumulative effect of these indicators is, or ought to be, unmistakable, but their clarity is apt to be impaired by the extraordinary richness and complexity of A.'s literary treatment of what (if the folklorists are right) was originally a quite simple story. The sources that he laid under contribution in writing *Cupid & Psyche* may be categorized under a number of (by no means mutually exclusive) headings:

(i) Folktale and myth.
(ii) Literary texts.
(iii) Platonizing philosophy.
(iv) Iconography.

Of these categories (i) and (ii) can be briefly dealt with. The 'folktale' elements in *Cupid & Psyche* – a Cinderella-type heroine with two malevolent elder sisters, the mysterious husband who is also (thought to be) a monster, the sequence of ordeals at the hands of a witch, etc. – have been identified as such largely because they are not attested in an immediately recognisable form in the extant corpus of Graeco-Roman legend and myth and find striking analogies in stories in modern collections of folktales.[76] That elements in the plot of *Cupid & Psyche* are of this character is undeniable, but their im-

---

was not a Christian innovation; the detection of hidden meanings in myth and early Greek poetry began in the 6th century B.C.

[75] Haight 52. Cf. Hooker *passim*. For a particularly eloquent (and probably little-known) interpretation which ascribes to A. 'some divination of the future' see Whittaker 1–8. Balme–Morwood pertinently note (8–9) that *Comus* shows that Milton had no difficulty in reading the story as an allegory of 'the salvation of the human soul through divine grace'. On the history of allegorizing interpretation of *Cupid & Psyche* see Heine 32–3. On A.'s awareness of allegory see below, pp. 27–8.

[76] See e.g. Walsh (1970) 193–4, Wright (J. R. G.) 273–82, both based on Swahn; and cf. Arnott (1962) 242–3.

portance has been exaggerated, as when it is observed of Zephyr's aerial ferry-service that 'This is so clearly a basic folk-lore theme that it is surprising that no trace of it has been found in the numerous collected versions of our tale';[77] *certa amittimus dum incerta petimus* (see Comm. 4.35.4n.). Fehling's provocative monograph, which contends that the 'folktale' motifs in *Cupid & Psyche* originated there – that is to say, so far from exploiting an existing corpus of folktale, A. helped to create it – is at the very least a salutary reminder of the exiguous nature of the evidence for some of these identifications and of the arbitrary character of the train of reasoning on which they are all too often based.[78] In any case, the ultimate source or sources of A.'s multifarious materials are less important and interesting than the use to which he can be shown on the evidence to have put them.[79]

There can be no clear line of division between folktale, legend, and myth;[80] and category (i) likewise shades off into category (ii). A.'s indebtedness to literary sources, both Greek and Roman, is illustrated sufficiently (it is hoped) in the Commentary. What should be stressed in the present context is that this is not simply a matter of embellishment or artful variation for its own sake but is crucial to the handling of the story. Thus A.'s characterization of Venus superimposes on the Platonic dichotomy to be discussed presently, Urania (Caelestis) / Pandemos (Vulgaris), the *persona* of the Virgilian Juno, affronted and vengeful, giving an additional edge to her persecution of Psyche; it also alternates with this the *persona* of the Lucretian Venus, lending a specifically Roman coloration to the originally Platonic conception of the higher kind of Love, to be subsumed in the sequel by the all-embracing figure of Isis. The 'punishment' of Psyche for her involuntary encroachment on the prerogatives of the goddess by exposure on

---

[77] Walsh (1970) 203; see Comm. 4.35.4n. Cf. e.g. Bettelheim 291, taking for granted A.'s 'even older sources' in folktale. This line of enquiry is richly documented in the pieces collected by Binder–Merkelbach; see more recently the monograph of Mantero.

[78] For some reservations see Dowden (1979). The chief merit of Fehling's work is his cogent demonstration (with due acknowledgement to Helm and others) of A.'s indebtedness to literary sources; see below.

[79] So, rightly, Fehling (9).

[80] On myth 'as a special form of the folktale' see e.g. Eliade 316; and cf. the various definitions of folklore in Funk & Wagnall, *Standard dictionary of folklore, mythology, and legend* (New York 1972).

a rock, to be carried off or devoured by a monster, was clearly suggested by the story of Andromeda.[81] Similarly the ordeals of the
golden wool and the descent to Hades are shaped on classical literary
models. Psyche herself, at the crucial moment of decision, is por-
trayed as an Ovidian heroine, a conflation of Althaea, Byblis, Hypermestra and Myrrha. Nor should it be overlooked that, as was noted
earlier, *Met.* is a novel and exemplifies many of the basic features
of the genre. A case in point, not generally recognized as such,
is Psyche's repeated and, as repeatedly, thwarted determination
on suicide, the classic refuge of the romantic heroine at the end of her
tether. Five attempts in one not very long story (Comm. 6.17.2n.),
in a writer less accomplished than A., might argue poverty of invention[82] or at best a stroke of gratuitous satire. We should rather
read this as reflecting a significant trait in Psyche's character, already
noted, her utter helplessness when thrown on her own resources. As a
parable of the feebleness of the human soul bereft of divine grace and
a warning against the sin of despair it says to the reader: *de te fabula.*

It is in categories (iii) and (iv) that the originality of A.'s invention
is most brilliantly evident.[83] Pausanias in Plato's *Symposium* had distinguished two Aphrodites, Urania (Heavenly, *Venus Caelestis*) and
Pandemos (Of the People, *Venus Vulgaris*), and two Eroses to correspond, their respective provinces being the love of souls and
bodies.[84] This passage is paraphrased by A. in the *Apology* (ch. 12);

[81] A point curiously overlooked by Dowden (1982*b*). Cf. Fehling 22–4.
Venus' persecution of the pregnant Psyche recalls not only Io (Helm (1914)
194–5 = 211–12, Merkelbach 105 = 394, Walsh (1970) 52–3, Fehling 22
and n. 49) but also Callisto and Semele: Comm. 6.9.4n.

[82] Compare Macaulay's painstaking computation of the number of
fainting-fits per character in Catherine Cuthbertson's *San Sebastiano* (G. O.
Trevelyan, *Life and letters* I (1923) 96; cf. *Letters* ed. T. Pinney II (1974) 51
n. 1).

[83] For a fuller discussion of (iii) see Kenney (1990). For possible allusions
to the *Symposium* and the *Phaedrus* in the magical episodes of the earlier books
see Anderson 80, and for speculation that Plato was a 'catalyst' in the ending
of the novel ibid. 82–5.

[84] Plat. *Symp.* 180d2–181b8. The devotees of A. Pandemos and her
corresponding Eros 'love bodies rather than souls and, for choice, those most
devoid of mind (ὡς ἂν δύνωνται ἀνοητοτάτων), only thinking
about achieving their object (διαπράξασθαι), never mind whether well
(καλῶς) or not' (181b2–6). The relationship of Lucius and Photis could

and in *Cupid & Psyche* he portrays these dichotomous deities con-
tending for Psyche – a human soul – just as in the body of the novel
the higher pleasure which is seen in the end to be the service of Isis
contends for the mastery of Lucius with the lower, servile, pleasures
typified by his infatuation with Photis. In *Cupid & Psyche* the power
which eventually wins the battle is Cupid, revealed in his higher,
Platonic, guise (Amor I),[85] and the power which loses is Venus
Vulgaris (Venus II).[86] It is this Cupid and this Venus which motivate
and control the action: Venus I (Caelestis) and Amor II (Vulgaris)
figure as largely decorative and (in Cupid's case especially) passive
foils[87] to their antithetical counterparts. This battle is what the story
is really about; A. however handles it in, as it were, counterpoint to
the ostensible plot, in which it is Psyche who is for the most part on
stage.[88]

The technical challenge posed by this undertaking was formidable,
and though it must be conceded that A. does not manage to integrate
the Platonic duality into the story with perfect smoothness,[89] nevertheless his achievement is a literary *tour de force*. It is thus all the more
remarkable that he was not content with the sources rehearsed so far,
but chose to compound his technical problems by drawing on (iv) the
iconographic tradition in order to deepen and enrich his message still
further. A.'s readers would have been familiar with a wide range of

hardly be more accurately or succinctly described. A.'s dual Cupid has
nothing to do with the *geminus Cupido* of the poets (cf. Mayer on Sen. *Phaedr.*
275).
  [85] '... even if there were many invisible husbands in folk tales, there were
none named Cupid, and none who behaved as Cupid did ... love is a
commitment on faith ... As religious faith is a conscious pursuit of
immortality, so love, according to Platonic doctrine, is an unconscious pursuit
of immortality; and neither pursuit is subject to reason' (Hooker 29).
  [86] For these terms and for a fuller analysis of the interaction between the
divine protagonists see Kenney (1990). Cf. also Rambaux 186–7, noting
that Venus was worshipped at Rome under several different guises.
  [87] Cf. Hooker 30.
  [88] See Walsh (1970) 198–9 for a helpful analysis. His division into five
'Acts' has been followed below and in the Commentary, though liberties have
been taken with their titles.
  [89] The concluding scene on Olympus is especially open to criticism on this
score: Kenney (1990) 195–7. The guise in which Cupid makes his submission to Jupiter is hardly that of a deity who has 'evolved' or 'matured'
(Rambaux 192–3) in the course of the action. His dual nature is in evidence
to the very end of the story.

works of art of every conceivable kind in which two symbolic figures, identified as Eros (Ἔρως) and the Soul (Ψυχή) are represented in a variety of situations, sometimes in harmony, sometimes in discord: now embracing (sometimes with nuptial concomitants), now one tormenting or being tormented by the other. These themes occur also in epigrams, particularly those of Meleager.[90] From the enormous extent and variety of the iconographic material it is apparent that there was no single myth of Eros and Psyche, rather a potentially unlimited range of applications of two highly versatile symbols, attractive to artists not only as profoundly suggestive but also as lending themselves to exploitation in innumerable forms, from the merely pretty or whimsical to the tragic or near-sadistic. The monuments do not yield a single coherent picture or narrative which can be posited as A.'s source for his story.[91] He had the acumen to perceive and the technical ability to turn effectively to account this rich and suggestive corpus of symbol and allegory and invest the protagonists in his basic story, if there really was such a thing,[92] with names and identities. 'It is through the figures of Cupid and Psyche that the folk tale has been reshaped to express meanings about love and the soul.'[93] The act of artistic recombination by which these, together with the literary and Platonic elements discussed above, were fused into a single integrated whole[94] represents an astonishing

---

[90] *A.P.* 5.57 (*HE* 4074–5), 12.80 (4082–7), 12.132*a* (4104–9), 12.132*b* (4110–17) (Schlam (1976) 17). For the iconography see Schlam ibid. 4–30 and his plates.

[91] Schlam (1976) 30, 32, 40.

[92] What Swahn has labelled 'The search for the lost husband'; cf. Schlam (1976) 2–3.

[93] Ibid. 3. This is a more satisfying interpretation than Fehling's (admittedly acute) suggestion that A. wrote *Cupid & Psyche* to provide these allegorical figures with a myth (14, 28). This completely fails to do justice to the Platonic dimension of the story, and Fehling's analysis of A.'s treatment, with its occasional inconsistencies (some of which can in fact be accounted for more satisfactorily), carries the implication of a hand-to-mouth method of composition which gravely underrates his technical skill.

[94] Less than perfectly integrated, as has been noted, but there are more important literary virtues than consistency. Nobody could tax A. with 'l'implacabile consequenziarietà dei mediocri' (Traina 58). Cf. Penwill 50–9, arguing however that the discrepancies show that A.'s purpose was not to illustrate Lucius' experiences through Psyche's but 'to point up a contrast' (51) between them. Cf. above, p. 14 n. 61.

feat of originality deserving more recognition than it has generally received.[95] It entitles him to a place in the annals of Latin literature alongside the two poets whom he evidently much admired and on whom he so often drew, Virgil and Ovid.

(c) Narrative voices

The story of Cupid and Psyche is an insertion in the main narrative, a retelling by Lucius – ostensibly *verbatim* – of a story overheard by him as told by a drunken old woman to comfort the captive Charite. There is a paradoxical discrepancy between the milieu of the old woman and Lucius-as-ass – the contemporary world of Rome and the provinces or at all events a recognizable travesty of it[96] – and Psyche's world of fairytale and myth, untrammelled by constraints of chronology or geography[97] and presided over by nameless kings of unlocated kingdoms and gods who don and shed Platonic and poetic *personae* with disconcerting facility and insouciance. The story is told by an 'omniscient narrator' – the only example of the use of this narrative technique in the novel.[98] The personality of the ostensible narratrix, the old woman, is nowhere detectable in the narrative itself.[99] She nevertheless has a part to play, albeit by way of ironical implication. As has been noted, the words in which she introduces her story, together with Lucius' superficial reaction to it, read in the light of the verbal echo of the prologue to the whole novel,[100] convey a

[95] Interpreters of *Cupid & Psyche* have been too prone to postulate a single *Vorlage* for the story, being 'wont to regard the other elements as incidental accretions in a hypothetical tradition or thoughtless additions by a clumsy borrower' (Schlam (1976) 2). To Schlam belongs the principal credit for perceiving the true nature and quality of A.'s achievement: see esp. ch. 17 'The metamorphosis of a folk tale' (31–40). If a criticism of his seminal monograph may be ventured, it is that it fails to do full justice to (though it certainly does not neglect) the role of the Platonic element in the story.

[96] See Millar and cf. Callebat (1968) 23 on 'la société moyenne et ... la basse société de l'époque, monde des artisans, paysans, marchands, esclaves'. Cf. above, p. 4.

[97] See Comm. 5.26–27n.

[98] Van der Paardt 81 ('as befits a *Märchen*'), Dowden (1982a) 420.

[99] See Comm. 6.24.2n.

[100] 4.27.8 *sed ego te narrationibus* lepidis *anilibusque fabulis protinus* auocabo ∼ 6.25.1 *dolebam ... quod pugillares et stilum non habebam qui* tam bellam *fabellam praenotarem*.

sardonic comment on his failure to profit from his experiences. She promises to distract Charite and succeeds in distracting Lucius; what is in fact a paradigm of his own predicament he treats as no more than an entertaining diversion.[101]

Nor is the presence of Lucius himself felt. Rather A. goes to some trouble to underline his unawareness that this is *de se fabula*. Hints to the reader such as the pointed references to *diuina/bona Prouidentia* (Comm. 5.3.1n.) are conveyed, so to say, over his head. His failure to learn by experience after the classical fashion of πάθει μάθος is not merely an ironical paradox: the author's use of *Cupid & Psyche* to emphasize it suggests that this is part of the essential message of the novel. Though the tone and subject-matter of *Cupid & Psyche* set it off from the rest of *Met.*, the presence of the author – 'le sourire complice du narrateur'[102] – is continually perceived. In this as in other respects A. resembles Ovid.[103] Ambiguity and irony repeatedly operate to put the alert reader on notice that his responses are being manipulated.[104] More overt hints are signalled by telltale adverbs, particularly *scilicet*.[105] The most striking, one might almost say blatant, manifestation of the authorial presence in *Cupid & Psyche* is the self-identification, supposedly through the voice of the old woman, of A. as *Milesiae conditor* at 4.32.6. This is on a par with the violations of dramatic illusion for immediate comic effect by poets from Aristophanes onwards. Less obtrusive but more numerous and as distinctly an intrusion into the

---

[101] Cf. Winkler 44–5; but though he identifies three separate levels of irony, the point of it does not emerge from his discussion. *Cupid & Psyche* is surely something better and more interesting than a 'funhouse [whatever that may be] of surprises about meaning'. Though there is undeniably an element of suspense in A.'s management of the story, it degrades the role of *Cupid & Psyche* in the novel to treat it merely as a 'detection thriller' (ibid. 90) about the identity of Psyche's husband. In any case, Winkler's discussion fails to grasp the nature of the identity question, which is essentially not *who?* (Cupid or a monster) but *which?* (Amor Caelestis or Vulgaris).

[102] Callebat (1968) 550.

[103] For the reader's continuous awareness of the poet in *Met.* cf. e.g. Kenney (1986) xxvii–xxviii.

[104] See Index s.v. 'Word-play', etc., Callebat (1968) 467–73.

[105] Winkler 66–7, citing Dowden (1982a) 422–5; Callebat (1968) 460–1. See Comm. 5.17.3, 5.23.5, 5.25.5, 5.26.5, 5.31.2, 6.1.5nn. It is noteworthy that these instances occur for the most part in the context of Psyche's extreme naivety. It should also be noted that *scilicet* is not always 'loaded' in this way; for 'straight' instances see 5.24.4, 5.26.3, 5.29.3, 6.8.7, 6.9.4.

timeless world of the fairytale are the references to contemporary or specifically Roman ideas and institutions.[106] Whether these sallies are to be ascribed to mere literary opportunism or to a conscious desire to maintain a direct rapport with the reader may be debated. In *Cupid & Psyche* A. was, as has been noted, employing the familiar Alexandrian technique of illuminating a larger literary whole by the inclusion of a self-contained but thematically relevant insert. The essence of this technique is that it should be employed in the Alexandrian manner, obliquely and allusively. The hints conveyed by the old woman's and Lucius' comments on the tale are indeed in that Alexandrian vein. The authorial nudge was also a characteristically Callimachean–Ovidian device.[107] It is not easy, however, to see how the rather obvious nudges noted here are calculated to enhance the reader's awareness of the relevance of *Cupid & Psyche* to the main story.[108] We do not really need these reminders of the 'real' world to which we and Lucius are abruptly returned with the birth of Voluptas.

(d) The conduct of the story

The tempo of the first 'Act'[109] (4.28–35) is brisk. In it two things are accomplished. Psyche is transported to what turns out to be the mysterious realm of Amor I;[110] and her enemy is identified as Venus II. This latter point is important, since Venus does not re-enter the story until Act III. In Act II (5.1–24) Psyche is tempted and falls. The initially idyllic relationship with her invisible but delectable husband is gradually undermined as her sisters, whom she is responsible for admitting to her paradise, work on her *simplicitas* and

[106] See Index s.v. 'Roman references' and cf. Gianotti 36 n. 12.

[107] Kenney (1986) xxvii–xxviii, Hinds 19.

[108] The rendezvous for claimants to the reward for turning Psyche in, *retro metas Murtias* (Comm. 6.8.2n.), is perhaps an exception which proves the rule if it underlines the fact that it is Venus II (Vulgaris) to whom Psyche (a human soul) is in bondage: Kenney (1990) 192–3.

[109] See above, p. 20 n. 88.

[110] Even the reader who has successfully identified the 'monster' described in the oracle cannot realize exactly what is to come, though the last sentence of Book IV (Comm. 4.35.4n.) should have reassured him that whatever fate awaits Psyche it can hardly be the misery and degradation devised for her by Venus.

curiositas, and shattered when she finally yields to them and disobeys his express orders. The build-up to this climax is engineered through a pattern of repeated warnings by Cupid interspersed with visits from the sisters. It is worth noting that, though they duly come in threes,[111] the spacing of the warnings and the visits is not strictly symmetrical: the sequence is first warning (5.5–6), first visit (5.7–10); second (5.11) and third (5.12) warnings; second (5.14–17) and third (5.17–20) visits. Act III (5.25–6.8.3) is the most discontinuous section of the story, especially as regards the elimination of the sisters[112] and the characterization of Venus, who re-enters as Venus II, pays a state call on Jupiter as Venus I, and on leaving Olympus reverts instantly to Venus II.[113] Act IV (6.8.4–21.2) corresponds formally to Act II in that, as Psyche was there tried (and found wanting) by Amor I, she is now tried by Venus II. The pattern of episodes in this Act is one of increasing length and elaboration, with Psyche growing ever more desperate as her ordeals become more formidable.[114] Though sustained throughout by the power of Cupid (Amor I) operating through various agents, she falls, not at but when safely over her last fence, a victim once again of her apparently ineradicable curiosity and silliness. This knot is cut by the miraculous intervention of Cupid (Amor I) in person, and the stage is set for Act V (6.21.3–6.24), in which all, or nearly all, the threads are drawn together and everybody lives happily ever after.

That the loose ends which obstinately decline to be tidily tucked

---

[111] Cf. below, n. 114.

[112] See Comm. 5.26–27n.

[113] See Comm. 6.7.2n., Kenney (1990) 191–2.

[114] This is where the folklorists have had a field-day. Attempts, for instance, have been made to reduce her ordeals to the canonical number of three – 'Die Dreizahl ist in den Märchen der Regel' (Reitzenstein 48 = 243 n. 11) – by explaining the Catabasis as a doublet of the mission to the Styx (cf. Walsh (1970) 212 and n. 3, Fehling 19 and n. 34). However, as noted above (p. 19), much of A.'s inspiration for these two episodes, as for the ordeal of the golden wool, is clearly literary. It ought also not to be overlooked that Psyche undergoes a preliminary ordeal in the shape of flogging and torture (cf. Comm. 6.9.3n.). *Ponderanda episodia, non numeranda.* Cf. Comm. 6.13.5n. on the 'water of life'. Fehling (17) ingeniously suggests Hera's persecution of Heracles as a model; cf. the analogies with the Virgilian Juno noted at Comm. 4.30n.

away[115] are not more numerous and more disturbing is an extra-ordinary tribute to A.'s literary skill. Classical literature offers few if any parallels to a book, one itself part of and intimately related to a larger literary whole, in which so many disparate elements are combined with such success into a coherent and moving narrative of profound human significance. If the basic plot does indeed derive – something that has never actually been proved – from the fathomless popular reservoir of folktale and fable, in A.'s hands it has trans-cended its anonymous origins. Rhetorical and literary enrichment were only to be expected from a writer of A.'s date and upbringing. What lifts the story into a class of its own is the stroke of genius which fused Platonizing philosophy and iconographic imagery to produce a book destined to take its place among the great allegories of the world. For this achievement alone Apuleius, as has already been said, deserves to rank as a literary artist with Ovid and Virgil. No critic has summed up the peculiar beauties of *Cupid & Psyche* more eloquently than Walter Pater:

> But set as one of the episodes in the main narrative, a true gem amid its mockeries, its coarse though genuine humanity, its burlesque horrors, came the tale of Cupid and Psyche, full of brilliant, life-like situations, *speciosa locis*, and abounding in lovely visible imagery (one seemed to see and handle the golden hair, the fresh flowers, the precious works of art in it!), yet full also of a gentle idealism, so that you might take it, if you chose, for an allegory. With a concentration of all his finer literary gifts, Apuleius had gathered into it the floating star-matter of many a delightful story.[116]

In the phrase 'if you chose' Pater puts his finger on the point. Apuleius has furnished the opportunity; it is for the reader to take it if he cares to.[117]

---

[115] See Kenney (1990) 187. Inconsistencies in *Met.* are of course not con-fined to *Cupid & Psyche*; see e.g. Perry 254–8.

[116] *Marius the Epicurean* (Everyman edn 1934) 36.

[117] Cf. Hunter 47 on Longus: '[he] has hinted at a second and deeper level of meaning which he challenges us to pursue'. It is worth adding that even Perry, dourly unreceptive to any suggestion that *Met.* has a message, concedes that 'in spite of its contradictions, the composite Apuleian narrative as a whole

(e) A note on allegory

On the simplest level, allegory is defined by the ancient authorities in etymological terms as meaning one thing and saying another: Isid. *Etym.* 1.37.22 *allegoria est alieniloquium: aliud enim sonat et aliud intellegitur;* cf. Quint. *I.O.* 9.2.5 *in tropis ponuntur uerba alia pro aliis, ut in* [seven tropes including metaphor, metonymy and allegory]. Cicero uses ἀλληγορίαις = 'in code' (*Att.* 2.20.3). It is this restricted sense that the scholiasts intend when they gloss a word or phrase in Virgil or Horace, as they frequently do, with '*allegorice*' or 'ἀλληγορικῶς'. However, the term was also used in a broader sense as defined by e.g. Cic. *Orat.* 94 *iam cum fluxerunt continuo plures translationes* [metaphors], *alia plane fit oratio; itaque genus hoc Graeci appellant* ἀλληγορίαν, echoed succinctly by Quint. *I.O.* 9.2.46 ἀλληγορίαν *facit continua* μεταφορά. It is this extended sense which is reflected in modern definitions such as 'a series of linked metaphors' or, more elaborately, 'a means of structuring language so as to produce continuously linked series of double or multiple meanings'.[118] In fact the examples of connected or continuous metaphor offered by Cic. *De or.* 3.166–7 show that what he (and rhetoricians and grammarians generally) meant by allegory in this sense was a small-scale trope of the kind employed e.g. by Horace (after Alcaeus) in the Ship of State Ode (*C.* 1.14; cf. Quint. *I.O.* 8.6.44). The influence of Plato must not be forgotten. Though he explicitly rejected the allegorizing interpretation of myth that had been vigorously pursued from the sixth century B.C. onwards, the Platonic myths themselves are a species of allegory. This is certainly true of the speech of Aristophanes in the *Symposium* (189c2–d6), the dialogue which was evidently in the forefront of A.'s mind when he was writing *Cupid & Psyche.*[119] However, important as these myths were as a model for A., continuous allegory on a large scale, designed to inform and to convey the 'real' message of a complete work of literature, is something rather different. Allegory of this sort is first found in Virgil's *Aeneid.* A.'s perception of allegory as it emerges from *Met.* far transcends the

is richer in suspense and dramatic surprise than was any one of its component parts' (281).

[118] Fletcher 41.

[119] See above, n. 25 for the 'framing' relationship.

narrow rhetorical conception with which his early training would
have made him familiar. It cannot in the nature of things be proved,
but it seems overwhelmingly probable that it was Virgil who opened
his eyes to its wider possibilities.[120] Ovid too may have contributed to
this awareness. His *Metamorphoses* is not an allegory in the sense that
the *Aeneid* is, but it was no more written to be read simply as an
anthology of entertaining stories than was A.'s.[121]

5. STYLE AND LANGUAGE[122]

A. was a professional rhetorician, writing for audiences themselves
trained both in the practice of effective communication and in the
techniques of critical appreciation. An enumeration of the various
tropes and figures of thought and speech employed by him in *Met.*
would comprise virtually the entire repertory of 'Asian' rhetoric (so
called) as it was cultivated in the Graeco-Roman world of his day.[123]
Nearly every feature of his style can be paralleled in the latinity of all
periods.[124] What makes him unique among Latin writers is the gusto
and lack of inhibition with which he handles these common resources.
Norden had no hesitation in awarding him the prize for stylistic
virtuosity and verbal prestidigitation.[125] It is a style calculated above
all, as promised in the prologue to *Met.*, to charm the ear: if ever a
Latin book cried out (as indeed most were intended) to be read aloud,
it is this one. It is above all a mixed style. Pater again:

   . . . full of the archaisms and curious felicities in which that gen-

---

[120] Cf. Kenney (1990) 198.

[121] Cf. Kenney (1986) xiv–xvii. See further J. Tate, 'Allegory, Greek' and
'Allegory, Latin', in *OCD*[2], Russell–Winterbottom Index III s.v. Allegory,
Hunter 46–7; *TLL* s. vv. *allegoria, allegoricus*.

[122] The brief characterization of Norden (1915) 600–5 is justly celebrated. Of the more recent standard monographs that of Médan, apart
perhaps from the section on rhythmical *clausulae* (274–304; see below,
pp. 30–1) has been largely superseded by the work of Bernhard and Callebat.
Purser (lxx–c) offers a serviceable brief conspectus; see also Walsh (1970)
63–6, Callebat (1978). On the special characteristics shared by A. with such
writers as Fronto and Tertullian and on so-called 'African' latinity see Brock
161–261 (and cf. below, n. 124), Raby 21–5, Dietrich 191–6, Lancel.

[123] Cf. Bernhard 91, 188, Raby 21.

[124] A point well brought out by Brock (loc. cit. above, n. 122).

[125] Norden (1915) 600: 'der virtuoseste Wortjongleur, den es gegeben hat'.

eration delighted, quaint terms and images picked fresh from the
early dramatists, the lifelike phrases of some lost poet preserved
by an old grammarian, racy morsels of the vernacular, and
studied prettinesses: all alike, mere playthings for the genuine
power and natural eloquence of the erudite artist, unsuppressed
by his erudition . . .[126]

Exuberance and richness are the hallmarks of A.'s vocabulary and
expression. Of the poet's traditional licence to innovate in the lexical
sphere, either by reviving old words or coining new ones, A. availed
himself with a freedom which might have caused Horace to purse his
lips[127] but which is very much in the spirit of two of the poets to whom
he more than once displays indebtedness in *Cupid & Psyche*, Lucretius
and, more particularly, Ovid.[128] However, his sparing use of Greek
words would have won Horace's approval;[129] in that connexion his
arch apology for making Apollo prophesy in Latin draws attention to
his own literary rectitude (Comm. 4.32.6n.). Almost as striking as
A.'s coinages is his readiness to use existing words in a hitherto
unexampled sense.[130] This again reflects his creative and poetic
attitude to the language, suggesting the experimental exploitation of
an adopted tongue, as by an Ennius or a Nabokov. In reviving old
words or forms which had fallen out of general use he showed himself
to be in tune with the archaizing tendencies of the age.[131] Nothing

[126] *Marius the Epicurean* (Everyman edn 1934) 33.

[127] *Epp.* 2.2.115–19; on need (*usus*) as the progenitor of new words see
Brink *ad loc.*

[128] Figures for *Cupid & Psyche* are: (1) Words first attested in A. (including
a handful of doubtful cases noted *ad loc.*): 46. (2) Words attested only in A.:
15. (3) *Hapax legomena*: 23. (For the identification of these categories in the
Commentary see above, p. x.)

(Bernhard's figure of a total of 233 *hapax legomena* in *Met.* as a whole
(138–41) must be treated as an approximation, but is of the right order.)

For the vocabulary of Book XI see Gwynn Griffiths (1975) 58–9 (25 *hapax
legomena*); and on A.'s neologisms Gargantini *passim*.

[129] Bernhard 143–5, Callebat (1968) 59–68; but many of these had long
been naturalized even in literary Latin. In *Cupid & Psyche* only *zygius* (4.33.4,
cf. 6.4.3) is a novelty.

[130] See Comm. on e.g. 4.28.3 *inaccessae*, 5.12.1 *florebat*, 6.8.2 *praedicatorem*
and Purser xcvi.

[131] See Comm. on e.g. 5.14.1 *consponsae*, 5.16.1 *sublimatae*, 5.29.1 *properiter*,
6.6.4 *Caelus* and Purser xciv; cf. Brock 25–35, Callebat (1964).

short of a complete tabulation of his usages would do justice to
A.'s catholic receptivity in matters linguistic and stylistic; but his
indebtedness, already glanced at more than once, to Ovid in particular merits special mention, for it speaks to a predilection which
helps to illuminate some of the highly individual qualities of this
unique novel.[132]

A.'s vocabulary is copious and recherché, and his phrasing often
elaborate in the extreme. Excessive striving for effect may occasionally
give rise to apparently strained expression,[133] but it is not often that
the intended sense is in real doubt. His syntax, if not always strictly
'classical', rarely poses problems.[134] In two respects, indeed, A.'s
Latin, compared with that of, say, Livy or Tacitus, might be called
reader-friendly. In the first place his sentence-structure is based on
co-ordination (parataxis) rather than subordination (hypotaxis): fully
periodic sentences à la Caesar or Cicero are a rarity.[135] Secondly he
writes expansively, with much pleonasm, variation and ampli-
fication.[136] Emphasis and colour are imparted by the lavish use of
alliteration and assonance and by careful attention to rhythm. In this
last respect A.'s practice is fully classical; the vast majority of his

---

[132] See Index s.v. 'Ovid' and Comm. on e.g. 5.1.3 *caelamen*, 5.10.6 *inacuit*,
5.16.4 *denupsit*, 5.20.2 *praeacutam*, 5.28.7 *inuestem*, 5.30.4 *rusticae*, 6.3.3
sublucidam. On all these features of A.'s lexis cf. Kenney (1984) xli.

[133] It is not always easy to decide when oddities of expression are due to A.
himself or to his copyists; more than one example of this dilemma is discussed
in the Commentary.

[134] Not all the usages adduced by Purser xcviff. as 'more or less unclassical'
deserve the description: e.g. *nudus* + gen. is found in Sallust and Ovid, *fungor* +
acc. in Terence, Nepos and Tacitus, etc. See Callebat (1968) 178–365;
especially interesting are his statistics for A.'s use of prepositions, particularly
de (206; cf. *TLL* s.v. 43.76ff.), where A. can be seen, as elsewhere, in the
forefront of the process by which Latin developed into the several Romance
vernaculars.

[135] Bernhard 37–9, citing from *Cupid & Psyche* 5.11.4, 5.20.2–5, 5.26.3,
6.22.3–5; one might add e.g. 4.35.4. However, none of these examples reads
in the least like Cicero, or indeed any other Latin writer; that A. 'understood
how to construct periods in the Ciceronian style' (Bernhard 39) may be true,
but it does not seem that he ever did so. On possible reasons for his predilection for parataxis see Gwynn Griffiths (1975) 64–5.

[136] Bernhard 55–87, using the rhetorical terminology of di-, tri-, tetracola,
etc. Virgilian and Ovidian 'theme and variation' must have played its part in
shaping A.'s phraseology.

sentences end with one of the recognized metrical cadences or *clausulae*.[137] This was of practical importance and not a matter of mere decoration or aural titillation. In a literature which was mostly intended to be listened to and which by the time of A. was written according to a scribal convention (adopted from the Greeks) in which there was no division between words, rhythm played an essential part in distinguishing the parts of a compound or complex sentence and especially in signalling the ends of clauses and periods.[138]

It is hardly possible and certainly unrewarding to attempt to isolate the various components of A.'s style with any degree of precision.[139] He wrote for effect and to please, and whatever served these ends was grist to his mill.[140] For all his evident mastery of the Greek-derived rules and techniques of rhetoric, the rich, often lush, exuberance of his expression is distinctively Roman. The earliest sacral and legal texts that have come down to us already reflect a conscious awareness of and pleasure in exploiting the native rhythms and sonorities of the Latin language.[141] These potentialities were from the earliest times of which we have knowledge turned to account by speakers in the courts, the Senate, and the popular assemblies.[142] This preliterary conditioning, with its built-in 'urge to impress, convince, and dominate the hearer',[143] imparted a set of characteristics to Latin literature which, though not suppressed completely, were in the 'higher' genres of literary composition disciplined and restrained by

---

[137] See *OCD*[2] s.v. 'Prose-rhythms'. Bernhard's figure is 92.5 per cent, leading him to conclude that A. stands almost alone among Latin prose writers in his cultivation of rhythmic expression (252). Médan, taking a somewhat different route, concludes that in about 69 per cent of his sentence-endings A. respects Ciceronian principles (303). This figure is almost identical with the total of Bernhard's most favoured categories: $-\cup--\cup\times$, $-\cup--\times$, $-\cup-\times$ and their resolutions (= 57 per cent) and $---\cup\times$ (= 12.5 per cent) (Bernhard 252).

[138] *CHCL* II (= *The early Republic* (1983)) 17.

[139] Callebat (1968) 9–10, 369.

[140] Bernhard 91.

[141] Cf. Norden (1915) 156–63, Pasquali 153–60, Wilkinson 25–34, Williams (G.) in *CHCL* II (= *The early Republic* (1983)) 53–5, De Meo ch. 3 'La lingua sacrale', esp. 154–66. For sound as a dominant feature of Latin poetry see Herescu *passim*.

[142] Leo (1913) 33.

[143] Palmer 76 on Plautus.

the Alexandrianizing and purist attitudes of Caesar, Cicero and the
Augustan poets, but which survived to surface triumphantly in the
work of A. and his contemporaries and successors, in the anonymous
Pervigilium Veneris and in the Christian hymnographers. What could
be more Apuleian than this extract from an unknown Republican
dramatist?

> caelum nitescere, arbores frondescere,
> uites laetificae pampinis pubescere,
> rami bacarum ubertate incuruescere,
> segetes largiri fruges, florere omnia,
> fontes scatere, herbis prata conuestirier.[144]

This is the native tradition, going back to the origins of a distinctively
Roman culture, in which the style of *Met.*, though profoundly affected
by the rhetorical conditioning which A. shared with his contemporaries,[145] is firmly rooted. *Ex Africa semper aliquid noui*: this novelty,
as always in the history of Latin literature, is a compound of old and
new, begotten by the artful operation of a vividly original intelligence
on the inherited riches of six or seven hundred years of linguistic and
literary development and experimentation.

An author's style can be appreciated only as it is actually experienced; labels and categories are of limited critical utility. Analysis
of a handful of passages may, it is hoped, assist the reader towards his
own individual appreciation, but it must again be emphasized that
there is no substitute for the educated and attentive ear.[146] The
affective impact of sound, rhythm, and balanced structure in *Cupid &*

---

[144] Cit. Cic. *Tusc.* 1.69 = *TRF* inc. inc. 133–7, Enn. *Scaen.* 151–5
Vahlen[2]; but the attribution to Ennius' *Eumenides* is treated sceptically by
Jocelyn (p. 285). On the poetical qualities of A.'s prose cf. Callebat (1978)
181–2 and on the archaic effect of such passages as 10.29.4 cf. id. (1964)
360. Raby (24) describes Lucius' address to Isis at 11.25.1–6 as 'a
rhythmical poem, anticipating or foreshadowing the poetry of the future'. If
A.'s verses at *Apol.* 6 (p. 7.16ff. Helm) had come down to posterity
anonymously, one wonders to what century they would have been attributed.

[145] See the useful summary at Bernhard 283–6, and for the 'Asianic'
characteristics commonly attributed to him cf. e.g. Quint. *I.O.* 12.10.12, Tac.
Dial. 18.4, Petron. 2.7.

[146] The best guide to the pronunciation of Latin is by W. S. Allen, *Vox
Latina* 2nd edn (Cambridge 1978).

Psyche is more clearly evident, as might be expected, in the speeches. A.'s treatment of speeches is unrealistic in that in general he makes no attempt to differentiate between speakers in terms of linguistic and stylistic registers.[147] He does, however, differentiate with great skill between the characters and their reaction to events, but the differentiation is rhetorical rather than linguistic. Even poor simple, naive, credulous Psyche is not found wanting in highly sophisticated eloquence when the occasion demands it: tragic pathos (4.34.3–6),[148] erotic blandishment (5.6.7–9), and formal prayer (6.2.4–6, 6.4.1–3) are all equally at her command. Venus is as much at home with comic rant (5.29.2–30.6)[149] as with epic indignation (4.30.1–3).[150] Jupiter's pompous delivery only lightly cloaks his sly hypocrisy (6.22.3–5). The lofty pathos with which Psyche's sisters express themselves contrasts ironically with the vulgar envy of their sentiments:

en orba et saeua et iniqua Fortuna!

[*exclamation + tricolon crescendo* > — ∪ | — — ×]

hocine tibi complacuit, ut utroque parente prognatae ⟨germanae⟩ diuersam sortem sustineremus?

[*indignant apostrophe + rhetorical question + alliteration* >
— ∪ — — ×][151]

et nos quidem quae natu maiores sumus maritis aduenis ancillae deditae[152]

[*subject in enclosing phrase* nos ... deditae; *highly rhythmical*

---

[147] Bernhard 4; but cf. Callebat (1968) 549, answered by Scobie (1975) 23–4. Whatever nuances careful analysis may purport to detect, the contrast with the extreme realism of Petronius' treatment of the dialogue in the *Cena Trimalchionis* could hardly be greater. In this respect Petronius is, of course, uniquely atypical; for the general avoidance in ancient literature of realism of expression see Kenney (1984) xlvii–xlviii.

[148] As brought out by Schissel's analysis; cf. however Comm. *ad loc.*

[149] With a bit of paratragedy thrown in for good measure at 30.3.

[150] Here, conversely, with a descent from generalized indignation to personal malice (§3 fin.).

[151] If *eodem* has fallen out of the text (see app. crit. and Comm. *ad loc.*) there is an effective opposition with *diuersam*.

[152] For A.'s free use of participles (here in preference to a subordinating construction) see Bernhard 41–6; cf. Comm. 6.20.1–2n.

writing coupled with assonance in the participial phrase: ◡—īs|
—◡ īs|——āe|—◡āe]

extorres et lare et ipsa patria degamus longe parentum uelut
exulantes,

[*predicate with enclosing structure chiastically arranged around central
verb: adj. + adverbial phrase   verb   adverbial phrase (with variation
of case from abl. to gen.) + (participial) adj. > —◡——*]

haec autem nouissime quam fetu satiante postremus partus
effudit,

[haec autem *picks up* nos quidem; *subject of second contrasting
sentence, parallel in sense, arrangement and construction with subject of
first sentence >* —◡|——×]

tantis opibus et deo marito potita sit,

[*main utterance parallel to* extorres . . . degamus . . . exulantes
with enclosing construction of different type in dicolon form >
◡—◡×; *an iambic clausula signalling only a light pause*]

quae nec uti recte tanta bonorum copia nouit?

[*the culminating cause of offence, syntactically an afterthought, but
summing up the real feeling behind the bitter deliberative question of the
main sentence >* —◡—|—×]   (5.9.2–4)

This passage immediately identifies the leading characteristic of
A.'s style, its flexibility. The parallelisms articulate the argument and
lend weight to the speaker's indignation, but they are not mechani-
cally contrived; and the sting in the tail of the last clause is a
masterly touch. The poisonous eloquence of the sisters – *nec tamen
eloquio lingua nocente caret* – is deployed just as effectively in the modes
of fulsome flattery (5.14.4–5), sisterly solicitude (5.17.2–18.3)
and crisp instruction (5.20.2–5).[153] The most elaborately mannered
writing in the story, apart from Psyche's prayers, is to be found in the
set-piece descriptions (*ecphraseis*) which form a standard feature in the
repertory of the orator, the poet and the novelist alike; but their effect
in each case, and the means by which it is achieved, leap to the eye

---

[153] This sentence is a *tour de force*, unusual in exemplifying something like a
real periodic structure, incorporating the classic sequence abl. abs. + *postquam*-
clause; but the main articulation is strung on a co-ordinated sequence of main
verbs *absconde . . . subde . . . mutuare . . . abscide*, with free use of participles.

and ear of the reader, and hardly call for detailed analysis. The same
is true of such obviously studied effects as

> nuntio Psyche lăetă flōrēbăt et diuinae subolis solācĭō plāudēbăt
> et futuri pignoris glōrĭā gēstĭēbăt et materni nominis
> dīgnĭtātĕ gāudēbăt,

which, though not unsubtle – for the fourfold repetition with variation
may be read as an ironical reflection of the naive and unthinking
quality of Psyche's joy[154] – hardly needs to be brought to the reader's
attention, on which indeed it positively forces itself. Less obvious, and
more instructive to consider, is A.'s stylistic conduct of narrative.

A particularly beautiful example is the concluding sentence of
Book IV:

> Psychen autem pauentem ac trepidantem et in ipso scopuli
> uertice deflentem[155]
> [*object in enclosing structure* + *tricolon crescendo articulated by
> participles*]
> mitis aura molliter spirantis Zephyri
> [*subject in a–A–adverb–b–B structure*][156]
> uibratis hinc inde laciniis et reflato sinu
> [*adverbial phrase used adnominally in participial a–A–b–B structure*]
> sensim leuatam suo tranquillo spiritu uehens
> [*object picked up by first (participial) verb*]
> paulatim per deuexa rupis
> [*adverbial phrase qualifying* uehens]
> excelsae uallis subditae florentis caespitis gremio
> [*adverbial phrase qualifying second (main) verb with enclosing a–A–
> participle–b–B–C structure*]
> leniter delapsam reclinat.
> [*object again picked up* + *main verb* > — — | ⏑ — ×]   (4.35.4)

Sense and syntax here move together in easy harmony, making a swift

---

[154] The famous quadruple variation at 11.14.2 on the theme 'I was at a
loss for words to express my feelings' is similarly not a case of elaboration
purely for its own sake.

[155] But see Comm. *ad loc.*

[156] For syntactically interlocking patterning of this kind in verse
see Kenney (1984) xlivf., lxiff.

but unhurried transition from Psyche's initial agitation to the image of tranquil repose which closes this book and ushers in the next. Subordination is avoided by the free use of participles, of which there are ten in the sentence.[157] As in the outburst of the sisters, balancing and enclosing structures are used flexibly to articulate the phases of the action. The sensuous languor of such a passage is in sharp contrast to the staccato portrayal of Psyche's conflicting feelings as she contemplates the murder of her husband:

> festinat differt, audet trepidat, diffidit irascitur,
>   [*three pairs of contrasting verbs in asyndeton*]
> et quod est ultimum,
>   [*emphatic underlining of paradox*]
> in eodem corpore odit bestiam, diligit maritum.
>   [*asyndetic and symmetrical dicolon with strongly rhythmical arti-*
>   *culation:* — — | — ◡ — ‖ — ◡ — | ◡ — ×]   (5.21.4)

Such syntactical variation is of the essence of A.'s conduct of the narrative. A striking example is the passage in which Venus, of whom nothing has been heard since her stately return to the sea (4.31.4–7), re-enters the story:

> interim, dum Psyche quaesitioni Cupidinis intenta populos circumibat, at ille uulnere lucernae dolens in ipso thalamo matris iacens ingemebat. tunc auis peralba illa gauia quae super fluctus marinos pinnis natat demergit sese propere ad Oceani profundum gremium. ibi commodum Venerem lauantem natantemque propter assistens indicat adustum filium eius graui uulneris dolore maerentem dubium salutis iacere, iamque per cunctorum ora populorum rumoribus conuiciisque uariis omnem Veneris familiam male audire, quod 'ille quidem montano scortatu, tu uero marino natatu secesseritis, ac per hoc non uoluptas ulla non gratia non lepos, sed incompta et agrestia et horrida cuncta sint, non nuptiae coniugales non amicitiae sociales non liberum caritates, sed enormis colluuies et squalentium foederum insuaue fastidium.'   (5.28.1–5)

---

[157] Reading *trepidantem* (see Comm. *ad loc.*) but counting *florentis* as an adjective. With *subditae* = 'which lay below' cf. *deditae* at 5.9.3 (above, p. 33 n. 152).

The first sentence neatly and economically writes Psyche out of and Cupid back into the story, using a simple subordination (*dum*-clause), the parallelism being discreetly reinforced by enclosing structures and (near)-rhyme: *dum Psyche ... circumibat, at*[158] *ille ... ingemebat*. The meddlesome tern, abruptly introduced with *tunc*,[159] appears from nowhere and plunges to where Venus is to be found. §§3–5 comprise a single long sentence in which the tern delivers its message, carefully articulated without rigidity, first by the parallel infinitives *iacere ... audire*, then, after a curious but effective modulation from indirect into direct speech, by the rhyming lexical rarities *scortatu ... natatu*, and finally in the elaborate peroration by standard rhetorical devices of balance and antithesis:

> *non* uoluptas ulla non gratia non lepos
> [*tricolon*]
> *sed* incompta et agrestia et horrida cuncta sint
> [*tricolon*]
> *non* nuptiae coniugales non amicitiae sociales non liberum caritates
> [*tricolon of adj.–noun pairs with rhyme*]
> *sed* ⟨infimarum sordium⟩[160] enormis colluuies et squalentium foederum insuaue fastidium.
> [*dicolon of adj.–noun phrases each with defining adj.–noun phrase in gen.* $> - \cup | - - \cup \times$]

What is especially impressive about this passage is the easy assurance with which A. modulates from swiftly moving narrative into a static depiction (and then back again).[161] Perhaps, however, no part of *Cupid & Psyche* better exemplifies A.'s complete mastery of the ways and means of the art of narrative than his brilliant summary treatment of Psyche's Catabasis and return (Comm. 6.20.1–4n.). Comparison with the tower's original instructions turns up not a single exact verbal repetition of words and phrases; A.'s précis is new

---

[158] But see Comm. *ad loc.*

[159] As often in *Met.*, a new development is precipitated by an apparently arbitrary and unmotivated agency, No doubt, however, A. expected his readers to remember Ovid's messenger-birds; see Comm. 5.28.2n.

[160] Paratore's supplement; see Comm. *ad loc.*

[161] In this too he resembles Ovid; cf. Kenney (1973) 137–40.

minted. There is much more to this than a *tour de force* for its own sake.
The careless ease of A.'s succinct paraphrase reflects the ease with
which Psyche, sustained by the unseen power of Cupid and doing
precisely what she has been told, accomplishes her mission. The
catastrophe which ensues when she offers to think for herself
(6.20.6) is all the more shattering for the contrast.

6. THE TEXT

Our knowledge of the text of *Met.* depends ultimately upon a single
source, an eleventh-century MS now at Florence, Laurentianus 68.2
F   (F). From this MS all other extant copies derive. Where its original
readings are defaced by correction or by wear and tear, they can be
restored from another Florentine MS of the twelfth or thirteenth
φ   century, Laurentianus 29.2 (φ), which was copied directly from F
when it was more legible than it is now. True or plausible readings
ς   found in the later MSS (ς) are likely to be due to conjecture. The
text of this edition is based on that of Robertson, but the readings
and conjectures of other editors and critics have not infrequently
been preferred to his. In a handful of places his spelling has been
normalized without comment, and the punctuation has been freely
revised. The apparatus criticus is a drastically selective and simplified
version of the information to be found in the editions of Helm,
Robertson and Paratore; the phrase 'alii alia' invites the interested
enquirer to refer to these sources. Those corrections registered in the
apparatus which are not discussed in the Commentary generally
represent small apparent improvements of the transmitted text with
no compelling arguments either for or against them. In so idiosyncratic
a writer as Apuleius anything like banalization of his text must be
carefully guarded against.

For a full discussion of the MS tradition see Robertson's edition,
which in this respect is definitive; a convenient summary is provided
by Marshall.

APVLEI METAMORPHOSEON
LIBRI IV 28 – VI 24

LIBER IV

28 Erant in quadam ciuitate rex et regina. hi tres numero filias
forma conspicuas habuere, sed maiores quidem natu, quamuis
gratissima specie, idonee tamen celebrari posse laudibus
2 humanis credebantur, at uero puellae iunioris tam praecipua
tam praeclara pulchritudo nec exprimi ac ne sufficienter quidem
3 laudari sermonis humani penuria poterat. multi denique
ciuium et aduenae copiosi, quos eximii spectaculi rumor
studiosa celebritate congregabat, inaccessae formonsitatis
admiratione stupidi et admouentes oribus suis dexteram
primore digito in erectum pollicem residente ut ipsam prorsus
4 deam Venerem uenerabantur religiosis adorationibus. iamque
proximas ciuitates et attiguas regiones fama peruaserat deam
quam caerulum profundum pelagi peperit et ros spumantium
fluctuum educauit iam numinis sui passim tributa uenia in
mediis conuersari populi coetibus, uel certe rursum nouo
caelestium stillarum germine non maria sed terras Venerem
29 aliam uirginali flore praeditam pullulasse. sic immensum
procedit in dies opinio, sic insulas iam proxumas et terrae
plusculum prouinciasque plurimas fama porrecta peruagatur.
2 iam multi mortalium longis itineribus atque altissimis
maris meatibus ad saeculi specimen gloriosum confluebant.
3 Paphon nemo, Cnidon nemo ac ne ipsa quidem Cythera ad
conspectum deae Veneris nauigabant; sacra deseruntur, templa
deformantur, puluinaria proteruntur, caerimoniae negleguntur;
incoronata simulacra et arae uiduae frigido cinere foedatae.

4.28.3 uenerabantur *add. post* Venerem *Crusius, post* religiosis *Stoll*   29.2
altissimi *uel* latissimis *Oudendorp*   3 deseruntur *ed. Ald.*: differuntur *Colvius*:
die p̄feruntur *F*: *alii alia*   proteruntur *Salmasius*: p̄feruntur *F*

THE METAMORPHOSES OF
APULEIUS BOOKS IV 28 – VI 24

BOOK IV

28 There were in a certain city a king and queen, who had three beautiful daughters. The two eldest were very fair to see, but their beauty was such that it was thought human praise could 2 do it justice. The loveliness of the youngest, however, was so perfect that human speech was too poor to describe or even 3 praise it satisfactorily. Indeed huge numbers of both citizens and foreigners, drawn together in eager crowds by the fame of such an extraordinary sight, were struck dumb with admiration of her unequalled beauty; and raising the right thumb and forefinger to their lips they would offer outright religious 4 worship to her as the goddess Venus. Meanwhile the news had spread through the nearby cities and adjoining regions that the goddess born of the blue depths of the sea and fostered by its foaming waves had made public the grace of her godhead by mingling with mortal men; or at least that, from a new fertilization by drops from heaven, not sea but earth had **29** grown another Venus in the flower of her virginity. And so this belief exceeded all bounds and gained ground from day to day, ranging, first through the neighbouring islands, then, as the report was extended, through a good part of the mainland and 2 most of the provinces. Now there came flocking many people by long journeys and deep-sea voyages to view this wonder of 3 the age. No one voyaged to Paphos or Cnidos or even Cythera to see the goddess herself; her rites were abandoned, her temples disfigured, her couches trampled, her worship neglected; her statues were ungarlanded, her altars shamefully cold and

41

4 puellae supplicatur et in humanis uultibus deae tantae numina
placantur, et in matutino progressu uirginis uictimis et epulis
Veneris absentis nomen propitiatur, iamque per plateas
commeantem populi frequentes floribus sertis et solutis
adprecantur.

5   haec honorum caelestium ad puellae mortalis cultum
inmodica translatio uerae Veneris uehementer incendit
animos, et inpatiens indignationis capite quassanti fremens
30 altius sic secum disserit: 'en rerum naturae prisca parens, en
elementorum origo initialis, en orbis totius alma Venus, quae
cum mortali puella partiario maiestatis honore tractor et
nomen meum caelo conditum terrenis sordibus profanatur!
2 nimirum communi nominis piamento uicariae uenerationis
incertum sustinebo et imaginem meam circumferet puella
3 moritura. frustra me pastor ille cuius iustitiam fidemque
magnus comprobauit Iuppiter ob eximiam speciem tantis
praetulit deabus. sed non adeo gaudens ista, quaecumque est,
meos honores usurpauerit: iam faxo eam huius etiam ipsius
inlicitae formonsitatis paeniteat.'

4   et uocat confestim puerum suum pinnatum illum et satis
temerarium, qui malis suis moribus contempta disciplina
publica flammis et sagittis armatus per alienas domos nocte
discurrens et omnium matrimonia corrumpens impune
5 committit tanta flagitia et nihil prorsus boni facit. hunc,
quanquam genuina licentia procacem, uerbis quoque insuper
stimulat et perducit ad illam ciuitatem et Psychen – hoc enim
31 nomine puella nuncupabatur – coram ostendit, et tota illa
prolata de formonsitatis aemulatione fabula gemens ac fremens
indignatione 'per ego te' inquit 'maternae caritatis foedera
deprecor, per tuae sagittae dulcia uulnera, per flammae istius

4 frequentes *ed. Iunt. 1512*: frequenter *F*   30.1 detractor *Shackleton Bailey*
2 nominis *Robertson*: numinis *F*   3 usurpauerit *uel* usurparit · *Oudendorp*:
usurpabit ς: usurpauit *F*   eam *add. post* faxo *Helm, pro* etiam *suppos.*
Jahn etiam] statim *Watt*   4 pro *add. ante* malis *Watt*   31.1 prolata
ς: perlata *F*

4 bereft of offerings. It was the girl to whom prayers were addressed, and in human guise that the power of the mighty goddess was placated. When she appeared each morning it was the name of Venus (who was far away) that was propitiated with sacrifices and banquets; and as she walked the streets the people crowded to adore her with garlands and flowers.

5   This outrageous transference of divine honours to the worship of a mortal girl kindled violent anger in the true Venus, and unable to contain her indignation, tossing her head and protesting in deep bitterness, she thus soliloquized:

30 'So much for me, the ancient mother of nature, first beginning of the elements, Venus nurturer of the whole world! I must share with a mortal girl the honour due to my godhead, and

2 my name, established in heaven, is profaned by earthly dirt! It seems that my name is to be worshipped in common and that I must put up with the obscurity of being adored by deputy,

3 publicly represented by a girl who is doomed to die! Much good it did me that the shepherd whose impartial fairness was approved by great Jove preferred me for my unrivalled beauty to such great goddesses! But she will be very sorry, whoever she is, that she has usurped my honours. I will see to it that she regrets this beauty of hers to which she has no right.'

4   So saying she summoned that winged son of hers, that most reckless of creatures, whose wicked behaviour flies in the face of public morals, who armed with torch and arrows roams by night through houses where he has no business, ruining marriages on every hand, committing heinous crimes with

5 impunity, and never doing anything good. Irresponsible as he already was by nature, she aroused him yet more by her words; and taking him to the city and showing him Psyche –

31 for this was the girl's name – she laid before him the whole story of this rival beauty. Groaning and crying out in indignation, 'By the bonds of a mother's love', she said, 'I implore you, by the sweet wounds of your arrows, by the honeyed burns made

2 mellitas uredines uindictam tuae parenti, sed plenam, tribue et
in pulchritudinem contumacem seueriter uindica idque unum
3 et pro omnibus unicum uolens effice: uirgo ista amore
fraglantissimo teneatur hominis extremi, quem et dignitatis et
patrimonii simul et incolumitatis ipsius Fortuna damnauit,
tamque infimi ut per totum orbem non inueniat miseriae suae
comparem.'
4 sic effata et osculis hiantibus filium diu ac pressule sauiata
proximas oras reflui litoris petit, plantisque roseis uibrantium
fluctuum summo rore calcato ecce iam profundum maris sudo
5 resedit uertice, et ipsum quod incipit uelle, set statim, quasi
pridem praeceperit, non moratur marinum obsequium:
6 adsunt Nerei filiae chorum canentes et Portunus caerulis
barbis hispidus et grauis piscoso sinu Salacia et auriga
paruulus delphini Palaemon; iam passim maria persultantes
7 Tritonum cateruae hic concha sonaci leniter bucinat, ille
serico tegmine flagrantiae solis obsistit inimici, alius sub oculis
dominae speculum progerit, curru biiuges alii subnatant. talis
ad Oceanum pergentem Venerem comitatur exercitus.

32 interea Psyche cum sua sibi perspicua pulchritudine nullum
decoris sui fructum percipit. spectatur ab omnibus, laudatur
ab omnibus, nec quisquam, non rex non regius nec de
plebe saltem cupiens eius nuptiarum petitor accedit.
2 mirantur quidem diuinam speciem, sed ut simulacrum fabre
3 politum mirantur omnes. olim duae maiores sorores, quarum
temperatam formonsitatem nulli diffamarant populi, procis
4 regibus desponsae iam beatas nuptias adeptae, sed Psyche uirgo
uidua domi residens deflet desertam suam solitudinem aegra
corporis, animi saucia, et quamuis gentibus totis complacitam
5 odit in se suam formonsitatem. sic infortunatissimae filiae
miserrimus pater suspectatis caelestibus odiis et irae superum

---

2 seueriter *Brantz*: reuerenter *F*   3 infimi ç: infirmi *F*   4 licoris (*i.e.*
liquoris) *Rohde*   profundum *Koehler*: profundi *F*   5 set statim *Robertson*: &
s. *F*: ei s. *Jahn*: id s. *Castiglioni*: alii alia   7 Solis?

2 by your torch, avenge your mother – avenge her fully. Punish mercilessly that arrogant beauty, and do this one thing willingly
3 for me – it is all I ask. Let this girl be ensnared by a burning love for the lowest of mankind, some creature cursed by Fortune in rank, in estate, in condition, some one so degraded that in all the world he can find no wretchedness to equal his own.'

4 With these words, she kissed her son with long kisses, open-mouthed and closely pressed, then returned to the nearest point of the sea-shore. And as she set her rosy feet on the surface of the moving waves, lo, the face of the deep sea became
5 bright and calm. Scarcely had she formed the wish when immediately, as if she had previously ordered it, her marine
6 attendance was prompt to appear. There came the daughters of Nereus singing in harmony, Portunus with his thick sea-green beard, Salacia, the folds of her robe heavy with fish, and little Palaemon astride his dolphin. On all sides squadrons of
7 Tritons cavorted over the sea. One softly sounded his loud horn, a second with a silken veil kept off the heat of her enemy the Sun, a third held his mistress's mirror before her face, and others yoked in pairs swam beneath her car. Such was the retinue that escorted Venus in her progress to Ocean.

32 Psyche meanwhile, for all her conspicuous beauty, had no advantage from it. Everyone gazed at her, everyone praised her, but no one, king, prince or even commoner, came as a
2 suitor desiring her in marriage. Though they admired her appearance as of a goddess, all admired her merely as they
3 would a statue finished to perfection. Long ago her two elder sisters, whose unremarkable looks had by no means been noised abroad, had been betrothed to kingly suitors and
4 achieved rich marriages; Psyche stayed at home an unmarried virgin mourning her abandoned and lonely state, sick in body and mind, hating that beauty of hers which had enchanted the
5 whole world. In the end the wretched girl's father, sorrowfully suspecting some divine visitation and fearing the anger of the

6 metuens dei Milesii uetustissimum percontatur oraculum, et
   a tanto numine precibus et uictimis ingratae uirgini petit
   nuptias et maritum. sed Apollo, quanquam Graecus et Ionicus,
   propter Milesiae conditorem sic Latina sorte respondit:

33   'montis in excelsi scopulo, rex, siste puellam
                   ornatam mundo funerei thalami.
                nec speres generum mortali stirpe creatum,
                   sed saeuum atque ferum uipereumque malum,
2   quod pinnis uolitans super aethera cuncta fatigat   5
                   flammaque et ferro singula debilitat,
                quod tremit ipse Iouis quo numina terrificantur
                   fluminaque horrescunt et Stygiae tenebrae.'

3 rex olim beatus affatu sanctae uaticinationis accepto piger
   tristisque retro domum pergit suaeque coniugi praecepta sortis
   enodat infaustae. maeretur, fletur, lamentatur diebus plusculis.
4 sed dirae sortis iam urget taeter effectus, iam feralium
   nuptiarum miserrimae uirgini choragium struitur, iam taedae
   lumen atrae fuliginis cinere marcescit, et sonus tibiae zygiae
   mutatur in querulum Ludii modum cantusque laetus hymenaei
   lugubri finitur ululatu, et puella nuptura deterget lacrimas
5 ipso suo flammeo. sic adfectae domus triste fatum cuncta
   etiam ciuitas congemebat luctuque publico confestim
   congruens edicitur iustitium.

34   sed monitis caelestibus parendi necessitas misellam Psychen
   ad destinatam poenam efflagitabat. perfectis igitur feralis
   thalami cum summo maerore sollemnibus toto prosequente
   populo uiuum producitur funus, et lacrimosa Psyche comitatur
2 non nuptias sed exequias suas. ac dum maesti parentes et

32.6 a *add. Price*   tanto *saepius sollicitatum*   33.3 pingens *Lipsius, quod utrum*
in F olim fuerit incertum   4 ludiimodum *F*: ludium *F² ut uid.*: Ludium
modum *Giarratano*   ipsa?

gods, consulted the most ancient oracle of Apollo at Miletus,
6 and implored the great god with prayers and sacrifices for
marriage and a husband for his slighted daughter. But Apollo,
though Greek and Ionian, in consideration for the writer of
a Milesian tale replied in Latin:

33   'On mountain peak, o king, expose the maid
          For funeral wedlock ritually arrayed.
        No human son-in-law (hope not) is thine,
          But something cruel and fierce and serpentine;
2   That plagues the world as, borne aloft on wings,
          With fire and steel it persecutes all things;
        That Jove himself, he whom the gods revere,
          That Styx's darkling stream regards with fear.'

3 The king who had once accounted himself happy, on hearing
the utterance of the sacred prophecy, returned home reluctant
and downcast and explained to his wife the instructions of the
inauspicious reply. There followed several days of mourning,
of weeping, of lamentation. But now the ghastly fulfilment of
4 the terrible oracle was upon them. The gear for the poor girl's
funereal bridal was now prepared; the flame of the torches
died down in black smoke and ash; the sound of the marriage-
pipe was changed to the plaintive Lydian mode; the joyful
marriage-hymn ended in lugubrious wailings; and the bride
5 wiped away her tears with her own bridal veil. The whole city
joined in lamenting the sad plight of the afflicted house, and
in sympathy with the general grief all public business was
immediately suspended.

34   But the bidding of heaven had to be obeyed, and the
unfortunate Psyche was required to undergo the punishment
ordained for her. Accordingly the ceremonies of her funereal
marriage were duly performed with the utmost sorrow, and
escorted by the entire populace Psyche was led forth, a living
corpse, and in tears joined in, not her wedding procession, but
2 her own funeral. While her parents, grief-stricken and stunned

tanto malo perciti nefarium facinus perficere cunctantur, ipsa
3 illa filia talibus eos adhortatur uocibus: 'quid infelicem
senectam fletu diutino cruciatis? quid spiritum uestrum, qui
magis meus est, crebris eiulatibus fatigatis? quid lacrimis
inefficacibus ora mihi ueneranda foedatis? quid laceratis in
uestris oculis mea lumina? quid canitiem scinditis? quid
4 pectora, quid ubera sancta tunditis? haec erant uobis egregiae
formonsitatis meae praeclara praemia. inuidiae nefariae letali
5 plaga percussi sero sentitis. cum gentes et populi celebrarent
nos diuinis honoribus, cum nouam me Venerem ore consono
nuncuparent, tunc dolere, tunc flere, tunc me iam quasi
peremptam lugere debuistis. iam sentio, iam uideo solo me
6 nomine Veneris perisse. ducite me et cui sors addixit scopulo
sistite. festino felices istas nuptias obire, festino generosum
illum maritum meum uidere. quid differo, quid detrecto
uenientem, qui totius orbis exitio natus est?'
35   sic profata uirgo conticuit ingressuque iam ualido pompae
2 populi prosequentis sese miscuit. itur ad constitutum scopulum
montis ardui, cuius in summo cacumine statutam puellam
cuncti deserunt, taedasque nuptiales, quibus praeluxerant,
ibidem lacrimis suis extinctas relinquentes deiectis capitibus
3 domuitionem parant. et miseri quidem parentes eius tanta
clade defessi, clausae domus abstrusi tenebris, perpetuae nocti
4 sese dedidere. Psychen autem pauentem ac trepidantem et in
ipso scopuli uertice deflentem mitis aura molliter spirantis
Zephyri uibratis hinc inde laciniis et reflato sinu sensim
leuatam suo tranquillo spiritu uehens paulatim per deuexa
rupis excelsae uallis subditae florentis caespitis gremio leniter
delapsam reclinat.

34.3 maceratis *Petschenig*   4 erant *Haupt*: erunt *F*: *alii alia*   35.4 trepidantem *F sed in* trepidam *corr. m*[1]   deflentem *F*: defluentem ç: deficientem *Helm*

by this great calamity, hesitated to complete the dreadful
3 deed, their daughter encouraged them herself: 'Why torture
your unhappy old age with prolonged weeping? Why weary
your spirit – my spirit rather – with repeated cries of woe?
Why disfigure with unavailing tears the faces which I revere?
Why by tearing your eyes do you tear mine? Why pull out your
white hairs? Why beat your breasts, those breasts which to me
4 are holy? Such, it seems, are the glorious rewards for you of my
incomparable beauty. Only now do you understand that you
5 are smitten by the deathly blow of a wicked jealousy. Then,
when nations and peoples were paying us divine honours,
when with one voice they were hailing me as a new Venus,
then you should have grieved, then you should have wept,
then you should have mourned me as already lost. Now I
understand, now I see that it is by the name of Venus alone
6 that I am destroyed. Take me and place me on the rock to
which destiny has assigned me. I cannot wait to enter on this
happy marriage, and to see that noble bridegroom of mine.
Why should I postpone, why should I shirk my meeting with
him who is born for the ruin of the whole world?'

35   After this speech the girl fell silent and, her step now firm,
2 joined the escorting procession. They came to the prescribed
crag on the steep mountain, and on the topmost summit they
placed the girl and there all abandoned her; leaving there too
the wedding torches with which they had lighted the way,
extinguished by their tears, with bowed heads they took their
3 way homeward. Psyche's unhappy parents, totally disheartened
by this great calamity, shut themselves away in the darkness of
their shuttered palace and abandoned themselves to perpetual
4 night. Her, however, fearful and trembling and lamenting her
fate there on the summit of the rock, the gentle breeze of softly
breathing Zephyr, blowing the edges of her dress this way and
that and filling its folds, imperceptibly lifted up; and carrying
her on his tranquil breath smoothly down the slope of the lofty
crag he gently let her sink and laid her to rest on the flowery
turf in the bosom of the valley that lay below.

LIBER V

1 Psyche teneris et herbosis locis in ipso toro roscidi graminis
suaue recubans, tanta mentis perturbatione sedata, dulce
conquieuit. iamque sufficienti recreata somno placido resurgit
2 animo. uidet lucum proceris et uastis arboribus consitum,
uidet fontem uitreo latice perlucidum; medio luci meditullio
prope fontis adlapsum domus regia est aedificata non humanis
3 manibus sed diuinis artibus. iam scires ab introitu primo dei
cuiuspiam luculentum et amoenum uidere te diuersorium.
nam summa laquearia citro et ebore curiose cauata subeunt
aureae   columnae,   parietes   omnes   argenteo   caelamine
conteguntur bestiis et id genus pecudibus occurrentibus ob os
4 introeuntium. mirus prorsum homo immo semideus uel certe
deus, qui magnae artis suptilitate tantum efferauit argentum.
5 enimuero pauimenta ipsa lapide pretioso caesim deminuto in
uaria picturae genera discriminantur: uehementer iterum ac
6 saepius beatos illos qui super gemmas et monilia calcant! iam
ceterae partes longe lateque dispositae domus sine pretio
pretiosae totique parietes solidati massis aureis splendore
proprio coruscant, ut diem suum sibi domus faciat licet sole
nolente: sic cubicula, sic porticus, sic ipsae ualuae fulgurant.
7 nec setius opes ceterae maiestati domus respondent, ut
equidem illud recte uideatur ad conuersationem humanam
magno Ioui fabricatum caeleste palatium.

2   inuitata Psyche talium locorum oblectatione propius accessit
et paulo fidentior intra limen sese facit, mox prolectante studio
pulcherrimae uisionis rimatur singula et altrinsecus aedium
horrea sublimi fabrica perfecta magnisque congesta gazis
2 conspicit. nec est quicquam quod ibi non est. sed praeter
ceteram tantarum diuitiarum admirationem hoc erat praecipue

5.1.2 medio *'fortasse ... expungenda' Price*   3 scires *uett. edd.*: scies *F*   id
genus *uix sanum*: omne genus *Vollgraff*: *alii alia*   4 prorsum magnae artis
homo *F*: *corr. Gruter*   6 domus faciat ς: domus faciant *F*: domi faciant
Castiglioni   ualuae *sscr.* ф: ualneç *F, unde* balneae *Eyssenhardt*   2.1 facit]
agit *Stewech*

BOOK V

1 In this soft grassy spot Psyche lay pleasantly couched in her bed of dewy turf and, her great disquiet of mind soothed, fell sweetly asleep. Presently, refreshed by a good rest, she rose
2 with her mind at ease. What she saw was a park planted with great tall trees and a spring of crystal-clear water. In the very centre of the garden, by the outflow of the spring, a palace had
3 been built, not by human hands but by arts divine. You could be sure at your first entry that you were looking at the splendid and delightful country-house of some god. For the coffering of the ceiling was of citron-wood and ivory artfully carved, and the columns supporting it were of gold; all the walls were covered in embossed silver, with wild beasts and other animals
4 confronting the visitor on entering. Truly it was a wonderful man or demigod or indeed god, who with such art had given
5 wild life to all that silver! Furthermore, the very floors were divided up into different kinds of pictures in mosaic of precious stones: twice indeed and more than twice marvellously happy
6 those who walk on gems and jewellery! The other parts of this house of inestimable price, extending far and wide, and all the walls, which were built of solid blocks of gold, shone with their own brilliance, so that the house furnished its own daylight, sun or no sun: such was the radiance of the rooms,
7 the colonnades, the very doors. The rest of the furnishings matched the magnificence of the building, so that it would seem fair to say that great Jove had built himself a heavenly palace to dwell among mortals.

2   Attracted by the delights of this place, Psyche approached and, becoming a little bolder, crossed the threshold; then allured by her joy in the beautiful spectacle she examined all the details. On the other side of the palace she discovered lofty storehouses crammed with rich treasure: there was nothing
2 that was not there. But in addition to the wonder that such wealth could exist, what was most astonishing was that this

mirificum, quod nullo uinculo, nullo claustro, nullo custode
3 totius orbis thensaurus ille muniebatur. haec ei summa cum
uoluptate uisenti offert sese uox quaedam corporis sui nuda et
'quid,' inquit 'domina, tantis obstupescis opibus? tua sunt
haec omnia. prohinc cubiculo te refer et lectulo lassitudinem
4 refoue et ex arbitrio lauacrum pete. nos, quarum uoces accipis,
tuae famulae sedulo tibi praeministrabimus nec corporis
3 curatae tibi regales epulae morabuntur.' sensit Psyche diuinae
Prouidentiae beatitudinem, monitusque uocis informis audiens
2 et prius somno et mox lauacro fatigationem sui diluit, uisoque
statim proximo semirotundo suggestu, propter instrumentum
3 cenatorium rata refectui suo commodum libens accumbit. et
ilico uini nectarei eduliumque uariorum fercula copiosa nullo
seruiente sed tantum spiritu quodam impulsa subministrantur.
4 nec quemquam tamen illa uidere poterat, sed uerba tantum
5 audiebat excidentia et solas uoces famulas habebat. post
opimas dapes quidam introcessit et cantauit inuisus et alius
citharam pulsauit, quae uidebatur nec ipsa. tunc modulatae
multitudinis conserta uox aures eius affertur, ut, quamuis
hominum nemo pareret, chorus tamen esse pateret.
4 finitis uoluptatibus uespera suadente concedit Psyche
cubitum. iamque prouecta nocte clemens quidam sonus aures
2 eius accedit. tunc uirginitati suae pro tanta solitudine metuens
et pauet et horrescit et quouis malo plus timet quod ignorat.
3 iamque aderat ignobilis maritus et torum inscenderat et
uxorem sibi Psychen fecerat et ante lucis exortum propere
4 discesserat. statim uoces cubiculo praestolatae nouam nuptam
interfectae uirginitatis curant. haec diutino tempore sic
5 agebantur. atque ut est natura redditum, nouitas per assiduam
consuetudinem delectationem ei commendarat et sonus uocis
incertae solitudinis erat solacium.

3.1 uocis informis *Groslot*: uoces informes *F* et *ante* prius *del. Toussaint*
3 *post* nectarei *add.* pocula *van der Vliet* tantum] tamquam *Bluemner* 5 conserta *Oudendorp*: conferta *F* chorum ς 4.1 clemens ς: demens *F*
5 nouitas] uiduitas *Jahn*: alii alia

vast treasure of the entire world was not secured by a single
3 lock, bolt or guard. As she looked at all this with much pleasure
there came to her a disembodied voice: 'Mistress, why are you
amazed at this great wealth? All of it is yours. Enter then your
bedchamber, relieve your fatigue in sleep, and go to your bath
4 when you are minded. We whose voices you hear are your
attendants who will diligently wait on you; and when you have
refreshed yourself a royal banquet will not be slow to appear
3 for you.' Psyche recognized her happy estate as sent by divine
Providence, and obeying the instructions of the bodiless voice
she dispelled her weariness first with sleep and then a bath.
2 There immediately appeared in front of her a semi-circular
seat; understanding from the dinner equipage that this provision
3 was for her entertainment she gladly took her place. Straightway course after course of wine like nectar and of different kinds
of food were placed before her, with no servant to be seen but
4 everything wafted as it were on the wind. She could see no one
but merely heard the words that were uttered, and her waiting
5 maids were nothing but voices to her. When the rich feast was
over, there entered an invisible singer, and another performed
on a lyre, itself invisible. This was succeeded by singing in
concert, and though not a soul was to be seen, there was
evidently a whole choir present.
4   These pleasures ended, and evening persuading, Psyche
went to bed. Night was well advanced when a gentle sound
2 was heard. Then, all alone as she was and fearing for her
virginity, Psyche quailed and trembled, dreading, more than
3 any possible harm, the unknown. Now there entered her
unknown husband; he had mounted the bed, made her his
4 wife, and departed in haste before sunrise. At once the voices
that were in waiting in the room tended the new bride's slain
5 virginity. Things went on in this way for some little time;
and, as nature has ordained, the novelty of her situation was
by custom rendered pleasurable to her, while the sound of the
unseen voice solaced her solitude.

6   interea parentes eius indefesso luctu atque maerore
consenescebant, latiusque porrecta fama sorores illae maiores
cuncta cognorant propereque maestae atque lugubres deserto
lare certatim ad parentum suorum conspectum adfatumque
5 perrexerant. ea nocte ad suam Psychen sic infit maritus
(namque praeter oculos et manibus et auribus eius nihil
2 non sentiebatur): 'Psyche dulcissima et cara uxor, exitiabile
tibi periculum minatur Fortuna saeuior, quod obseruandum
3 pressiore cautela censeo. sorores iam tuae mortis opinione
turbatae tuumque uestigium requirentes scopulum istum
protinus aderunt, quarum si quas forte lamentationes acceperis,
neque respondeas immo nec prospicias omnino; ceterum mihi
quidem grauissimum dolorem, tibi uero summum creabis
4 exitium.' annuit et ex arbitrio mariti se facturam spopondit,
sed eo simul cum nocte dilapso diem totum lacrimis ac
5 plangoribus misella consumit, se nunc maxime prorsus perisse
iterans, quae beati carceris custodia septa et humanae
conuersationis colloquio uiduata nec sororibus quidem suis de
se maerentibus opem salutarem ferre ac ne uidere eas quidem
6 omnino posset. nec lauacro nec cibo nec ulla denique
refectione recreata flens ubertim decessit ad somnum.

6   nec mora, cum paulo maturius lectum maritus accubans
eamque etiam nunc lacrimantem complexus sic expostulat:
2 'haecine mihi pollicebare, Psyche mea? quid iam de te tuus
maritus expecto, quid spero? et perdia et pernox nec inter
3 amplexus coniugales desinis cruciatum. age iam nunc ut uoles,
et animo tuo damnosa poscenti pareto. tantum memineris
4 meae seriae monitionis, cum coeperis sero paenitere.' tunc illa
precibus et dum se morituram comminatur extorquet a marito
cupitis adnuat, ut sorores uideat, luctus mulceat, ora conferat.
5 sic ille nouae nuptae precibus ueniam tribuit et insuper

5.1 eius nihil non *Watt post Traube* (is nihil non) *et Terzaghi* (nihil non): Ius
nichil *F*: is nihilo setius *Haupt*: ut praesentius nihil *Robertson: alii alia*   6.2
post pernox *add*. fles *Watt*, maeres *uel* luges *uel* doles *Kenney*

6   Meanwhile her parents were worn away with ceaseless grief
and sorrow; and as the story spread abroad her elder sisters
learned of the whole affair. Immediately, sad and downcast,
they left home and vied with each other in their haste to see
5   and talk to their parents. That night her husband spoke to
Psyche – for by her hands and ears, though not by her eyes, his
2   presence was completely felt – as follows: 'Sweetest Psyche, my
dear wife, Fortune in yet more cruel guise threatens you with
mortal danger: I charge you to be most earnestly on your
3   guard against it. Your sisters, believing you to be dead, are
now in their grief following you to that mountain-top and will
soon be there. If you should hear their lamentations, do not
answer or even look that way, or you will bring about heavy
4   grief for me and for yourself sheer destruction.' She agreed and
promised to do her husband's bidding; but as soon as he and
night had vanished together, the unhappy girl spent the whole
5   day crying and mourning, constantly repeating that now she
was utterly destroyed: locked up in this rich prison and deprived
of intercourse or speech with human beings, she could not
bring comfort to her sisters in their sorrow or even set eyes on
6   them. Unrevived by bath or by food or any other refreshment
and weeping abundantly she retired to rest.

6   It was no more than a moment before her husband, earlier
than usual, came to bed and found her still weeping. Taking
2   her in his arms he remonstrated with her: 'Is this what you
promised, my Psyche? What am I, your husband, now to
expect from you? What am I to hope? All day, all night, even
3   in your husband's arms, you persist in tormenting yourself. Do
then as you wish and obey the ruinous demands of your heart.
Only be mindful of my stern warning when – too late – you
4   begin to be sorry.' Then with entreaties and threats of suicide
she forced her husband to agree to her wishes: to see her
5   sisters, to appease their grief, to talk with them. So he yielded
to the entreaties of his new bride, and moreover allowed her to

   quibuscumque uellet eas auri uel monilium donare concessit,
6 sed identidem monuit ac saepe terruit ne quando sororum
   pernicioso consilio suasa de forma mariti quaerat neue se
   sacrilega curiositate de tanto fortunarum suggestu pessum
7 deiciat nec suum postea contingat amplexum. gratias egit
   marito iamque laetior animo 'sed prius' inquit 'centies moriar
   quam tuo isto dulcissimo conubio caream. amo enim et
   efflictim te, quicumque es, diligo aeque ut meum spiritum, nec
8 ipsi Cupidini comparo. sed istud etiam meis precibus, oro,
   largire et illi tuo famulo Zephyro praecipe simili uectura
9 sorores hic mihi sistat', et imprimens oscula suasoria et
   ingerens uerba mulcentia et inserens membra cogentia haec
   etiam blanditiis astruit: 'mi mellite, mi marite, tuae Psychae
10 dulcis anima.' ui ac potestate Venerii susurrus inuitus
   succubuit maritus et cuncta se facturum spopondit atque
   etiam luce proxumante de manibus uxoris euanuit.

7 at illae sorores percontatae scopulum locumque illum quo
   fuerat Psyche deserta festinanter adueniunt ibique difflebant
   oculos et plangebant ubera, quoad crebris earum heiulatibus
2 saxa cautesque parilem sonum resultarent. iamque nomine
   proprio sororem miseram ciebant, quoad sono penetrabili
   uocis ululabilis per prona delapso amens et trepida Psyche
   procurrit e domo et 'quid' inquit 'uos miseris lamentationibus
3 necquicquam effligitis? quam lugetis, adsum. lugubres uoces
   desinite et diutinis lacrimis madentes genas siccate tandem,
4 quippe cum iam possitis quam plangebatis amplecti.' tunc
   uocatum Zephyrum praecepti maritalis admonet. nec mora,
   cum ille parens imperio statim clementissimis flatibus innoxia
5 uectura deportat illas. iam mutuis amplexibus et festinantibus

---

5 donare] donis ornare *Traube*: donis donare *Baehrens*   9 cogentia $F^{a.c.}$ ut
uid.: cohibentia φ   10 etiam] iam '*uir doctus*' *ap. Oudendorp*

present them with whatever she liked in the way of gold or
6 jewels; repeatedly, however, warning her and terrifying her
again and again: she must never be induced by the evil advice
of her sisters to try to discover what her husband looked like or
allow impious curiosity to hurl her down to destruction from
the heights on which Fortune had placed her and so for ever
7 deprive her of his embraces. Psyche thanked her husband and,
happier now in her mind, 'Indeed', she said, 'I shall die a
hundred deaths before I let myself be robbed of this most
delightful marriage with you. For I love and adore you to
distraction, whoever you are, as I love my own life; Cupid
8 himself cannot compare with you. But this too I beg you to
grant me: order your servant Zephyr to bring my sisters to
9 me as he brought me here' – and planting seductive kisses,
uttering caressing words, and entwining him in her enclosing
arms, she added to her endearments 'My darling, my husband,
10 sweet soul of your Psyche.' He unwillingly gave way under
the powerful influence of her murmured words of love, and
promised to do all she asked; and then, as dawn was now near,
he vanished from his wife's arms.

7   The sisters enquired the situation of the rock where Psyche
had been abandoned and hurriedly made their way there;
where they started to cry their eyes out and beat their breasts,
so that the rocky crags re-echoed their ceaseless wailings.
2 They went on calling their unhappy sister by name, until the
piercing noise of their shrieks carried down the mountainside
and brought Psyche running out of the palace in distraction,
crying 'Why do you destroy yourselves for no reason with
3 miserable lamentation? I whom you mourn, I am here. Cease
your sad outcry, dry now your cheeks so long wet with tears;
for now you can embrace her for whom you were grieving.'
4 Then she summoned Zephyr and reminded him of her husband's
order. On the instant he obeyed her command and straightway
on his most gentle breeze brought them to her unharmed.
5 Then they gave themselves over to the enjoyment of embraces

sauiis sese perfruuntur et illae sedatae lacrimae postliminio
6 redeunt prolectante gaudio. 'sed et tectum' inquit 'et larem
nostrum laetae succedite et afflictas animas cum Psyche uestra
8 recreate.' sic allocuta summas opes domus aureae uocumque
seruientium populosam familiam demonstrat oculis et auribus
earum lauacroque pulcherrimo et inhumanae mensae lautitiis
2 eas opipare reficit, ut illarum prorsus caelestium diuitiarum
copiis affluentibus satiatae iam praecordiis penitus nutrirent
3 inuidiam. denique altera earum satis scrupulose curioseque
percontari non desinit, quis illarum caelestium rerum dominus,
4 quisue uel qualis ipsius sit maritus. nec tamen Psyche
coniugale illud praeceptum ullo pacto temerat uel pectoris
arcanis exigit, sed e re nata confingit esse iuuenem quendam et
speciosum, commodum lanoso barbitio genas inumbrantem,
plerumque rurestribus ac montanis uenatibus occupatum,
5 et ne qua sermonis procedentis labe consilium tacitum pro-
deretur, auro facto gemmosisque monilibus onustas eas statim
uocato Zephyro tradit reportandas.

9   quo protenus perpetrato sorores egregiae domum redeuntes
iamque gliscentis inuidiae felle fraglantes multa secum
2 sermonibus mutuis perstrepebant. sic denique infit altera: 'en
orba et saeua et iniqua Fortuna! hocine tibi complacuit,
ut utroque parente prognatae germanae diuersam sortem
3 sustineremus? et nos quidem quae natu maiores sumus maritis
aduenis ancillae deditae extorres et lare et ipsa patria degamus
4 longe parentum uelut exulantes, haec autem nouissima, quam
fetu satiante postremus partus effudit, tantis opibus et deo
marito potita sit, quae nec uti recte tanta bonorum copia
5 nouit? uidisti, soror, quanta in domo iacent et qualia monilia,
quae praenitent uestes, quae splendicant gemmae, quantum
6 praeterea passim calcatur aurum. quodsi maritum etiam tam

8.1 oculis et *add. van der Vliet* 4 rebus *post* rurestribus *add. Watt* 9.2
eodem *add. post* prognatae *Michaelis, post* utroque *Paratore: alii alia* germanae
add. Robertson, sorores *Jahn* tam *ante* diuersam *add. Crusius*

and eager kisses; and the tears which they had restrained now
6 broke out again at the coaxing of their joy. 'But now', said
Psyche, 'enter in happiness my house and home and with your
8 sister restore your tormented souls.' With these words she
showed them the great riches of the golden palace and let
them listen to the retinue of slave-voices, and refreshed them
sumptuously with a luxurious bath and the supernatural
2 splendours of her table. They, having enjoyed to the full this
profusion of divine riches, now began deep in their hearts to
3 cherish envy. Thus one of them persisted in asking with
minute thoroughness who was the master of this heavenly
4 household and who or what was Psyche's husband. Psyche,
however, did not in any way violate her husband's orders or
banish them from her secret heart, but improvised a story that
he was a handsome young man whose beard had only just
begun to grow and that he spent most of his time hunting over
5 the countryside and the mountains. Then, fearing that if the
conversation were to be prolonged some slip would give away
her secret thoughts, she loaded them with goldwork and
jewellery, immediately summoned Zephyr, and handed them
over to him for their return journey.

9   No sooner said than done. The worthy sisters on their return
home were now inflamed by the poison of their growing envy,
and began to exchange noisy complaints. So then the first
2 started: 'See how blind and cruel and unjust is Fortune! –
content, it seems, that sisters of the same parents should fare
3 so differently. Here are we, the elder sisters, handed over to
foreign husbands as slaves, banished from our home, our own
4 country, to live the life of exiles far from our parents; while she,
the youngest, the offspring of a late birth and flagging fertility,
is to enjoy huge wealth and a god for husband, though she
does not even know how to make proper use of this store of
5 happiness. You saw, sister, all the priceless necklaces, the
resplendent stuffs, the sparkling gems, the gold everywhere
6 underfoot. If this husband of hers is as handsome as she says,

formonsum tenet ut affirmat, nulla nunc in orbe toto felicior
uiuit. fortassis tamen procedente consuetudine et adfectione
roborata deam quoque illam deus maritus efficiet. sic est
7 hercules, sic se gerebat ferebatque. iam iam sursum respicit
et deam spirat mulier, quae uoces ancillas habet et uentis
8 ipsis imperitat. at ego misera primum patre meo seniorem
maritum sortita sum, dein cucurbita caluiorem et quouis
puero pusilliorem, cunctam domum seris et catenis obditam
custodientem.'

10 suscipit alia: 'ego uero maritum articulari etiam morbo
complicatum curuatumque ac per hoc rarissimo uenerem
2 meam recolentem sustineo, plerumque detortos et duratos in
lapidem digitos eius perfricans, fomentis olidis et pannis
sordidis et faetidis cataplasmatibus manus tam delicatas istas
adurens, nec uxoris officiosam faciem sed medicae laboriosam
3 personam sustinens. et tu quidem, soror, uideris quam patienti
uel potius seruili – dicam enim libere quod sentio – haec
perferas animo: enimuero ego nequeo sustinere ulterius tam
4 beatam fortunam allapsam indignae. recordare enim quam
superbe, quam adroganter nobiscum egerit et ipsa iactatione
inmodicae ostentationis tumentem suum prodiderit animum
5 deque tantis diuitiis exigua nobis inuita proiecerit confestimque
praesentiam nostram grauata propelli et efflari exsibilarique
6 nos iusserit. nec sum mulier nec omnino spiro, nisi eam
pessum de tantis opibus deiecero. ac si tibi etiam, ut par est,
inacuit nostra contumelia, consilium ualidum requiramus
7 ambae. iamque ista quae ferimus non parentibus nostris ac nec
ulli monstremus alii, immo nec omnino quicquam de
8 eius salute norimus. sat est quod ipsae uidimus quae
uidisse paenituit, nedum ut genitoribus et omnibus populis
tam beatum eius differamus praeconium. nec sunt enim

7 imperitat *F*: imperat φ   10.3 allapsam *Helm*: conlapsam *F*: allatam
Lipsius   5 praesentiam nostram *Price*: praesentia nostra *F*   6 ac] at
Castiglioni   8 paenitet *van der Vliet*

she is the happiest woman alive. Perhaps, though, as he learns to know her and his love is strengthened, her god-husband will make her too a goddess. Yes indeed, that's it: that explains her

7 behaviour and her attitude. She looks in the air and gives off an aura of goddess already, this woman who has voices for

8 slaves and lords it over the winds themselves. And I, poor wretch, have been vouchsafed a husband older than my father, bald as a pumpkin and puny as a child, who keeps the whole house shut up with bolts and bars.'

10 Her sister took up the refrain: 'And I have to put up with a husband bent double by rheumatism and so hardly ever able

2 to pleasure me. I have constantly to massage his twisted, stone-hard, fingers, spoiling these delicate hands of mine with stinking compresses and filthy bandages and loathsome plasters – so that mine is not the dutiful appearance of a wife

3 but the toilsome part of a sick-nurse. It is for you, sister, to consider how patiently – or rather slavishly, for I shall say frankly what I think – *you* can bear this; as for me, I can no longer stand the sight of such good fortune befalling one so

4 unworthy of it. Do you remember the pride, the arrogance of her treatment of us? How in the display of her immoderate

5 ostentation she revealed her puffed-up heart? With what bad grace she tossed us a few scraps of her huge wealth and then without more ado, weary of our company, ordered us to be

6 thrust – blown – whistled away? As I'm a woman, as I live, I will hurl her down to ruin from her great riches. And if you too, as you are entitled to do, have taken offence at her contemptuous treatment of us, let us together devise strong

7 measures. Let us not show these presents to our parents or to anybody else, and let us pretend not to know even if she is alive

8 or dead. Enough that we have seen what we wished we hadn't, without spreading this happy news of her to them and to the rest of the world. You aren't really rich if nobody knows that

9 beati quorum diuitias nemo nouit. sciet se non ancillas sed
sorores habere maiores. et nunc quidem concedamus ad
maritos, et lares pauperes nostros sed plane sobrios reuisamus,
denique cogitationibus pressioribus instructae ad superbiam
poeniendam firmiores redeamus.'

11   placet pro bono duabus malis malum consilium totisque illis
tam pretiosis muneribus absconditis comam trahentes et
proinde ut merebantur ora lacerantes simulatos redintegrant
2 fletus. ac sic parentes quoque redulcerato prorsum dolore
raptim deterrentes uesania turgidae domus suas contendunt
dolum scelestum immo uero parricidium struentes contra
3 sororem insontem. interea Psychen maritus ille quem nescit
rursum suis illis nocturnis sermonibus sic commonet: 'uidesne
quantum tibi periculum minatur? uelitatur Fortuna eminus,
ac nisi longe firmiter praecaues mox comminus congredietur.
4 perfidae lupulae magnis conatibus nefarias insidias tibi
comparant, quarum summa est ut te suadeant meos explorare
5 uultus, quos, ut tibi saepe praedixi, non uidebis si uideris. ergo
igitur si posthac pessimae illae lamiae noxiis animis armatae
uenerint – uenient autem, scio – neque omnino sermonem
conferas, et si id tolerare pro genuina simplicitate proque
animi tui teneritudine non potueris, certe de marito nil
6 quicquam uel audias uel respondeas. nam et familiam nostram
iam propagabimus et hic adhuc infantilis uterus gestat nobis
infantem alium, si texeris nostra secreta silentio, diuinum, si
12 profanaueris, mortalem.' nuntio Psyche laeta florebat et
diuinae subolis solacio plaudebat et futuri pignoris gloria
2 gestiebat et materni nominis dignitate gaudebat. crescentes
dies et menses exeuntes anxia numerat et sarcinae nesciae

9 denique ς: diuque F: alii alia   11.2 prorsum] rursum van der
Vliet post dolore add. discruciatos ex. gr. Shackleton Bailey deterrentes uix
sanum: deserentes Colvius raptim ante uesania transp. Castiglioni, ante contendunt Damsté; sed nisi illud quoque aut explices aut corrigas aut auferas, frustra haec
et similia   3 minatur add. van der Vliet   4 magnis] malignis Kroll   6
propagauimus 'Edd. Rom. & Aldi. Nec male' Oudendorp   12.2 in ante
sarcinae add. Michaelis

9 you are rich. She will learn that she has elder sisters, not servants. Now let us return to our husbands and go back to our homes – poor but decent – and then thinking things over seriously let us equip ourselves to return yet more resolute to punish her insolence.'

11   The two wicked women thought well of this bad plan, and having hidden all their precious gifts, tearing their hair and clawing their cheeks (just as they deserved) they renewed their

2 pretence of mourning. And having in this way quite reinflamed their parents' grief and abruptly discouraged them, they made off to their homes swollen with mad rage, to devise their wicked – or I should say murderous – plot against their innocent

3 sister. Meanwhile Psyche's mysterious husband once more warned her in their night-time conversation: 'Do you not see your great danger? Fortune is now engaging your outposts, and if you do not stand very firmly on your guard she will

4 soon be grappling with you hand to hand. These faithless she-wolves are trying as hard as they can to lay a horrible trap for you; their one aim is to persuade you to try to know my face – but if you do see it, as I have often told you, you will not

5 see it. So then if those vile witches come, as I know they will, armed with their noxious designs, you must not even talk to them; but if because of your natural lack of guile and tenderness of heart you are unequal to that, at least you must refuse to

6 hear or answer any questions about your husband. For before long we shall increase our family; your womb, until now a child's, carries a child for us in its turn – who, if you hide our secret in silence, will be divine, but if you divulge it, will be

12 mortal.' Hearing this Psyche, blooming with happiness, clapped her hands at the consoling thought of a divine son, exulting in the glory of this pledge to be and rejoicing in the

2 dignity of the name of mother. Anxiously she counted the growing tale of days and months as they passed, and as she learned to bear her unfamiliar burden she marvelled that from

rudimento miratur de breui punctulo tantum incrementulum
locupletis uteri.

3   sed iam pestes illae taeterrimaéque Furiae anhelantes
uipereum uirus et festinantes impia celeritate nauigabant. tunc
4 sic iterum momentarius maritus suam Psychen admonet: 'en
dies ultima et casus extremus! sexus infestus et sanguis
inimicus iam sumpsit arma et castra commouit et aciem
derexit et classicum personauit; iam mucrone districto iugulum
5 tuum nefariae tuae sorores petunt. heu quantis urguemur
cladibus, Psyche dulcissima! tui nostrique miserere religiosaque
continentia domum maritum teque et istum paruulum nostrum
6 imminentis ruinae infortunio libera. nec illas scelestas feminas,
quas tibi post interneciuum odium et calcata sanguinis foedera
sorores appellare non licet, uel uideas uel audias, cum in
morem Sirenum scopulo prominentes funestis uocibus saxa
personabunt.'

13   suscipit Psyche singultu lacrimoso sermonem incertans:
'iam dudum, quod sciam, fidei atque parciloquio meo
perpendisti documenta, nec eo setius adprobabitur tibi nunc
2 etiam firmitas animi mei. tu modo Zephyro nostro rursum
praecipe fungatur obsequia, et in uicem denegatae sacrosanctae
3 imaginis tuae redde saltem conspectum sororum. per istos
cinnameos et undique pendulos crines tuos, per teneras et
teretis et mei similes genas, per pectus nescio quo calore
feruidum sic in hoc saltem paruulo cognoscam faciem tuam:
4 supplicis anxiae piis precibus erogatus germani complexus
indulge fructum et tibi deuotae Psychae animam gaudio
5 recrea. nec quicquam amplius in tuo uultu requiro, iam nil
officiunt mihi nec ipsae nocturnae tenebrae: teneo te, meum
6 lumen.' his uerbis et amplexibus mollibus decantatus maritus

4 en add. van der Vliet, imminet Michaelis, adest Kronenberg et ante sexus del. van
der Vliet: alii alia   13.1 parciloquii mei ς   2 obsequia Fᵃ·ᶜ·: obsequio
ς   4 deuotę ******* F: deuote dicateque ς: deuote careque φ   6 se
ante facturum add. Helm, omnia se van der Vliet

a fleeting pinprick should come so great a growth of her rich womb.

3   But now those plagues, foulest Furies, breathing viperine poison and eager in their unnatural haste, had started their voyage; and once more her transitory husband warned Psyche:

4   'The day of reckoning and the last chance are here. Your own sex, your own flesh and blood, are the enemy, arrayed in arms against you; they have marched out and drawn up their line, and sounded the trumpet-call; with drawn sword

5   your abominable sisters now make for your throat. What disasters press upon us, sweetest Psyche! Have pity on yourself and on us both; with strict restraint save your home, your husband, yourself and this little son of ours from the catastrophe

6   that threatens us. Do not look at, do not listen to, those wicked women, whom it is not right for you to call sisters, after their murderous hatred, their spurning of blood-ties, when like the Sirens aloft on their crag they make the rocks ring with their deadly voices.'

13   Her voice muffled by sobs and tears, Psyche replied: 'More than once, I believe, you have assessed the proofs of my loyalty and discretion, but none the less now too you shall approve my

2   strength of mind. Only once more order our Zephyr to do his duty, and instead of your own sacred appearance that I am

3   refused let me at least behold my sisters. By those fragrant locks that hang so freely, by those soft smooth cheeks so like mine, by that breast warm with hidden heat, as I hope to see

4   your face at least in this little one: be swayed by the dutiful prayers of an anxious suppliant, allow the enjoyment of a sisterly embrace, and restore with joy the soul of your devoted

5   Psyche. As to your face, I ask nothing more; even the darkness

6   of night does not blind me; I have you as my light.' Enchanted by her words and her soft embrace, her husband dried her

lacrimasque eius suis crinibus detergens se facturum spopondit
et praeuertit statim lumen nascentis diei.

14   iugum sororium consponsae factionis ne parentibus quidem
uisis recta de nauibus scopulum petunt illum praecipiti cum
uelocitate nec uenti ferentis oppertae praesentiam licentiosa
2 cum temeritate prosiliunt in altum. nec immemor Zephyrus
regalis edicti, quamuis inuitus, susceptas eas gremio spirantis
3 aurae solo reddidit. at illae incunctatae statim conferto
uestigio domum penetrant complexaeque praedam suam
sororis nomen ementientes thensaurumque penitus abditae
4 fraudis uultu laeto tegentes sic adulant: 'Psyche, non ita
ut pridem paruula, et ipsa iam mater es. quantum, putas,
boni nobis in ista geris perula! quantis gaudiis totam
5 domum nostram hilarabis! o nos beatas quas infantis aurei
nutrimenta laetabunt! qui si parentum, ut oportet, pulchritudini
responderit, prorsus Cupido nascetur.'

15   sic adfectione simulata paulatim sororis inuadunt animum,
statimque eas a lassitudine uiae sedilibus refotas et balnearum
uaporosis fontibus curatas pulcherrime triclinio mirisque illis
2 et beatis edulibus atque tuccetis oblectat. iubet citharam loqui:
psallitur; tibias agere: sonatur; choros canere: cantatur. quae
cuncta nullo praesente dulcissimis modulis animos audientium
3 remulcebant. nec tamen scelestarum feminarum nequitia
uel illa mellita cantus dulcedine mollita conquieuit, sed
ad destinatam fraudium pedicam sermonem conferentes
dissimulanter occipiunt sciscitari qualis ei maritus et unde
4 natalium, secta cuia proueniret. tunc illa simplicitate nimia
pristini sermonis oblita nouum commentum instruit aitque
maritum suum de prouincia proxima magnis pecuniis
negotiantem iam medium cursum aetatis agere interspersum

14.2 leniter *ante* spirantis *add. van der Vliet*   3 incunctanter *Colvius*   sororis
nomen ementientes *Wolf*: sororum nomen ementientes *Price*: sorores nomine
mentientes *F*   4 et] en *Plasberg* geri *Novák*   15.1 a *add. Price, ex*
Helm lassitudinem *Castiglioni* pulcherrimo *Colvius*

tears with his hair, promised to do as she asked, and then by his swift departure forestalled the light of the dawning day.

14 The two sisters, pledged accomplices, without even visiting their parents, disembarked and made their way at breakneck speed straight to the well-known rock, where, without waiting for their conveying wind to appear, they launched themselves

2 with wanton daring into the void. However, Zephyr, heeding though reluctantly his royal master's commands, received them into the embrace of his sighing breeze and brought them

3 to the ground. Without stopping they immediately entered the palace in close order and, embracing their victim, these women who belied the name of sister, hiding their rich store of

4 treachery under smiling faces, began to fawn on her: 'Psyche, not little Psyche as before, so you too are a mother! What a blessing for us do you suppose you carry in this little pocket!

5 With what joy will you gladden our whole house! What happiness for us to enjoy raising this marvellous child! If he is, as he ought to be, as fair as his parents, it will be a real Cupid that is to be born.'

15 With such a pretence of affection did they gradually make their way into their sister's heart. Immediately she sat them down to recover from the fatigues of their journey, provided warm baths for their refreshment, and then at table regaled them splendidly with all those wonderful rich eatables and

2 savoury delicacies of hers. She gave an order, and the lyre played; another, and there was pipe-music; another, and the choir sang. All these, with nobody to be seen, soothed with

3 their sweet strains the hearts of the listeners. Not that the malice of the wicked sisters was softened or laid to rest even by the honeyed sweetness of the music; directing their conversation towards the trap their guile had marked out they craftily began to ask Psyche about her husband, his birth, his occupa-

4 tion. She in her excessive silliness, forgetting what she had said before, concocted a new story and told them that her husband was a prosperous merchant from the neighbouring province, a

5   rara canitie. nec in sermone isto tantillum morata rursum
    opiparis muneribus eas onustas uentoso uehiculo reddidit.
16   sed dum Zephyri tranquillo spiritu sublimatae domum
    redeunt, sic secum altercant: 'quid, soror, dicimus de tam
2   monstruoso fatuae illius mendacio? tunc adolescens modo
    florenti lanugine barbam instruens, nunc aetate media candenti
    canitie lucidus. quis ille quem temporis modici spatium
3   repentina senecta reformauit? nil aliud repperies, mi soror,
    quam uel mendacio ista pessimam feminam confingere uel
    formam mariti sui nescire; quorum utrum uerum est, opibus
4   istis quam primum exterminanda est. quodsi uiri sui faciem
    ignorat, deo profecto denupsit et deum nobis praegnatione ista
    gerit. certe si diuini puelli (quod absit) haec mater audierit,
5   statim me laqueo nexili suspendam. ergo interim ad parentes
    nostros redeamus et exordio sermonis huius quam concolores
    fallacias adtexamus.'
17   sic inflammatae, parentibus fastidienter appellatis et nocte
    turbatis uigiliis perdita, matutino scopulum peruolant et
    inde solito uenti praesidio uehementer deuolant lacrimisque
2   pressura palpebrarum coactis hoc astu puellam appellant: 'tu
    quidem felix et ipsa tanti mali ignorantia beata sedes incuriosa
    periculi tui, nos autem, quae peruigili cura rebus tuis
3   excubamus, cladibus tuis misere cruciamur. pro uero namque
    comperimus nec te, sociae scilicet doloris casusque tui, celare
    possumus immanem colubrum multinodis uoluminibus
    serpentem, ueneno noxio colla sanguinantem hiantemque
4   ingluuie profunda, tecum noctibus latenter adquiescere. nunc
    recordare sortis Pythicae, quae te trucis bestiae nuptiis

16.1 altercant *'forsan'* Oudendorp: altercantur Wouwere: altercantes F   2 in-
struens] induens Watt: nutriens Bluemner   3 ista Salmasius: istam F   utrum
utrum Rittershausen: utrumcumque Luetjohann   17.1 turbatis uigiliis
perdita Gruter: turbatis uigiliis perditae F: turbata uigiliis peracta (perditae
tamen retento) Grimal: alii alia   uehementer] uehentis Salmasius: uehentes
Eyssenhardt

5   middle-aged man with a few white hairs here and there. But
she did not dwell on this for more than a moment or two, but
again returned them to their aerial conveyance loaded with
rich gifts.

16   No sooner were they on their way home borne aloft by
Zephyr's calm breath than they began to hold forth to each
other: 'Well, sister, what is one to say about that silly creature's
2   fantastic lies? Last time it was a youth with a beard of new
down, now it's a middle-aged man with white hair. Who is this
whom so short an interval has suddenly transformed into an
3   old man? Take it from me, sister, either the wretched girl is
telling a pack of lies or she doesn't know what her husband
looks like. Whichever it is, she must be got out of those riches
4   of hers at once. If she doesn't know his shape, obviously it is
a god she has married and it is a god whom her pregnancy
brings us. For sure, if she is called – God forbid – the mother
5   of a divine child, I'll straightway hang myself. Meanwhile
then let us go back to our parents, and on to the warp of this
conversation let us weave the most colourable yarn that we
can.'

17   On fire with this idea they greeted their parents distantly
and, having spent a disturbed and wakeful night, in the morning
they flew to the rock, from which with the accustomed assistance
of the wind they swooped down in a fury, and rubbing their
eyelids to bring on the tears they cunningly accosted the girl:
2   'There you sit, happy and blessed in your very ignorance of
your misfortune, careless of your danger, while we are on
guard with unceasing watchfulness over your welfare, and
3   suffer acute torments in your distress. For we have it as a
certain fact, and partners of your troubles and misfortunes
as we are we cannot conceal it from you, that it is an immense
serpent, writhing its manifold coils, its bloody jaws dripping
deadly poison, its maw gaping deep, that sleeps with you each
4   night undiscovered. Remember now the Pythian oracle, which
proclaimed that you were destined to wed a wild beast. Many

destinatam esse clamauit. et multi coloni quique circumsecus
uenantur et accolae plurimi uiderunt eum uespera redeuntem
18 e pastu proximique fluminis uadis innatantem. nec diu blandis
alimoniarum obsequiis te saginaturum omnes adfirmant, sed
cum primum praegnationem tuam plenus maturauerit uterus,
2 opimiore fructu praeditam deuoraturum. ad haec iam tua est
existimatio, utrum sororibus pro tua cara salute sollicitis
adsentiri uelis et declinata morte nobiscum secura periculi
3 uiuere an saeuissimae bestiae sepeliri uisceribus. quodsi te
ruris huius uocalis solitudo uel clandestinae ueneris faetidi
periculosique concubitus et uenenati serpentis amplexus
delectant, certe piae sorores nostrum fecerimus.'

4   tunc Psyche misella utpote simplex et animi tenella, rapitur
uerborum tam tristium formidine; extra terminum mentis suae
posita prorsus omnium mariti monitionum suarumque
5 promissionum memoriam effudit et in profundum calamitatis
sese praecipitauit tremensque et exsangui colore lurida tertiata
19 uerba semihianti uoce substrepens sic ad illas ait: 'uos quidem,
carissimae sorores, ut par erat, in officio uestrae pietatis
permanetis, uerum et illi qui talia uobis adfirmant non
2 uidentur mihi mendacium fingere. nec enim umquam uiri mei
uidi faciem uel omnino cuiatis sit noui, sed tantum nocturnis
subaudiens uocibus maritum incerti status et prorsus lucifugam
tolero, bestiamque aliquam recte dicentibus uobis merito
3 consentio. me namque magnopere semper a suis terret
aspectibus malumque grande de uultus curiositate praeminatur.
4 nunc si quam salutarem opem periclitanti sorori uestrae
potestis adferre, iam nunc subsistite; ceterum incuria sequens
prioris prouidentiae beneficia conrumpet.'

5   tunc nanctae iam portis patentibus nudatum sororis
animum facinerosae mulieres, omissis tectae machinae latibulis,
destrictis gladiis fraudium simplicis puellae pauentes

peasants and hunters of the region and many dwellers nearby have seen him returning from feeding and bathing in the
18 waters of the neighbouring river. They all say that it will not be for long that he will go on fattening you so compliantly, but that as soon as the fullness of your womb brings your pregnancy to maturity and you are that much more rich and enjoyable a
2 prize, he will devour you. This being so, it is for you to decide whether to take the advice of your sisters who are worried for your life, and avoid death by living in security with us, or to be
3 entombed in the entrails of a savage monster. However, if it is the musical solitude of this countryside and the stinking perilous intimacy of clandestine love and the embraces of a venomous serpent that please you, anyway your loving sisters will have done their duty.'

4 Then poor Psyche, simple and immature creature that she was, was seized by fear at these grim words. Beside herself, she totally forgot all her husband's warnings and her own promises,
5 and plunged herself headlong into an abyss of calamity. Trembling, her face bloodless and ghastly, she scarcely managed
19 to whisper from half-opened lips after several attempts: 'Dearest sisters, you are constant in your loving duty, as befits you, and I believe that those who have told you these things are not
2 lying. For I have never seen my husband's face and I have no idea where he comes from; only at night, attentive to his voice, do I submit to a husband of unknown condition – one who altogether shuns the light; and when you say that he is some
3 sort of wild beast, I can only agree with you. For he constantly terrifies me with warnings not to try to look at him, and threatens me with a fearful fate if I am curious about his
4 appearance. So if you can offer some way of escape to your sister in her danger, support her now: for indifference at this point will undo the benefits of your earlier concern.'

5 So, the gates thrown open, these wicked women occupied Psyche's defenceless heart, and discarding under-cover assaults drew the swords of their treachery and attacked the

20 cogitationes inuadunt. sic denique altera: 'quoniam nos
originis nexus pro tua incolumitate ne periculum quidem
ullum ante oculos habere compellit, uiam qua sola deducit iter
2 ad salutem diu diuque cogitatam monstrabimus tibi. nouaculam
praeacutam adpulsu etiam palmulae lenientis exasperatam
tori qua parte cubare consuesti latenter absconde, lucernamque
concinnem completam oleo claro lumine praemicantem subde
3 aliquo claudentis aululae tegmine, omnique isto apparatu
tenacissime dissimulato, postquam sulcatum trahens gressum
cubile solitum conscenderit iamque porrectus et exordio somni
4 prementis implicitus altum soporem flare coeperit, toro
delapsa nudoque uestigio pensilem gradum paullulatim
minuens, caecae tenebrae custodia liberata lucerna, praeclari
5 tui facinoris opportunitatem de luminis consilio mutuare, et
ancipiti telo illo audaciter, prius dextera sursum elata, nisu
quam ualido noxii serpentis nodum ceruicis et capitis abscide.
6 nec nostrum tibi deerit subsidium, sed cum primum illius
morte salutem tibi feceris, anxie praestolatae aduolabimus
cunctisque istis opibus tecum relatis uotiuis nuptiis hominem
te iungemus homini.'
21 tali uerborum incendio flammata uiscera sororis iam prorsus
ardentis deserentes ipsae protinus tanti mali confinium sibi
2 etiam eximie metuentes flatus alitis impulsu solito porrectae
super scopulum ilico pernici se fuga proripiunt statimque
3 conscensis nauibus abeunt. at Psyche relicta sola, nisi quod
infestis Furiis agitata sola non est, aestu pelagi simile
maerendo fluctuat, et quamuis statuto consilio et obstinato
animo iam tamen facinori manus admouens adhuc incerta
consilii titubat multisque calamitatis suae distrahitur affectibus.

20.1 ne *add. Petschenig*   qua *Jahn*: quę *F*   iter *del. Gruter*, quae *retento*   2 concinne ς   3 sulcatum trahens gressum *Robertson*: sulcato intrahens gressus
F, unde sulcatos intrahens gressus ς: *alii alia*   5 abscide ς: abscinde *F*
6 anxie *Robertson*: anxiae *F*   praestolatae aduolabimus *van der Vliet*: praestolabimus *F*: praestolabimur ς   opibus ς: sociis *F, unde* ocius ς   21.1
flammatam uiscera sorores iam prorsus ardentem *Robertson dubitanter*

20 panic-stricken thoughts of the simple-minded girl. Thus one began: 'Since the tie of our relationship forbids us to consider danger when your safety is at stake, we shall show you the only
2 way that can save you, one that we have long planned. Take a very sharp blade and give it an additional edge by caressing it on your palm, then surreptitiously hide it on your side of the bed. Make ready a lamp and fill it with oil, then when it is
3 burning brightly put it under cover of a jar of some kind. Keep all these preparations absolutely secret. When he comes, trailing his furrowed course, and mounts the bed as usual, as he lies outstretched and, folded in his first heavy sleep, begins
4 to breathe deeply, slip out of bed and with bare feet taking tiny steps one by one on tiptoe, free the lamp from its prison of blind darkness; consulting the light as to the best moment for
5 your glorious deed, with that two-edged weapon, boldly, your right hand first raised high, with powerful stroke, there where the deadly serpent's head and neck are joined – cut them
6 apart. Our help will not be wanting; the instant you have secured yourself by his death, we shall be anxiously awaiting the moment to fly to you; then, taking all these riches back along with you, we shall make a desirable marriage for you, human being to human being.'

21 Their sister had long been on fire; these words kindled her heart to a fierce flame. Her sisters immediately left her, fearing
2 acutely to be found anywhere near such a crime. Carried as usual on the wings of the wind and laid down on the rock, they betook themselves swiftly to flight and immediately embarked
3 and sailed away. But Psyche, alone now except for the savage Furies who harried her, was tossed to and fro in her anguish like the waves of the sea. Though she had taken her decision and made up her mind, now that she came to put her hand to the deed she began to waver, unsure of her resolve, torn by the
4 conflicting emotions of her plight. Now she was eager, now she

4 festinat differt, audet trepidat, diffidit irascitur et, quod est
ultimum, in eodem corpore odit bestiam, diligit maritum.
uespera tamen iam noctem trahente praecipiti festinatione
5 nefarii sceleris instruit apparatum. nox aderat et maritus
aduenerat priusque Veneriis proeliis uelitatus altum in soporem
descenderat.

22 tunc Psyche et corporis et animi alioquin infirma Fati tamen
saeuitia subministrante uiribus roboratur, et prolata lucerna et
2 adrepta nouacula sexum audacia mutatur. sed cum primum
luminis oblatione tori secreta claruerunt, uidet omnium
ferarum mitissimam dulcissimamque bestiam, ipsum illum
Cupidinem formonsum deum formonse cubantem, cuius
aspectu lucernae quoque lumen hilaratum increbruit et
3 acuminis sacrilegi nouaculam paenitebat. at uero Psyche tanto
aspectu deterrita et impos animi marcido pallore defecta
tremensque desedit in imos poplites et ferrum quaerit
4 abscondere, sed in suo pectore; quod profecto fecisset, nisi
ferrum timore tanti flagitii manibus temerariis delapsum
euolasset. iamque lassa, salute defecta, dum saepius diuini
5 uultus intuetur pulchritudinem, recreatur animi. uidet capitis
aurei genialem caesariem ambrosia temulentam, ceruices
lacteas genasque purpureas pererrantes crinium globos
decoriter impeditos, alios antependulos, alios retropendulos,
quorum splendore nimio fulgurante iam et ipsum lumen
6 lucernae uacillabat; per umeros uolatilis dei pinnae roscidae
micanti flore candicant et quamuis alis quiescentibus extimae
plumulae tenellae ac delicatae tremule resultantes inquieta
7 lasciuiunt; ceterum corpus glabellum atque luculentum et
quale peperisse Venerem non paeniteret. ante lectuli pedes
iacebat arcus et pharetra et sagittae, magni dei propitia tela.

21.5 aderat] erat *van der Vliet*: aduenerat *Frassinetti*   aduenerat *Price ex cod. iam
deperdito*: aderat *F*: *an delendum?*   priusque *Kronenberg*: primisque ς: primusque
F   Veneriis *Rohde*: ueneris *F*   in *add. post* altum *Paratore, post* uelitatus *Vulcanius*
22.1 mutatur *Jahn*: mutatum φ: mutauit *F^{p.c.}*   2 nouaculum paenitebat
Lipsius: nouacula paenitebat *Weyman, uix minus probabiliter*: nouacula praenitebat *F*

would put it off; now she dared, now she hesitated; now she
was in despair, now in a rage; and in a word in one and the
same body she loathed the monster and loved the husband.
However, when evening ushered in the night, she hurried to
5 prepare for her dreadful deed. Night came, and with it her
husband, who, having first engaged on the field of love, fell
into a deep sleep.

22   Then Psyche, though naturally weak in body and mind,
rallied her strength as cruel Fate reinforced it, brought out the
2 lamp, seized the blade, and took on a man's courage. But as
soon as the light was presented and the secret of their bed
became plain, what she saw was of all wild beasts the most soft
and sweet of monsters, none other than Cupid, the fair god
fairly lying asleep. At the sight the flame of the lamp was itself
gladdened and flared up, and her blade began to repent its
3 blasphemous edge. Psyche herself was unnerved at the sight
and was no longer mistress of herself: feeble, pale, exhausted,
trembling, she crouched down and tried to hide the steel – in
4 her own bosom; and she would certainly have done it, had not
the steel in fear of such a crime slipped and flown out of her
rash hands. Now, worn out and utterly lost as she was, yet as
she gazed and gazed on the beauty of the god's face, her spirits
5 returned. She saw a rich head of golden hair dripping with
ambrosia, a milk-white neck, and rosy cheeks over which there
strayed coils of hair becomingly arranged, some hanging in
front, some behind, shining with such extreme brilliance that
6 the lamplight itself flickered uncertainly. On the shoulders of
the flying god wings sparkled dewy-white with glistening
sheen, and though they were at rest the soft delicate down at
7 their edges quivered and rippled in incessant play. The rest of
the god's body was smooth and shining and such as Venus
need not be ashamed of in her son. At the foot of the bed lay a
bow, a quiver and arrows, the gracious weapons of the great
god.

23   quae dum insatiabili animo Psyche, satis et curiosa, rimatur
atque pertrectat et mariti sui miratur arma, depromit unam
2 de pharetra sagittam et punctu pollicis extremam aciem
periclitabunda trementis etiam nunc articuli nisu fortiore
pupugit altius, ut per summam cutem rorauerint paruulae
3 sanguinis rosei guttae. sic ignara Psyche sponte in Amoris
incidit amorem. tunc magis magisque cupidine fraglans
Cupidinis prona in eum efflictim inhians patulis ac petulantibus
4 sauiis festinanter ingestis de somni mensura metuebat. sed
dum bono tanto percita saucia mente fluctuat, lucerna illa,
siue perfidia pessima siue inuidia noxia siue quod tale corpus
contingere et quasi basiare et ipsa gestiebat, euomuit de
summa luminis sui stillam feruentis olei super umerum dei
5 dexterum. hem audax et temeraria lucerna et amoris uile
ministerium, ipsum ignis totius dominum aduris, cum te
scilicet amator aliquis, ut diutius cupitis etiam nocte potiretur,
6 primus inuenerit! sic inustus exiluit deus uisaque detectae fidei
colluuie prorsus ex osculis et manibus infelicissimae coniugis
tacitus auolauit.

24   at Psyche statim resurgentis eius crure dextero manibus
ambabus adrepto sublimis euectionis appendix miseranda et per
nubilas plagas penduli comitatus extrema consequia tandem
2 fessa delabitur solo. nec deus amator humi iacentem deserens
inuolauit proximam cupressum deque eius alto cacumine sic
3 eam grauiter commotus adfatur: 'ego quidem, simplicissima
Psyche, parentis meae Veneris praeceptorum immemor, quae
te miseri extremique hominis deuinctam cupidine infimo
4 matrimonio addici iusserat, ipse potius amator aduolaui tibi. sed
hoc feci leuiter, scio, et praeclarus ille sagittarius ipse me telo meo
percussi teque coniugem meam feci, ut bestia scilicet tibi uiderer
et ferro caput excideres meum quod istos amatores tuos oculos

23.1 satis curiosa ζ: s. curiose *Watt*: s. cupida et curiosa *Weyman*   punctu *Flor-*
idus: puncto *F*   5 dominum *F^{a.c.}*: deum ζ   6 defectae *Jahn*: deceptae
Helm: alii alia   osculis *Crusius*: oculis *F*   24.4 tuos] tui *Castiglioni*

23   Psyche could not restrain herself, in her innate curiosity, from examining and handling and admiring her husband's

2 weapons. She took one of the arrows out of the quiver and tried the point by pricking her thumb; but as her hands were still trembling she used too much force, so that the point went right

3 in and tiny drops of red blood bedewed her skin. Thus unknowingly Psyche through her own act fell in love with Love. Then ever more on fire with desire for Desire she hung over him gazing in her distraction and devoured him with quick wanton kisses, fearing all the time that he might wake

4 up. But while she was thus, carried away by this enjoyment, the prey of her conflicting passions, that lamp, either through basest treachery, or in jealous malice, or because it longed itself to touch such a form and as it were to kiss it, disgorged from its spout a drop of hot oil on to the right shoulder of the

5 god. What! Rash and daring lamp, vile slave of love, to burn the lord of universal fire himself, when it must have been a lover who first invented the lamp so that he could enjoy his

6 desires for longer even at night! The god, thus burned, leaped up, and seeing his confidence betrayed and sullied, flew off from the loving embrace of his unhappy wife without saying a word.

24   But as he rose Psyche immediately seized his right leg with both hands, a wretched passenger in his lofty flight; trailing attendance through the clouds she hung on below, but finally

2 in her exhaustion sank to the ground. Her divine lover did not abandon her as she lay there, but alighting in a nearby cypress

3 he spoke to her from its lofty top with deep emotion: 'Simple-minded Psyche, forgetting the orders of my mother Venus, who commanded that you should be constrained by desire for the lowest of wretches and bound to a degrading marriage, I

4 myself flew to you instead as your lover. But this I did, I know, lightly; I, the famous archer, wounded myself with my own weapons and made you my wife – so that you might, it seems, look on me as a monster and cut off that head which carries

5 gerit. haec tibi identidem semper cauenda censebam, haec
beniuole remonebam. sed illae quidem consiliatrices egregiae
tuae tam perniciosi magisterii dabunt actutum mihi poenas, te
uero tantum fuga mea puniuero.' et cum termino sermonis
pinnis in altum se proripuit.

25   Psyche uero humi prostrata et, quantum uisu poterat, uolatus
mariti prospiciens extremis affligebat lamentationibus animum.
sed ubi remigio plumae raptum maritum proceritas spatii fecerat
alienum, per proximi fluminis marginem praecipitem sese dedit.
2 sed mitis fluuius in honorem dei scilicet qui et ipsas aquas urere
consueuit metuens sibi confestim eam innoxio uolumine super
3 ripam florentem herbis exposuit. tunc forte Pan deus rusticus
iuxta supercilium amnis sedebat complexus Echo montanam
deam eamque uoculas omnimodas edocens reccinere; proxime
ripam uago pastu lasciuiunt comam fluuii tondentes capellae.
4 hircuosus deus sauciam Psychen atque defectam, utcumque
casus eius non inscius, clementer ad se uocatam sic permulcet
5 uerbis lenientibus: 'puella scitula, sum quidem rusticanus et
upilio sed senectutis prolixae beneficio multis experimentis
instructus. uerum si recte coniecto, quod profecto prudentes uiri
diuinationem autumant, ab isto titubante et saepius uacillante
uestigio deque nimio pallore corporis et assiduo suspiritu immo
6 et ipsis marcentibus oculis tuis amore nimio laboras. ergo mihi
ausculta nec te rursus praecipitio uel ullo mortis accersitae
genere perimas. luctum desine et pone maerorem precibusque
potius Cupidinem deorum maximum percole et utpote
adolescentem delicatum luxuriosumque blandis obsequiis
promerere.'

26   sic locuto deo pastore nulloque sermone reddito sed adorato
tantum numine salutari Psyche pergit ire. sed cum aliquam
multum uiae laboranti uestigio pererrasset, inscia quodam

---

5 identidem *ante* beniuole *transp. van der Vliet*   25.1 uisu φ: uisi *F*
prosequens *Michaelis*   5 marcentibus *Price*: maerentibus *F*   6 accersitae
Barth: accersito te *F*   26.1 cum *add. Gronovius*   inscia *Vogel*: inscio *F*

5 these eyes that love you. This is what I repeatedly advised you to be constantly on your guard against; this is what I repeatedly warned of in my concern for you. But those worthy counsellors of yours shall speedily pay the price of their pernicious teaching; your punishment shall merely be that I shall leave you.' And with these last words he launched himself aloft on his wings.

25 Psyche, as she lay and watched her husband's flight for as long as she could see him, distressed herself with bitter lamentation. But when distance had taken him from her as he soared away on his winged oarage, she threw herself from

2 the bank of a nearby stream. But the gentle river, in respect it would seem for the god who is wont to scorch even water, and fearing for himself, immediately bore her unharmed on his

3 current and landed her on his grassy bank. It happened that the country god Pan was sitting on the top of the bank with the mountain nymph Echo in his arms teaching her to repeat all kinds of song. By the bank his kids browsed and frolicked at

4 large, cropping the greenery of the river. The goat-god, aware (no matter how) of her plight, called the lovesick and suffering Psyche to him kindly and caressed her with soothing words:

5 'Pretty child, I may be a rustic and a herdsman, but age and experience have taught me a great deal. If I guess aright – and this indeed is what learned men style divination – from these tottering and often uncertain steps of yours, and from your deathly pallor, and from your continual sighing, and from

6 your swimming eyes, you are desperately in love. Listen to me then, and do not try to destroy yourself again by jumping off heights or by any other kind of unnatural death. Cease to weep, lay aside your grief; rather adore in prayer Cupid, greatest of gods, and strive to earn his favour, young, wanton and pleasure-loving that he is, through tender service.'

26 These were the words of the herdsman-god. Psyche made no reply, but having worshipped his saving power went on her way. But when she had wandered far with toilsome steps,

tramite iam die labente accedit quandam ciuitatem, in qua
2 regnum maritus unius sororis eius optinebat. qua re cognita
Psyche nuntiari praesentiam suam sorori desiderat; mox inducta
mutuis amplexibus alternae salutationis expletis percontanti
3 causas aduentus sui sic incipit: 'meministi consilium uestrum,
scilicet quo mihi suasistis ut bestiam, quae mariti mentito
nomine mecum quiescebat, prius quam ingluuie uoraci me
4 misellam hauriret, ancipiti nouacula peremerem. set cum
primum, ut aeque placuerat, conscio lumine uultus eius aspexi,
uideo mirum diuinumque prorsus spectaculum, ipsum illum
deae Veneris filium, ipsum inquam Cupidinem, leni quiete
5 sopitum. ac dum tanti boni spectaculo percita et nimia uoluptatis
copia turbata fruendi laborarem inopia, casu scilicet pessumo
6 lucerna feruens oleum rebulliuit in eius umerum. quo dolore
statim somno recussus, ubi me ferro et igni conspexit armatam,
"tu quidem" inquit "ob istud tam dirum facinus confestim toro
7 meo diuorte tibique res tuas habeto, ego uero sororem tuam" – et
nomen quo tu censeris aiebat – "iam mihi confarreatis nuptiis
coniugabo" et statim Zephyro praecipit ultra terminos me
domus eius efflaret.'

27 necdum sermonem Psyche finierat, et illa uesanae libidinis
et inuidiae noxiae stimulis agitata, e re concinnato mendacio
fallens maritum, quasi de morte parentum aliquid comperisset,
2 statim nauem ascendit et ad illum scopulum protinus pergit et
quamuis alio flante uento caeca spe tamen inhians, 'accipe
me,' dicens 'Cupido, dignam te coniugem et tu, Zephyre,
3 suscipe dominam' saltu se maximo praecipitem dedit. nec
tamen ad illum locum uel saltem mortua peruenire potuit.
nam per saxa cautium membris iactatis atque dissipatis et
proinde ut merebatur laceratis uisceribus suis alitibus bestiisque
4 obuium ferens pabulum interiit. nec uindictae sequentis poena
tardauit. nam Psyche rursus errabundo gradu peruenit ad

---

7 eius] ocius *Kronenberg*   27.1 et *post* finierat *add. Koziol*, at *Jahn*   e re
concinnato *ς*: freconcinnato *F*: praeconcinnato *ς*: e re nata concinnato
Augello

without realizing it she came by a certain path as day waned
to the city ruled over by the husband of one of her sisters.

2 On discovering this, Psyche had herself announced to her
sister. She was ushered in, and after the exchange of greetings
and embraces she was asked why she had come. Psyche

3 replied: 'You remember the advice you both gave me, in which
you persuaded me to kill with two-edged blade the monster
who lay with me under the false name of husband, before he

4 swallowed me up, poor wretch, in his greedy maw. I agreed;
but as soon as with the conniving light I set eyes on his face,
I saw a wonderful, indeed divine, spectacle, the son of Venus

5 himself, I mean Cupid, in deep and gentle slumber. But as,
thrilled by the glorious sight and troubled by excess of pleasure,
I suffered from inability to enjoy it, by the unhappiest of
chances the lamp spilt a drop of boiling oil on to his shoulder.

6 Aroused instantly from sleep by the pain and seeing me armed
with steel and flame, "For this foul crime," he said, "leave my

7 bed this instant and take your chattels with you; I shall wed
your sister (and he named you) in due form." And immediately
he ordered Zephyr to waft me outside the boundaries of his
palace.'

27   Before Psyche had finished speaking, her sister, stung by her
frantic lust and malignant jealousy, concocted on the spot a
story to deceive her husband, to the effect that she had had
news of her parents' death, and immediately took ship and

2 hurried to the well-known rock. There, though quite a different
wind was blowing, yet besotted with blind hope she cried
'Receive me, Cupid, a wife worthy of you, and you, Zephyr,

3 uphold your mistress', and threw herself over with a leap. But
not even in death did she reach the place she sought: for as she
fell from one rocky crag to another she was torn limb from
limb, and she died providing a banquet of her mangled flesh,
as she so richly deserved, for the birds of prey and wild beasts.

4 The second vengeance soon followed. For Psyche again in her
wanderings arrived at another city, where her second sister

5 ciuitatem aliam, in qua pari modo soror morabatur alia. nec
setius et ipsa fallacie germanitatis inducta et in sororis
sceleratas nuptias aemula festinauit ad scopulum inque simile
mortis exitium cecidit.

28   interim, dum Psyche quaesitioni Cupidinis intenta populos
circumibat, at ille uulnere lucernae dolens in ipso thalamo
2 matris iacens ingemebat. tunc auis peralba illa gauia quae
super fluctus marinos pinnis natat demergit sese propere ad
3 Oceani profundum gremium. ibi commodum Venerem
lauantem natantemque propter assistens indicat adustum
filium eius graui uulneris dolore maerentem dubium salutis
4 iacere, iamque per cunctorum ora populorum rumoribus
conuiciisque uariis omnem Veneris familiam male audire,
quod 'ille quidem montano scortatu, tu uero marino natatu
5 secesseritis, ac per hoc non uoluptas ulla non gratia non lepos,
sed incompta et agrestia et horrida cuncta sint, non nuptiae
coniugales non amicitiae sociales non liberum caritates, sed
enormis colluuies et squalentium foederum insuaue fastidium.'
6 haec illa uerbosa et satis curiosa auis in auribus Veneris fili
lacerans existimationem ganniebat. at Venus irata solidum
7 exclamat repente: 'ergo iam ille bonus filius meus habet
amicam aliquam? prome agedum, quae sola mihi seruis
amanter, nomen eius quae puerum ingenuum et inuestem
sollicitauit, siue illa de Nympharum populo seu de Horarum
numero seu de Musarum choro uel de mearum Gratiarum
8 ministerio.' nec loquax illa conticuit auis, sed 'nescio,' inquit
'domina: puto puellam – si probe memini, Psyches nomine
9 dicitur – efflicte cupere.' tunc indignata Venus exclamauit uel
maxime: 'Psychen ille meae formae succubam, mei nominis

28.1 interim dum] interdum *Colvius*   at *del.* ς   3 marcentem *van der Vliet*
5 *ante* enormis *lacunam indicauit van der Vliet*, infimarum sordium (sordium *iam*
Brakman) *add. Paratore*   colluuies *Jahn*: gluuies *F*: illuuies *Scioppius*, eluuies
Beroaldus, utrumque probabiliter   8 puto puellam, si probe memini, Psyches
nomine dici: illam dicitur efflicte cupere *Robertson*   eum efflicte cupere *Helm*:
efflicte eum perire *Traube*: *alii alia*

5 likewise lived. She too was no less readily taken in by her sister's ruse, and eager to supplant her in an unhallowed marriage she hastened to the rock and fell to a similar death.

28   Meanwhile, as Psyche scoured the earth, bent on her search for Cupid, he lay groaning with the pain of the burn in his
2 mother's chamber. At this point a tern, that pure white bird which skims over the sea-waves in its flight, plunged down
3 swiftly to the very bottom of the sea. There sure enough was Venus bathing and swimming; and perching by her the bird told her that her son had been burned and lay suffering from
4 the sharp pain of his wound and in peril of his life. Now throughout the whole world the good name of Venus' whole family was besmirched by all kinds of slanderous reports. People were saying 'He has withdrawn to whoring in the
5 mountains, you to swimming in the sea; and so there is no pleasure anywhere, no grace, no charm, all is rough, savage, uncouth. There are no more marriages, no more mutual friendships, no children's love, nothing but endless squalor
6 and repellent, distasteful and sordid couplings.' Such were the slanders this garrulous and meddlesome bird whispered in Venus' ear to damage her son's honour. Venus was quite
7 furious and exclaimed: 'So then, this worthy son of mine has a mistress? Out with it, my only faithful servant, the name of this creature who has debauched a simple childish boy – is it one of the tribe of the Nymphs or one of the number of the Hours or one of the choir of the Muses or one of my attendant
8 Graces?' The voluble bird was not slow to reply: 'I do not know, my lady; but I think it is a girl called Psyche (if I remember
9 rightly) whom he loves to distraction.' Venus, outraged, cried out loud: 'Psyche, is it, my rival in beauty, the usurper of my

aemulam uere diligit? nimirum illud incrementum lenam me
putauit cuius monstratu puellam illam cognosceret.'

29 haec quiritans properiter emergit e mari suumque protinus
aureum thalamum petit et reperto, sicut audierat, aegroto
2 puero iam inde a foribus quam maxime boans 'honesta' inquit
'haec et natalibus nostris bonaeque tuae frugi congruentia, ut
primum quidem tuae parentis immo dominae praecepta
calcares, nec sordidis amoribus inimicam meam cruciares,
3 uerum etiam hoc aetatis puer tuis licentiosis et immaturis
iungeres amplexibus, ut ego nurum scilicet tolerarem inimicam.
4 sed utique praesumis nugo et corruptor et inamabilis te solum
5 generosum nec me iam per aetatem posse concipere. uelim
ergo scias multo te meliorem filium alium genituram, immo ut
contumeliam magis sentias aliquem de meis adoptaturam
uernulis, eique donaturam istas pinnas et flammas et arcum et
ipsas sagittas et omnem meam supellectilem, quam tibi non ad
6 hos usus dederam: nec enim de patris tui bonis ad instructionem
30 istam quicquam concessum est. sed male prima a pueritia
inductus es et acutas manus habes et maiores tuos irreuerenter
pulsasti totiens et ipsam matrem tuam, me inquam ipsam,
parricida denudas cotidie et percussisti saepius et quasi
uiduam utique contemnis nec uitricum tuum fortissimum
2 illum maximumque bellatorem metuis. quidni? cui saepius in
angorem mei paelicatus puellas propinare consuesti. sed iam
faxo te lusus huius paeniteat et sentias acidas et amaras istas
3 nuptias. sed nunc inrisui habita quid agam? quo me conferam?
quibus modis stelionem istum cohibeam? petamne auxilium
ab inimica mea Sobrietate, quam propter huius ipsius luxuriam
4 offendi saepius? at rusticae squalentisque feminae conloquium
prorsus horresco. nec tamen uindictae solacium undeunde
5 spernendum est. illa mihi prorsus adhibenda est nec ulla alia,

29.4 et *post* corruptor *del. Rohde*   5 me *post* alium *add. Helm*   30.1 a
post prima *add. Michaelis, post* male *Weyman*   prima tu a *Frassinetti ex* φ (p. tua)
4 at *Jahn*: aut *F*   prorsus adhibendum est horresco *F: corr. Luetjohann*   5 et
post explicet *del. Luetjohann*

name, whom he in truth loves? I suppose this sprig took me
for a go-between to introduce him to the girl?'

29   With such protests she hurriedly left the sea and straightway
went to her golden bedchamber, where she found her ailing
son as she had been told. Hardly had she passed through the
2 door when she started to shout at him: 'Fine goings-on, these,
a credit to our family and your character for virtue! First
you ride roughshod over your mother's – I should say your
sovereign's – orders, by not tormenting my enemy with a base
3 amour; then you, a mere child, actually receive her in your
vicious adolescent embraces, so that I have to have my enemy
4 as my daughter-in-law. I suppose you think, you odious good-
for-nothing seducer, that you are the only one fit to breed and
5 that I'm now too old to conceive? Let me tell you, I'll bear
another son much better than you – better still, to make you
feel the insult more, I'll adopt one of my household slaves and
give *him* those wings and torch, and bow and arrows too, and
all that gear of mine, which I didn't give you to be used like
6 this – for there was no allowance for this outfit from your
30 father's estate. But you were badly brought up from a baby,
quarrelsome, always insolently hitting your elders. Your own
mother, me I say, you expose every day, you parricide, often
striking me and despising me, it seems, as an unprotected
female – and you have no fear of your stepfather, that mighty
2 warrior. Naturally, seeing that you are in the habit of providing him with girls, to torment me with his infidelities. But I'll
see to it that you are sorry for these games and find that this
3 marriage of yours has a sour and bitter taste. But now, thus
mocked, what am I to do? Whither am I to turn? How am I to
control this reptile? Am I to seek assistance from my enemy
Sobriety, whom I have so often offended through this creature's
4 wantonness? No, I positively refuse to deal with such an
uncouth and unkempt female. But the solace of revenge is
5 not to be scorned, whatever its source. Her aid and nobody
else's I must enlist, to administer severe correction to this

quae castiget asperrime nugonem istum, pharetram explicet et
sagittas dearmet, arcum enodet, taedam deflammet, immo et
6 ipsum corpus eius acrioribus remediis coerceat. tunc iniuriae
meae litatum crediderim cum eius comas quas istis manibus
meis subinde aureo nitore perstrinxi deraserit, pinnas quas in
meo gremio nectarei fontis infeci praetotonderit.'

31   sic effata foras sese proripit infesta et stomachata biles
Venerias. sed eam protinus Ceres et Iuno continantur
uisamque uultu tumido quaesiere cur truci supercilio tantam
2 uenustatem micantium oculorum coerceret. at illa 'opportune'
inquit 'ardenti prorsus isto meo pectori uolentiam scilicet
perpetraturae uenitis. sed totis, oro, uestris uiribus Psychen
illam fugitiuam uolaticam mihi requirite. nec enim uos utique
domus meae famosa fabula et non dicendi filii mei facta
3 latuerunt.' tunc illae non ignarae quae gesta sunt palpare
Veneris iram saeuientem sic adortae: 'quid tale, domina,
deliquit tuus filius ut animo peruicaci uoluptates illius
4 impugnes et, quam ille diligit, tu quoque perdere gestias? quod
autem, oramus, isti crimen si puellae lepidae libenter adrisit?
an ignoras eum masculum et iuuenem esse uel certe iam quot
sit annorum oblita es? an, quod aetatem portat bellule, puer
5 tibi semper uidetur? mater autem tu et praeterea cordata
mulier filii tui lusus semper explorabis curiose et in eo
luxuriem culpabis et amores reuinces et tuas artes tuasque
6 delicias in formonso filio reprehendes? quis autem te deum, quis
hominum patietur passim cupidines populis disseminantem,
cum tuae domus amores amare coerceas et uitiorum muliebrium
7 publicam praecludas officinam?' sic illae metu sagittarum
patrocinio gratioso Cupidini quamuis absenti blandiebantur.

30.6 in *ante* meo *add. Cornelissen*   31.2 uolentiam *Markland*: uiolentiam *F*
dicenda *Petrus Faber, fort. recte*   3 non ignarae *Price*: iam gnarae *Damsté*:
gnarae *Beroaldus*: ignarae *F*   4 portas *van der Vliet*   6 cum tuae domus
eqs. dubitanter refinxit Robertson; u. Comm.

good-for-nothing, to undo his quiver, blunt his arrows, unstring his bow, put out his torch, and to himself apply more stringent

6 corporal remedies. I shall believe that full reparation has been made for his insolence to me only when she has shaved off the locks to which I have so often imparted a golden sheen by my caressing hands, and cut off the wings which I have imbued with nectar from my own breast.'

31 With these words she rushed violently out in a fury of anger such as befitted Venus. But immediately she was met by Ceres and Juno, who seeing her with congested face asked why she repressed the beauty of her shining eyes under a lowering

2 forehead. To which she answered 'You come just at the right moment to satisfy the desire with which this heart of mine burns. Do, I pray you, with might and main find that runaway fly-by-night Psyche for me – for *you* can't possibly be unaware of the scandal of my house and of what my son – not that he

3 deserves the name – has been doing.' They, knowing full well what had happened, tried to soothe Venus' violent rage: 'Madam, what has your son done so heinous that you should so obstinately thwart his pleasures and be eager even to

4 destroy the one he loves? Is it really a crime, for Heaven's sake, to have been so ready to smile at a nice girl? Don't you know that he is a young man? You must have forgotten how old he is now. Perhaps because he carries his years so prettily,

5 he always seems a boy to you? Are you, a mother and what is more a woman of sense, to be for ever enquiring minutely into his diversions, reproving his wantonness, arraigning his love-affairs, condemning in your fair son your own arts and

6 pleasures? Gods and men alike will find it intolerable that you spread desire broadcast throughout the word, while you impose a bitter constraint on love in your own family and deny

7 it admission to your public academy of gallantry.' In this way, fearful of his arrows, did they flatter Cupid in his absence with their ingratiating defence of his cause. But Venus took it ill

sed Venus indignata ridicule tractari suas iniurias praeuersis
illis alterorsus concito gradu pelago uiam capessit.

LIBER VI

1 Interea Psyche uariis iactabatur discursibus, dies noctesque
mariti uestigationibus intenta et quanto magis inquieta animi,
tanto cupidior iratum licet si non uxoriis blanditiis lenire certe
2 seruilibus precibus propitiare. et prospecto templo quodam in
ardui montis uertice 'unde autem' inquit 'scio an istic meus
degat dominus?' et ilico derigit citatum gradum, quem
defectum prorsus adsiduis laboribus spes incitabat et uotum.
3 iamque nauiter emensis celsioribus iugis puluinari sese
proximam intulit. uidet spicas frumentarias in aceruo et alias
4 flexiles in corona et spicas hordei uidet. erant et falces et
operae messoriae mundus omnis, sed cuncta passim iacentia et
incuria confusa et, ut solet aestu, laborantium manibus
5 proiecta. haec singula Psyche curiose diuidit et discretim semota
rite componit, rata scilicet nullius dei fana caerimoniasue
neclegere se debere sed omnium beniuolam misericordiam
corrogare.

2   haec eam sollicite seduloque curantem Ceres alma
deprehendit et longum exclamat protinus: 'ain, Psyche
2 miseranda? totum per orbem Venus anxia disquisitione tuum
uestigium furens animi requirit teque ad extremum supplicium
expetit et totis numinis sui uiribus ultionem flagitat; tu uero
rerum mearum tutelam nunc geris et aliud quicquam cogitas
3 nisi de tua salute.' tunc Psyche pedes eius aduoluta et uberi
fletu rigans deae uestigia humumque uerrens crinibus suis
4 multiiugis precibus editis ueniam postulabat: 'per ego te
frugiferam tuam dexteram istam deprecor, per laetificas

6.1.1 intenta et quanto magis add. van der Vliet   animi Robertson: animo F
3 puluinari Kenney: puluinaribus F   uidet et spicas hordei Helm: uidet s. h.
Giarratano: et s. h. Norden. suspicari licet lacunam plurium uocabulorum   5 semota
Rohde: remota F   caerimoniasue Robertson: caeremonias F: et c. ς: ac c.
Hildebrand

that her grievances should be treated so lightly, and cutting them short made off quickly in the other direction, towards the sea.

BOOK VI

1 Psyche meanwhile was wandering hither and thither, searching night and day for her husband; and the sicker she was at heart, the more eager she was, if she could not mollify him by wifely endearments, at least to appease his anger by the
2 entreaties of a slave. Seeing a temple on the top of a steep hill, 'Perhaps,' said she, 'my lord lives there?', and straightway she quickly made for it, her pace, which had flagged in her
3 unbroken fatigues, now urged on by hope and desire. Having stoutly traversed the lofty slopes she approached the shrine. There she saw ears of corn, some heaped up, some woven into
4 garlands, together with ears of barley. There were also sickles and all kinds of harvesting gear, all lying anyhow in neglect and confusion and looking (as happens in summer) as if they
5 had just been dropped from the workers' hands. All these things Psyche carefully sorted, separated each in its proper place, and arranged as they ought to be, thinking evidently that she should not neglect the shrines or worship of any god but should implore the goodwill and pity of all of them.

2   She was diligently and busily engaged on this task when bountiful Ceres found her and with a long-drawn sigh said:
2 'So, poor Psyche! There is Venus in her rage dogging your footsteps with painstaking enquiries through the whole world, singling you out for dire punishment, and demanding revenge with the whole power of her godhead; and here are you taking charge of my shrine and thinking of anything rather than your
3 own safety.' Psyche fell down before her, and bedewing her feet with a flood of tears, her hair trailing on the ground, she
4 implored the goddess's favour in an elaborate prayer: 'I beseech you, by this your fructifying hand, by the fertile rites messium caerimonias, per tacita secreta cistarum et per

5 famulorum tuorum draconum pinnata curricula et glebae
Siculae sulcamina et currum rapacem et terram tenacem
et inluminarum Proserpinae nuptiarum demeacula et
luminosarum filiae inuentionum remeacula et cetera quae
silentio tegit Eleusinis Atticae sacrarium, miserandae Psyches
6 animae supplicis tuae subsiste. inter istam spicarum congeriem
patere uel pauculos dies delitescam, quoad deae tantae
saeuiens ira spatio temporis mitigetur uel certe meae uires
3 diutino labore fessae quietis interuallo leniantur.' suscipit
Ceres: 'tuis quidem lacrimosis precibus et commoueor et
opitulari cupio, sed cognatae meae, cum qua etiam foedus
antiquum amicitiae colo, bonae praeterea feminae, malam
2 gratiam subire nequeo. decede itaque istis aedibus protinus et
quod a me retenta custoditaque non fueris optimi consule.'
3   contra spem suam repulsa Psyche et afflicta duplici maestitia
iter retrorsum porrigens inter subsitae conuallis sublucidum
lucum prospicit fanum sollerti fabrica structum, nec ullam
uel dubiam spei melioris uiam uolens omittere sed adire
4 cuiuscumque dei ueniam sacratis foribus proximat. uidet dona
pretiosa ac lacinias auro litteratas ramis arborum postibusque
suffixas, quae cum gratia facti nomen deae cui fuerant dicata
testabantur. tunc genu nixa et manibus aram tepentem
4 amplexans detersis ante lacrimis sic adprecatur: 'magni Iouis
germana et coniuga, siue tu Sami, quae sola partu uagituque
et alimonia tua gloriatur, tenes uetusta delubra, siue celsae
Carthaginis, quae te uirginem uectura leonis caelo commeantem
2 percolit, beatas sedes frequentas, seu prope ripas Inachi, qui te
iam nuptam Tonantis et reginam dearum memorat, inclitis
3 Argiuorum praesides moenibus, quam cunctus oriens Zygiam

2.6 leuentur *Rohde*: leuigentur *Kenney*   3.3 subsitę *F*: subditae *Salmasius*
4 ac *Jahn*: hęc *F^{a.c.}*: et ç   amplexans *F^{a.c.}* *ut uid.*: amplexa φ   4.1 quae
sola *Salmasius*: .quęrula *F*   2 dearum *uel* decorum *F*: deorum *corr. ex*
decorum φ

5 of harvest, by the inviolate secrets of the caskets, by the winged
chariot of your dragon-servants, by the furrows of the Sicilian
fields, by the car that snatches and the earth that catches, by
your daughter Proserpine's descent to her lightless wedding
and her return to bright discovery, and all else that the sanc-
tuary of Attic Eleusis conceals in silence, support the pitiful
6 spirit of your suppliant Psyche. Allow me to hide for only a
very few days among these heaps of corn, until the great
goddess's fierce anger is soothed by the passing of time or at
least until my strength is recruited from the fatigues of long
3 suffering by an interval of rest.' Ceres answered: 'Your tearful
prayers indeed move me and make me wish to help you, but I
cannot offend my kinswoman, with whom I cherish a long-
standing friendship, and who is moreover an excellent creature.
2 Leave then this place at once and think yourself lucky that you
are not my prisoner.'

3   Disappointed and rebuffed, the prey of a double sadness,
Psyche was retracing her steps, when through the half-light of
a wood in a valley which lay before her she saw a temple built
with cunning art. Not wishing to neglect any way, however
doubtful, towards better hopes but willing to implore the
favour of any and every god, she drew near to the holy entrance.
4 There she saw precious offerings and cloths lettered in gold
affixed to trees and to the doorposts, attesting the name of the
goddess to whom they were dedicated in gratitude for her aid.
Then kneeling and embracing the yet-warm altar, she wiped
4 away her tears and prayed: 'Sister and consort of great Jove,
whether you are at home in your ancient shrine on Samos,
which alone glories in having seen your birth, heard your first
cries, and nourished your infancy; or whether you dwell in
your rich abode in lofty Carthage, which worships you as a
2 virgin riding the heavens on a lion; or whether by the banks of
Inachus, who hails you now as bride of the Thunderer and
queen of goddesses, you rule over the famous citadel of Argos,
3 you who are worshipped by the whole East as Zygia and whom

ueneratur et omnis occidens Lucinam appellat, sis meis
extremis casibus Iuno Sospita meque in tantis exanclatis
laboribus defessam imminentis periculi metu libera. quod
4 sciam, soles praegnatibus periclitantibus ultro subuenire.' ad
istum modum supplicanti statim sese Iuno cum totius sui
numinis augusta dignitate praesentat et protinus 'quam
uellem' inquit 'per fidem nutum meum precibus tuis
5 accommodare. sed contra uoluntatem Veneris nurus meae,
quam filiae semper dilexi loco, praestare me pudor non sinit.
tunc etiam legibus quae seruos alienos profugos inuitis
dominis uetant suscipi prohibeor.'

5 isto quoque Fortunae naufragio Psyche perterrita nec
indipisci iam maritum uolatilem quiens, tota spe salutis
2 deposita, sic ipsa suas cogitationes consuluit: 'iam quae
possunt alia meis aerumnis temptari uel adhiberi subsidia, cui
nec dearum quidem quanquam uolentium potuerunt prodesse
3 suffragia? quorsum itaque tantis laqueis inclusa uestigium
porrigam quibusque tectis uel etiam tenebris abscondita
magnae Veneris ineuitabiles oculos effugiam? quin igitur
masculum tandem sumis animum et cassae speculae renuntias
fortiter et ultroneam te dominae tuae reddis et uel sera
4 modestia saeuientes impetus eius mitigas? qui scis an etiam
quem diu quaeritas illic in domo matris repperias?' sic ad
dubium obsequium immo ad certum exitium praeparata
principium futurae secum meditabatur obsecrationis.

6 at Venus terrenis remediis inquisitionis abnuens caelum
petit. iubet construi currum quem ei Vulcanus aurifex subtili
fabrica studiose poliuerat et ante thalami rudimentum nuptiale
munus obtulerat limae tenuantis detrimento conspicuum et
2 ipsius auri damno pretiosum. de multis quae circa cubiculum
dominae stabulant procedunt quattuor candidae columbae et

5 opem *ante* praestare *add. Cornelissen*, praesidium *van der Vliet*   profugos φ²:
pfugas *F*   5.3 quorsum *F^{a.c.} ut uid., sicut coni. Mercier*: quo rursum *F^{p.c.}*
4 scis *Philomathes*: scias *F*   6.1 instrui *Oudendorp*

all the West calls Lucina: be in my desperate need Juno who
Saves, and save me, worn out by the great sufferings I have
gone through, from the fear of the danger that hangs over
me. Have I not been told that it is you who are wont to come
uncalled to the aid of pregnant women when they are in peril?'
4 As she supplicated thus, Juno immediately manifested herself
in all the awesome dignity of her godhead and replied: 'Believe
5 me, I should like to grant your prayers. But I cannot for shame
oppose myself to the wishes of my daughter-in-law Venus,
whom I have always loved as a daughter. Then too I am
prevented by the laws which forbid me to receive another
person's runaway slaves against their master's wishes.'

5   Psyche was completely disheartened by this second shipwreck
of her fortunes, and with no prospect of finding her winged
husband she gave up all hope of salvation. She took counsel
2 with herself thus: 'Now what other aid can I try or bring to
bear on my distresses, seeing that not even the goddesses'
3 influence can help me, though they would like to? Trapped in
such a net, whither can I turn? In what shelter, even hidden
away in the dark, can I hide to escape the unavoidable eye of
great Venus? No; I must finally summon up a man's spirit,
boldly renounce my empty remnants of hope, give myself
up voluntarily to my mistress, and appease her violence by
4 submission, late though it be. And perhaps he whom I have so
long sought may be found there in his mother's house.' So,
prepared for submission with all its dangers, indeed for certain
destruction, she thought over how she should begin the prayer
she would utter.

6   Venus, however, discarded earthbound expedients in her
search and set off for heaven. She ordered to be prepared the
car that Vulcan the goldsmith had lovingly perfected with
cunning workmanship and given her as a betrothal present – a
work of art made notable by what his refining tools had pared
2 away, valuable through the very loss of gold. Of the many
doves quartered round their mistress's chamber there came

hilaris incessibus picta colla torquentes iugum gemmeum
3 subeunt susceptaque domina laetae subuolant. currum deae
prosequentes gannitu constrepenti lasciuiunt passeres et ceterae
quae dulce cantitant aues melleis modulis suaue resonantes
4 aduentum deae pronuntiant. cedunt nubes et Caelus filiae
panditur et summus Aether cum gaudio suscipit deam, nec
obuias aquilas uel accipitres rapaces pertimescit magnae
Veneris canora familia.

7 tunc se protinus ad Iouis regias arces derigit et petitu
superbo Mercuri dei uocalis operae necessariam usuram
2 postulat. nec rennuit Iouis caerulum supercilium. tunc ouans
ilico, comitante etiam Mercurio, Venus caelo demeat eique
3 sollicite serit uerba: 'frater Arcadi, scis nempe sororem
tuam Venerem sine Mercuri praesentia nil unquam fecisse
nec te praeterit utique quanto iam tempore delitescentem
ancillam nequiuerim repperire. nil ergo superest quam tuo
praeconio praemium inuestigationis publicitus edicere.
4 fac ergo mandatum matures meum et indicia qui possit
agnosci manifeste designes, ne si quis occultationis illicitae
crimen subierit, ignorantiae se possit excusatione defendere.'
5 haec simul dicens libellum ei porrigit ubi Psyches nomen
continebatur et cetera. quo facto protinus domum facessit.

8 nec Mercurius omisit obsequium. nam per omnium ora
populorum passim discurrens sic mandatae praedicationis
2 munus exequebatur: 'si quis a fuga retrahere uel occultam
demonstrare poterit fugitiuam regis filiam, Veneris ancillam,
nomine Psychen, conueniat retro metas Murtias Mercurium
3 praedicatorem, accepturus indiciuae nomine ab ipsa Venere
septem sauia suauia et unum blandientis adpulsu linguae
4 longe mellitum.' ad hunc modum pronuntiante Mercurio

---

4 Caelus *Kenney*: caelum *F*   Aether *non* aether *edendum*   cedunt ... deam *post*
familia *transp. Bintz*   7.5 haec *Price*: et *F*   facessit *Scioppius*: secessit *F*

forth four all white; stepping joyfully and twisting their coloured
necks around they submitted to the jewelled yoke, then with
3 their mistress on board they gaily took off. The car was attended
by a retinue of sportive sparrows wantoning with their noisy
chatter, and of other sweet-voiced birds who, singing in honey-
toned strains, harmoniously proclaimed the arrival of the
4 goddess. The clouds part, Heaven opens for his daughter and
highest Aether joyfully welcomes the goddess; great Venus'
tuneful entourage has no fear of ambushes from eagles or
rapacious hawks.

7   She immediately headed for Jove's royal citadel and with
haughty request demanded an essential loan – the services of
2 Mercury, the loud-voiced god. Jove nodded his dark brow,
and she in triumph left heaven then and there with Mercury,
3 to whom she earnestly spoke: 'Arcadian brother, you know
well that your sister Venus has never done anything without
Mercury's assistance, and you must be aware too of how long
it is that I have not been able to find my skulking handmaid.
All we can do now is for you as herald to make public
4 proclamation of a reward for her discovery. Do my bidding
then at once, and describe clearly the signs by which she can
be recognized, so that if anybody is charged with illegally
concealing her, he cannot defend himself with the plea of
5 ignorance'; and with these words she gave him a paper with
Psyche's name and the other details. That done, she returned
straight home.

8   Mercury duly obeyed her. Passing far and wide among the
peoples he carried out his assignment to make proclamation as
2 ordered: 'If any man can recapture or show the hiding-place
of a runaway king's daughter, the slave of Venus, by name
Psyche, let him report to Mercury the crier behind the South
3 turning-point of the Circus, and by way of reward for his
information he shall receive from Venus herself seven sweet
kisses and an extra one deeply honeyed with the sweetness of
4 her thrusting tongue.' This proclamation of Mercury's and

tanti praemii cupido certatim omnium mortalium studium
adrexerat. quae res nunc uel maxime sustulit Psyches omnem
5 cunctationem. iamque fores ei dominae proximanti occurrit
una de famulitione Veneris nomine Consuetudo statimque
6 quantum maxime potuit exclamat 'tandem, ancilla nequissima,
dominam habere te scire coepisti? an pro cetera morum
tuorum temeritate istud quoque nescire te fingis quantos
7 labores circa tuas inquisitiones sustinuerimus? sed bene, quod
meas potissimum manus incidisti et inter Orci cancros iam
ipsos haesisti datura scilicet actutum tantae contumaciae
9 poenas', et audaciter in capillos eius inmissa manu trahebat
eam nequaquam renitentem. quam ubi primum inductam
oblatamque sibi conspexit Venus, latissimum cachinnum
extollit et qualem solent furenter irati, caputque quatiens et
2 ascalpens aurem dexteram, 'tandem' inquit 'dignata es socrum
tuam salutare? an potius maritum, qui tuo uulnere periclitatur,
interuisere uenisti? sed esto secura, iam enim excipiam te ut
bonam nurum condecet', et 'ubi sunt' inquit 'Sollicitudo atque
3 Tristities ancillae meae?' quibus intro uocatis torquendam
tradidit eam. at illae sequentes erile praeceptum Psychen
misellam flagellis afflictam et ceteris tormentis excruciatam
4 iterum dominae conspectui reddunt. tunc rursus sublato risu
Venus 'et ecce' inquit 'nobis turgidi uentris sui lenocinio
commouet miserationem, unde me praeclara subole auiam
5 beatam scilicet faciat. felix uero ego quae in ipso aetatis meae
flore uocabor auia et uilis ancillae filius nepos Veneris audiet.
6 quanquam inepta ego quae frustra filium dicam: impares enim
nuptiae et praeterea in uilla sine testibus et patre non
consentiente factae legitimae non possunt uideri ac per hoc
spurius iste nascetur, si tamen partum omnino perferre te
patiemur.'

8.5 ei dominae *Rohde*: eius dominae *F*: dominae ei *Oudendorp*: dominae *Price*:
alii alia   famulitio *Roaldus*   9.1 latissimum ς: laetissimum *F*   furenter
F[1] *marg.* φ: frequenter *F text.*   4 set ecce *Jahn*: en ecce *Bluemner*   6 quae
add. van der Vliet

the desire for such a reward aroused eager competition all
over the world. Its effect on Psyche was to put an end to all her
5 hesitation. As she neared her mistress's doors she was accosted
by one of Venus' household named Habit, who on seeing her
6 cried out at the top of her voice: 'At last, you worthless slut,
have you begun to realize you have a mistress? Or will you
with your usual impudence pretend you don't know how much
7 trouble we have had looking for you? A good thing you've
fallen into *my* hands; you're held in the grip of Orcus, and you
can be sure you won't have to wait long for the punishment
9 of your disobedience.' So saying, she laid violent hands on
Psyche's hair and dragged her inside unresisting. As soon as
Venus saw her brought in and presented to her, she laughed
with wide open mouth, as people do in a rage; and shaking her
2 head and scratching her right ear, 'So,' she said, 'you have
finally condescended to pay your respects to your mother-in-
law? Or have you come to visit your husband, who lies under
threat of death from the wound you have given him? But don't
worry, I am going to receive you as befits a good daughter-in-
law.' Then, 'Where are Care and Sorrow, my handmaids?',
3 she asked. They were called in, and Psyche was handed over to
them to be tormented. In obedience to their mistress's orders
they whipped the wretched girl and afflicted her with every
other kind of torture, and then brought her back to face the
4 goddess. Venus, laughing again, exclaimed: 'Look at her,
trying to arouse my pity through the allurement of her swollen
belly, whose glorious offspring is to make me, if you please, a
5 happy grandmother. Happy indeed, to be called grandmother
in the flower of my age and to hear the son of a vile slave styled
6 Venus' grandson! But I'm a fool to speak of a son: the marriage
is not between equals, and what is more took place in the
country, without witnesses, and without his father's consent,
and cannot be held to be legitimate. So it will be born a bastard,
if indeed I allow you to bear it at all.'

10   his editis inuolat eam uestemque plurifariam diloricat
capilloque disciso et capite conquassato grauiter affligit, et
accepto frumento et hordeo et milio et papauere et cicere et
lente et faba commixtisque aceruatim confusisque in unum
2   grumulum sic ad illam: 'uideris enim mihi tam deformis
ancilla nullo alio sed tantum sedulo ministerio amatores tuos
3   promereri: iam ergo et ipsa frugem tuam periclitabor. discerne
seminum istorum passiuam congeriem singulisque granis rite
dispositis atque seiugatis ante istam uesperam opus expeditum
4   approbato mihi.' sic assignato tantorum seminum cumulo
ipsa cenae nuptiali concessit. nec Psyche manus admolitur
inconditae illi et inextricabili moli, sed immanitate praecepti
5   consternata silens obstupescit. tunc formicula illa paruula
atque ruricola certa difficultatis tantae laborisque miserta
contubernalis magni dei socrusque saeuitiam execrata
discurrens nauiter conuocat corrogatque cunctam formicarum
6   accolarum classem: 'miseremini Terrae omniparentis agiles
alumnae, miseremini et Amoris uxori puellae lepidae
7   periclitanti prompta uelocitate succurrite.' ruunt aliae superque
aliae sepedum populorum undae summoque studio singulae
granatim totum digerunt aceruum separatimque distributis
dissitisque generibus e conspectu perniciter abeunt.

11   sed initio noctis e conuiuio nuptiali uino madens et fraglans
balsama Venus remeat totumque reuincta corpus rosis
2   micantibus, uisaque diligentia miri laboris 'non tuum,' inquit
'nequissima, nec tuarum manuum istud opus, sed illius cui tuo
immo et ipsius malo placuisti', et frusto cibarii panis ei
3   proiecto cubitum facessit. interim Cupido solus interioris
domus unici cubiculi custodia clausus coercebatur acriter,
partim ne petulanti luxurie uulnus grauaret, partim ne cum

10.1 accepto] accersito *van der Vliet*   5 certa *Eyssenhardt post Stewech* (certa
iam) *et Oudendorp* (certa tum): certata *F*   11.3 unici] inuii *Heinsius: alii
alia*

10   With these words, she flew at Psyche, ripped her clothes to
shreds, tore her hair, boxed her ears and treated her cruelly.
Then she took wheat and barley and millet and poppy-seed
and chick-peas and lentils and beans, mixed them thoroughly
2 all together in a single heap, and told Psyche: 'Since it seems
to me that, ugly slave that you are, you can earn the favours of
your lovers only by diligent drudgery, I myself will now put
3 your merit to the test. Sort out this random heap of seeds, and
let me see the work completed by this evening, with each kind
4 of grain properly arranged and separated.' And handing over
the enormous heap of grains, Venus went off to a wedding-
dinner. Psyche did not offer to touch the disordered and
unmanageable mass but stood in silent stupefaction, stunned
5 by this monstrous command. Then an ant, that tiny country-
dweller, grasping the size of the problem, pitying the plight of
the great god's bedfellow and execrating her mother-in-law's
cruelty, rushed round eagerly to summon and convene the
6 whole assembly of the local ants. 'Have pity,' she cried,
'nimble children of Earth the all-mother, have pity and run
with all speed to the aid of the sweet girl-wife of Love in her
7 peril.' In wave after wave the six-footed peoples poured in and,
each one vying with the other, they sorted out the whole heap
grain by grain, separated and distributed the seed by kinds,
and vanished swiftly from view.

11   At nightfall Venus returned from the banquet flushed with
wine, fragrant with perfume and garlanded all over in brilliant
roses. When she saw how diligently the wondrous task had
2 been performed, 'Worthless wretch!', she exclaimed, 'this is
not your doing or the work of your hands, but his whose fancy
you have taken – the worse indeed for you, and for him'; and
throwing Psyche a crust of coarse bread she took herself to
3 bed. Meanwhile Cupid was under strict guard, in solitary
confinement in one room at the back of the palace, partly to
stop him from aggravating his wound through his impetuous
passion, partly to stop him from seeing his beloved. So then

sua cupita conueniret. sic ergo distentis et sub uno tecto
4 separatis amatoribus tetra nox exanclata. sed Aurora
commodum inequitante uocatae Psychae Venus infit talia:
'uidesne illud nemus, quod fluuio praeterluenti ripisque longis
5 attenditur, cuius imi frutices uicinum fontem despiciunt? oues
ibi nitentis auri uero decore florentes incustodito pastu
6 uagantur. inde de coma pretiosi uelleris floccum mihi confestim
quoquo modo quaesitum afferas censeo.'

12   perrexit Psyche uolenter non obsequium quidem illa functura
sed requiem malorum praecipitio fluuialis rupis habitura. sed
inde de fluuio musicae suauis nutricula leni crepitu dulcis
aurae diuinitus inspirata sic uaticinatur harundo uiridis:
2 'Psyche tantis aerumnis exercita, neque tua miserrima morte
meas sanctas aquas polluas nec uero istud horae contra
3 formidabiles oues feras aditum, quoad de solis fraglantia
mutuatae calorem truci rabie solent efferari cornuque acuto et
fronte saxea et non nunquam uenenatis morsibus in exitium
4 saeuire mortalium; sed dum meridies solis sedauerit uaporem
et pecua spiritus fluuialis serenitate conquieuerint, poteris sub
illa procerissima platano, quae mecum simul unum fluentum
5 bibit, latenter abscondere. et cum primum mitigata furia
laxauerint oues animum, percussis frondibus attigui nemoris
lanosum aurum repperies, quod passim stirpibus conexis
obhaerescit.'

13   sic harundo simplex et humana Psychen aegerrimam
salutem suam docebat. nec auscultatu paenitendo indiligenter
instructa illa cessauit, sed obseruatis omnibus furatrina facili
flauentis auri mollitie congestum gremium Veneri reportat.
2 nec tamen apud dominam saltem secundi laboris periculum

---

4 caelum *ante* inequitante *add. Wernicke*   praeterfluenti *Colvius*   5 frutices
van der Vliet post Luetjohann (inuii frutices): gurgites *F. locus multifarie
uexatus*   auri uero decore *Robertson*: auri ** cole (ue *eras. ut uid.*) *F*: auriue cole
φ: aurique colore ς: *alii alia*   12.2 istud horae *Salmasius*: istius ore *F*
3 efferari *Colvius*: efferri *F*   4 te *post* latenter *add.* ς, *post* poteris *Novák*
13.1 impaenitendo *Petschenig*   indiligenter *Robertson*: diligenter *F*

the two lovers, though under the same roof, were kept apart
4 and endured a melancholy night. As soon as Dawn took horse,
Venus summoned Psyche and said: 'You see that wood which
stretches along the banks of the river which washes it in
5 passing, and the bushes at its edge which look down on the
nearby spring? Sheep resplendent with fleece of real gold
6 wander and graze there unguarded. Of that precious wool
I suggest you get a tuft by hook or by crook and bring it to me
directly.'

12   Psyche set out willingly, not indeed as expecting to fulfil her
task, but meaning to find a respite from her sufferings by
throwing herself from a rock into the river. But then from the
river a green reed, source of sweet music, divinely inspired by
2 the gentle whisper of the soft breeze, thus prophesied: 'Psyche,
tried by much suffering, do not pollute my holy waters by your
pitiable death. This is not the moment to approach these
3 fearsome sheep, while they are acquiring heat from the blazing
sun and are maddened by fierce rage, with their sharp horns
and stone-hard foreheads, and frequently with their poisonous
4 bites, attacking and killing men. However, until the midday
heat of the sun abates and the flock is quietened by the soothing
breeze off the river, you can hide under that tall plane which
5 drinks the current together with me. Then, when their rage is
calmed and they relax their attention, shake the branches of
the nearby trees, and you will find the golden wool which
sticks everywhere in their entwined stems.'

13   So this open-hearted reed in its humanity showed the
unfortunate Psyche the way to safety. She paid due heed to
its salutary advice and acted accordingly: she did everything
she was told, and with easy larceny brought back to Venus a
2 heaped-up armful of the golden softness. Not that, from her
mistress at least, the successful outcome of her second trial

secundum testimonium meruit, sed contortis superciliis
3 subridens amarum sic inquit: 'nec me praeterit huius quoque
facti auctor adulterinus. sed iam nunc ego sedulo periclitabor
an oppido forti animo singularique prudentia sis praedita.
4 uidesne insistentem celsissimae illi rupi montis ardui uerticem,
de quo fontis atri fuscae defluunt undae proxumaeque
conceptaculo uallis inclusae Stygias inrigant paludes et rauca
5 Cocyti fluenta nutriunt? indidem mihi de summi fontis penita
scaturrigine rorem rigentem hauritum ista confestim defer
urnula.' sic aiens crustallo dedolatum uasculum insuper ei
grauiora comminata tradidit.

14   at illa studiose gradum celerans montis extremum petit
tumulum certe uel illic inuentura uitae pessimae finem. sed
cum primum praedicti iugi conterminos locos appulit, uidet
2 rei uastae letalem difficultatem. namque saxum immani
magnitudine procerum et inaccessa salebritate lubricum mediis
3 e faucibus lapidis fontes horridos euomebat, qui statim proni
foraminis lacunis editi perque procliue delapsi et angusti
canalis exarato contecti tramite proxumam conuallem latenter
4 incidebant. dextra laeuaque cautibus cauatis proserpunt ecce
longa colla porrecti saeui dracones inconiuae uigiliae luminibus
5 addictis et in perpetuam lucem pupulis excubantibus. iamque
et ipsae semet muniebant uocales aquae. nam et 'discede' et
'quid facis? uide' et 'quid agis? caue' et 'fuge' et 'peribis'
6 subinde clamant. sic impossibilitate ipsa mutata in lapidem
Psyche, quamuis praesenti corpore, sensibus tamen aberat et
inextricabilis periculi mole prorsus obruta lacrumarum etiam
extremo solacio carebat.

15   nec Prouidentiae bonae graues oculos innocentis animae

---

2 inquit] incipit *Stoll*: infit *Robertson*   4 rauca *Lipsius*: pauca *F*   5 defer
urnula ς: defer surnula *F*: deferas urnula *Jahn*   14.1 celerans φ: cele*rans
F (b *an* r *eras. incert.*)   tumulum ς: cumulum *F*   inuentura uitae *Beroaldus*:
inuitς *F*   3 exarato *Petschenig*: exarto *F*   conlecti *Michaelis*   4 e *ante*
cautibus *add. Robertson dubitanter*   ecce *Walter*: et *F*   saeui] saeuiunt saeui
Purser: saeuiunt *Frassinetti. alii alia*   15.1 graues] acres *Watt*

earned her any approval. Venus bent her brows and with an
3 acid smile said: 'I am not deceived: this exploit too is that
lecher's. Now however I am going to put myself out to discover
if your heart is really stout and your prudence unequalled.
4 You see the top of the steep mountain that looms over that
lofty crag, from which there flow down the dark waters of a
black spring, to be received in a basin of the neighbouring
valley, and then to water the marshes of Styx and feed the
5 hoarse streams of Cocytus? Thence, just where the spring
gushes out on the very summit, draw off the ice-cold water and
bring it to me instantly in this jar.' So saying she gave her an
urn hollowed out from crystal, adding yet direr threats.

14   Psyche eagerly quickened her pace towards the mountain-
top, to find at least an end of her wretched existence there. But
as soon as she approached the summit indicated by Venus, she
2 saw the deadly difficulty of her enormous task. There stood a
rock, huge and lofty, too rough and treacherous to climb; from
3 jaws of stone in its middle it poured out its grim stream, which
first gushed from a sloping cleft, then plunged steeply to be
hidden in the narrow channel of the path it had carved out
for itself and so to fall inconspicuously into the neighbouring
4 valley. To left and right she saw emerging from the rocky
hollows fierce serpents with long necks outstretched, their eyes
constrained to unwinking vigilance, for ever on the watch and
5 incessantly wakeful. And now the very water defended itself in
speech, crying out repeatedly 'Depart' and 'What are you
doing? Look out' and 'What are you about? Take care' and
6 'Fly' and 'You'll die.' Psyche was turned to stone by the very
impossibility of her task, and though her body was present her
senses were elsewhere: overwhelmed completely by the weight
of dangers she was powerless to cope with, she was even
deprived of tears, the last consolation.

15   But the suffering of this innocent soul did not escape the
august eyes of Providence. For that regal bird of almighty

latuit aerumna. nam supremi Iouis regalis ales illa repente
2 propansis utrimque pinnis affuit rapax aquila, memorque
ueteris obsequii, quo ductu Cupidinis Ioui pocillatorem
Phrygium substulerat, opportunam ferens opem deique numen
in uxoris laboribus percolens alti culminis Diales uias deserit
3 et ob os puellae praeuolans incipit: 'at tu, simplex alioquin et
expers rerum talium, sperasne te sanctissimi nec minus
truculenti fontis uel unam stillam posse furari uel omnino
4 contingere? diis etiam ipsique Ioui formidabiles aquas istas
Stygias uel fando comperisti, quodque uos deieratis per
5 numina deorum deos per Stygis maiestatem solere. sed
cedo istam urnulam', et protinus adrepta complexaque
festinat libratisque pinnarum nutantium molibus inter genas
saeuientium dentium et trisulca uibramina draconum remigium
6 dextra laeuaque porrigens nolentes aquas et ut abiret innoxius
praeminantes excipit, commentus ob iussum Veneris petere
eique se praeministrare, quare paulo facilior adeundi fuit
copia.

16 sic acceptam cum gaudio plenam urnulam Psyche Veneri
citata rettulit. nec tamen nutum deae saeuientis uel tunc
2 expiare potuit. nam sic eam maiora atque peiora flagitia
comminans appellat renidens exitiabile: 'iam tu quidem
magna uideris quaedam mihi et alta prorsus malefica, quae
3 talibus praeceptis meis obtemperasti nauiter. sed adhuc istud,
mea pupula, ministrare debebis. sume istam pyxidem', et
dedit; 'protinus usque ad inferos et ipsius Orci ferales Penates
4 te derige. tunc conferens pyxidem Proserpinae "petit de te
Venus" dicito "modicum de tua mittas ei formonsitate uel ad
5 unam saltem dieculam sufficiens. nam quod habuit, dum
filium curat aegrotum, consumpsit atque contriuit omne." sed

15.1 supremi *Modius*: primi *F*   3 sperasne *Stewech*: sperasq; *F*: speras quippe
Jahn: *alii alia*   5 et protinus ζ: set protinus *F*   adrepta complexaque *Leo*
(eaque arrepta complexaque *iam Higtius*): adreptam completamque *F*: adreptam
completum aquae *Hildebrand* (arreptam completum aqua *iam Oudendorp*): *alii
alia*

Jove, the ravisher eagle, suddenly appeared with outspread
2 wings, and remembering his former service, how prompted
by Cupid he had stolen the Phrygian cupbearer for Jupiter,
brought timely aid. In honour of the god's power, in his wife's
distress he left Jove's pathways in the heights, and gliding
3 down before the girl he addressed her: 'Do you, naive as you
are and inexperienced in such things, hope to be able to steal
a single drop of this most holy and no less terrible spring, or
4 even touch it? You must have heard that this water of Styx is
feared by the gods themselves, even Jupiter, and that the oaths
which mortals swear by the power of the gods, the gods swear
5 by the majesty of Styx. Give me that urn' – and seizing and
holding it he took off, and poising himself on his mighty
hovering wings he steered to left and right between the raging
6 jaws and flickering three-forked tongues of the dragons, to
draw off the waters, though they resisted and warned him to
retreat while he could do so in safety – he pretending meanwhile
that he had been ordered to fetch it by Venus and that he
was in her service; and thus it was a little easier for him to
approach.

16   Psyche joyfully received the full urn and speedily took it
back to Venus. Even then however she could not satisfy the
2 wishes of the cruel goddess. Threatening her with yet worse
outrages, she addressed Psyche with a deadly smile: 'I think
you must be some sort of great and profoundly accomplished
witch, having so promptly carried out orders like these of
3 mine. But you still have to do this service for me, my dear.
Take this casket' (giving it to her) 'and off with you to the
4 Underworld and the ghostly abode of Orcus himself. Present it
to Proserpine and say "Venus requests that you send her a little
5 of your beauty, enough at least for a single short day. For the
supply that she had, she has quite used up and exhausted in
looking after her ailing son." Come back in good time, since I

haud immaturius redito, quia me necesse est indidem delitam
theatrum deorum frequentare.'

17 tunc Psyche uel maxime sensit ultimas fortunas suas et
uelamento reiecto ad promptum exitium sese compelli manifeste comperit. quidni? quae suis pedibus ultro ad Tartarum
2 Manesque commeare cogeretur. nec cunctata diutius pergit ad
quampiam turrim praealtam, indidem sese datura praecipitem:
sic enim rebatur ad inferos recte atque pulcherrime se posse
3 descendere. sed turris prorumpit in uocem subitam et 'quid te'
inquit 'praecipitio, misella, quaeris extinguere, quidque iam
4 nouissimo periculo laborique isto temere succumbis? nam si
spiritus corpore tuo semel fuerit seiugatus, ibis quidem
profecto ad imum Tartarum, sed inde nullo pacto redire
18 poteris. mihi ausculta. Lacedaemo Achaiae nobilis ciuitas non
longe sita est: huius conterminam deuiis abditam locis quaere
2 Taenarum. inibi spiraculum Ditis et per portas hiantes
monstratur iter inuium, cui te limine transmeato simul
commiseris iam canale derecto perges ad ipsam Orci regiam.
3 sed non hactenus uacua debebis per illas tenebras incedere,
sed offas polentae mulso concretas ambabus gestare manibus
4 at in ipso ore duas ferre stipes. iamque confecta bona
parte mortiferae uiae continaberis claudum asinum lignorum
gerulum cum agasone simili, qui te rogabit decidentis sarcinae
fusticulos aliquos porrigas ei, sed tu nulla uoce deprompta
5 tacita praeterito. nec mora, cum ad flumen mortuum uenies,
cui praefectus Charon protenus expetens portorium sic ad
6 ripam ulteriorem sutili cumba deducit commeantes. ergo et
inter mortuos auaritia uiuit nec Charon ille Ditis exactor
tantus deus quicquam gratuito facit, set moriens pauper
uiaticum debet quaerere, et aes si forte prae manu non fuerit,
7 nemo eum expirare patietur. huic squalido seni dabis nauli

17.3 quidue *Castiglioni*   18.3 at] et *uel* atque *Watt*   6 Ditis exactor
Robertson: ditis & pater *F*: Ditis portitor *Gronovius*: *alii alia*

must make myself up from it before going to the theatre of the gods.'

17 Then indeed Psyche realized that her last hour had come and knew that all disguise was at an end and that she was being openly sent to immediate destruction. That was clear, seeing that she was being forced to go on her own two feet even

2 to Tartarus and the shades. Without further delay she made her way to a certain lofty tower, meaning to throw herself off it: for in that way she thought she could most directly and

3 neatly descend to the Underworld. But the tower suddenly broke into speech: 'Why, poor wretch, do you seek to destroy yourself by a headlong fall? Why recklessly give up at this last

4 perilous ordeal? Once your soul is separated from your body, then indeed you will go straight to the pit of Tartarus, from

18 which you cannot possibly return. Listen to me. Not far from here is Sparta, a famous city of Greece. Near to it, hidden in a

2 trackless countryside, you must find Taenarum. There is to be seen the breathing-hole of Dis, and through its gaping portals the forbidden road; once you have passed the threshold and entrusted yourself to it you will fare by a direct track to the

3 very palace of Orcus. But you must not go through that darkness empty-handed as you are; you must carry in your hands cakes of barley meal soaked in wine and honey, and in

4 your mouth two coins. When you have gone a good part of the infernal road you will meet a lame donkey loaded with wood with a lame driver; he will ask you to hand him some sticks fallen from the load, but you must say nothing and pass by in

5 silence. Directly after that you will come to the river of death. Its harbour-master is Charon, who ferries wayfarers to the other bank in his boat of skins only on payment of the fee

6 which he immediately demands. So it seems avarice lives even among the dead, and a great god like Charon, Dis's Collector, does nothing for nothing. A poor man on his deathbed must make sure of his journey-money, and if he hasn't got coppers

7 to hand, he won't be allowed to expire. To this unkempt old

nomine de stipibus quas feres alteram, sic tamen ut ipse sua
8 manu de tuo sumat ore. nec setius tibi pigrum fluentum
transmeanti quidam supernatans senex mortuus putris
adtollens manus orabit ut eum intra nauigium trahas, nec tu
19 tamen inlicita adflectare pietate. transito fluuio modicum te
progressam textrices orabunt anus telam struentes manus
paulisper accommodes, nec id tamen tibi contingere fas est.
nam haec omnia tibi et multa alia de Veneris insidiis orientur,
2 ut uel unam de manibus omittas offulam. nec putes futile istud
polentacium damnum leue; altera enim perdita lux haec tibi
3 prorsus denegabitur. canis namque praegrandis teriugo et
satis amplo capite praeditus immanis et formidabilis tonantibus
oblatrans faucibus mortuos, quibus iam nil mali potest facere,
frustra territando ante ipsum limen et atra atria Proserpinae
4 semper excubans seruat uacuam Ditis domum. hunc offrenatum
unius offulae praeda facile praeteribis ad ipsamque protinus
Proserpinam introibis, quae te comiter excipiet ac benigne, ut
5 et molliter assidere et prandium opipare suadeat sumere. sed
tu et humi reside et panem sordidum petitum esto, deinde
nuntiato quid adueneris susceptoque quod offeretur rursus
6 remeans canis saeuitiam offula reliqua redime ac deinde auaro
nauitae data quam reseruaueras stipe transitoque eius fluuio
recalcans priora uestigia ad istum caelestium siderum redies
7 chorum. sed inter omnia hoc obseruandum praecipue tibi
censeo, ne uelis aperire uel inspicere illam quam feres pyxidem
uel omnino diuinae formonsitatis abditum curiosius temptare
thensaurum.'
20　　　sic turris illa prospicua uaticinationis munus explicuit.
nec morata Psyche pergit Taenarum sumptisque rite stipibus
2 illis et offulis infernum decurrit meatum transitoque per
silentium asinario debili et amnica stipe uectori data neglecto
supernatantis mortui desiderio et spretis textricum subdolis

19.6 reseruaueris *Robertson*　recalcans F^1 *marg. ut uid.* ς: recolens φ　7
curiosius temptare thensaurum *Castiglioni*: curiosius thensaurum *F*: c. scrutari
t. *van der Vliet*: rimari c. t. *Brakman*: c. explorare t. *Watt*

man you must give one of your coins as his fare, making him

8 take it himself from your mouth. Likewise, while you are crossing the sluggish stream, an old dead man swimming over will raise his decaying hands to ask you to haul him abroad; but you must not be swayed by pity, which is forbidden to you.

19 When you are across and have gone a little way, some old women weavers will ask you to lend a hand for a moment to set up their loom; but here too it is forbidden for you to become involved. For all these and many other ruses will be inspired

2 by Venus, to make you drop one of your cakes. Don't think the loss of a paltry barley cake a light thing: if you lose one you will

3 thereby lose the light of the sun. For a huge dog with three enormous heads, a monstrous and fearsome brute, barking thunderously and with empty menace at the dead, whom he can no longer harm, is on perpetual guard before the threshold and dark halls of Proserpine, and watches over the empty

4 house of Dis. Him you can muzzle by letting him have one of your cakes; passing him easily by you will come directly to Proserpine, who will receive you kindly and courteously,

5 urging you to take a soft seat and join her in a rich repast. But you must sit on the ground and ask for some coarse bread; when you have eaten it you can tell her why you have come,

6 and then taking what you are given you can return. Buy off the fierce dog with your other cake, and then giving the greedy ferryman the coin you have kept you will cross the river and retrace your earlier path until you return to the light of heaven

7 above. But this rule above all I bid you keep: do not open or look into the box that you bear or pry at all into the hidden store of divine beauty.'

20 So this far-sighted tower accomplished its prophetic task. Psyche without delay made for Taenarum, where she duly equipped herself with coins and cakes and made the descent to

2 the Underworld. Passing in silence the lame donkey-driver, paying her fare to the ferryman, ignoring the plea of the dead swimmer, rejecting the crafty entreaties of the weavers, and

precibus et offulae cibo sopita canis horrenda rabie domum
3 Proserpinae penetrat. nec offerentis hospitae sedile delicatum
uel cibum beatum amplexa sed ante pedes eius residens
humilis cibario pane contenta Veneriam pertulit legationem.
4 statimque secreto repletam conclusamque pyxidem suscipit et
offulae sequentis fraude caninis latratibus obseratis residuaque
5 nauitae reddita stipe longe uegetior ab inferis recurrit. et
repetita atque adorata candida ista luce, quanquam festinans
obsequium terminare, mentem capitur temeraria curiositate et
6 'ecce' inquit 'inepta ego diuinae formonsitatis gerula, quae nec
tantillum quidem indidem mihi delibo uel sic illi amatori meo
21 formonso placitura', et cum dicto reserat pyxidem. nec
quicquam ibi rerum nec formonsitas ulla, sed infernus somnus
ac uere Stygius, qui statim coperculo reuelatus inuadit eam
crassaque soporis nebula cunctis eius membris perfunditur et
2 in ipso uestigio ipsaque semita conlapsam possidet. et iacebat
immobilis et nihil aliud quam dormiens cadauer.

sed Cupido iam cicatrice solidata reualescens nec diutinam
suae Psyches absentiam tolerans per altissimam cubiculi quo
3 cohibebatur elapsus fenestram refectisque pinnis aliquanta
quiete longe uelocius prouolans Psychen accurrit suam
detersoque somno curiose et rursum in pristinam pyxidis
sedem recondito Psychen innoxio punctulo sagittae suae
4 suscitat et 'ecce' inquit 'rursum perieras, misella, simili
curiositate. sed interim quidem tu prouinciam quae tibi matris
meae praecepto mandata est exsequere nauiter, cetera egomet
uidero.' his dictis amator leuis in pinnas se dedit, Psyche uero
confestim Veneri munus reportat Proserpinae.

22   interea Cupido amore nimio peresus et aegra facie matris

21.1 releuatus *Rohde*   2 solidata *Rohde*: solida *F*

lulling the fearsome rage of the dog with her cake, she arrived
3 at the palace of Proserpine. She declined her hostess's offer of a
soft seat and rich food, and sitting on the ground before her
feet, content with a piece of coarse bread, she reported Venus'
4 commission. The box was immediately taken away to be filled
and closed up in private, and given back to Psyche. By the
device of the second cake she muzzled the dog's barking, and
giving the ferryman her second coin she returned from the
5 Underworld much more briskly than she had come. Having
regained and adored the bright light of day, though in haste to
complete her mission, she madly succumbed to rash curiosity.
6 'What a fool I am,' said she, 'to be carrying divine beauty and
not to help myself even to a tiny bit of it, so as perhaps to
21 please my beautiful lover.' So saying she opened the box.
But she found nothing whatever in it, no beauty, but only
an infernal sleep, a sleep truly Stygian, which when uncovered
by the removal of the lid at once took possession of her and
diffused itself in a black cloud of oblivion throughout her
whole body, so that overcome by it she collapsed on the spot
2 where she stood in the pathway, and lay motionless, a mere
sleeping corpse.

But Cupid's wound had now healed and, his strength
returned, he could no longer bear to be parted for so long
from Psyche. He escaped from the high window of the room
3 in which he was confined; and, his wings having been restored
by his long rest, he flew off at great speed to the side of his
Psyche. Carefully wiping off the sleep and replacing it where it
had been in the box, he roused her with a harmless prick from
4 one of his arrows. 'See, poor wretch,' he said, 'how you had,
once again, been ruined as before by curiosity. But meanwhile
you must complete the mission my mother assigned you with
all diligence; the rest I will see to.' So saying, her lover nimbly
took flight, while Psyche quickly took back Proserpine's gift to
Venus.

22   Meanwhile Cupid, eaten up with love, looking ill, and

suae repentinam sobrietatem pertimescens ad armillum redit
alisque pernicibus caeli penetrato uertice magno Ioui supplicat
2 suamque causam probat. tunc Iuppiter prehensa Cupidinis
buccula manuque ad os suum relata consauiat atque sic ad
3 illum 'licet tu,' inquit 'domine fili, numquam mihi concessu
deum decretum seruaris honorem, sed istud pectus meum quo
leges elementorum et uices siderum disponuntur conuulneraris
assiduis ictibus crebrisque terrenae libidinis foedaueris casibus
4 contraque leges et ipsam Iuliam disciplinamque publicam
turpibus adulteriis existimationem famamque meam laeseris
in serpentes, in ignes, in feras, in aues et gregalia pecua serenos
5 uultus meos sordide reformando, at tamen modestiae meae
memor quodque inter istas meas manus creueris cuncta
perficiam, dum tamen scias aemulos tuos cauere, ac si qua
nunc in terris puella praepollet pulchritudine, praesentis
beneficii uicem per eam mihi repensare te debere.'

23   sic fatus iubet Mercurium deos omnes ad contionem
protinus conuocare, ac si qui coetu caelestium defuisset, in
poenam decem milium nummum conuentum iri pronuntiare.
quo metu statim completo caelesti theatro pro sede sublimi
2 sedens procerus Iuppiter sic enuntiat: 'dei conscripti Musarum
albo, adolescentem istum quod manibus meis alumnatus sim
profecto scitis omnes. cuius primae iuuentutis caloratos
impetus freno quodam coercendos existimaui; sat est cotidianis
eum fabulis ob adulteria cunctasque corruptelas infamatum.
3 tollenda est omnis occasio et luxuria puerilis nuptialibus
pedicis alliganda. puellam elegit et uirginitate priuauit: teneat,
possideat, amplexus Psychen semper suis amoribus perfruatur.'
4 et ad Venerem conlata facie 'nec tu,' inquit 'filia, quicquam
contristere nec prosapiae tantae tuae statuque de matrimonio

22.1 sociam Sobrietatem *Robertson*   2 consauiatur?   23.3 habeat *ante*
teneat *add. Brantz*

dreading his mother's new-found austerity, reverted to type.
On swift wings he made his way to the very summit of heaven
2 and pleaded his cause as a suppliant to great Jupiter. Jupiter
took Cupid's face in his hand, pulled it to his own, and kissed
3 him, saying: 'In spite of the fact, dear boy, that you have never
paid me the respect decreed by the agreement of the gods, but
have constantly shot and wounded this breast of mine by
which the behaviour of the elements and the movements of
the heavenly bodies are regulated, defiling it repeatedly with
4 lustful adventures on earth, compromising by low intrigues
my reputation and character in defiance of the laws, the Lex
Julia included, and of public morals, changing my majestic
features into the base shapes of snakes, of fire, of wild animals,
5 of birds and of farmyard beasts – yet in spite of all, remembering
my clemency and that you grew up in my care, I will do what
you ask. But you must take care to guard against your rivals;
and if there is now any pre-eminently lovely girl on earth, you
are bound to pay me back with her for this good turn.'

23 So saying, he ordered Mercury to summon all the gods
immediately to assembly, proclaiming that if anyone failed
to attend this heavenly meeting they would be liable to a
fine of ten thousand sesterces. This threat straightway filled
the divine theatre; and Jupiter towering on his lofty throne
2 announced his decision. 'Conscript deities enrolled in the
register of the Muses, you undoubtedly know this young
man well, how I have reared him with my own hands. I
have decided that the hot-blooded impulses of his first youth
must be somehow bridled; his name has been besmirched
for long enough in common report for adultery and all kinds
3 of wantonness. We must take away all opportunity for this
and fetter his youthful excess in the bonds of marriage. He
has chosen a girl and had her virginity: let him hold her, have
4 her, and embracing Psyche for ever enjoy his beloved.' Then
turning to Venus, 'Daughter,' he said, 'do not be downcast or
fear for your great lineage or social standing because of this

mortali metuas. iam faxo nuptias non impares sed legitimas et
5 iure ciuili congruas,' et ilico per Mercurium arripi Psychen et
in caelum perduci iubet et porrecto ambrosiae poculo 'sume,'
inquit 'Psyche, et immortalis esto, nec umquam digredietur a
tuo nexu Cupido sed istae uobis erunt perpetuae nuptiae.'
24   nec mora, cum cena nuptialis affluens exhibetur.
accumbebat summum torum maritus Psychen gremio suo
complexus, sic et cum sua Iunone Iuppiter ac deinde per
2 ordinem toti dei. tunc poculum nectaris Ioui quidem suus
pocillator ille rusticus puer, ceteris uero Liber ministrabat;
3 Vulcanus cenam coquebat; Horae rosis et ceteris floribus
purpurabant omnia, Gratiae spargebant balsama, Musae
quoque canora personabant; Apollo cantauit ad citharam,
Venus suaui musicae superingressa formonsa saltauit, scaena
sibi sic concinnata, ut Musae quidem chorum canerent aut
tibias inflarent, Saturus et Paniscus ad fistulam dicerent.
4   sic rite Psyche conuenit in manum Cupidinis et nascitur illis
maturo partu filia, quam Voluptatem nominamus.

4 iuri *Jahn*   5 iubet et porrecto φ (et *add. m²*): iubet porrecto *F*   24.2
quod uinum deorum est *post* nectaris *F, secl. Wouwere*   3 *post* personabant
add. post dapes *uel* inter dapes *Helm,* tunc *Robertson*   superingressa] suppari
gressu *Scaliger*   aut tibias *Oudendorp*: tibias *F*: et t. *Hildebrand*: tibiasue *Heinsius*:
Gratiae t. *Wiman*   inflaret . . . diceret ς

marriage with a mortal. I shall arrange for it to be not unequal
5 but legitimate and in accordance with the civil law.' Then he
ordered Psyche to be brought by Mercury and introduced into
heaven. Handing her a cup of ambrosia, 'Take this, Psyche,'
he said, 'and be immortal. Never shall Cupid leave the tie that
binds you, but this marriage shall be perpetual for you both.'

24   No sooner said than done: a lavish wedding-feast appeared.
In the place of honour reclined Psyche's husband, with his
wife in his arms, and likewise Jupiter with his Juno, and then
2 all the other gods in order of precedence. Cups of nectar were
served to Jove by his own cupbearer, the shepherd-lad, and to
3 the others by Liber; Vulcan cooked the dinner; the Seasons
made everything colourful with roses and other flowers; the
Graces sprinkled perfumes; the Muses discoursed tuneful
music. Then Apollo sang to the lyre, and Venus, fitting her
steps to the sweet music, danced in all her beauty, having
arranged a production in which the Muses were chorus and
played the tibia, while a Satyr and a little Pan sang to the
shepherd's pipe.

4   Thus was Psyche married to Cupid with all due observance,
and when her time came there was born to them a daughter,
whom we call Pleasure.

COMMENTARY

The story is told to Charite, held prisoner by a band of robbers, by their housekeeper, described as *delira et temulenta ... anicula* (6.25.1). She introduces it with the words *Sed ego te narrationibus lepidis anilibusque fabulis protinus auocabo.* See Introd. pp. 13, 22–3

Act I Psyche Innocens

IV

4.28.1 Erant in quadam ciuitate rex et regina: 8.1.5 *erat in proxima ciuitate iuuenis natalibus praenotabilis* ..., Tac. *Ann.* 13.45.1 *erat in ciuitate Sabina Poppaea.* Beginnings of this kind are no doubt as old as the art of narrative itself: e.g. Hdt. 1.6.1, Xen. *Anab.* 1.1.1 (Helm (1914) 191 = 205–6; cf. Dowden (1982*a*) 425, Fehling 79–88). They are particularly associated with the novel: Xen. *Eph.* 1.1.1 'There was in Ephesus a leading citizen called Lycomedes', Petron. 111.1 *matrona quaedam Ephesi tam notae erat pudicitiae* ..., Hist. *Apoll. reg. Tyr.* (6th c. A.D.?) 1 *fuit quidam rex in ciuitate Antiochiae nomine Antiochus*; but cf. also e.g. Ov. *Met.* 14.320–1 *Picus in Ausoniis, proles Saturnia, terris | rex fuit*, 1.689–91, 13.750. On the geographical vagueness of the story cf. 5.26–27n.　　**ciuitate** 'city', the usual sense in A. and late Latin generally, but already classical: *OLD* s.v. 3, *TLL* s.v. 1232.75ff. *ciuitas* (46 exx. in *Met.*) ousted *urbs* (6) and *oppidum* (2) to give It. *città*, Fr. *cité*, Eng. *city*.　　**gratissima specie:** ablative of quality or description, used, as often, adnominally (H–S 118). English says '*of* charming appearance'.

4.28.2 For the heroine's ideal beauty and its effects cf. Chariton's description of Callirhoe: 'Her loveliness was not human but divine, not that of some nymph of the sea or the mountains, but of Aphrodite Parthenos herself. Report of this wonderful sight was everywhere, and suitors came flocking to Syracuse, kings and the sons of tyrants, not only from Sicily but from Italy and Epirus and its peoples' (1.1.2); also Longus 4.33.3–4 (Daphnis and Chloe), Heliod. 2.33.3 (Chariclea), Callim. fr. 67.9–14 Pfeiffer, Musaeus, *Hero and Leander*

116

55–85. Cf. below, §3n.   **iunioris** 'youngest', cf. 9.37.1 *e tribus iunior*, as not uncommonly in later (Christian) Latin: *TLL* s.v. *iuuenis* 737.76ff.   **nec ... ac ne ... quidem:** 4.21.2 *neque clamore ac ne ululatu quidem*, 4.10.1 *neque subleuare neque dimouere ac ne perfringere quidem*, al. (some 24 instances in *Met.*: Hijmans al. 159). Cf. 4.29.3n.   **sufficienter:** (*) here, anon. *Decl. in Catil.* 74, and in the Digest; later frequent.   **penuria** 'because of its poverty', causal ablative: H–S 132.

4.28.3 denique 'indeed', 'in fact': *TLL* s.v. 530.68ff. Cf. 5.8.3n.   **copiosi** 'numerous', 'many'; cf. 4.20.4 *canes ... copiosi*, 8.17.3, 10.20.2, an unclassical and otherwise rare use of the plural: *TLL* s.v. 913.4–18, 914.24–46, Callebat (1968) 153–4. Cf. 5.3.3n.   **inaccessae** 'unequalled', lit. 'unapproachable'; first used by A. in this transferred sense: *TLL* s.v. 807.79–82.   **formonsitatis:** this spelling of *formosus* and its derivatives is usual in A.'s MSS. It was condemned by the ancient grammarians but is well attested in inscriptions and Virgil's capital MSS: 'The only remotely plausible etymology for *-ōsus* favours *-onsus*' (Coleman 39). *formosus*, 'rigorously avoided by the epic poets', occurs 23 times in Ovid's *Metamorphoses* (Knox 53–4).   **admouentes ... residente** (lit.) 'raising their right hands to their lips with the index finger resting on the upright thumb'; cf. Plin. *N.H.* 28.25 *in adorando dextram ad osculum referimus*, Butler–Owen on A. *Apol.* 56.15 (p. 64.1 Helm). For this reaction cf. Chariton's description of the reception of Callirhoe: 'When she appeared, the whole crowd were thunderstruck (θάμβος ... κατέλαβεν), like hunters in the wild surprised by Artemis, and many of them prostrated themselves (προσεκύνησαν)' (1.1.16) ... 'Leonas and the others were astonished, and some thought her a goddess, for there was a report that Aphrodite was appearing in the neighbourhood' (1.14.1); cf. 3.2.17, 4.7.5, 5.9.1, and for the comparison with a divinity Heliod. 1.2.1 and Maillon *ad loc.*, Xen. *Eph.* 1.1–2, 1.12.1, 2.2.4. See Helm (1914) 191 = 206, Rohde (1914) 162 n. 1, suggesting Callimachus' story of Acontius and Cydippe as the original model for such scenes; cf. especially Chariton 1.1.5 on Chaereas ~ Callim. frr. 68, ?534 Pfeiffer, Aristaen. *Ep.* 1.10.9–14 Mazal on Acontius; and see 4.29.2–3n. A. may also have had in mind Virgil's description of Camilla: *illam omnis tectis agrisque effusa iuuentus | turbaque*

miratur matrum et prospectat euntem | attonitis inhians animis ... (*Aen.*
7.812–14).   **primore digito:** usually taken as referring to the
first, i.e. index finger; so *OLD* s.v. 1b. This gesture (sc. with the other
fingers outspread) is still in use to signify approval, e.g. by (stage)
chefs. The alternative interpretation, as suggested by Purser (cf. *TLL*
s.v. *digitus* 1127.50), that all the finger-tips are brought together with
the thumb, entails that *primore digito* is 'poetic' or collective singular
for *primoribus digitis* (cf. *OLD* ibid. 2b). Precise parallels for such a
usage with *digitus* are lacking: in the passage of Naevius (*Com.* 79
Ribbeck[3]) cited by *TLL* ibid. 1122.80–1 the natural sense is 'hand'.
Venerem uenerabantur: etymological word-play of the kind that A.
had inherited from the Alexandrian tradition and took particular
delight in. Cf. Plaut. *Poen.* 278 *hanc equidem Venerem uenerabor, Rud.*
305, 1348–9. Crusius' placing of the restored verb immediately
after *Venerem* neatly accounts for its omission by haplography and is
supported by the Plautine parallels (Pasoli 193–5). Cf. below, §4n.

4.28.4 ros spumantium fluctuum: an allusion to the etymology
of her Greek name: 'Aphrodite she is called ... because she grew in
the foam (ἐν ἀφρῶι | θρέφθη)' (Hes. *Theog.* 195–7). See below.
numinis sui passim tributa uenia (lit.) 'by the grace of her godhead
freely granted'; *uenia* is vox propria of divine favours (*OLD* s.v. 1a).
There may be etymological word-play at work (cf. above, §3n.): cf.
Ernout–Meillet s.v. *uenia*, Pasoli 200–4 and n. 22.   **nouo caelestium stillarum germine:** at first sight an elaborate periphrasis for
rain (cf. e.g. Lucret. 1.250–1), but *nouo* identifies a delicate allusion to
an indelicate myth, the story of her birth. Cronus, having castrated
his father Uranus, threw his genitals into the sea, where they en-
gendered Aphrodite, while from the drops of blood which fell on the
earth there sprang (among others) the race of Giants (Hes. *Theog.*
176–200). Cf. 2.8.6 *illa caelo deiecta, mari edita, fluctibus educata* ...
Venus, 10.31.2 *corpus candidum quod caelo demeat, amictus caerulus quod mari
remeat, Perv. Ven.* 9–11 *tunc cruore de superno spumeo pontus globo | caerulas
inter cateruas inter et bipedes equos | fecit undantem Dionen de marinis imbribus.*
Cf. 6.6.4n.   **germine** 'sprouting', 'germination', perhaps with a
glance at the sense 'semen': *TLL* s.v. *germen* 1924.1–14.   **uirginali
flore praeditam:** and therefore one up on Venus.   **pullulasse**
'grow', with *Venerem aliam* as internal or cognate accusative, the only

occurrence of the word in A. The sequence *germine* ... *flore* ... *pullulasse* sustains the image of fertilization and growth.

4.29.1 There is a remarkable parallel at Tac. *Ann.* 12.36.2 *unde fama eius* [Caratacus] *euecta insulas et proximas prouincias peruagata per Italiam quoque celebratur*, with the same alliterative repetition of *p*. For Fame broadcasting reports of the heroine's beauty see Molinié's index s.v. Φήμη.   **immensum** 'hugely', 'enormously': *OLD* s.v.² On the neuter of adjectives used adverbially see H–S 40.   **procedit** signals the beginning of the story proper, the historic present being A.'s usual narrative tense; contrast the scene-setting function of ch. 28 and the descriptive imperfects of §§2–3. See also 5.2.1, 5.7.1nn. **terrae** 'the continent', 'the mainland': *OLD* s.v. 1c. It is unsafe to infer from any of this that the *ciuitas* was on an island (Hoevels 18); cf. 4.32.5, 5.24.1nn.

4.29.2–3 The picture is that of worshippers flocking to a great festival such as that of the Delian Apollo: cf. Chariton, cit. 4.28.2n., Musaeus, *Hero and Leander* 42–54 and Kost *ad loc.* Again, the model may have been Callimachus' Acontius and Cydippe (Rohde (1914) 162 n. 1): cf. Callim. fr. 71 Pfeiffer, where Pfeiffer cites Thuc. 3.104.3. Cf. 4.28.2n. and below, §4n.

4.29.2 altissimis maris meatibus 'journeys over the deep sea' = *altissimi m.m.*, a particularly harsh example of enallage or transferred epithet (Bell 315–29, Bernhard 215). Oudendorp's correction to *altissimi* is easy but destroys the balance of the phrase; his *latissimis* (which he preferred) suggests inappropriately that the voyagers wandered Ulysses-like far and wide over the ocean.

4.29.3 A paradoxical reversal of Ovid's description of Venus' neglect of her own shrines under the influence of her passion for Adonis: *capta uiri forma non iam Cythereia curat | litora, non alto repetit Paphon aequore cinctam | piscosamue Cnidon grauidamue Amathunta metallis* (*Met.* 10.529–31; see Bömer *ad loc.* and cf. Helm (1914) 199 = 218–19). A. omits Amathus (cf. Catull. 36.11–15) and rearranges the list to culminate with the goddess' birthplace Cythera, from which she took her commonest secondary name in literary Latin, Cytherea. Cf. also Ov. *Am.* 2.17.4 *quae Paphon et fluctu pulsa Cythera tenet*. There may also be a distant echo of Catull. 64.35–6 *deseritur Cieros, linquunt Pthiotica Tempe | Crannonisque domos et moenia Larisaea*.   **nemo ... nemo ... nauigabant:** for similar anomalous plurals with singular pronouns see H–S 437. For *nemo ... nemo ... ac ne ... quidem* cf. 10.12.1 and 4.28.2n.   **deseruntur:** the reading of the Aldine (recommended by Colvius) gives a suitably strong sense; Colvius' own *differuntur* ('Forte non male etiam'), 'put off', is comparatively tame.   **uiduae** 'bereft', 'deprived', sc. of offerings; but the literal sense 'widowed' may also be felt, underlining the fact that it is *Venus* who is thus slighted.

4.29.4 supplicatur 'supplication is made', impersonal passive: 4.33.3n.   **in matutino progressu:** possibly an echo of the notice attracted by Acontius: 'he was noticed by his lovers when he went to school or the bath' (Callim. fr. 68 Pfeiffer; cf. 4.28.3, 4.29.2–3nn.). For this adoration, in addition to Chariton (cit. 4.28.2n.), cf. Xen. *Eph.* 1.1.3 'They treated the young man [Habrocomes] like a god and some even prostrated themselves (προσεκύνησαν) at the sight of him and worshipped', 1.12.1 'The population of Rhodes gathered and admired the young pair [Habrocomes and Anthia] ... some said it was a visit from the gods and prostrated themselves'. Cf. Rohde (1914) 162 n. 1.   **uictimis et epulis:** possibly blood-sacrifices and bloodless offerings respectively (Hoevels 20 and n. 29). **populi** 'people', the individuals making up a crowd: cf. 4.32.3, 5.10.8, 6.10.7, al.; and cf. 4.34.5n. Ovid is fond of the plural of *populus* in this sense (Bömer on *Met.* 6.179). See H–S 21 and cf. 4.32.4 *gentibus totis* and n.   **floribus sertis et solutis:** 10.32.3 *iaculis floris serti et soluti deam suam* [Venus] *propitiantes*, Catull. 63.66–7 (Attis before his mutilation) *mihi floridis corollis redimita domus erat, | linquendum ubi esset orto mihi sole cubiculum*, Heliod. 3.3.8 'the girls threw him [Theagenes] fruit and flowers to attract his favour', Chariton 8.1.12 (Rohde (1914) 162 n.1).

4.29.5 incendit animos: Virg. *Aen.* 1.50 *talia flammato secum dea* [Juno] *corde uolutans ...*; see 4.30n. For Venus as a jealous goddess cf. Prop. 2.28.9–10 *num sibi collatam doluit Venus? illa peraeque | prae se formosis inuidiosa dea est* and for the neglect of love as motivating plot and punishment cf. Xen. *Eph.* 1.1, Callimachus' *Acontius and Cydippe* ('le commencement de la littérature romanesque', A. Couat cit.

Dalmeyda xix n. 1), and the exx. at Grimal (1963) 14–15; Hoevels 22.   **capite quassanti:** Virg. *Aen.* 7.292 *tum quassans caput haec effundit pectore dicta.* On Virgil's Juno as a model for A.'s Venus see next n.

4.30 A.'s portrayal of Venus is profoundly indebted to both Lucretius and Virgil. Her opening words identify her as the universal creative principle hymned in the opening lines of the *De rerum natura.* However, her vindictive indignation at the slight put upon her irresistibly recalls the Virgilian Juno: so Price 234 'Virgilius (ex quo hunc locum delineasse Apulejus videtur) . . .' Just as Venus' is the first speech in the story, so Juno's is the first in the *Aeneid* (1.37–49), and it is her vow of vengeance against Psyche that motivates the plot just as Juno's motivates that of the epic (cf. *Aen.* 7.292–322). 'The reader who has followed Apuleius attentively thus far may be prompted to anticipate the vast dimensions of Psyche's future suffering' (Horsfall 41). Ovid also seems to have been in A.'s mind, both his adaptation or parody (Tatum (1979) 49 n. 40) of *Aen.* 1.37–49 at *Met.* 3.262–72 and Latona's complaint at 6.206–13 (also noted by Price ibid.). See below, §§1, 3nn.

4.30.1 en rerum naturae . . . alma Venus, quae . . .: the expression is unmistakably Lucretian: *rerum naturae* ~ *rerum naturam* (Lucret. 1.21, al.), *origo initialis* ~ *rerum genitalis origo* (5.176), *alma Venus* (1.2). Rhetoric and tone, however, owe more to Virgil and Ovid: *Aen.* 7.308–10 (Juno) *ast ego, magna Iouis coniunx, nil linquere inausum | quae potui infelix, quae memet in omnia uerti, | uincor ab Aenea, Met.* 6.206–9 (Latona) *en ego uestra parens, uobis animosa creatis | et nisi Iunoni nulli cessura deorum, | an dea sim dubitor perque omnia saecula cultis | arceor . . . aris.* Venus' words are echoed and varied in Isis' epiphany at 11.5.1; cf. 11.2.1 *seu tu caelestis Venus,* 11.25.3–4, and Introd. pp. 15–16. On *alma* cf. 6.2.1n.   **en:** both the speeches of Allecto, the Fury sent by Juno to stir up war in Latium, begin with *en* (*Aen.* 7.452, 545): *quasi demonstrantis particula est, per quam intelligimus eam multa cogitasse et sic prorupisse . . .* (Serv. on *Aen.* 4.534). The word is not found in Lucretius.   **prisca:** a favourite word of Ovid's (29 instances), with overtones of old-fashioned morality (*OLD* s.v.[1] 3b) which are amusingly at odds with Venus' subsequent actions.   **elementorum** 'elements' (not as in Lucretius 'particles'), i.e. land, sea, and air; cf.

Longus 2.7.2 (of Eros), cit. 4.33.2.7n.   **initialis:** (*), but the
word is attested for Varro by 'Probus' on Virg. *Ecl.* 6.31 (p. 344.6
Thilo).   **orbis totius alma** = *quae totum orbem alo*; *alma* = *altrix*
(Price 234, Horsfall 41). For this active sense *TLL* s.v. 1703. 74–5
registers only *A.L.* 21.224 R.[2] = 8.224 Shackleton Bailey (who,
however, emends it away; cf. *H. S. C. P.* 84 (1980) 177–98).   **cum
mortali puella ... tractor** 'I am dealt with by having to share my
honour with a mortal girl'; Purser's 'I am dragged in the dust (like a
captive slave ...)' hardly suits *partiario ... honore*. However, the
expression is odd and Shackleton Bailey's *detractor* (172) (but A.'s
MSS prefer the spelling *detrecto*) deserves consideration.   **caelo
conditum:** with a glance at her parentage (4.28.4n.); cf. *OLD* s.v.
condo 11a.

4.30.2 nimirum 'evidently', heavily sarcastic.   **nominis:** Venus
sarcastically reflects that she is worshipped at least in name; cf.
4.29.4. *numinis* blunts the contrast and the point.   **uicariae
uenerationis incertum** 'the uncertainty of being worshipped by
deputy', genitive of definition. For substantival *incertum* + genitive see
TLL s.v. 886.8–28.   **moritura:** the emphasis on Psyche's mortal
status contrasts with the proclamation of omnipotence and omni-
presence with which the speech began and embodies a threat which in
the sequel is all but realized. The future participle stands for a relative
clause: cf. H–S 390, 6.8.3n.

4.30.3 pastor: Paris, who was ordered by Zeus (Jupiter) to decide
the palm of beauty between Aphrodite (Venus), Hera (Juno) and
Athene (Minerva). The reference to his *iustitia* and *fides* can only be
ironical, for by carrying off Helen (the bribe for his verdict in Venus'
favour) when she was already married to Menelaus he precipitated
the Trojan War and all the woes that ensued; cf. e.g. Hector's bitter
reproaches at Hom. *Il.* 3.39–57, Hor. *C.* 3.3.19 *fatalis incestusque
iudex*, and Lucius' rhetorical digression at 10.33.1.   **non adeo
gaudens:** a combination of Graecism (= οὐ χαίρουσα: LSJ
s.v. χαίρω II) and idiomatic Latin understatement (*non adeo* = 'not
very', i.e. not at all, far from it).   **usurpauerit** 'she will find that
she has usurped'; the future perfect (Oudendorp's correction:
usurpabit is also possible) may emphasize the certainty of the outcome:
K–S 1 147. Cf. however 5.24.5n.   **faxo** = *fecero*, an old form

surviving in classical writers in this sort of phrase: Ov. *Met.* 3.271
(Juno) *fallat eam faxo*, Claud. 20 (*In Eutrop.* 2).143–4 *largis haec
gaudia faxo | compensent lacrimis*. For the paratactic construction without
ut after *facio*, *uolo* et sim. see H–S 530–1 and cf. 5.6.4n. There are
significant echoes of this threat at 5.30.2, 6.23.4 (see nn.).

4.30.4–31.3 Venus enlists the aid of Cupid, whom she orders to
punish Psyche by making her fall in love with the most miserable
wretch he can find. A.'s model for the episode was the scene in the
Aeneid in which Venus causes Dido to fall in love with Aeneas by
substituting Cupid for Ascanius (1.657–84); that scene was itself
modelled on the scene in Apollonius' *Argonautica* in which Aphrodite,
instigated by Hera and Athene, asks Eros to make Medea fall in love
with Jason (3.111–66) (cf. also Ach. Tat. 8.12.4–5). A. had
evidently read Apollonius, and his picture of Cupid as seen through
Venus' eyes is more Hellenistic than Virgilian (Webster *passim*). 'In
Apollonius, Cupid is a naughty boy, who has to be bribed to obey:
Virgil made him a heartless accomplice in a heartless plot' (Austin on
Virg. *Aen.* 1.664ff.). This summary of his activities combines conventional literary attributes (wings, torch, bow) with specifically
Roman ideas and terminology (*disciplina publica, matrimonia corrumpens*,
etc.). See General Index s.v. 'Roman references'.

4.30.4 puerum suum: he is not identified by name until Psyche
sees him (5.22.2n.).   **pinnatum:** 3.22.5 (Lucius to Photis) *perfice
ut meae Veneri Cupido pinnatus adsistam tibi*, Cic. *N.D.* 3.58 (Proserpina)
pinnatum Cupidinem genuisse dicitur (see Pease *ad loc.*), Virg. *Aen.* 1.663
his aligerum dictis adfatur Amorem, Mosch. 1.16 'winged like a bird he
flits from one victim to another', Prop. 2.12.5–6 *idem non frustra
uentosas addidit alas, | fecit et humano corde uolare deum*, Ov. *Am.* 2.9.49 *tu
leuis es multoque tuis uentosior alis*, *A.A.* 1.233–6, Eubulus fr. 41 and
Hunter *ad loc.*; Bömer on Ov. *Met.* 1.466, Lier 18, Pichon 229, *LIMC*
III 1.851 (Eros), 953 (Cupid).   **satis temerarium** 'most reckless': *satis* is A.'s favourite intensifier: cf. 5.8.3 *satis scrupulose*, 5.23.1,
5.28.6 *satis curiosa*, 1.24.6 *sat pol diu est* 'it's an age', 3.21.1 *satis trepida*
'in a great taking', *OLD* s.v. 9b, Callebat (1968) 540–1.   **malis
suis moribus:** Mosch. 1.8 κακαὶ φρένες 'wicked disposition'. For
Watt's addition of *pro* cf. 5.11.5 and *OLD* s.v. 16b.   **disciplina
publica:** repeated by Jupiter at 6.22.4.   **flammis et sagittis**

armatus: Hor. *C.* 2.8.14–15 *Cupido,* | *semper ardentis acuens sagittas* (see N–H *ad loc.*), Mosch. 1.18–23, Ov. *Am.* 2.9.5 *cur tua fax urit, figit tuus arcus amicos?*, Sen. *Phaedr.* 276–7 *impotens flammis simul et sagittis* | *iste lasciuus puer*, Chariton 4.7.6, Ach. Tat. 1.11.3, 2.4.5, 2.5.2, 4.7.3; Bömer on Ov. *Met.* 1.461, Lier 31–2, *LIMC* III 1.852, 878–82 (Eros 332–87), 954, 973–7 (Cupid 132–71). Hellenistic poets rang endless changes on these conceits: Kenney (1970) 382 = 253. On the wounds of love cf. 4.31.1 *dulcia uulnera* and 4.32.4n.

4.30.5 uerbis ... stimulat: Virg. *Aen.* 7.330 *quam* [the Fury Allecto] *Iuno his acuit uerbis*; cf. 4.30.1n. on *en.* Juno's ensuing description of Allecto's powers would apply equally to Cupid: *tu potes unanimos armare in proelia fratres* | *atque odiis uersare domos, tu uerbera tectis* | *funereasque inferre faces, tibi nomina mille,* | *mille nocendi artes* (335–8). This is Venus II stirring Amor II into action; cf. 5.24.4n., Introd. p. 20.   **Psychen:** given the significance of the name (Introd. p. 16), · its casual introduction when the story is well advanced must be deliberate (cf. Brotherton 44). Her role hitherto has been entirely passive; with Venus' departure she will emerge (4.32.1) as the protagonist of the next episode.

4.31.1 prolata 'laid before him'; *profero* is the appropriate word for a recital of grievances amounting to a criminal charge (*OLD* s.v. 5c) rather than *perfero*, which is used of delivering a message vel sim. (*OLD* s.v. 2a).   **gemens ac fremens:** she is almost comically vehement.   **per ego te ... foedera** = *per foedera ego te*; the hyperbaton (displacement of normal word-order) throws the pronouns into high emotional relief – 'it is I (your mother), who implore you'; cf. 6.2.3. See *OLD* s.v. *per* 10b, Pease and Austin on Virg. *Aen.* 4.314. Her words recall Venus' appeal to Cupid at *Aen.* 1.664–6 *nate, meae uires, mea magna potentia, solus* | *nate patris summi qui tela Typhoea temnis,* | *ad te confugio et supplex tua numina posco.*   **dulcia uulnera ... mellitas uredines:** an oxymoron (pointed contradiction) of a kind much favoured by Hellenistic epigrammatists: Kenney (1970) 382–3 = 253–4. All such expressions are variations on Sappho's description of Eros as γλυκύπικρον ἀμάχανον ὄρπετον 'bittersweet uncontrollable beast' (fr. 130.2 L–P); cf. Catull. 68.18 (Venus) *quae dulcem curis miscet amaritiem* and Fordyce *ad loc.*, 2.10.2 (Photis to Lucius) *dulce et amarum gustulum carpis* etc., Longus 1.18.1

'her mouth is sweeter than honeycomb, but her kiss is sharper than a bee's sting'. *uredo* properly = 'scorching' of plants by frost or of the skin by a sting vel sim.   **sed plenam** 'and (I mean) a full one'; for this emphatic use of *sed* (predominantly colloquial) see *OLD* s.v. 3a and cf. below, §5 *set statim*.

4.31.2 seueriter: some editors retain F's *reuerenter*; but Venus is less interested in respectful compliance than in revenge.   **in pulchritudinem ... uindica:** for the classical construction with accusative of the offence; elsewhere in *Met.* of the offender, 2.27.4, 3.3.9, 8.13.5. Cf. *OLD* s.v. *uindico* 5b, c.   **unum et pro omnibus unicum:** Virg. *Aen.* 3.435–6 (Helenus to Aeneas) *unum illud tibi, nate dea, proque omnibus unum | praedicam.* A. characteristically compounds his model with a colloquial touch, the heightening of *unus* with *unicus*, as at Catull. 73.6 *qui me unum atque unicum amicum habuit*, Plaut. *Asin.* 208, al. (Bernhard 168, 229).

4.31.3 fraglantissimo: A.'s MSS tend to spell both *flagro* (the sense here) and *fragro* in this way: see Hijmans al. Appendix II (210–11). **extremi** 'lowest', cf. 5.24.3, 3.5.6 *extremos latrones* and Helm *ad loc.*; used of slaves by Seneca (*Dial.* 5.37.2) and the jurist Ulpian (*notae extremae, Dig.* 47.10.15.44). See *OLD* s.v. 5.   **incolumitas** 'sa personne même' (Vallette); the word connotes both physical health and safety and also the possession of civil rights (*TLL* s.v. 983.39–52).

4.31.4–7 Venus' return to the sea. This is the first of a number of elaborate descriptions (*ecphraseis*) in the story; it is complemented by her aerial progress at 6.6. It is not purely decorative, though A. clearly delighted in rococo embellishment for its own sake. The epicizing tone underlines Venus' current Apollonian–Virgilian *persona*, which contrasts with her Lucretian entrance (4.30n.) and reappearance (6.6, 6.7.3nn.). A.'s models are Homer (*Il.* 13.27–31: Poseidon, 18.37–49: catalogue of Nereids), Moschus (*Europa* 115–24: Zeus as bull), and Virgil (*Aen.* 5.816–26: Neptune); he may also have known the famous sculptured group by Scopas depicting Neptune and his retinue (Plin. *N.H.* 36.26). Venus herself is figured in art as drawn by Tritons (*LIMC* II 1.118 (Aphrodite 1211)) and swans (ibid. 1212) over the sea; for *Venus marina* in art

cf. also Amat 125. Claudian produces an even more elaborate
version at 10 (*Epithalam. Hon. Aug.*).144–79. Cf. Hoevels 34–5
and nn.

4.31.4 sic effata: an epicizing tag; cf. 5.31.4, Virg. *Aen.* 2.524, 4.30,
al., *TLL* s.v. *effor* 198.46ff.; *haec ecfatus* Enn. *Ann.* 46, 57 Skutsch.
Cf. 4.35.1, 6.23.1nn.   **pressule (†)** 'avidement' (Vallette) rather
than 'with gentle pressure' (*OLD* s.v.), as shown by *osculis hiantibus
. . . diu*; cf. 10.21.2 *exosculata pressule*. This parting is modelled on that
at A.R. 3.149–50 (cf. 6.22.2n.), but Venus' kiss here is not exactly
maternal – but how could the embrace of this mother and this son
(Venus II and Amor II: 4.30.5n.) be anything but 'erotic'? Cf. 3.19.5
(Lucius to Photis) *cum . . . sic tuis . . . hiantibus osculis teneas uolentem*.
'Aphrodite does not just order her son to do her dirty work for her, she
seduces him sexually to do so' (Bettelheim 293). Cf. 5.28.7n.
reflui litoris 'the tidal shore', i.e. the shore of the sea; cf. Claud. 7
(*Hon. III Cons.*).58 *Tethyos alternae refluas calcauit harenas*, where *refluas*
= 'tidal' rather than 'ebbing' ('the wave-swept strand', Platnauer);
re- can equally well refer to either direction of the tide. However,
Rohde's *licoris* (= *liquoris*) deserves consideration: cf. Hor. *C.*
3.3.46–7 *. . . oras, qua medius liquor | secernit Europen ab Afro*. For the
pleonasm *orae . . . litoris* cf. Virg. *G.* 2.44, *Aen.* 3.396 *litoris oram*.
plantisque roseis: Moero, *A.P.* 6.189.1–2 (*HE* 2679–80)
'Hamadryad (?) Nymphs, ambrosial daughters of the river who tread
these depths for ever with rosy feet (αἳ . . . ῥοδέοις στείβετε ποσσὶν
ἀεί) . . .' The ability to walk on water is a manifestation of divinity:
Hom. *Il.* 13.29–30 (Poseidon's horses), 20.228–9 (the mares of
Erichthonius), Matt. 14.25ff., etc.; cf. Bühler on Mosch. *Eur.* 114
(Zeus as bull) 'stepping out over the sea with hooves unwetted.'
profundum: Koehler's correction restores sense and point. The
instant calming of the sea is a standard feature of such descriptions:
Mosch. *Eur.* 115 'at his approach the sea became still' (∼ Hom. *Il.*
13.29: see Bühler *ad loc.* and cf. also *Il.* 18.61–7), Virg. *Aen.* 5.820–1
subsidunt undae tumidumque sub axe tonanti | sternitur aequor aquis, Lucian
78 (*Dial. Mar.*).15.3. One of Aphrodite's titles was Εὔπλοια 'She
of the fair voyage'; cf. Lucret. 1.8 *tibi rident aequora ponti*. This was also
one of the roles of Isis; see the Isiac aretalogy at Walsh (1970) 252–3,
items 41, 47, 48. With F's *profundi* this essential point is lost, and

Venus takes her seat − on what? Presumably on the car to be mentioned presently (§7), an implausibly elliptical feature in this elaborately written passage. **sudo** 'clear', perhaps with a play on the popular etymology *se-udus* 'dry'; the wave-crests subside, there is no spray, and Venus does not wet her feet (Augello (1977−9) 175−80).

4.31.5 ipsum quod incipit uelle: another attribute of divinity; Ov. *Met.* 8.619 *quidquid superi uoluere peractum est* and Bömer *ad loc.* It is unclear whether *ipsum* is subject ('her escort was prompt to appear, the very thing she was (just) beginning to wish') or object ('her escort did not delay (to carry out) the very thing . . .') of *moratur*; the first seems more natural. Cf. 5.2.4 *nec . . . epulae morabuntur* 'will not be slow to appear'. **set statim** 'and that speedily'; above, §1n. Robertson's correction neatly provides the emphasis lacking in F's *et*. **obsequium:** (*) in concrete sense = *ministri* (*TLL* s.v. 184.54ff., Callebat (1968) 59); cf. §7 *exercitus*.

4.31.6 The participants in this marine cortège are mostly traditional: Virg. *Aen.* 5.240−2 *Nereidum Phorcique chorus Panopeaque uirgo | et pater ipse manu magna Portunus euntem | impulit*, 823−4 *et senior Glauci chorus Inousque Palaemon | Tritonesque citi Phorcique exercitus omnis* (see Williams *ad loc.*). *Nereus* was father of the sea-nymphs (Nereids) by Doris; *Portunus* (sometimes identified with Neptune) was god of harbours (*portus*); *Salacia* (*ab salo*, Varr. *L.L.* 5.72; *quod salum ciet*, Festus pp. 436, 437 L.) was an old Roman goddess of the sea; *Palaemon* (often depicted in art astride a dolphin, as here) was originally Melicertes, son of Athamas and Ino, changed into a sea-god by Neptune (Ov. *Met.* 4.531−42). Cf. A. *Apol.* 31 (p. 37.21ff., Helm) *Neptunus cum Salacia et Portuno et omni choro Nerei*. Portunus and Palaemon were commonly identified in the learned tradition (Ov. *F.* 6.547), but A. was no doubt less concerned with mythological accuracy than with the general effect and the sound of the names, Greek and Latin being mixed with abandon. The Tritons were Neptune's attendants. **Nerei filiae:** Mosch. *Eur.* 118−19 'The Nereids arose from the sea and mounted on the sea-beasts went all in procession'. Moschus and A. omit the list of their names traditional in epic (Hom. *Il.* 18.39−48, Virg. *Aen.* 5.825−6). **caerulis barbis:** the plural apparently connotes luxuriance, as at Petron. 99.5 *barbis*

horrentibus nauta (Walsh (1978) 22).   **grauis piscoso sinu:** like
other sea-gods and goddesses Salacia is identified with the sea itself;
sinus = both 'fold' of her garment and 'bay', 'gulf' of the ocean.
auriga paruulus: he is figured as a small boy, as Melicertes was
before his metamorphosis (above).   **delphini:** Mosch. *Eur.* 117
'dolphins somersaulted joyfully over the waves'.   **iam passim
maria persultantes:** Lucret. 1.14 *inde* [inspired by Venus] *ferae
pecudes persultant pabula laeta.*   **Tritonum:** Triton was the son of
Poseidon (Neptune) and Amphitrite (with whom Salacia was
sometimes identified): Hes. *Theog.* 930–3. Plural Tritons figured in
Scopas' group (above, §§4–7n.) and (for the first time in literature)
in Moschus: *Eur.* 123–5 'there thronged round him [Poseidon]
Tritons, the sonorous trumpeters of the sea, sounding a marriage-
song on their long shells'. They were human above the waist, piscine
below: Virg. *Aen.* 10.210–12.

4.31.7 concha sonaci: their usual attribute: Mosch. *Eur.* (cit.
previous n.), Virg. *Aen.* 6.171–4, 10.209–10, Ov. *Met.* 1.333–8.
inimici: to her complexion, for sun-tan in the ancient world was
cultivated only by men (cf. Philostratus' description of Galatea, *Imag.*
2.18.4); and to her native element; but also recalling the fact that it
was the all-seeing Sun who had given away her affair with Mars:
Hom. *Od.* 8.302, Ov. *A.A.* 2.573–4, *Met.* 4.171–4, 190–2 *exigit
indicii memorem Cythereia poenam | inque uices illum, tectos qui laesit amores, |
laedit amore pari.*   **speculum progerit:** 11.9.2 ... *aliae, quae
nitentibus speculis pone tergum reuersis uenienti deae* [Isis] *obuium
commonstrarent obsequium.* The mirror is a familiar attribute of Venus
(Callim. *Hymn* 5.21–2 and Bulloch *ad loc.*, A.R. 1.745–6), but is
less common in art than might be expected (*LIMC* II 1.60–1
(Aphrodite 494–6).   **curru ... subnatant:** they swim under and
buoy up (*curru* dative: 6.23.4n.) her car; the construction is analogous
to that with e.g. *subicio, succedo.*   **ad Oceanum:** her birthplace
(4.28.4nn.) but not her usual home.   **exercitus:** Virg. *Aen.* 5.824
Phorci ... exercitus omnis.

4.32.1 interea: the standard signal of a change of scene, especially
favoured by Virgil (Kenney on *Moret.* 52). The abrupt transition
helps to gloze over the fact that Cupid flatly disobeys his mother's
orders, something which emerges only gradually from the narrative

and is not explicitly acknowledged until 5.24.3–4 (see n. and Introd. p. 20). Cf. the equally abrupt transition at 6.22.1 (6.22–24n.). **cum** 'along with', carrying the colloquial nuance 'she and that beauty of hers': *OLD* s.v. *cum*[1] 3c, Callebat (1968) 199.   **sua sibi** 'her very own', an old colloquial usage in which *sibi* is equivalent to an indeclinable emphatic particle: cf. 1.10.3 *in suis sibi domibus*, 7.28.1, 9.30.4; Lindsay on Plaut. *Capt.* 5, *OLD* s.v. *se*[1] 2a, H–S 94. Cf. below, §4 in *se suam*, 5.1.6n.   **nec** 'but (nobody)': *OLD* s.v. *neque* 5, Hijmans al. 24–5. Latin conjunctions often take their tone (here adversative) from the context: cf. Kenney on Lucret. 3.150, Courtney on Juv. 3.102.   **nec ... saltem** = *ne ... quidem*; cf. 5.27.3 *nec ... uel saltem mortua*, 6.13.2 *nec tamen ... saltem*, al., Callebat (1968) 334–5.   **petitor accedit** 'came seeking', 'came as a suitor'; *petitor* is predicative.

4.32.2 ut simulacrum fabre politum: a stock compliment (Rohde (1914) 165 and n. 2; add Ach. Tat. 5.11.5, Heliod, 2.33.3); cf. Eur. *Hec.* 560–1, Rufinus, *A.P.* 5.15 (IV Page, q.v.), Petron. 126.16–17, Ov. *Am.* 1.7.51–2. A. may well have had Euripides' *Andromeda* in mind (4.33nn.): 'I see the image of a girl ... a statue by a cunning hand (σοφῆς ἄγαλμα χειρός)', fr. 125 Nauck[2]; cf. Ov. *Met.* 4.672–6, Ach. Tat. 3.7.2.   **nulli diffamarunt populi** = *populi* [4.29.4n.] *haudquaquam diff.*; for this emphatic adverbial use of *nullus* cf. e.g. 8.19.2 *nulli scitis?* 'Haven't you any idea?', 9.30.6 *nullus respondit dominus* 'There came no answer at all from the master', Catull. 8.14 *cum rogaberis nulla* 'when you will not be courted at all'; *OLD* s.v. 6.

4.32.3 beatas: the sisters later take a rather different view: 5.9–10. **adeptae:** understand *erant*.

4.32.4 aegra corporis, animi saucia: Enn. *Medea* 216 Jocelyn *Medea animo aegro amore saeuo saucia*, a phrase which 'appealed to later Latin poets' (Jocelyn *ad loc.*, q.v.). For the wounding metaphor cf. 5.23.4 *saucia mente*, 10.2.5 *uulnus animi*, 4.31.1 *tuae sagittae dulcia uulnera* and 4.30.4n.; Lucret. 4.1048 ... *corpus, mens unde est saucia amore*, Virg. *Aen.* 4.1–2 *at regina graui iamdudum saucia cura | uulnus alit uenis et caeco carpitur igni* (see Pease and Austin *ad loc.*), *OLD* s.v. *saucius* 5a, Kenney (1970) 382–4 = 253–5, Calboli 76. The language

underlines the paradox that Psyche is sick for *lack* of love. For the
genitives of respect cf. e.g. 5.18.4 *animi tenella*, 5.22.1 *et corporis et
animi . . . infirma*: H–S 75.   **gentibus totis** 'everybody'; for *gentes*
plural (> French *les gens*) cf. 4.29.4 *populi* and n. *toti = omnes* (>
French *tous*, Italian *tutti*) as at 5.1.6 *toti . . . parietes*, and frequently
elsewhere in *Met.*: *OLD* s.v. *totus* 6, H–S 203, Bömer on Ov. *Met.*
1.253.   **odit . . . suam formonsitatem:** another paradox; when
the heroine of romance curses her beauty it is because it attracts too
much (unwelcome) attention (4.34.5n.).

4.32.5 sic 'this being the case': *OLD* s.v. 9a.   **infortunatissimae:**
the superlative only here and at 4.27.2.   **dei Milesii:** Apollo,
who had a famous oracle at Didyma near Miletus. Resort to an oracle
in such circumstances was standard practice, in life as in literature
(Helm (1914) 194 = 210); but one cannot help being reminded
once again of Cydippe (Callim. fr. 75.20–37 Pfeiffer; cf. 4.28.3,
4.29.2–3, 4nn.). However, we are justified, in the light of later
developments (5.25.4, 6.10.5nn.), in inferring that Cupid is already
at work behind the scenes (Hoevels 43–4). In that case the last two
lines of the oracle (and choice of metre? see next n.) may hint that
Apollo has been blackmailed. Geographical inferences about the
location of the *ciuitas* (Dietze 140) are misplaced; see 4.29.1n.

4.32.6 ingratae 'displeasing': *OLD* s.v. 3.   **propter Milesiae**
(*) **conditorem:** that is, as a favour to A., who respects the literary
proprieties so far as to refrain from introducing a passage of Greek (as
distinct from proper names or words of Greek derivation) into a Latin
book (cf. 9.39.3–7, where the soldier's Greek is translated). However, in doing so he goes out of his way to shatter the dramatic illusion
(for all this is supposed to be narrated by the drunken housekeeper)
for immediate humorous effect, underlined perhaps by the rare
technical term *Milesia* sc. *fabula* (Bernhard 161); cf. *Hist. Aug.* 12
(Jul. Capitol.).11.8, 12.12, Tert. *De an.* 23.4. The god at least
replies in metre, even if in the wrong language. (In fact, the Delphic
oracle at least never used elegiacs (Parke–Wormell II xxii); but cf.
Heliod. 2.26.5, 2.35.5, 8.11.2–3; the oracle at Xen. *Eph.* 1.6.2 is in
hexameters.) On *Met.* as a 'Milesian' tale see Introd. pp. 7–8.

4.33 The punishment of Psyche's involuntary hybris is to be exposed
on a rock for a monster to carry off, like Andromeda or Hesione

(Grimal (1963) 15). On the popularity of the Andromeda story see
Mayer on Sen. *Phaedr.* 1035–48. The allusive description of Cupid
as the monster exploits his attributes to make him sound like a fire-
breathing dragon; ambiguity was the stock-in-trade of oracles.

4.33.1.2 ornatam mundo funerei thalami 'adorned in the gear
of a funereal marriage', a conceit exploited by Manilius in his descrip-
tion of Andromeda: *hic hymenaeus erat, solataque publica damna | priuatis
lacrimans ornatur uictima poenae | induiturque sinus non haec ad uota paratos, |
uirginis et uiuae rapitur sine funere funus* (5.545–8). So too Achilles
Tatius in his description of a picture of Andromeda: 'She stood in a
wedding dress like a bride adorned for Death' (3.7.5). Cf. also Ar.
Thesm. 1034–5 (a parody of Euripides' *Andromeda*) 'not with bridal
but with binding song', Iphigenia at Lucret. 1.95–9 (Hoevels 46
n. 101), Polyxena at Sen. *Tro.* 1132–52 (Herrmann 17). Cf. below,
§4n.

4.33.1.3 mortali stirpe creatum: Lucret. 1.733 *ut uix humana uideatur
stirpe creatus*, Virg. *Aen.* 10.543 *Vulcani stirpe creatus*, Ov. *Met.* 1.760
caelesti stirpe creatus (cf. 3.543, 14.699). Oracular ambiguity: *nec . . .
mortali* = both 'inhuman' and 'immortal'.

4.33.1.4 Every word in this verse is loaded with double meaning
(Helm (1914) 185–6 = 198).   **saeuum:** a stock epithet of love or
Cupid: 2.16.6 *sagittam saeui Cupidinis*, 8.2.7 *flamma saeui Amoris*, 10.2.5
saeuienti deo, Virg. *E.* 8.47 *saeuus Amor docuit* etc., Ov. *Am.* 1.1.5, 1.6.34,
2.10.19, *A.A.* 1.18, *Rem.* 530, *Her.* 7.190, [Tib.] 3.4.65, 66, Ov. *Met.*
1.453 *saeua Cupidinis ira*, Tib. 2.4.6 *uror, io, remoue saeua puella faces*; Lier
29–30, Pichon 257–8. In the event it is Venus who is to earn the title
twice given her by Horace, *mater saeua Cupidinum, C.* 1.19.1, 4.1.5; cf.
Prop. 3.24.13 *saeuo Veneris torrebar aeno.*   **ferum:** Bion 13.13 κακόν
ἐντι τὸ θηρίον 'cet animal est méchant', Meleager, *A.P.* 5.177.1
(*HE* 4190) κηρύσσω τὸν Ἔρωτα τὸν ἄγριον 'I cry the fierce Eros',
Alexis fr. 245.12 Kock ἡ σφοδρότης δὲ θηρός 'violent as a wild
beast'; Ov. *Am.* 1.2.8 *possessa ferus pectora uersat Amor*, 3.1.20, *A.A.* 1.9,
Her. 16.126, *Rem.* 267; Pichon 147.   **atque:** in elegy of the
classical period almost never unelided: Platnauer 78–82.
uipereumque: suggesting the 'bridegroom as serpent' motif later
exploited by the sisters (5.17.3–18.3) but also with a reference
to Sappho's famous description of Eros as a creeping thing

(ὄρπετον, fr. 130 L–P) and perhaps to the idea of love as a poison: Virg. *Aen.* 1.688 *occultum inspires ignem fallasque ueneno*, Prop. 2.12.19 *intactos isto satius temptare ueneno*. **malum:** ostensibly 'monster' (*OLD* s.v.[1] 7c, *TLL* s.v. *malus* 229.31–42); but Love himself is styled κακόν, *malum*: A.R. 3.129 (Aphrodite to Eros) ἄφατον κακόν, Prop. 1.5.28, 1.9.18, 3.17.10, Ov. *Rem.* 526; cf. *Am.* 2.9.26 *usque adeo dulce puella malum est*, Pichon 195.

4.33.2.5–6 See 4.30.4n.

4.33.2.7 Oracular ambiguity wears thin here, for love was the only power in the mythological universe of which this was true: Ov. *Met.* 5.369–70 (Venus to Cupid) *tu superos ipsumque Iouem, tu numina ponti | uicta domas* etc., Hes. *Theog.* 121–2 'He subdues the mind and sensible counsel of all the gods and all mankind', Longus 2.6.2 'Not even Zeus has such power. He rules the elements, the stars, his fellow gods', Chariton 6.3.2, Ach. Tat. 1.2.1 'How the brat rules heaven and earth and sea!', Heliod. 4.10.5 and Rattenbury *ad loc.*, Men. fr. 198.1–2 Koerte, Asclepiades, *A.P.* 5.64.5–6 (*HE* 858–9), Meleager, *A.P.* 12.101.6 (4545), Virg. *E.* 10.69 *omnia uincit Amor*, Sen. *Phaedr.* 186–94 and Mayer *ad loc.*; cf. *Hom. hym.* 5 (Aphrod.).36–40, Bömer on Ov. *Met.* 1.464. Cf. also the Greek magical prayer cited by Reitzenstein 150–1, with a range of epithets embracing both the cosmic and the anthropomorphic attributes of Eros. This is the universal cosmogonic Eros (Guthrie IV 382–3) in trivialized literary guise. 'A reader with even a smattering of Plato would recognise [the] "monster" as Cupid' (Tatum (1979) 50); see Introd. pp. 19–20. **Iouis** = *Iuppiter* (archaic).   **quo** refers to *Iouis* rather than to the 'monster'; see translation.

4.33.2.8 fluminaque ... et Stygiae tenebrae 'the dark stream of Styx'; this can be taken as an example of the 'explicative' use of conjunctions, *et* = 'i.e.', or as hendiadys ('the resolution of a complex expression into its parts': Moore 273; cf. Serv. on Virg. *Aen.* 1.61); see Bell 258–61, H–S 782–3. Rivers are just as much subject to the power of love as other gods (5.25.2n.) and not even Styx, whose name was associated with στυγερός 'hateful' (Hes. *Theog.* 775–6), an oath by whom even the gods feared to break (Hom. *Il.* 15.37–8), is immune. Cf. Mosch. 1.14 'he can shoot as far as Acheron and the palace of Hades'.

4.33.3 piger 'slow', 'reluctant'; cf. Ov. *Her.* 18.210 *tunc piger ad nandum, tunc ego cautus ero, OLD* s.v. 3a. Lipsius' *pigens*, which editors generally print, is objectionable on two grounds: (i) the present participle is nowhere else attested, which would not be decisive if it gave satisfactory sense; but (ii) the king should not be feeling 'displeased', 'irked' (*OLD* s.v. *piget* e) but grieved and despondent. **maeretur, fletur, lamentatur:** impersonal passives; 'there is mourning' etc. A relatively uncommon usage in the present tense (not however as rare as suggested by H–S 418), here conveying that the whole scene was one of grief. Cf. 4.35.1 *itur* and n. Elsewhere in A. *lamentor* is, as usual, deponent; here it is used passively by assimilation to the other verbs, but the active form is not uncommon in Christian Latin and was probably colloquial: *TLL* s.v. 903.33ff., 73–5, Callebat (1968) 298. For the expression as a whole cf. (one of the transmitted versions of) Enn. *Ann.* 498 Skutsch *maerentes flentes lacrumantes ac/commiserantes* (Bernhard 67 n. 25).

4.33.4 The paradox of the wedding that is also a funeral (above, §1. 2n.) is now exploited in terms recalling a favourite topic of Hellenistic epigram, the bride who dies on her wedding day: Antipater of Sidon, *A.P.* 7.711 (*HE* 548–55), Erinna, *A.P.* 7.712 (1789–96), Meleager, *A.P.* 7.182 (4680–7), Philip, *A.P.* 7.186 (*GP* 2795–800); Sen. *Contr.* 6.6 *uersae sunt in exsequias nuptiae mutatusque genialis lectus in funebrem, subiectae rogo felices faces,* Ach. Tat. 1.13.5–6, 3.10.5, Heliod. 2.29.3–4, 10.16.10, Xen. *Eph.* 1.6.2 (v. 6), 3.7.2, Sil. *Pun.* 13.547. See Szepessy *passim.* Again, Callimachus' Cydippe may also be lurking here: Ov. *Her.* 21.157–72, Aristaen. 1.10.85–6 Mazal 'Her parents were faced with a funeral instead of a marriage'. The conceit of death as a bridal is far older: Soph. *Ant.* 813–16, Seaford 106–7. **zygiae** 'of marriage' (Greek ζυγόν 'yoke'), for the usual *iugalis* (4.26.5); (‡), but cf. 6.4.3n. **Ludii** 'the Lydian', sc. mode or strain; but here apparently neuter as at 10.31.5 *tibicen Doricum canebat bellicosum, Flor.* 4 (p. 5.15–16 Helm), cf. Pausan. 9.12.5 τὸ ... καλούμενον Λύδιον; with *modum* the expression is slightly pleonastic, but A. is apt to sacrifice precision and economy to balanced phrasing. On the Lydian mode as appropriate for mourning cf. [Plut.] *De musica* 15.1136c, citing Plat. *Rep.* 3.398e. **deterget lacrimas ipso suo flammeo:** a fresh twist to the paradox: Psyche is a live participant in her own funeral. For *ipso* read *ipsa*?

4.33.5 luctu: dative with *congruens*.   **iustitium:** a specifically Roman term for a suspension of judicial and public business.

4.34.1 uiuum producitur funus: cf. Manil. 5.548 (cit. 4.33.1.2n.). A. may also have recollected Ovid's exploitation of the idea of exile as death, especially *Tr.* 1.3.89 *egredior, siue illud erat sine funere ferri* [= *efferri*].

4.34.3–6 Psyche's speech, highly implausible in terms of consistent characterization (Médan 350), is that of a tragic heroine such as Iphigenia or Macaria or Polyxena (4.33.1.2n.), doomed to be sacrificed for the people: cf. Eur. *Heracl.* 500–34, 574–96, *I.A.* 1374–8, Ov. *Met.* 13.457–73 (and see Bömer *ad loc.*). We may also discern an echo of a philosophical–rhetorical commonplace on excess in mourning: cf. Lucian 40 (*On grief*).16 'Wretch, why do you make such an outcry? ... Cease tearing your hair and scratching your face.'

4.34.3 qui magis meus est: Eur. *Alc.* 882–4 'I envy the unmarried and the childless, who have but one life (ψυχή), a moderate burden of anxious care', Sen. *Ep.* 104.2 *cum sciam spiritum illius* [Paulina] *in meo uerti, incipio, ut illi consulam, mihi consulere.* The idea is most familiar in its erotic guise: Plut. *Amat.* 759d 'Cato [!] used to say that the soul of the lover dwelt in that of the beloved' (cf. id. *Ant.* 946d), Callim. *A.P.* 12.73 (*HE* 1057–62), Catulus p. 43 Morel *aufugit mi animus; credo ut solet ad Theotimum | deuenit,* Ov. *Met.* 3.473 (Narcissus to his reflection) *duo concordes anima moriemur in una,* 11.388 (husband and wife) *animas ... duas ut seruet in una* and Bömer *ad loc.*; cf. Petron. 79.8 *transfudimus hinc et hinc labellis | errantes animas,* Rufinus, *A.P.* 5.14 (III Page, q.v.), Ach. Tat. 2.8.2, 2.37.9–10, Xen. *Eph.* 1.9.6; Bréguet *passim,* Lilja 195–7. Cf. below. This is the first of a series of plays on her name: *spiritus* = ψυχή; cf. 5.6.7n.   **ora ... foedatis:** Virg. *Aen.* 11.86 (Acoetes mourning Pallas) *pectora nunc foedans pugnis, nunc unguibus ora,* 4.673 (Anna mourning Dido), 12.871 (Juturna mourning Turnus).   **quid laceratis in uestris oculis mea lumina** 'Why do you torture my eyes by weeping yourselves?', a fresh variant of the 'two souls in one' conceit. Cf. Ov. *Am.* 1.7.60 (a verse productive of much misunderstanding when taken seriously) *sanguis erat lacrimae, quas dabat illa, meus,* Her. 13.80 *ne meus ex illo corpore sanguis*

eat, A. *Met.* 8.12.1 *haec est illa dextera quae meum sanguinem fudit.*
ubera sancta: a tragic motif, reminiscent of Clytemnestra's famous
appeal to Orestes: Aesch. *Cho.* 896–8, Eur. *El.* 1206–7 and Garvie,
Denniston *ad locc.*; cf. Hom. *Il.* 22.82–3, Chariton 3.5.6.

4.34.4 erant etc. 'these were the ⟨destined⟩ rewards', sc. of your
care and love. Haupt's correction gives pointed sense to F's rather flat
erunt. Cf. Hor. *Epp.* 1.4.6 *non tu corpus eras sine pectore*, Prop. 1.13.34 *non
alio limine dignus eras* and Fraenkel 324 and n. 3, arguing that the
imperfect in such cases is a Graecism (*contra* Fedeli on Prop. *loc. cit.*).
Add Ov. *Am.* 1.6.64 *sollicito carcere dignus eras* and Barsby *ad loc.*
('imperfect of fact just recognized'). **percussi ... sentitis** =
percuti uos sentitis: cf. Virg. *Aen.* 2.377 *sensit medios delapsus in hostes* and
Austin *ad loc.* A Graecism, but A.'s model is no doubt Virgil.

4.34.5 gentes et populi: cf. 4.29.4, 4.32.4nn., but this, like 5.31.6
(q.v.), is perhaps a borderline case. **iam sentio, iam uideo:**
Catull. 67.16 *ut quiuis sentiat et uideat.* **nomine Veneris** 'through
being called Venus', but also ironically 'in the name of V.', 'by V.'s
orders' (*OLD* s.v. *nomen* 14a). Psyche, though she does not fully
realize it, is the victim of a personal vendetta. The fatal beauty of the
heroine is a leitmotiv of the Greek novels: Chariton 2.2.6, Xen. *Eph.*
2.1.3, 2.11.4, 5.5.5, 5.7.2 (Dietze 144).

4.34.6 istas ... illum: variation for its own sake; there is no difference in the degree of bitterness. **quid differo, quid detrecto ...:**
the indicative is sometimes preferred to the deliberative subjunctive
in rhetorical questions: cf. 5.6.2 *quid ... expecto, quid spero?*, 5.16.1 *quid
... dicimus ...?*, Catull. 1.1 *cui dono lepidum nouum libellum?*, Virg. *Aen.*
7.359 *exulibusne datur ducenda Lauinia Teucris?* and Fordyce *ad loc.* (On
the need to distinguish carefully between rhetorical and real questions
see Pease on Virg. *Aen.* 4.534 *en quid ago?*) **exitio natus:** Prop.
2.22.4 *o nimis exitio nata theatra meo*, Tib. 1.5.48 *uenit in exitium callida lena
meum*, Ov. *Am.* 1.1.22 *in exitium spicula facta meum* (Love's arrows). For
nascor + dative = 'am destined for' see *OLD* s.v. 14.

4.35.1 sic profata: an epicizing tag; Virg. *Aen.* 4.364 *sic ... profatur*,
Lucan 9.251, 584 *sic ille profatus*, 2.337, 4.701 *sic ... profatur*, V.F.
2.289, 3.534 *sic ... profatur*, Stat. *Theb.* 5.103 *sic ... profari*, Sil. *Pun.*
1.124, 3.570, 4.419, al. *sic ... profatur*; Ov. *Met.* 9.473, Sil. *Pun.* 3.674

ita . . . profatur. Cf. 4.31.4, 6.23.1nn.   **ingressuque . . . ualido:** like
a true heroine; cf. Polyxena's dying speech at Eur. *Hec.* 547–52.
itur: 10.12.1 *itur . . . ad illud sepulchrum,* Virg. *Aen.* 6.179 *itur in antiquam
siluam.* The echo is specifically Virgilian: Ovid does not use the
impersonal passive *itur* in *Met.*

4.35.2 statutam: like a sacrificial victim: Hor. *Sat.* 2.3.199–200 *cum
pro uitula statuis dulcem Aulide natam | ante aras . . .,* Liv. 1.45.6 *bouem Romam
actam deducit ad fanum Dianae et ante aram statuit.*   **domuitionem:** i.e.
domum itionem, and so transmitted at Cic. *Div.* 1.68 *reditum ac domum
itionem dari,* but generally spelled in MSS as one word. An expression
apparently resurrected from Republican latinity by A. (6 occurrences,
all in *Met.*): *TLL* s.v. *domu(m)itio.* For the acc. in this and similar
expressions see Pease on Cic. *loc. cit.*

4.35.4 Psyche's transition from wretchedness to blissful repose is
beautifully managed in one artful, though syntactically simple,
sentence, with an extraordinary proliferation of words connoting
gentleness and peace (Bernhard 179): *mitis . . . molliter . . . sensim . . .
tranquillo . . . paulatim . . . leniter.* See Introd. pp. 35–6. That Zephyrus
should be given the task of carrying her off would not surprise readers
conversant with the stories of Boreas and Orithyia (Plat. *Phaedr.*
229b–c, A.R. 1.212–15, Ov. *Met.* 7.702–10) or indeed Zephyrus
himself (Ov. *F.* 201–4 and Bömer *ad loc.*); and the rescuer of
Andromeda was airborne. Cf. Wright (J. R. G.) 273 n. 4, citing Call.
fr. 110. 51–9 Pfeiffer, Catull. 66.51–8. Folktale (Walsh (1970) 203) is
irrelevant. In some genealogies Zephyrus was Eros' father: Alcaeus fr.
327 L–P.   **trepidantem:** this is rhetorically superior to *trepidam,*
which interrupts the sequence of participles on which the sentence is
strung (cf. Paratore 31–3). For the pattern cf. perhaps Ov. *Met.*
8.363–4 *trepidantem et terga parantem | uertere.*   **in ipso . . . uertice**
'there on the summit'; for this emphatic use of *ipse* see Kenney on
Lucret. 3.128–9 and cf. 5.1.1n.   **deflentem:** though *defleo* is not
infrequently found = 'lament' without an object expressed (*TLL* s.v.
359.37–55), *defluentem* (Oudendorp ex recc.) or *deficientem* (Helm) may
be what A. wrote.   **uibratis hinc inde laciniis et reflato sinu
sensim leuatam:** like Europa as depicted in art (*LIMC* IV 1.77–88
(Europe 1 22–213)) and literature: Mosch. *Eur.* 129–30 'Europa's
robe bellied out like a ship's sail and bore up' (ἐλαφρίζεσκε ~

leuatam) the girl', Ov. *Met.* 2.875 (the last verse of the book: see 5.1n.) *tremulae sinuantur flamine uestes* – a reassuring echo, since Europa was to be *uxor inuicti Iouis* (Hor. *C.* 3.27.73).   **deuexa** [neuter plural] **rupis** = *deuexam rupem*; cf. 1.2.2 *ardua montium* = *arduos montes*, 3.28.6 *auia montium*, Liv. 9.3.1 *aduersa montium* and see e.g. Austin on Virg. *Aen.* 1.422 *strata uiarum*. Cf. 5.7.23 *saxa cautium* and n.

Act II Psyche Nocens

V

5.1 This description of Cupid's palace belongs in a tradition of such *ecphraseis* (4.31.4–7n.) which goes back to Homer's account of the palace and gardens of Alcinous (*Od.* 7.84–132; cf. the much briefer treatment of the palace of Menelaus, 4.43–6), imitated by Apollonius in his description of the palace of Aeetes (3.215–37; in later epic cf. e.g. Cleopatra's palace at Lucan 10.111–26). The setting of the palace amid grass, trees and water (§§1–2; cf. 4.17.3 *lucos consitos et specus roridos et fontes amoenos*) is a typical example of the ideal literary landscape conventionally styled the *locus amoenus* (Curtius 195–200, Schönbeck *passim*); cf. 6.14.2–3n. One of the most celebrated of all such landscapes formed the setting of Plato's dialogue *Phaedrus*, which A. may very well have had in mind here (Hunter 109 n. 43, Kenney (1990) 193 n. 59); the place was famous as the scene of the rape of Orithyia by Boreas (cf. 4.35.4n.). For other gardens in the novelists see Longus 2.3.3–4, 4.2–3, Ach. Tat. 1.1, 1.15 (Rohde (1914) 545 n. 1, Grimal (1969) 64–70, 353–424). For much of the detail of his treatment A. is indebted not only to Homer but also to Ovid, more especially to his description of the palace of the Sun at the beginning of *Met.* 2 (see Bömer *ad loc.*). Descriptions of fine houses almost constituted a genre in its own right within the ecphrastic rhetorical tradition, as in Statius' *Siluae* and Pliny's famous letter about his villa (Pavlovskis *passim*).

5.1.1 in ipso toro 'on a veritable bed'; 4.35.4n.   **suaue ... dulce** 'pleasantly ... sweetly'; cf. 10.32.3 *suaue mulcentibus*, Virg. *E.* 3.63 *suaue rubens hyacinthus*. This adverbial use of the neuter singular dates its popularity from Catullus' *dulce ridentem* (51.5); cf. H–S 40. **conquieuit:** her sleep is interpreted by Grimal (on 5.3.1) as 'une figure de la mort'. To take it in this way is to blur the point of the *infernus somnus* at 6.26.1 (see n.). Nothing could be more natural in ordinary human terms than that Psyche should yield to physical and emotional fatigue at this point; cf. Prop. 1.3.3–4 *qualis et accubuit primo Cepheia somno | libera iam duris cotibus Andromede*.

5.1.2 uidet ...: cf. 5.22.5. The focus of the description narrows from the whole grove to the spring, then to the palace itself, and then (§3 *ab introitu primo*) inside, where again the mind's eye of the reader is conducted from ceiling via the walls to the floor. Cf. 5.22.5–7n.
lucum proceris et uastis arboribus consitum: 'describing a grove', *ponere lucum* (Pers. 1.70; cf. Jenkinson *ad loc.*) was a stock poetic ploy, as Horace sardonically noted (*A.P.* 16–18 and Brink *ad loc.*); cf. e.g. Callim. *Hymn* 6 (*Dem.*). 25–30 and Hopkinson *ad loc.*, Virg. *Aen.* 1.441–9, Prop. 4.4.3–6, Ov. *Am.* 3.1.1–4, *A.A.* 3.687–92, *F.* 2.165–6, *Met.* 1.568–76 (with Bömer *ad loc.*), Lucan 3.399–425, al.
fontem uitreo latice perlucidum: Ov. *Met.* 3.161 *fons sonat a dextra tenui perlucidus unda*, *Ep. Sapph.* 157–8 *est nitidus uitroque magis perlucidus omni | fons sacer* etc.   **medio luci meditullio:** Price (245) thought *medio* superfluous, as indeed it is, but that is no reason for believing that A. did not write it. His usual phrase admittedly is *in ipso meditullio*: 3.27.2, 7.19.4, 10.32.1, 11.24.2. Water is the most essential element of the *locus amoenus* (cf. e.g. Hom. *Od.* 6.291–2, 7.129–31, Theoc. 7.136–7, Ov. *Met.* 3.407–12), hence is properly placed in the middle of the scene and of the three stages of the description; cf. Ov. *Am* 3.1.3 *fons sacer in medio*, *F.* 2.166 *in medio* [*luco*] *gelidae fons erat altus aquae*, Ach. Tat. 1.1.5 'In the middle of the meadow in the picture [n.b.] flowed a stream', 1.15.6, cf. 1.2.3.   **prope fontis adlapsum:** just the site a rich Roman would choose: see Statius' description of Manilius Vopiscus' villa (*Silvae* 1.3), situated within convenient reach of the Aqua Marcia (64–7) and straddling the Anio (24–33) (Pavlovskis 17–19). Cf. Prop. 3.2.14, cit. below, §3n.

5.1.3 scires 'one could be sure', a characteristic Ovidian idiom (*Am.* 1.13.47, *F.* 2.419, *Met.* 1.162, 6.23) not found in the other Augustan poets (Bömer on *Met.* 1.162) and in view of the prevalent Ovidian influence hereabouts (cf. below, n. on *subeunt*) to be preferred to *scies* (dubiously supported by *putabis* and *credes*, in different syntactical contexts, at 2.4.4, 9). **laquearia:** elaborate ceilings were synonyr̄ ous with architectural magnificence: Lucret. 2.28 *laqueata aurataque ̣empla* (cf. *OLD* s.v. *laqueatus*), Virg. *Aen.* 1.726 *dependent lychni laquearibus aureis*, Hor. *C.* 2.18.1−5 *non ebur neque aureum | mea renidet in domo lacunar, | non trabes Hymettiae | premunt columnas ultima recisas | Africa* (N–H *ad loc.* and on 2.16.11), Prop. 3.2.11−14 *quod non Taenariis domus est mihi fulta columnis, | nec camera auratas inter eburna trabes, | nec mea Phaeacas aequant pomaria siluas, | non operosa rigat Marcius antra liquor*, Ov. *Met.* 2.3 (cit. below), Lucan 10.112−13. **subeunt aureae columnae:** columns of imported marble were much admired; cf. Hor., Prop. *locc. cit.* (previous n.), Ov. *Met.* 2.1 *regia Solis erat sublimibus alta columnis*; with *aureae* A. goes one better. He has borrowed *subeunt* from Ovid's description of the metamorphosis of Baucis and Philemon's cottage at *Met.* 8.700−2 *furcas subiere columnae, | stramina flauescunt, adopertaque marmore tellus | caelataeque fores aurataque tecta uidentur*; but he has changed the sense from 'replace' (*OLD* s.v. 9b) to 'support' (2a). **aureae ... argenteo:** gold and silver were of course liberally employed in the decoration of grand houses (cf. above on *laquearia*), but as a literary feature this goes back to Homer (*Od.* 7.88−91; cf. 4.45−6). Here however A. evidently has in mind Ovid's description of the palace of the Sun at *Met.* 2.2−4 *clara micante auro flammasque imitante pyropo, | cuius ebur nitidum fastigia summa tegebat, | argenti bifores radiabant lumina ualuae*; and with *caelamine* here cf. ibid. 5−6 *Mulciber illic | aequora caelarat*, 8.702 (cit. previous n.). Cf. below, §6n. on *ualuae*. The use of *caelamen* for prose *caelatura* first appears in Ovid, *Met.* 13.291. **id genus** 'similar'; cf. 2.1.5 *boues et id genus pecua*, 3.17.4 *omne genus aromatis*, al. *id* (*hoc, quod, omne*) *genus* is practically equivalent to an indeclinable adjective (*OLD* s.v. *genus* 13a). The meaning is obscure: if *pecudes* has its ordinary sense of domestic animals, *id genus* is contradictory. In this setting one might expect hunting scenes (Amat 128 n. 3). Hence *omne genus* (Vollgraff) and other attempts at correction.

5.1.4 efferauit: the rare word (in poetry only at Sen. *Phoen.* 206, [Sen.] *Oct.* 787, Stat. *Ach.* (cit. below); but see 6.12.3 and n.) exploits the contrast between (wild) subject-matter and (civilized) material: cf. Stat. *Ach.* 1.425 *ereptum superis Mars efferat aurum*, which may have suggested the conceit to A. This style of decoration is Near Eastern rather than classical: cf. Apul. *De Mundo* 26 (p. 162.6–7 Thomas), Philostr. *Vit. Apoll.* 2.20, Fick 379–81, Amat 128–9, Hoevels 63–4.

5.1.5 lapide pretioso ... gemmas et monilia: Sen. *Ep.* 86.7 (on contemporary luxury in baths) *eo deliciarum peruenimus ut nisi gemmas calcare nolimus*, *Dial.* 9.1.8 *domus ... qua calcantur pretiosa*, 4.35.5, *Ep.* 16.8 *non tantum habere tibi liceat sed calcare diuitias*, Lucan 10.116–17 (Cleopatra's banqueting hall) *tota ... effusus in aula | calcabatur onyx*, Stat. *Silv.* 1.3.53 (Manilius Vopiscus' villa) *calcabam necopinus opes*, Mart. 12.50.4 *calcatus ... tuo sub pede lucet onyx.* See *OCD*[2] s.v. 'Mosaic'. **uehementer:** 'immensely', 'marvellously', qualifying *beatos* (*OLD* s.v. 4b), not = *certe, profecto. uehementer* is itself qualified by *iterum ac saepius*: the effect is satirical (cf. previous n.).   **super ... calcant:** the first attested use of *calco* intransitive; cf. Callebat (1968) 238. Contrast 5.9.5 *calcatur aurum*.

5.1.6 iam: transitional, hardly more emphatic than Greek δέ. **sine pretio pretiosae** 'pricelessly priceful', an Apuleian oxymoron; *sine pretio* properly = 'gratis'.   **totique:** a case where the basic sense 'whole' can be seen shading into or co-existing with the secondary sense 'all' (4.32.4n.). *All* the walls were *completely* of gold. **ut diem suum sibi domus faciat:** Hom. *Od.* 7.84–5 'There was a radiance as of the sun or the moon in the lofty palace of Alcinous' (cf. 4.45–6). *domus faciat*, the old vulgate correction of F's *domus faciant*, gives a more straightforward sense than Castiglioni's *domi faciat*. For *suum sibi* cf. 4.32.1n., but here *sibi* can be construed regularly with *faciat*.   **licet sole nolente:** the conceit recurs in Corippus' *ecphrasis* of Justinus' Sophiae palace: *In laud. Iustini* 1.100–1 *rutili non indiga solis | uel solis dicenda domus*; cf. 4.116 (on the curule chair) *lumen habens sine sole suum*, and see Stache on 1.98. For *licet* = 'though' + ablative absolute see H–S 140–1; it is an extension of the use with adjectives (*OLD* s.v. 4c, K–S II 446).   **ualuae:** Ov. *Met.* 2.4 *argenti bifores radiabant lumine ualuae*, Hom. *Od.* 7.88 'Gold were the doors that guarded the palace', Cic. *Verr.* 2.4.124 *confirmare hoc ... possum, ualuas magnificentiores, ex auro atque ebore perfectiores, nullas umquam ullo in templo fuisse* etc. Though the Romans were notoriously epicures in their bathing (cf. Sen. *Ep.* 86.7, cit. above, §5n.), *balneae* (Eyssenhardt, after F's *ualneę*) are out of place here.

5.2.1 talium locorum 'such a locality'; for this use of the plural for a single place see *OLD* s.v. *locus* 1b.   **accessit ... facit:** cf. 5.24.2 *inuolauit ... adfatur*, 6.13.1 *cessauit ... reportat.* Conversely 5.23.1–2 *depromit ... pupugit*, 5.31.1 *continantur ... quaesiere.* For the treatment of tenses in A.'s narrative cf. Bernhard 152–3, Callebat (1968) 427–32, Dragonetti 72–9; though variation between perfect and historic present is ancient (Blase 103), arbitrary variation with connexion by *et*, *-que* et sim., as here, seems to have been a Petronian innovation (Blase 105, H–S 307). See also Mellet 152–60, arguing that A. uses the perfect to emphasize moments of dramatic tension; cf. 5.7.1n.   **intra limen sese facit** 'betakes herself across the threshold'. Cf. 10.32.4 *ut primum ante iudicis conspectum facta est ...*; a colloquial use of *facio* explained by Donatus on Ter. *Ph.* 635 *'haec hinc facessat' pro 'hinc se faciat' id est abeat, ut 'huc se faciat' huc accedat significat*; cf. *TLL* s.v. 119.31–8. Price (249) compared Greek ἔξω ποιεῖν 'put outside' at Acts 5.34: see Arndt–Gingrich s.v. ποιέω I.e.γ, comparing Xen. *Cyr.* 4.1.3. Stewech proposed *sese agit*, attested in Virgil (cf. Serv. on *Aen.* 9.693 *iuxta ueteres 'se agebat' pro 'ueniebat'*) and comedy (*OLD* s.v. *ago* 3a), but there is no reason to deny A. this colloquialism.   **rimatur singula** ~ 2.26.2 *rimabar singula*; cf. Virg. *Aen.* 8.618 *oculos per singula uoluit*, 1.453 *lustrat ... singula.*   **altrinsecus aedium** = 3.17.3, the only two instances of the word used as a preposition + gen., perhaps a Graecism (Callebat (1968) 240); cf. 5.9.3n.   **nec est quicquam quod ibi non est** 'nothing exists that is not there', but the words can also = 'what is not there is nothing', i.e. does not exist; with what follows (cf. below, §3n.) an allusive reminder of the universality and all-sufficiency of love when experienced in its true and highest form. It is through seeking what she (wrongly) thinks she lacks that Psyche is to come to grief.

5.2.2 nullo uinculo etc.: the riches of Love are freely accessible to all who submit to him. This palace without locks, bolts or doorkeeper is reminiscent of Ovid's palace of Sleep: *Met.* 11.609 *(ianua) nulla domo tota est, custos in limine nullus.*   **totius orbis thensaurus:** on Love as a blessing to mankind see Plat. *Symp.* 178a–b, Plut. *Amat.* 762b.

5.2.3 corporis sui nuda: genitive of respect; cf. Ov. *Met.* 12.512–13 *nudus | arboris Othrys erat* and Bömer *ad loc.*, 4.32.4, 5.2.4nn.   **quid ... tantis obstupescis opibus?:** Calp. Sic. 7.40–1 *quid te stupefactum*

... | *ad tantas miraris opes?*   **tua sunt haec omnia:** on the face of it a conventional formula of hospitality, but to the attentive reader an ominous echo of the words of Byrrhena to Lucius at 2.5.1 *tua sunt ... cuncta quae uides.* He too is examining a wonderful house and he too falls victim, as Psyche is to do, to ignoble curiosity. Each is warned, each is trusted; both fail the test. See Introd. p. 11.   **prohinc (*)** 'therefore'; otherwise only at Boeth. *Subst. bon.* 11.   **te refer** 'take yourself': the force of the prefix is not felt. Cf. *OLD* s.v. *refero* 14, where however 'direct' not 'redirect' should be read. Cf. 5.9.7 *sursum respicit* 'looks up'.

5.2.4 corporis curatae tibi (lit.) 'when you are cared for in respect of your body'; for the genitive of respect (4.32.4n.) with *curo* cf. 5.4.4 *interfectae uirginitatis curant.*

5.3.1 diuinae Prouidentiae ~ 6.15.1 *Prouidentiae bonae.* In view of the emphasis on the *prouidentia* of Isis in the priest's address to Lucius (11.15.4; cf. 11.5.4, 11.12.1, 11.18.1), the word must be given its full value (and a capital letter). Psyche is under the protection of a power which *foresees* the danger awaiting her; she repeatedly shows herself blind and deaf to its warnings. This power is in fact Cupid, as becomes clear (cf. 5.19.4, 6.15.1). On Pronoia in Chariton cf. Rohde (1914) 525 n. 4. For *Prouidentia* as a power that also rewards and punishes see 3.3.8, 9.27.1, 10.12.5; at 9.1.5 it is practically equivalent to Fortune. Cf. Apul. *De Plat.* 1.12 esp. *unde si quid prouidentia geritur, id agitur et fato, et quod fato terminatur, prouidentia debet susceptum uideri* (p. 95.22ff. Thomas).   **et ... et:** she follows her instructions to the letter.   **fatigationem sui** = *f. suam*, an unclassical usage favoured by A.; see K–S 1 598–9, Callebat (1968) 262–3.

5.3.2 semirotundo (*) suggestu: a piece of furniture known from its shape (C) as a *sigma*: Mart. 10.48.6, 14.87.1. There is an implication of a seat of honour; cf. 5.6.6 *de tanto fortunarum suggestu* and *OLD* s.v. 1b. Is there here a hint of the *subterraneum semirotundum* of Lucius' symbolic Catabasis (11.6.6)?

5.3.3 copiosa 'numerous' as well as 'lavish', as at 2.19.3; cf. 4.28.3, 5.1.6nn.   **quodam** = *aliquo*, 'a' (Graur 380); cf. for this weakened sense of *quidam* 5.8.4, 6.1.2, 6.16.2 (ibid. 379).

5.3.5 inuisus 'unseen', a very rare sense in classical authors, but relatively common in Christian Latin: *TLL* s.v.   **alius** = *alter*, as at 5.10.1, 5.27.4; see *TLL* s.v. 1648.70ff., Callebat (1968) 286.   **quae uidebatur nec ipsa** 'which too was invisible'; *nec* = *ne* ... *quidem*, as frequently in Livy and the Augustan poets and subsequently: *OLD* s.v. *neque* 2b, H–S 450, Callebat (1968) 333–4.   **modulatae multitudinis conserta uox** 'the combined voice(s) of a harmonious throng'; *modulatus* is used unusually of the singers rather than the song.   **aures:** acc. with *affertur*; cf. e.g. 5.4.1 *aures ... accedit*. **hominum nemo** 'not a soul'; cf. Ter. *Eun.* 757, Cic. *Att.* 8.2.4 (Callebat (1968) 526).   **pareret ... pateret:** both words can = 'appear', 'be visible': *OLD* s.vv. 5, 6a. *pateret* is used practically = *uideretur* with prolative infinitive both for the sake of the word-play (not impaired by the difference in quantity *pār-* ... *păt-*) and with an additional play on the sense 'be (logically) evident': *OLD* s.v. 6c.

5.4.1 uespera suadente: Virg. *Aen.* 2.9, 4.81 *suadentque cadentia sidera somnos*, Ov. *Her.* 7.55 *pelago suadente uiam*, *Met.* 10.688 *iter longum requiescere suasit*.   **clemens ... sonus** 'a gentle sound', an unexampled use of *clemens*: but attempts to justify F's *demens* do not carry conviction, and in view of Cupid's subsequent behaviour, an emphasis on *clementia* is surely not inappropriate. Cf. 5.7.4 (*Zephyri*) *clementissimis flatibus*.

5.4.2 pro 'by reason of', 'because of': *OLD* s.v.[1] 17.   **quouis malo plus timet quod ignorat:** proverbial; Publ. Syr. s13 *semper plus metuit animus ignotum malum*, Livy 9.24.8 *nox ... quae omnia ex incerto maiora territis ostentat*, 28.44.3 *maior ignotarum rerum est terror*, Tac. *Ann.* 4.62.3 *latior ex incerto metus*; cf. Ov. *Her.* 1.71 *quid timeam ignoro, timeo tamen omnia demens*.

5.4.3 ignobilis 'unknown', picking up *quod ignorat* (previous n.), but also in the familiar sense as an ironical authorial reference to the outcaste wretch whom Cupid was supposed to furnish as Psyche's lover. Her husband's identity is not to be explicitly revealed until she disobeys him and lights the lamp (5.22); but the double entendres of the oracle, to say nothing of the hint dropped by Psyche herself in her innocence at 5.6.7, are calculated to have given the game away to the intelligent reader long before then.   **inscenderat ...**

fecerat ... discesserat: the pluperfects suggest a hurried and clandestine consummation, a hint perhaps of (what will later emerge) a guilty conscience (5.24.4n.). Cf. below, §6 *cognorant ... perrexerant*. **uxorem sibi ... fecerat:** the classical and poetical restraint with which their lovemaking is handled contrasts markedly with the tone of the erotic episodes in the main narrative of the novel, especially that between Lucius and Photis. Such sensuality as is displayed is all on Psyche's side, when she uses her charms to her own undoing, to persuade Cupid against his better judgement to let her see her sisters: 5.6.9, 5.13.5–6. Cf. 5.21.5n.

5.4.4 cubiculo: locative ablative. **interfectae uirginitatis:** Longus 3.19.2 'She [Chloe] will be bloodstained as if slain' (καθάπερ πεφονευμένη del. Castiglioni; cf. ibid. 3.20.1), Heliod. 1.18.5 'you will kill her', sc. by defloration. The metaphor was a favourite with Christian writers, as Price's n. illustrates; see now Fowler (D.). For the genitive cf. 5.2.4n.

5.4.5 atque 'And indeed', emphatic: *OLD* s.v. 2a. **ut est natura redditum** 'as is usually the case', lit. 'as has been brought about by nature'; cf. *OLD* s.v. *reddo* 16a. The perfect is 'gnomic': H–S 318–19. **nouitas ... commendarat** (lit.) 'novelty through habit had made delight agreeable to her'; the general drift is clear but the expression, even for A., is strained, and the text may be corrupt. Cf. however for the idea Sen. *Ep.* 114.9 *commendatio ex nouitate et soliti ordinis commutatione captatur* (cit. Helm). **consuetudinem:** probably with a play on the secondary sense 'love', 'sexual intercourse'; for habit as an ally of love cf. Walsh (1970) 212 n. 2, 6.8.5n.

5.4.6 illae: 5.7.1n.

5.5.1 ea nocte: sc. of the day of the sisters' homecoming. **infit** 'began', an epic word (*TLL* s.v. 1447.3–10) favoured by A. (13 occurrences: Hijmans al. 186); cf. 4.35.1n., 5.9.1, 6.11.4, 6.13.2n., 6.23.1n. **nihil non sentiebatur** 'she felt everything', i.e. she experienced her husband with all her senses, except sight. Watt's is the simplest, and one of the most palaeographically plausible, of the numerous solutions (Paratore *ad loc.* lists 19) that have been suggested; the truth is irrecoverable. Cf. 5.17.3n.

5.5.2 Fortuna saeuior: 11.15.2 (the priest to Lucius) *eat nunc et summo furore saeuiat et crudelitati suae materiam quaerat aliam*; cf. 6.28.3, 7.16.1, 8.24.1, 11.12.1, Hor. *Sat.* 2.2.126 *saeuiat atque nouos moueat Fortuna tumultus*, *C.* 3.29.49 *Fortuna saeuo laeta negotio*, al., and on the story of Lucius as 'in a way built around Fortune' cf. Kajanto (1981) 551, Fry 168 'un fil conducteur'. For the role of Fortune (Τύχη) in the ancient novel see e.g. Heliod. 5.4.1, 5.6.3, al.; Rohde (1914) 296–305, Molinié Index s.v. Τύχη. As a rule Aphrodite and Fortune/Fate (5.22.1n.) play opposing roles (but cf. Fry 154 n. 56); in A. they are virtually identified (Tatum (1979) 50, 59), as Eros is identified with Fate at Xen. *Eph.* 1.10.2 (cf. Dalmeyda *ad loc.*). On Fortune, Providence and Fate in A. and *Met.* see Fry *passim*.

5.5.3 tuumque uestigium requirentes ~ 6.2.2 *Venus ... tuum uestigium ... requirit.*   **scopulum ... aderunt:** cf. 2.10.6 *cubiculum tuum adero. adsum* + accusative is almost unique to A. (*TLL* s.v. *assum* 917.67–9), on the analogy of verbs of motion such as *accedo* (5.4.1 *sonus aures eius accedit*). Cf. 5.6.1 *lectum ... accubans* and n.   **istum:** A.'s use of *iste* is exceptionally varied and flexible (Callebat (1968) 274), but it is perhaps unlikely that it here stands for the definite article (cf. *TLL* s.v. 510.55–72), as *ille* apparently does on occasion (5.7.1n.). Rather it = 'that (of yours)', the crag that Psyche knew from being exposed there (so Callebat (1968) 270–1).   **neque respondeas ... nec prospicias:** for the classical *ne ... neue*; cf. 6.12.2 *neque ... polluas nec ... feras*, 6.23.4 *nec ... contristere nec ... metuas*, Plaut. *Men.* 221 *neque defiat neque supersit*, Lindsay 102–3, Bennett 1 170, K–S 1 194. Cf. 5.6.6 *ne ... neue ... nec*. This solemn injunction to harden the heart against appeals foreshadows the instructions given to Psyche about her journey to Hades (6.18.4, 6.18.8, 6.19.1); it also recalls the ordeal of Tamino in *The Magic Flute*. **ceterum** '(for) otherwise': cf. 5.19.4. In this sense rare in classical writers but common in the Digest and Christian Latin: *TLL* s.v. 972–973.16. Cf. Helm (1957).   **exitium** ~ §2 *exitiabile*.

5.5.4 dilapso: the word suits both the departure of night and the slipping away of a person: *OLD* s.v. *dilabor* 1b, 2c, 3.

5.5.5 nec ... quidem: if (which is doubtful) the MSS can be trusted on such a point, A.'s usage varied arbitrarily between this form and the classical *ne ... quidem*; cf. e.g. 6.5.2, 6.20.6. However, here (with *ac ne ... quidem* following) and elsewhere (e.g. 1.25.3, cf. Vitruv. 2.6.5) *nec* may have an additional connective function, i.e. *nec ... quidem* is the negative form of *et ... quidem*. See K–S II 45–5, H–S 450, Powell on Cic. *Sen.* 27. Examples of this usage tend to be emended away by modern editors; cf. Woodman on Vell. 2.67.1.

5.6.1 nec mora, cum ...: cf. 5.7.4, 6.18.5, 6.24.1; a favourite phrase of A.'s (17 occurrences: *TLL* s.v. 1 *mora* 1471.58). The poets generally prefer asyndeton with *nec mora* (*TLL* ibid. 37–51), but cf. Prop. 4.8.51 *nec mora, cum totas resupinat Cynthia ualuas*. Callebat (1968) 445–6. **lectum ... accubans:** this instance of *accubo* + accusative seems to be unique, but cf. 6.24.1 *accumbebat summum torum maritus*, al. Cf. 5.5.3n.

5.6.2 quid ... expecto, quid spero?: 4.34.6n. **et ... cruciatum:** a verb seems to be wanted after *pernox*, either one meaning 'weep' (*fles* Watt, *ploras* van der Vliet; but A. does not use *ploro*) or 'mourn' (*maeres/luges/doles* Kenney) or, less probably, one to govern *cruciatum* (*sumis* Leo; but the expression – 'bring anguish on yourself' (?) – seems odd). **perdia et pernox:** 9.5.5 *at ego misera pernox et perdia* (Scaliger: *per diem* F), Gell. 2.1.2. **nec:** 5.3.5n.

5.6.3 animo ... pareto: *animus* = θυμός, the appetitive part of the soul (*anima* = ψυχή); the expression is reminiscent of Plato's description of the man 'who is ruled by desire' (*Phaedr.* 238e). A. would have been familiar with the Platonic doctrine 'that the soul is complex and righteousness consists in a harmonious order and working together of its parts' (Guthrie IV 300). Contrast the innocent irony of Psyche's words at §9 below, *tuae Psychae dulcis anima*. Cf. *OLD* s.v. *pareo* 3. *pareto* is the 'future' imperative (H–S 340–1), used for its weight and solemnity. In his summary of Plat. *Symp.* 180d2–e2 at *Apol.* 12 A. had described Venus Vulgaria as *truci ... perculsorum animalium serua corpora complexu uincientem* (p. 14. 5–6 Helm); cf. Kenney (1990) 176–7, 190. The image of man as the slave of his passions was not of course exclusively Platonic; cf. e.g. Plaut. *Trin.* 308 *si animus hominem pepulit, actumst: animo seruit, non sibi*, an echo of the Stoa (Grimal (1986) I 289); and cf. 5.31.2n. **paenitere:** here personal (*OLD* s.v. 3a); A. usually prefers the commoner impersonal construction, but see 5.22.2n.

5.6.4 dum ... comminatur 'by threatening': *OLD* s.v. *dum* 4a.
se morituram: threats of or attempts at suicide are a stock feature of
the Greek romances; cf. Petronius' burlesque at *Sat.* 94.8–15. Psyche
makes several unsuccessful attempts (5.22.4, 5.25.2, 6.12.1, 6.14.1,
6.17.2); it is ironical that when she finally succeeds, it is involuntarily
(6.21.1). Cf. 5.16.4n., Introd. p. 19.   **extorquet ... adnuat:** *ut*
is omitted on the analogy of constructions with verbs such as *faxo*
(4.30.3n.), *uolo, iubeo* (H–S 530–1). Cf. below, §8 *praecipe ... sistat*,
5.13.2 *praecipe fungatur*, 5.26.7 *praecipit ... efflaret*, 5.29.5 *uelim ...
scias*, 6.2.6 *patere ... delitescam*, 6.7.4 *fac ... matures*, 6.11.6 *afferas
censeo*, 6.16.4 *petit ... mittas*, 6.18.4 *rogabit ... porrigas*, 6.19.1 *orabunt
... accommodes* (Callebat (1968) 107, Bernhard 51–2).   **ora
conferat** 'converse', on the analogy of *sermonem/-es conferre*: cf. 5.11.5
neque omnino sermonem conferas (*OLD* s.v. *confero* 12c).   **cupitis** 'what
she wanted', 'her desires', neuter plural; cf. 5.23.5, Tac. *Ann.* 4.3.1,
9.18.3 *ni ... cupito potiatur*, 6.11.3n.

5.6.5 quibuscumque uellet ... auri uel monilium 'with whatever
(items) of gold or jewels she liked'; the construction of the partitive
genitives is slightly harsh, and *donis ornare* (Traube) or *donis donare*
(Baehrens) is tempting.

5.6.6 monuit ac ... terruit ... quaerat ... deiciat ... contingat:
such irregular sequences of tenses, not uncommon in Plautus (Bennett
1 341) and found sporadically in classical Latin (H–S 550–1), are
relatively rare in *Met.* (Callebat (1968) 361–2). Contrast 5.26.7n.
ne ... neue ... nec: a conflation of orthodox constructions; cf.
5.5.3n. *neue* occurs only three times in *Met.* (7.5.5, 8.8.8): Callebat
(1968) 96.   **suasa:** A. commonly constructs *suadeo* with the accusative
rather than the dative; cf. 5.11.4 *ut te suadeant*.   **sacrilega curiositate:**
the first overt reference to the failing which, along with her naivety
(5.11.5n.), is to prove Psyche's undoing. See Introd. p. 15. *curiositas*
is found once only in earlier Latin, at Cic. *Att.* 2.12.2; A. may have
reinvented the word (Labhardt 209–10).

5.6.7 caream 'deprive myself of': *OLD* s.v. 4.   **spiritum** =
animam = Psyche; cf. 4.34.3n.   **te, quicumque es ... comparo:**
under the obvious surface irony of Psyche's words a second and
fundamental layer can be detected. In spite of her professions she
is ignorant of the true nature and value of love (Love); as yet her

devotion to her unknown husband is purely physical. See below, §9
and 5.19.3, 5.23.3nn. Here too there are Platonic undertones; cf.
Phaedr. 255d.

5.6.8 praecipe ... sistat: above, §4n.

5.6.9 Psyche tempts Cupid physically as Photis had tempted Lucius
(2.7.7, 2.10.2: see Introd. pp. 11–12). Hers is the love that desires
bodies (Eros Pandemos), Cupid's that which desires souls (E.
Uranios); cf. Plat. *Symp.* 181b3–5. Her words are doubly ironic: *anima*
and ψυχή were common lovers' endearments, but her ignorance of
what *Psychae ... anima* implies – that only a complete and perfect
union with Love can save her – contrasts with Cupid's awareness of
the implications of his words to her at §3 (see n.). The whole scene, as
Price (256–7) noted, recalls Venus' shameless tempting of *her* husband
Vulcan at Virg. *Aen.* 8.387–406.   **imprimens oscula ... inserens
membra:** Ov. *Met.* 10.558–9 (Venus and Adonis) *inque sinu iuuenis
posita ceruice reclinis | sic ait ac mediis interserit oscula uerbis* – but the
sensual temperature of A.'s adaptation is higher than that of the
model.   **cogentia** is pointedly ambiguous: her embrace encloses
him and bends him to her will. *cohibentia*, suggesting merely restraint,
is less forceful.   **Psychae:** cf. 5.13.4 *Psychae animam*, but 6.2.5 *Psyches
animae*; the MSS vary between the two forms, with a preference for the
Greek gen. in *-es*. This may or may not reflect A.'s usage.

5.6.10 susurrus: on A.'s apparently arbitrary variation between
2nd and 4th decl. forms see Callebat (1968) 122; cf. 5.27.5n.   **inuitus:**
Cupid's reluctant agreement to Psyche's imprudent wish recalls that
of Photis to the importunity of Lucius (3.15.3, 3.20.1–2). That Cupid
himself should fall in love is a paradox (underlined by *Venerii*) exploited
by Hellenistic epigrammatists: Anon. *A.P.* 12.112 (*HE* 3710–11),
Meleager, *A.P.* 5.179 (4028–37), 12.113 (4312–13), 12.144 (4554–7).
Cf. his own words at 5.24.4 and n.   **atque etiam etc.** 'and finally,
as dawn was near ...'; cf. *TLL* s.v. *etiam* 935.81–3. But the simple
correction *iam* of Oudendorp's learned friend may well be right.
proxumante: (*); later quite common.

5.7.1 illae: sc. those previously mentioned, no doubt in this case
with a pejorative connotation as at 5.4.6; but here and elsewhere *ille*
in A. can be seen (*pace* Löfstedt I 361) well on its way to its eventual

destiny as the Romance definite article: see *TLL* s.v. 355.81ff., especially 357.23ff., Lindsay 46, Bernhard 114. The most natural English rendering will often be 'the', as here. Cf. below, §5n.

fuerat ... deserta = *erat deserta*, cf. 6.3.4 *fuerant dicata*; such 'double' pluperfects are common in A.; they were particularly affected by Ovid, mainly for metrical convenience (Bömer on *Met.* 3.228), but were generally avoided (Livy being a notable exception) by careful stylists: N–W III 142–5, Blase 220–2, Callebat (1968) 303. Cf. 6.3.2n.

adueniunt ... difflebant ... plangebant: the tenses are here not arbitrarily varied (5.2.1n.); having arrived, they begin to weep ...; cf. 5.22.2 *increbruit* (an instantaneous reaction) ... *paenitebat* (repented and went on repenting).

5.7.2 nomine proprio ... ciebant: like mourners calling the dead back to life; cf. 8.7.2 *fratrem denique addito nomine lugubri ciere*, Kenney on Lucret. 3.468, Hoevels 88 n. 105. **ululabilis (*):** otherwise only in Ammianus (6 instances). **amens et trepida:** she is in no fit state to withstand the danger they represent. **quam lugetis adsum:** Virg. *Aen.* 1.595 *quem quaeritis adsum*.

5.7.5 sese 'each other'; cf. 5.9.1, 5.16.1 *secum*, *OLD* s.v. *se*[1] 8. **illae sedatae** 'which had been restrained'; *illae* with the participle has almost the force of the Greek article. Cf. above, §1n. and *TLL* s.v. *ille* 358.76ff. **postliminio (*)** 'once again'; this weakened adverbial sense is rare even after A.: *TLL* s.v. *postliminium* 236.45–50.

5.7.6 sed 'But now': *OLD* s.v. 2c. **tectum ... et larem nostrum ... succedite:** Virg. *Aen.* 1.627 (Dido to the Trojans) *tectis ... succedite nostris*, *G.* 3.344 *tectumque laremque*; *lar* has very much the flavour of English 'home'. **animas cum Psyche uestra recreate:** this suggests another play on Psyche = 'soul', but the point is elusive. Is it that they might join in the quest for salvation?

5.8.1 oculis et auribus: if the transmitted text is read, *auribus* connotes vision as well as hearing, a harsh and pointless zeugma (see Kenney on Lucret. 3.614) quite alien to A.'s expansive style (cf. 5.12.4n.). Van der Vliet's supplement offers an easy correction. **inhumanae** 'supernatural', 'divine', a sense found only here and at

11.14.5, where it is used of the expression on the face of the priest as he addresses Lucius.

5.8.3 denique 'thus', as at 5.9.1 and frequently elsewhere in A.: *TLL* s.v. 533.10–51, Callebat (1968) 325, Cf. 4.28.3n., van der Paardt 42–3.   **satis scrupulose** 'pretty thoroughly'; 4.30.4n. **-ue** 'and', esp. common with *quis, qui, quid* etc.: Löfstedt I 348 n. 1. Conversely, for disjunctive *-que* see Fordyce on Catull. 45.6–7, *OLD* s.v. 7; for *uel = et* cf. Callebat (1968) 331.

5.8.4 exigit 'drive out', i.e. forget, an instance of the idiom in which Latin says 'do' for 'allow to be done': Kenney on Lucret. 3.490 and *Addenda* (p. 250). Cf. *inumbrantem* below.   **e re nata** 'on the spur of the moment'; this sense of the phrase seems to originate with A., in whom it is frequent. In classical Latin it = 'in the circumstances' (*OLD* s.v. *nascor* 4c). Cf. 5.27.1 *e re concinnato mendacio* and n.   **lanoso barbitio** (†) **genas inumbrantem** (lit.) 'shadowing his cheeks with a woolly beard'. Adolescent fuzz was a stock feature of poetical descriptions of youthful male beauty from Homer onwards: 7.5.2 (the disguised Tlepolemus), Hom. *Il.* 4.348, *Od.* 10.279, Theoc. 6.3, 11.9 (Cyclops), 15.85 (Adonis) (see Gow *ad locc.*), Heliod. 7.10.4, Lucret. 5.888–9 *iuuentas | ... molli uestit lanugine malas*, Virg. *Aen.* 10.324–5 *flauentem prima lanugine malas ... Clytium*, Ov. *Met.* 9.398 *paene puer dubiaque tegens lanugine malas* (Bömer *ad loc.*), al. A. rings the changes *more suo* on the familiar theme: *lanosus* occurs only here of a beard, *barbitium* is found only here and at 11.8.3, and *inumbro* is a recherché exaggeration, later imitated by Claudian (1 (*Pan. Olybr. et Prob.*).69–70). It may possibly be modelled on Eur. *Phoen.* 63 ἐπεὶ δὲ τέκνων γένυς ἐμῶν σκιάζεται (Bernhard 203); but the metaphor is commoner in Greek: see Flaccus, *A.P.* 12.26.5 (*GP* 3855) and Gow–Page *ad loc.* For the idiom in *inumbrantem* cf. above on *exigit*.   **rurestribus:** the distinction between different types of hunting seems pointless and indeed improbable, since the mountains were the traditional scene of the sport; cf. e.g. Sen. *Phaedr.* 1–8. Hence Watt's addition of *rebus* is very tempting, giving a rational distinction 'farming and hunting'.

5.8.5 labe 'slip', 'mistake', a very rare sense almost wholly confined to A.: *TLL* s.v. *labes* 769.38–42. It may be the sense intended by

Virgil at *Aen.* 2.97 *hinc mihi prima mali labes* 'the first slip towards disaster'; see Austin *ad loc.*   **facto** 'worked': *OLD* s.v. *factus*[1] 4a.

5.9–10 Cupid's warning is now justified: the sisters are seen to be actuated by an unholy combination of greed, thwarted lust, envy and spite. However, A.'s treatment is the reverse of solemn: the tone of their dialogue is reminiscent of Herodas and Theocritus' *Adoniazusae.* These are not princesses wedded to kings (4.32.3) but termagant bourgeoises tethered to elderly and inadequate pantaloons (5.9.8, 5.10.1–2). Though some of this may be due to literary opportunism, the ignobility of these instruments of a malignant Fortune can be read as corresponding to the sordid circumstances of Lucius' downfall (Introd. p. 11).

5.9.1 egregiae: heavily ironical; cf. 5.24.4n.   **fraglantes:** 4.31.3n. **multa ... perstrepebant** 'held forth noisily and at length'; *multa* is adverbial accusative (H–S 37–8).   **secum** = *inter se*: 5.7.1n. **denique:** 5.8.3n.   **infit:** 5.5.1n.

5.9.2–4 See Introd. pp. 33–4.

5.9.2 en orba et saeua et iniqua Fortuna: ironical, for they are her instruments (5.5.2 and n.).   **orba:** sc. *oculis,* *uisu,* sim.; for this absolute sense see *TLL* s.v. 927.74–928.3, Löfstedt II 374–6. For Fortune's blindness cf. 7.2.4 *caecam et prorsus exoculatam ... Fortunam,* 8.24.1 *Fortuna ... in me caecos detorsit oculos.* It was proverbial (Otto s.v. *fortuna* 1), but the idea is especially important in *Met.,* in which Fortune is the antitype of provident and beneficent Isis; cf. the words of the priest to Lucius at 11.15.2–3 *Fortunae caecitas ... ad religiosam istam beatitudinem inprouida produxit malitia ... in tutelam iam receptus es Fortunae, sed uidentis, quae suae lucis splendore ceteros etiam deos illuminat ... uideant inreligiosi, uideant et errorem suum recognoscant: en ecce pristinis aerumnis absolutus Isidis magnae prouidentia gaudens Lucius de sua Fortuna triumphat.* On *Prouidentia* see 5.3.1n.   **utroque parente:** the sense is clear, but edd. have generally felt that the Latinity is suspect. There is no agreement on what is missing: the most likely candidate is *eodem* = 'each parent the same', sc. for all three sisters; cf. Livy 44.30.2 *fratres duos, Platorem utroque parente, Carauantium matre eadem natum habuit.*

5.9.3 et nos quidem 'We, for instance', 'Take our case': *OLD* s.v. *et*

11.   **maritis aduenis ancillae deditae:** they make themselves sound like prisoners of war.   **longe parentum:** for *a* + ablative, a Graecism (H–S 271), Callebat (1968) 241; cf. 5.30.6n., 8.29.6 *intus aedium*.

5.9.4 fetu satiante 'by a wearying birth', a recherché variant on *effetus*. The suggestion is that she is degenerate; cf. Lucret. 2.1150 ff. *iamque adeo fracta est aetas, effetaque tellus | uix animalia parua creat* etc. **nec:** 5.3.5n.   **uti recte:** philosophical language; Psyche has no moral right to her good fortune, cf. e.g. Hor. *C.* 4.9.46–9 *rectius occupat | nomen beati, qui deorum | muneribus sapienter uti | . . . callet*, Sen. *Phaedr.* 442–3 *perdere est dignus bona | qui nescit uti*. The sister speaks truer than she knows (cf. *deo marito*); it is because Psyche cannot cope with what has befallen her that she comes to grief.

5.9.5 quanta = *quot*: *OLD* s.v. *quantus* 2d. See Fedeli on Prop. 1.5.10; add e.g. Ov. *Am.* 1.14.24, Stat. *Theb.* 2.460–1. Cf. 6.10.4 *tantorum*. **iacent ... praenitent ... splendicant (*) ... calcatur:** the use of the indicative for the subjunctive in indirect questions was predominantly colloquial but occurs sporadically in the poets: H–S 537–40, Callebat (1968) 356–8. Cf. 4.34.6n. *splendico* otherwise only at ps.-Aug. *Serm.* 2.1.3 Cailleau.

5.9.6 consuetudine: 6.8.5n.   **deam quoque ... efficiet:** more irony, for this is precisely what eventually happens; and the sister is shrewd enough to realize, what Psyche is too perversely naive to grasp, her unknown husband's divinity.   **hercules:** an imprecation normally used by men; but cf. 2.26.4, 9.16.3 for breaches of this 'rule'.

5.9.7 sursum respicit 'looks up'; the force of the prefix is not felt (5.2.3n.).   **deam spirat** 'gives off the air of a goddess': *OLD* s.v. *spiro* 6b, Müller 27–8, 83–4, H–S 39–40. The idea is reinforced by the word-play in *uoces ... uentis* following.   **imperitat:** the frequentative form adds emphasis. A. uses *imperito* nowhere else in *Met.*, *impero* only at 2.26.5; each verb occurs some half-dozen times in his other works.

5.9.8 cucurbita caluiorem: with an additional suggestion of 'nothing between the ears': 1.15.2 *nos cucurbitae caput non habemus ut pro te moriamur*, Petron. 39.12, Sen. *Apoc.* ed. Eden pp. 3–4.   **domum**

... custodientem: in a society in which girls tended to marry young this situation was classic: cf. Catull. 17.12–14 *insulsissimus est homo, nec sapit pueri instar | bimuli tremula patris dormientis in ulna. | cui cum sit uiridissime nupta flore puella* eqs. However, her complaint about bolts and bars seems to reflect Aristophanes' or Menander's Athens, or perhaps the demi-monde of Augustan elegy, rather than contemporary Roman society; and in fact she can evidently come and go freely.

5.10.1 uenerem meam recolentem (lit.) 'renewing his homage to my charms', with a play on *Venus* as goddess and = 'sexual attraction/ activity'.   **sustineo ... sustinens:** the apparently inadvertent repetition of a word (here in a different sense) without rhetorical point is very rare in *Met.*; Bernhard 154 cites only this passage and 5.25.5 (doubtfully relevant) from *Cupid & Psyche*.

5.10.3 uideris (lit.) 'you will look to it', i.e. on your head be it if you choose to put up with such treatment. Cf. 9.16.1 *de iste quidem ... tecum ipse uideris*, Cic. *Phil.* 2.118 *sed de te tu uideris: ego de me ipse profitebor*, Sen. *Apoc.* 10.4 *uideris, Iuppiter*. Ovid is particularly fond of this idiomatic use of the future perfect in the 3rd person, *uiderit*: see Bömer on *F.* 2.782, Blase 183–5, Callebat (1968) 101–2. Cf. 6.21.4 *cetera egomet uidero* and n., 5.24.5n.   **allapsam** 'falling on', 'befalling'. Helm's conjecture is supported by Amm. 14.10.15 *adlapsa felicitate*; F's *conlapsam* gives hardly tolerable sense. Lipsius' *collatam* also deserves consideration (Paratore 38–9).

5.10.5 praesentiam nostram: with *grauor* 'object to', 'find trouble-some', sim. the accusative is the normal construction: *OLD* s.v. 4b, *TLL* s.v. 2314.17–47.

5.10.6 nec sum mulier ... nisi ...: Ov. *Met.* 3.271 *nec sum Saturnia, si non ...*, Plaut. *Men.* 471 *non hercle is sum qui sum, ni ...*, Petron. 81.6 *aut uir ego liberque non sum, aut ...*   **pessum ... deiecero** ~ 5.6.6 *pessum deiciat*.   **inacuit:** found in literary writers only here and at Ov. *Rem.* 307 *haec tibi per totos inacescant omnia sensus*.

5.10.7 non ... ac nec ...: cf. 4.28.2, 5.3.5nn. *non* for *nec* in pro-hibitions is too common to have a marked colloquial flavour: H–S 337.

5.10.8 nedum ut ... differamus: cf. 9.39.7 *nedum ut rebus amplioribus idoneus uideatur*. Such expressions with *nedum* are essentially negative purpose clauses = 'lest (not to be thought of) we divulge'; *ut* is an optional reinforcement ('a curious piece of surplusage', Nettleship 179). Cf. Ogilvie on Liv. 3.14.6, Roby §1658, K–S II 67.   **omnibus populis:** 4.29.4n.   **nec sunt ... nouit:** Sen *Ep.* 94.71 *inritamentum est omnium in quae insanimus admirator et conscius ... ambitio et luxuria et impotentia scaenam desiderant.*

5.10.9 denique is the simplest correction of *diuque*, which is unduly strong for 'at our leisure', 'prenons notre temps' (Vallette).

5.11.1 totisque 'all': 4.32.4n.   **illis** 'their': 5.7.1n.

5.11.2 prorsum 'quite', 'absolutely' is odd; van der Vliet's *rursum* is tempting.   **deterrentes:** F's reading is barely defensible: (i) it is oddly qualified by *raptim*; (ii) *deterreo* ought to connote discouragement from some contemplated course of action, which does not seem in point here; (iii) *quoque* refers closely to *parentes*: in addition to whom were they discouraged?; (iv) how could they be discouraged by 'reinflaming their grief' (*redulcerato ... dolore*)? No correction hitherto proposed is really convincing (*quoque* being the chief stumbling block), and the transmitted text is kept and translated *faute de mieux*.

5.11.3 uidesne 'do you not see ...?'; a negative nuance must sometimes be read into positive questions, as in English 'are you aware?' = presumably you are not. Cf. Plaut. *Amph.* 433 *uincon argumentis te non esse Sosiam?*, Ov. *Met.* 10.681–2 *dignane cui grates ageret, | cui turis honorem | ferret, Adoni, fui?*   **minatur:** a verb is necessary, and van der Vliet's supplement accounts simply for the omission: the copyist's eye leapt from 'min*atur*' to 'uelit*atur*' (parablepsy). For the indicative in indirect questions cf. 5.9.5n.   **uelitatur ... congredietur:** for the military imagery cf. 5.12.4, 5.14.3, 5.15.1, 5.19.5 and (the priest to Lucius) 11.15.5. Ironically, it was Cupid himself and lovers who were figured in the literary tradition as engaged in warfare: 5.21.5n.   **longe** 'very', as at 1.21.5, 6.8.3; a sense peculiar to A., *pace* Callebat (1968), citing (535) Stat. *Theb.* 10.140, on which see Williams *ad loc.*

5.11.4 lupulae (†): an Apuleian diminutive of *lupa*, with the same overtones of prostitution.   **ut te suadeant:** for the more classical

construction with inf. (Callebat (1968) 341). For *suadeo* + acc. see
5.6.6n.   **non uidebis si uideris:** i.e. he will disappear; the oracular
paradox emphasizes the warning against Psyche's *curiositas*, her
passion to know what she is forbidden to know. There is a similar
paradox at 11.15.5 (the priest to Lucius) *nam cum coeperis deae seruire,
tunc magis senties fructum tuae libertatis.* Here, however, there is a second
layer of meaning: she will not recognize him if she sees him, i.e. she
will not understand the revelation of the true nature of Love, for
which she is not ready.

5.11.5 ergo igitur: a pleonasm much favoured by A. adopted from
Plautus: *TLL* s.v. 775.5–8, Callebat (1968) 530–1.   **neque:** 5.3.5n.
simplicitate: the first reference to this recurrent theme.   **nil
quicquam** 'nothing whatever'; cf. 4.21.4 *nemo quisquam*; a pleonastic
colloquial usage: Hijmans al. 162, K–S I 652, H–S 802, MacCary–
Willcock on Plaut. *Cas.* 1008.   **uel ... uel:** for the classical *aut ...
aut*: K–S II 105. *aut* in fact occurs in *Met.* twice only, *uel* nearly 200
times: Hijmans al. 187, H–S 501. Cf. 5.12.6 *nec ... uel uideas uel audias*,
5.16.3.

5.11.6 diuinum: a clear enough hint, one would have thought; cf.
5.17.3n.

5.12.1 See Introd. p. 35.   **florebat** 'bloomed', 'brightened'; an
unusual, perhaps unique use of the word applied to a person, but cf.
6.11.5 *oues ... auri ... decore florentes* and 5.22.6n. 'Became exhilarated'
(*OLD* s.v. 4; Gell. 7.13.4 is not really parallel) is insufficiently physical;
TLL s.v. 918.45–6 classifies this passage under the rubric 'de corpore,
vultu', but in the other examples the part of the body is specified.
solacio: ablative of cause rather than dative; cf. Ov. *Tr.* 5.12.7 *exigis
ut Priamus natorum funere plaudat* (but Ovid probably wrote *in funere*).
Cf. below, §2 *rudimento*.

5.12.2 sarcinae nesciae rudimento 'through the new experience of
her unfamiliar burden'; *rudimento* is causal or instrumental ablative.
Michaelis's supplement *in* gives slightly easier Latin. For the passive
sense of *nescius* see *OLD* s.v. 4.   **miratur:** Psyche's naive wonder,
symptom of her *simplicitas*, contrasts with the understanding that she
(almost fatally) lacks. Unthinking admiration was a leading trait in
Lucius' character; he and Psyche are both culpably innocent (Tatum

(1979) 39, 60). **de breui punctulo (†):** cf. 6.21.3 *Psychen innoxio punctulo sagittae suae suscitat*, Sen. *Phaedr.* 281–2 *non habet latam data plaga frontem,* | *sed uorat tectas penitus medullas*. The phrase refers both to the short-lived pain of defloration (Graves: 'the mere breach of her maidenhead') and (an authorial irony, for Psyche as yet knows nothing of them or him) to Cupid's arrows (5.24.4n.). The interpretation preferred by most editors = 'temporis breui punctulo' (cf. 9.39.1 *puncto breuissimo*) is pointless and in view of 6.21.3 (cit. above) improbable. *punctulum* occurs otherwise only at Isid. *Orig.* 16.9.7. **tantum incrementulum (‡)** (lit.) 'so great a growthlet', a striking oxymoron. Cf. Venus' description of Cupid as *incrementum* (5.28.9n.)

5.12.3 Furiae: an appropriate description for the instruments of a Junonian Venus: 4.30.1n. **uipereum uirus:** cf. 4.33.1.4n. They, not Cupid, are the real serpents in this Eden. The Furies are often represented with snakes for hair. **nauigabant:** cf. 5.14.1, 5.21.2, 5.27.1. The geography of the tale is vague: 5.26–27n. **momentarius (*)** 'transitory'; literally 'brief', possibly with an ironical reference to their imminent separation. *momentarius* also in A.'s contemporary Papinian (*Dig.* 34.1.8).

5.12.4 en dies ultima ...: the transmitted text has Cupid begin his speech with implausible abruptness and entails a pointless and uncharacteristic zeugma (5.8.1n.). Of the several treatments proposed, van der Vliet's is the most economical. **personauit:** contrast 7.13.3 *personui*. Such forms are not confined to late Latin (N–W III 376); see Hor. *Sat.* 1.8.41 *resonarint*, Manil. 5.656 (the Andromeda passage) *resonauit* and Bentley and Housman *ad locc.*

5.12.6 uel ... uel: 5.11.5n. **in morem Sirenum:** the Sirens, half women, half birds, lured mariners to destruction by their song: *OCD*[2] s.v. 'Sirens'. Their first appearance in literature is in Homer (*Od.* 12.39–54, 154–200), but A. is thinking of Virgil (*Aen.* 5.864 *scopulos Sirenum*) or Ovid (*Met.* 14.88 *Sirenum scopulos*); in Homer they sit 'in a meadow'. A. may possibly be recalling Socrates' comparison of the cicadas to the Sirens: their song lulls the hearer to sleep 'because of mental indolence' (*Phaedr.* 259a; cf. Ferrari 28).

5.13.1 singultu ... incertans: Ov. *Rem.* 598 *ruptaque singultu uerba* *loquentis erant*, *Met.* 11.420 *singultu . . . pias interrumpente querellas*, *Tr.* 1.3.42 *singultu medios impediente sonos*. Virgil does not use *singultus* of weeping. *incerto* is attested twice in Republican drama and once elsewhere in A. (11.16.10): *TLL* s.v.   **quod sciam** 'as far as I know' (*quod = quoad*): *OLD* s.v. *scio* 1c. This limiting or restrictive use of the subjunctive is old and idiomatic (Roby §§1692−4, K−S 11 307−8, Bennett 1 295−6), but the phrase strikes an oddly formal note here.   **fidei atque parciloquio (‡) . . . documenta** 'proofs of (lit. 'for') my loyalty and discretion'. For this adnominal use of the dative to connect two nouns (emended away in late MSS) see K−S 1 346, H−S 95−6; but the examples cited by commentators are generally in a predicative construction ('*as* a proof . . .', '*to be* a proof . . .') and so less harsh than this one; cf. 9.18.2 *supplex eum medellam cruciatui deprecatur*. Cf. however Plaut. *Mil.* 271 *illic est Philocomasio custos meu' conseruos*, 1431 PY. *quis erat igitur?* SC. *Philocomasio amator*, Cic. *Phil.* 13.15 *receptui signum . . . audire non possumus* (but cf. Roby liii*b*), Liv. 9.18.5 *nullane haec damna imperatoriis uirtutibus ducimus?*

5.13.2 praecipe fungatur: 5.6.4n.   **obsequia:** cf. 6.12.1 *obsequium . . . functura* (Paratore 39−40); for *fungor* + accusative see *TLL* s.v. 1586.63ff.

5.13.3−6 As she speaks she caresses him. After her words here her credulity in allowing her sisters to persuade her that (even in the daytime) her husband is a monster verges on the imbecile; cf. Helm (1914) 171 = 177 n. 4.

5.13.3 cinnameos: (*).   **mei** stands for *meis* (*genis*) by so-called 'compendious comparison'. In this form it goes back to Homer, *Il.* 17.51 κόμαι Χαρίτεσσιν ὁμοῖαι 'hair like (that of) the Graces'; cf. Vell. 2.41.2 *dissimilem . . . fortunae suae indutus habitum* and Woodman *ad loc.*, K−S 11 566−7, H−S 826.   **sic:** normally in wishes or prayers *sic* introduces 'a *quid pro quo* which is to operate on the fulfilment of the speaker's own request' (N−H on Hor. *C.* 1.3.1; cf. *OLD* s.v. 8d). Here it sums up the adjuration = 'per faciem tuam quam in hoc saltem paruulo cognoscam'. Psyche's wish to see her husband's features in her child (a topos: Catull. 61.214−18, on which see Fedeli 114−15) is not a stipulation: see Vallette *ad loc.* A. was no doubt thinking of the famous words of Dido to Aeneas, Virg.

Aen. 4.328–9 *si quis mihi paruulus aula | luderet Aeneas, qui te tamen ore referret* . . .

5.13.4 deuotae: this is followed in F by an erasure, probably covering a mistaken repetition of the same word. The presumed lacuna is variously filled in the later MSS (and by edd.). See Helm and Robertson *ad loc.*, Dowden (1980) 223–4. **Psychae animam:** 5.6.9n.

5.13.5 nec quicquam . . . requiro 'And I ask nothing . . .': *OLD* s.v. *neque* 3a. **in** 'as to', lit. 'in the matter of': *OLD* s.v. 42. **nec:** 5.3.5n. **meum lumen:** cf. [Tib.] 3.19.11–12 *tu mihi curarum requies, tu nocte uel atra | lumen*, *TLL* s.v. 1821.52–63. There is an ironical hint of the language of mystical revelation (6.2.5n.); Psyche is still far from a true understanding of where her salvation really lies.

5.13.6 This too is reminiscent of Venus' seduction of Vulcan (5.6.9n.). **suis crinibus detergens:** so Anthia dries her tears with Habrocomes' hair, Xen. *Eph.* 1.9.5–6; cf. also perhaps Luke 7.37–8, John 12.3. **se facturum:** Helm's supplement restores A.'s usage: cf. 5.5.4, 5.6.10.

5.14.1 consponsae factionis (lit.) 'forming a pledged party', genitive of definition. *conspondeo* is an old and rare word, otherwise unattested in the literary tradition between Naevius and Ausonius: *TLL* s.v. **de nauibus:** 5.12.3n. **nec:** 5.3.5n. **ferentis** 'to carry them', but also 'favourable': *OLD* s.v. *ferens* 1. **licentiosa cum temeritate:** a foreshadowing of their eventual fate (5.27).

5.14.2 quamuis inuitus ~ 5.6.10 *inuitus . . . maritus*.

5.14.3 incunctatae 'undelaying'; the word is found nowhere else, but the formation of negative adjectives from *in-* + perfect participle is an Ovidian mannerism (Kenney (1973) 124) which may well have appealed to A. Less recherché is Colvius' *incunctanter*, a word used seven times elsewhere in *Met.* and relatively common in late Latin. However, when, as here, A. uses three adverbial phrases in a row, variation (adjective – adverb – adjective/noun phrase) is rather what we should expect. **conferto uestigio** 'in close order', a military turn of phrase (5.11.3n.) to express their grim determination; it varies the usual *conferto gradu* (8.29.6, Tac. *Ann.* 12.35.6). **sororis**

nomen ementientes: Wolf's correction (essentially anticipated by Price 268) restores idiom and sense to F's awkward *sorores nomina mentientes*. Cf. Gell. 1.2.7 *nomen ementirentur* ed. Ascens. 1517: *nomine mentirentur* VR. *ementior* in A. otherwise only at *Apol.* 17 (p. 20.19 Helm).   **thensaurumque ... abditae fraudis:** contrast 5.2.2 *totius orbis thensaurus.* Cf. Plaut. *Merc.* 163, 641 *thensaurum ... mali*, Eur. *Ion* 923–4.   **adulant:** for the classical *adulantur*: *TLL* s.v. 877.58–64.

5.14.4 perula: the sisters' arch vulgarity is tinged with authorial irony: they are indeed preoccupied with what there is 'in the bag' for them.

5.14.5 aurei: gold is a natural symbol of excellence (LSJ s.v. χρύσεος III, *OLD* s.v. *aureus* 5), but this is the grandchild of *Venus aurea* (Virg. *Aen.* 10.16, Ov. *Her.* 16.35, al.; cf. Hom. *Il.* 3.64, al.) and the child of *aureus Amor* (Ov. *Am.* 2.18.36, al.). Cf. 5.22.5 *capitis aurei genialem caesariem*, 5.29.1n.   **Cupido nascetur:** 5.6.7n.

5.15.1 a lassitudine: Price's supplement (269) mends the grammar simply and economically; Helm's *ex* is almost equally plausible. Castiglioni's *lassitudinem* (rec. Robertson) introduces an accusative of respect (K–S I 285–92, H–S 36–8) of a kind not easy to parallel. **fontibus** = *aquis*, a poeticism: *TLL* s.v. *fons* 1024.38–52.   **-que ... et ... atque:** for *-que ... et* (most commonly without any intervening words) see H–S 515, K–S II 37, Brink on Hor. *A.P.* 196; for *-que ... atque* see H–S 516, K–S II 37, Bömer on Ov. *Met.* 4.429–30.   **illis** 'those (of hers)'.

5.15.2 psallitur ... sonatur ... cantatur: 4.33.3n.   **agere** 'perform': *OLD* s.v. 20.   **choros canere** '(ordered) the choir to sing' (cf. *tibias agere*) rather than '(ordered) (them) to sing songs'. For *chori* of a single group cf. Stat. *Ach.* 1.622 *consedere chori* 'the dancers sat down', 4.29.4 *populi* and n.

5.15.3 mellita ... mollita: the mellifluous assonance accentuates their callousness.   **sermonem conferentes** 'directing the conversation' (*OLD* s.v. *confero* 3a), not the usual sense of the phrase (5.6.4n.).   **unde natalium:** for the classical *unde natus*, perhaps on the analogy of *unde gentium* et sim.: *OLD* s.v. *gens* 4a, H–S 53.   **secta cuia:** inverted for the sake of the chiasmus with *unde natalium*.

cuius (adj.) properly = 'whose?', here practically = *qua* 'which?', 'what?'. The word is not uncommon in comedy; Virgil was derided for introducing it to poetry at *E.* 3.1 *cuium pecus? an Meliboei?* It survived in colloquial Latin (Coleman *ad loc.*). The ablative of origin with *prouenio* is on the analogy of established usage with *natus, ortus* et sim.: H–S 104–5.

5.15.4 simplicitate nimia: something of an understatement. Psyche's improvisations illustrate the age-old truth that liars should have a good memory (Otto s.v. *mendax* 1). The abl. is causal.   **de prouincia proxima:** cf. 4.29.1n.   **magnis pecuniis negotiantem** 'in a large way of business', ablative of means.   **interspersum (†) rara canitie:** the tacking on of this touch – 'merely corroborative detail, intended to give artistic verisimilitude to an otherwise bald and unconvincing narrative' – at the end of the description is eloquent of the hasty character of Psyche's ill-starred improvisation, after which she bundles her sisters off the premises (§5) as quickly as she can.

5.16.1 sublimatae 'borne aloft'; the word is found before A. only in Ennius, Cato and the non-literary Vitruvius.   **secum:** 5.9.1n. **altercant:** Oudendorp's correction eliminates an un-Apuleian anomaly in F's *altercantes*: it is not characteristic of him to 'understand' a finite verb of saying. Wouwere's *altercantur* is equally plausible, but A. has a slight preference for the active over the deponent form.   **quid ... dicimus?** 'what are we to say?': 4.34.6n.

5.16.2 florenti lanugine barbam instruens (lit.) 'equipping his beard with blooming down', a strange and forced use of *instruo*, though perhaps defensible if *instruens* is taken as = *instructus*: 5.8.4n. Blümner's *nutriens* is tempting; cf. Hor. *Sat.* 2.3.35 *pascere barbam.* **aetate media** '(a man) of middle age', descriptive or qualifying ablative: H–S 118–19.

5.16.3 mi soror: cf. 4.26.1 *mi parens*, 4.27.5, 9.16.1 *mi erilis*, 8.8.7 *mi coniux.* The use of *mi*, properly the masculine vocative of *meus*, with feminine nouns, was expressly interdicted by ancient grammarians, but occurs sporadically in late (Christian) Latin: N–W II 368–9, Hijmans al. 191. In this A. seems to have led the way: *TLL* s.v. *meus*

9ᴵ4.39–53.   **uel ... uel:** 5.11.5n.   **utrum** 'whichever' = *utrumcumque*: *OLD* s.v. *uter*[3] 2c, N–W ii 540.

5.16.4 denupsit: this uncommon word is first attested at Ov. *Met.* 12.196 (Bömer *ad loc.*).   **audierit** 'is to be called', cf. 6.9.5 *uilis ancillae filius nepos Veneris audiet*: *OLD* s.v. 5a.   **me ... suspendam:** like the heroine of a tragedy (Soph. *Ant.* 54 πλεκταῖσιν ἀρτάναισι 'with twisted noose') or indeed of a novel: cf. Chariclea's threats at Heliod. 1.8.3, 6.8.6, 8.7.3, and the fate of Arsace at 8.15.2. For *laqueo nexili* cf. 8.22.4 *laqueum sibi nectit*, 8.31.2 *mortem sibi nexu laquei comparabat*. Cf. 5.6.4n.

5.16.5 exordio ... adtexamus: more corroborative detail ... Their metaphor exploits the literal and figurative senses of *exordium, concolor* and *adtexo* (*OLD* s. vv.); cf. English 'spin a yarn'. The warp (basis) of their plan is their determination to strip Psyche of her good fortune. **quam concolores:** cf. 5.20.5 *nisu quam ualido*, for the classical *quam* + superlative (*OLD* s.v. 7b): K–S ii 480, H–S 164, 590, Callebat (1968) 538–9.

5.17.1 fastidienter (‡): they are too preoccupied to display affection ('elles saluent leur parents du bout des lèvres', Vallette).   **nocte turbatis uigiliis perdita** 'the night having been passed fruitlessly in disturbed wakefulness'; Gruter's correction restores sense and form to the sentence by the deletion of one letter. Editors who keep *perditae* and construe it with *peruolant* ('flew in desperate haste') fail to recognize that *matutino* must stand first in its sub-clause to answer *nocte*. An alternative possibility is Grimal's *nocte turbata uigiliis peracta* (however he confusingly retains *perditae*) 'a night disturbed with wakefulness having been passed', for which cf. Ov. *Am.* 1.2.3 *uacuus somno noctem, quam longa, peregi*.   **scopulum:** accusative after verb of motion: cf. 5.5.3n.   **uehementer deuolant:** the manner of their throwing themselves over might be violent, but the speed of their descent was not under their control. Hence Salmasius' *uehentis* (cf. 4.35.4 *uehemens* F, corr. φ); cf. 5.14.1 *uenti ferentis*. To read *uehentes* 'riding' (Eyssenhardt) is also possible.   **lacrimisque ... coactis:** Virg. *Aen.* 2.196 (Sinon's) *lacrimis ... coactis*, Ov. *Am.* 1.8.89 *discant oculi lacrimare decenter*, *Met.* 6.628 *oculi lacrimis maduere coactis*. For *pressura palpebrarum* cf. Ter. *Eun.* 67–8 *una ... falsa lacrimula⸗ | quam*

oculos terendo misere uix ui expresserit, Ov. *Met.* 13.132–3 (Ulysses)
manuque simul ueluti lacrimantia tersit | lumina; Dickens, *The Pickwick
Papers* 'As Mr Weller said this, he inflicted a little friction on his right
eyelid, with the sleeve of his coat, after the most approved manner of
actors when they are in domestic pathetics.'

5.17.2 ignorantia ... incuriosa: authorial irony. It is precisely the
combination of *simplicitas* (her failure to understand the character
either of her husband or her sisters) and her *curiositas* (her insistence
on prying into forbidden things) that is to ruin her.   **incuriosa
periculi:** genitive of respect, as at 5.18.2 *secura periculi*, 5.21.3 *incerta
consilii*.

5.17.3 A. seems to go out of his way to compound the improbabilities
and so to accentuate Psyche's *simplicitas*. She is apparently led to
accept the proposition (which her experience should have refuted:
5.5.1, 5.11.6, 5.13.3–6nn.) that her husband keeps his serpentine
form *by night* (5.19.2, 5.20.3–4), for that is evidently what she expects
to see when she uncovers the light (5.22.2). The sisters too evidently
expect her to see a monster, or they would instruct her to do the
murder in the dark, and they know the words of the oracle (see
below); but their language appears to suggest that they do not believe
their own story (5.16.5 *fallacias*). A. seems less concerned with con-
structing a probable plot than with exploiting deliberately created
ambiguity. Attribution of a serpent's form to the husband recalls the
oracle (4.33.1.4 and n.). The sisters terrify Psyche with its literal
sense; its true meaning is revealed to her the more dramatically when
she sees him as he really is. For details of the description A. probably
had Virgil's snakes uppermost in his mind: *Aen.* 2.204–8 *immensis
orbibus angues | incumbunt pelago pariterque ad litora tendunt; | pectora quorum
inter fluctus arrecta iubaeque | sanguineae superant undas, pars cetera pontum |
pone legit sinuatque immensa uolumine terga*, G. 3.425–6 *anguis | squamea
conuoluens sublato pectore terga ...*, 430–1 *piscibus atram | improbus
ingluuiem ranisque loquacibus explet ...*, 433 *flammantia lumina torquens ...*,
439 *linguis micat ore trisulcis*; cf. Ov. *Met.* 3.32–4, 37–42 and Bömer *ad
locc.*   **scilicet** 'as you know', but also an ironical authorial nudge;
the reader is better informed than Psyche of the reasons for their
involvement. See Introd. p. 23.   **multinodis:** (*).   **ueneno ...
colla sanguinantem** 'its neck running with bloody poison'; the

details are recombined from Virgil (*Aen.* 2.206–7 *iubae* ... | *san-guineae*, 210 *oculos suffecti sanguine*) and Ovid (*Met.* 3.85–6 *uenenifico sanguis manare palato* | *coeperat*) without much regard for even poetic herpetology; the object is to make Psyche's flesh creep.   **colla:** the common 'poetic' plural for singular, accusative of respect with *sanguinantem*.   **latenter** 'without your realizing it'; Greek would say λανθάνει συγκοιμώμενος. The contrast between the horrific elaboration of the preceding description and the laconic adverb produces a humorous anticlimax.

5.17.4 Pythicae: the oracle was at Miletus, but in this serpentine context it is appropriate to refer to Apollo by his cult-title 'Slayer of the Python'; the Python was the dragon which guarded the Delphic oracle until Apollo killed and took over from it.   **circumsecus (†)** 'round about'; only in *Met.*

5.18.1 saginaturum ... deuoraturum: sc. *eum esse.*   **opimiore fructu praeditam** 'endowed with a richer fruit', with the senses 'profit' and 'enjoyment' also felt: *OLD* s.v. *fructus* 3, 5, 6.

5.18.2–3 This is in the best style of family dialectic: 'Of course it's your affair, and if that's your idea of pleasure, don't let *us* influence you, but don't say we didn't do our best ...'

5.18.2 secura periculi: 5.17.2n.   **sepeliri:** Lucret. 5.993 *uiua uidens uiuo sepeliri uiscera busto* and Costa *ad loc.*

5.18.3 uocalis: to be taken with *solitudo* rather than with *ruris.* **nostrum** 'our duty': *OLD* s.v. *noster* 8a.

5.18.4 misella ... simplex et animi tenella ~ 5.11.5 *pro genuina simplicitate proque animi tui temeritudine.* The diminutives accentuate her helplessness.   **animi:** 4.32.4n.

5.18.5 in profundum ... praecipitauit: an act of spiritual suicide, with a hint of her later bodily attempts (5.25.1, 6.17.2 and nn.). **semihiante uoce** (lit.) 'with voice half-open', i.e. coming from half-opened lips. This seems easier than postulating a special sense 'choked', 'strangled' (*OLD* s.v.).   **substrepens (‡)** evidently = 'muttering', 'whispering'. *strepo* = 'make a loud noise', and its compounds generally convey this sense, but cf. Calp. Sic. 4.2 *sub hac platano quam garrulus adstrepit humor.*

5.19.1 quidem ... uerum: much like Greek μὲν ... δέ; *uerum* is connective rather than adversative.   **ut par erat** 'as is proper', a common idiomatic use of the imperfect and pluperfect indicative: cf. e.g. Ter. *Hec.* 867–8 *hic quos par fuerat resciscere | sciunt*, Cic. *De fin.* 4.2 *illud erat aptius, aequum cuique concedere*. Cf. the common *tempus erat* (N–H on Hor. *C.* 1.37.4). See Blase 149–52, K–S I 173, H–S 320–1, 327–8.

5.19.2 nec ... uel: cf. 3.11.1, 6.20.3 and Purser *ad loc.*, *OLD* s.v. *neque* 7f.   **cuiatis** 'of what country', ante-classical form of *cuias*. **subaudiens (*)** 'submitting to'; the word is found nowhere else in this sense, and = 'understand (something omitted)' it is a technical term of commentators. A. seems to have (re)coined it *ad hoc*, perhaps on the model of Gk ὑπακούω: for *audio* = 'obey' see *OLD* s.v. 11. Souter's *obaudiens* (= *oboediens*: *TLL* s.v. 133.60.5) is an easy but unnecessary normalization.

5.19.3 Psyche's misinterpretation of her husband's solemn warnings shows that she has not learned to trust him, she does not yet know him: cf. 5.6.7, 5.23.6nn., Hoevels 91.   **me namque:** Castiglioni's correction of F's *meque* provides a needed connexion. For postponed *namque* cf. 5.17.3, 6.19.3, al. (Paratore *ad loc.*).   **de** 'on account of': *OLD* s.v. 14, *TLL* s.v. 65.47ff., esp. for A. 66.38–42, Callebat (1968) 201–2.   **praeminatur:** (*).

5.19.4 ceterum: 5.5.3n.   **prouidentiae:** the antithesis of the true *Prouidentia* (5.3.1n.). Her words are heavily ironical: their intervention undoes the effects of Cupid's *prouidentia*.

5.19.5 portis patentibus = Virg. *Aen.* 2.266; for a possible allusion to the fall of Troy cf. Harrison 266–7.   **tectae machinae latibulis:** in the context (5.11.3n.) the suggestion of siege-engines (*uineae*) at work is appropriate, but the figurative sense of *machina*, perhaps here verging on its Christian meaning 'temptation' (*TLL* s.v. 12.42–68), is also felt.

5.20.1 qua: no satisfactory parallel is forthcoming for the construction with *quae*: *uia iter (de)ducit* is not idiomatic Latin. Jahn's simple correction is adopted in preference to Gruter's more drastic (but not on that account improbable) deletion of *iter*.

5.20.2–5 Psyche is given her orders. The long sentence in which this is done is artfully constructed to sweep her (and the reader) unfalteringly on to the final decisive word. Instrument (*nouacula*) and act (*abscide*) frame the instructions. Cf. Introd. p. 34 n. 153.

5.20.2 nouaculam: perhaps a knife rather than a razor; cf. below, §5 *ancipiti telo*, 5.26.3 *ancipiti nouacula*.   **praeacutam:** A. is fond of the word (four other instances in *Met.*); its only previous occurrence in a literary writer in a non-technical or non-military context is at Ov. *Met.* 7.131 *praeacutae cuspidis hastas*.   **lenientis exasperatam:** the somewhat strained expression accentuates the paradox that the gentle caressing motion of the hand imparts an additional edge. **concinnem** (‡) 'made ready' = *concinnatam*. A. elsewhere uses *concinnus*; the old vulgate reading *concinne* 'neatly' deserves consideration.   **praemicantem:** (*).

5.20.3 sulcatum trahens gressum: Ov. *Met.* 15.725–6 *litoream tractu squamae crepitantis harenam | sulcat*, evidently the source of A.'s expression; as often, he 'improves' on his model, for *gressus* is properly (and almost universally: *TLL* s.v. 2327.25–7) reserved for animals with feet. Robertson notes that with the exception of *Flor.* 10 (p. 16.11 Helm) A. never uses *gressus* in the pl.; that instance, looked at in its context, is clearly a special case. F's *intrahens* may be right; the word is otherwise reliably attested only at 11.23.3 (*TLL* s.v.)   **exordio somni prementis implicitus:** *premo* is common of sleep (*OLD* s.v. 18), but with *implicitus* it suggests an image of wrestling: Stat. *Theb.* 6.889–90 *mox latus et firmo celer implicat ilia nexu, | poplitibus genua inde premens* . . .   **altum soporem flare:** Virg. *Aen.* 9.326 *toto proflabat pectore somnum*, Theoc. 24.47 ὕπνον βαρὺν ἐκφυσῶντας; Virg. *Aen.* 8.27, Ov. *Met.* 7.667 *sopor altus habebat* (Bömer *ad loc.*).

5.20.4 pensilem gradum paullulatim (†) minuens (lit.) 'reducing tinily your raised-up tread', i.e. walking on tiptoe with very small steps. For *pensilem* cf. 3.21.3 *suspenso et insono uestigio* and *OLD* s.v. *suspendo* 6b.   **tenebrae:** the first instance of the very rare use of the singular. N–W 1 712 offer only four other examples.

5.20.5 dextera . . . elata: Virg. *Aen.* 10.414–15 (a different gesture, however) *dextram fulgenti deripit ense | elatam in iugulum*.   **quam ualido:** 5.16.5n.   **nodum** 'joint'; cf. Plin. *N.H.* 11.217 *nodos* . . .

corporum qui uocantur articuli. The anatomical precision is characteristic of epic warfare, as Price (276) pointed out, comparing Hom. *Il.* 14.465–6; cf. Ov. *Met.* 1.717–18 *uulnerat ense | qua collo est confine caput.*

5.20.6 praestolatae aduolabimus: the anomaly involved in accepting the archaic *praestolabimus* (F), given A.'s otherwise consistent use of the deponent form, seems pointless, and the easy restoration *praestolabimur* (ς) does not yield positive enough sense: there should be a promise of action. Van der Vliet's correction neatly solves the difficulty.   **opibus:** cf. 5.2.3, 5.8.1, 5.9.4, 5.10.6, 5.16.3 (Paratore 45–6). *ocius*, though closer to F's *sociis*, gives inferior sense, though the use of comparative for positive ('pretty quickly') is idiomatic: *OLD* s.v. *ociter* 2b, H–S 168–9, cf. 6.21.3 *longe uelocius.* Cf. 5.26.7n.   **uotiuis (*)** 'longed-for'; cf. 7.13.1 *tota ciuitas ad uotiuum conspectum effunditur, OLD* s.v. *uotum* 3, Callebat (1968) 154–5; Hor. *Sat.* 2.6.1 *hoc erat in uotis* 'this is what I always wanted'.

5.21.1 'Leaving the heart of their sister, (who was) already burning, (now) kindled to flame by their fire of words ...' The sense is clear, the expression, with *uiscera* as the grammatical object of *deserentes,* odd. Of the suggested corrections Robertson's *flammatam uiscera sorores iam prorsus ardentem* deserves consideration.

5.21.2 porrectae '(finding themselves) stretched out'; cf. 4.35.4 *delapsam reclinat,* 5.1.1 *recubans.*   **conscensis nauibus:** 5.12.3n.

5.21.3–4 'It is the psychological portrayal of the irresolute heroine so notably painted in Euripides' *Medea* and in Seneca's drama, and so frequently imitated in the Greek romances' (Walsh (1970) 206 and n. 2, citing Eur. *Med.* 1042ff., Sen. *Med.* 893ff., Ach. Tat. 2.25, Xen. *Eph.* 2.5; add Apollonius' Medea, A.R. 3.751–801). A.'s prime inspiration, however, is clearly Ovid (cf. Helm (1914) 199 = 218):

   (*a*) *relicta sola, nisi quod infestis Furiis* etc.: *Met.* 6.430–1, 595 (Procne), 8.481–511 (Althaea) (see Bömer *ad locc.*); *Her.* 2.117–20, 6.45–6, 7.96, 11.103. For the expression cf. *Am.* 1.6.34 *solus eram, si non saeuus adesset Amor.*

   (*b*) *aestu pelagi simile maerendo fluctuat: Met.* 8.470–4 (Althaea); *Her.* 21.41–2 (Cydippe); *Am.* 2.10.9–10.

   (*c*) *festinat differt* etc.: *Met.* 9.523–7 (Byblis), 10.369–76 (Myrrha).

(*d*) *in eodem corpore odit bestiam, diligit maritum*: *Met.* 8.463, 475 (Althaea) *pugnant materque sororque … incipit esse tamen melior germana parente.*
A.'s description of Psyche's state can indeed be summed up best in one Ovidian phrase used of Byblis: *incertae tanta est discordia mentis*, *Met.* 9.630. Her situation most closely resembles that of Hypermestra among Ovid's heroines, but little or no specific similarity with *Her.* 14 is detectable (see, however, below, §3n.). For a comparable depiction of a woman torn by warring passions cf. 10.3.2. See also below, §4n.

5.21.3 simile 'like': 5.1.1n.   **maerendo** 'in her grieving'; the ablative (of means) of the gerund is used as an equivalent for the present participle: cf. Virg. *Aen.* 2.6–8 *quis talia fando | … | temperet a lacrimis?* and Austin *ad loc.* Cf. 6.15.4n., Callebat (1968) 319 (but his other exx. are not strictly parallel).   **quamuis** qualifies *statuto* and *obstinato*, 'though fixed her purpose …'; cf. 5.22.6 *quamuis … quiescentibus*, 5.27.2 *quamuis … flante*, al., H–S 385.   **statuto consilio** = 7.4.1.   **manus admouens:** Ov. *Her.* 14.48 (Hypermestra) *admoui iugulo tela paterna tuo.*   **incerta consilii:** 5.17.2n.

5.21.4 audet trepidat: Ov. *Met.* 8.82 (Scylla) *tenebris … audacia creuit*, 9.527 (Byblis) *in uultu est audacia mixta pudore.*

5.21.5 nox aderat et maritus aduenerat: the repetition of *aderat* in F's text is feeble and pointless. Van der Vliet proposed *nox erat*, a common introductory formula (Hor. *Epod.* 15.1, Virg. *Aen.* 3.147, 4.522, Ov. *F.* 2.792 (see Bömer *ad loc.*), [Ov.] *Am.* 3.5.1); but *nox aderat* occurs in Ovid (*F.* 4.331), and if a verb is needed with *maritus* it should be pluperfect to parallel *descenderat*, as at e.g. 5.4.3 *aderat … inscenderat … fecerat … discesserat.* Possible alternatives are to delete the second *aderat* or to read *aduenerat … aderat* (Frassinetti; but *aduenio* seems to be used with *dies* rather than *nox*).   **priusque Veneriis proeliis uelitatus:** sense is restored by Kronenberg's *prius* (*primis* can only mean that he fell asleep before their lovemaking was completed), elegance by Rohde's *Veneriis*: cf. 2.6.6 *nexu … Venerio*, 10.34.5 *amplexu Venerio*, al., 6.1.1 *uxoriis blanditiis.* The metaphor of love as warfare was common in both Greek and Latin literature (Lier 33–4, Spies *passim*, Murgatroyd *passim*). For its application to lovemaking, as here, cf. e.g. Prop. 2.1.13–14, 2.22.34, 4.8.88, Ov. *Am.* 3.7.71–2, Petron.

129.1,130.4, Mart. 10.38.6–8; and in A. 9.20.2 *prima stipendia Veneri militabant nudi milites*, and especially the encounters of Lucius and Photis (2.10.6, 2.15.6, 2.16.5, 2.17.3; cf. Spies 76, Adams 158–9). Here the application is restrained: cf. 5.4.3n.   **altum in soporem:** 5.20.3 and n. Paratore's placing of *in* accounts more easily for its disappearance (after *-m*, a common phenomenon).

5.22.1 corporis et animi ... infirma: 4.32.4n.   **alioquin** 'in general': *OLD* s.v. 2a, 6.15.3n. A. has a penchant for this word: some 35 instances in *Met.*   **Fati ... saeuitia:** cf. 5.5.2 *Fortuna saeuior* and n. The distinction between Fate and Fortune is frequently blurred: Virg. *Aen.* 8.334 *Fortuna omnipotens et ineluctabile Fatum* and Fordyce *ad loc.*; on Ovid see Kajanto (1961), esp. 29, on Lucan Ahl 297–305, and cf. Introd. pp. 4, 14   **subministrante:** sc. *uires*.   **sexum audacia mutatur** 'changes her sex in her daring' (accusative of the object after *mutatur* middle) or 'is changed by daring as to her sex' (accusative of respect); cf. Virg. *Aen.* 1.658 *faciem mutatus et ora Cupido* and Austin *ad loc.* Is Psyche the accomplice of Fate or its plaything?

5.22.2 This tableau recalls Ov. *Met.* 10.472–4 (the recognition of Myrrha by her father) *cum tandem Cinyras auidus cognoscere amantem* | *post tot concubitus inlato lumine uidit* | *et scelus et natam* ...; cf. also Parthen. 17.6 (Periander and his mother), noted by Fehling 25 n. 58.   **oblatione:** (*).   **omnium ... bestiam:** recalling and finally explaining the words of the oracle (4.33.1–2) and refuting those of her sisters (5.18.2).   **ipsum illum Cupidinem** 'Cupid, his very self'; cf. 5.26.4 *ipsum illum deae Veneris filium*. For *ille* used of a god see *OLD* s.v. 4b. The mysterious husband is now finally identified by name: Kenney (1990) 175 n. 1, 183, 5.23.3n.   **formonsum ... formonse cubantem:** cf. the Homeric κεῖτο μέγας μεγαλωστί 'great he greatly lay' (*Il.* 16.776; cf. 18.26–7, *Od.* 24.40), Heliod. 1.17.6 ἔκειτο κακὴ κακῶς 'bad she badly lay'. The adverb is found otherwise only at Prop. 2.3.17.   **lumen ... increbruit:** understandably, for it has up to now been denied its traditional role as confidant and voyeur: 2.11.3 (Photis speaking) *hac enim sitarchia nauigium Veneris indiget sola, ut in nocte peruigili et oleo lucerna et uino calix abundet*, 8.10.6 *te nullo lumine conscio ad meum perducet cubiculum*, Ar. *Eccl.* 7–11 (and Ussher *ad loc.*), Asclep. *A.P.* 5.7 (*HE* 846–9), Meleager, *A.P.* 5.8 (4348–53), al., Mart. 10.38.7–8,

14.39; Lier 43−5. Cf. 5.23.5 *amoris uile ministerium.*   **nouaculam paenitebat:** the joyful reaction of the lamp is complemented by the abashment of the knife; cf. below, §4. F's *nouacula praenitebat* gives wholly inappropriate sense and less than elegant syntax. It is possible, however, that A. wrote *nouacula paenitebat* (Weyman): see 5.6.3n.

5.22.3 marcido pallore defecta 'overcome with the pallor of faintness'; cf. 5.25.4 *sauciam ... atque defectam* (*OLD* s.v. *defectus*[1] 1) and contrast §4 *salute defecta* and n. Her symptoms are classical, those of a woman in love: 10.2.6 (cit. 5.25.5n.).

5.22.4 timore tanti flagitii: because she is the bride of Love; cf. 5.25.2n. The knife, no less than the river and her various helpers in her ordeals, owns the power of the god.   **salute defecta** 'forsaken (as she was) by salvation' (*OLD* s.v. *deficio* 2a), i.e. believing herself utterly lost.   **recreatur animi:** 2.11.5 *recreabar animi*, 11.22.4 *recreatus animi* and 4.32.4n.

5.22.5−7 A.'s bravura description of the sleeping Cupid incorporates standard features of the Hellenistic, 'elegiac', boy-god, notably the emphasis on his wings (4.30.4n.). The total effect is quite unelegiac, recalling rather the enumeration of the attributes of Isis at 11.3.4−4.3. The radiant beauty of the sleeping figure, made effulgent by a series of words denoting light and colour, inspires wonder and awe; a sense of latent power is made explicit in the concluding reference to *magni dei propitia tela*. Conformably with standard rhetorical doctrine and practice the description begins with the head and proceeds downwards (Kenney on *Moret.* 32−5; cf. 5.1.2n.): the living god is treated as a work of art. Cf. the description of Chariclea at Heliod. 1.2.2 and Maillon *ad loc.*

5.22.5 uidet ~ 5.1.2.   **aurei:** 5.14.5n.   **genialem** 'rich', 'abundant'; both the common connotation of joyfulness (A. is fond of the word in this sense) and the special association with marriage and procreation are felt.   **ambrosia:** the Homeric gods used ambrosia not only as a food but also as perfume and unguent: Hom. *Il.* 14.170, 16.670, 680, *Od.* 4.445; Virg. *G.* 4.415 *liquidum ambrosiae defundit odorem*, *Aen.* 12.419, al. Cf. 6.23.5n.   **ceruices lacteas ... pererrantes crinium globos:** Virg. *Aen.* 10.137−8 *fusos ceruix cui lactea crinis*

| *accipit*, 8.659–60 *aurea caesaries . . . tum lactea colla.* For the plural
ceruices cf. Quint. *I.O.* 8.3.35 *ueteres pluraliter appellabant*, Löfstedt 1 31.
pererrantes: Prop. 2.1.7 *seu uidi ad frontem sparsos errare capillos . . .*,
2.22.9 *siue uagi crines puris in frontibus errant . . .* With *decoriter* (*)
impeditos following the effect is one of artful disorder, the god represented as a statue or painting (cf. above, §§5–7n.).   **antependulos**
(†) . . . **retropendulos** (‡): both Apuleian coinages, the first also at
2.23.7.   **quorum splendore . . . lumen lucernae uacillabat:** the
emphasis on hair recalls Lucius' fetishistic excursus on the subject
apropos of Photis (2.8–9); but Cupid's tresses exude unearthly
power.

5.22.6 roscidae 'dewy', sc. in appearance; they gleam like dew on
grass or flowers. Cf. Virg. *E.* 4.30 *roscida mella* ('refers to the surface
texture', Coleman *ad loc.*), Plin. *N.H.* 26.47 *roscida lanugine* 'dew-
like tufts'.   **flore** 'bloom', 'brightness'; cf. 5.12.1n., *TLL* s.v.
932.15–31. Lucretius' *flammai . . . flore* (1.900) is different, being
modelled directly on Greek πυρὸς ἄνθος.   **plumulae tenellae:**
the diminutives are both descriptive in their own right and contribute
to the series of *l*-sounds which help to give the passage its sensuous
quality (as in Lucius' description of Photis at 2.7.3); cf. below, §7
glabellum . . . lectuli.   **inquieta** 'restlessly': 5.9.1n.

5.22.7 ceterum corpus etc.: a typical ecphrastic motif, cf. e.g. Ov.
Am. 1.5.23 (having recounted Corinna's charms from shoulder to
thigh) *singula quid referam? nil non laudabile uidi*, Stat. *Silv.* 1.5.57 *quid
nunc . . . referam?*, Plin. *Ep.* 3.6.3 (on a statue) *talia denique omnia,
ut possint artificum oculos tenere, delectare imperitorum.*   **glabellum** (*):
2.17.2 (Photis) *glabellum feminal rosea palmula . . . obumbrans*, *Flor.* 3
(p. 4.16–17 Helm) *Apollo . . . corpore glabellus.* The word is otherwise
attested only in Martianus Capella (2.132).   **iacebat:** as usual in
Latin, the verb takes the number of the nearest element, here *arcus*, of
a compound subject.   **magni dei propitia tela:** what in his
mother's eyes are the toys of a naughty unbiddable child (4.30.4,
4.31.1, 5.29.5, 5.30.5) are now seen as the attributes of a mighty god;
cf. 5.25.6 *Cupidinem deorum maximum percole.* The word *deus* occurs five
times in chh. 22–3 (Wlosok 75 n. 6; her figure is six, but see 5.23.5n.).
propitia is here not merely 'a conventional word applied to the
graciousness of the pleasures of love' (Purser) but an acknowledgement of Cupid's immense power for good.

5.23.1 satis et curiosa '(who was), as well, extremely curious', sc. by nature; *et = etiam*; *OLD* s.v. 5a (but see crit. n.). For *satis* = 'very' cf. 4.30.4n. 'Psyche not only gazed rapturously at the wondrous weapons of Cupid, but (her besetting sin) was full of curiosity also to know what they were' (Purser on 6.14.4). *insatiabili* preceding helps to underline the point.   **depromit ... pupugit:** 5.2.1n.

5.23.2–3 This is indebted to Ovid's description of the wounding of Venus: *Met.* 10.525–8 *namque pharetratus dum dat puer oscula matri,* | *inscius exstanti destrinxit harundine pectus.* | *laesa manu natum dea reppulit;* | *altius actum* | *uulnus erat specie primoque fefellerat ipsam* (Helm (1914) 199 = 218); cf. 10.636–7 (Atalanta) *utque rudis primoque cupidine tacta* | *quid facit ignorans amat et non sentit amorem.*

5.23.2 punctu 'by pricking'; Floridus' correction is inescapable. Oudendorp explained *puncto pollicis* = 'on the tip of her thumb', but there is no parallel for this sense of *punctum*.   **periclitabunda:** (†). **articuli** 'hand': *OLD* s.v. 2b.

5.23.2 ignara ... sponte: the oxymoron is pointed; it was her own act but done in ignorance of its implications and consequences.   **in Amoris ... amorem:** Cupid is now for the first time explicitly identified as Love (Rambaux 200), but the revelation has been brought about through disobedience; cf. Kenney (1990) 183. 'Beauty was for both Cupid and Psyche the necessary condition of falling in love ... Psyche did not fall in love with Cupid until she saw him and could recognize his beauty ... What she had experienced before the recognition of Cupid was mere "pleasure" ...; what she felt after falling in love was an overwhelming urge to pursue Cupid forever ... It was an ambition that could only be fulfilled by immortality in his divine company' (Hooker 38).   **fraglans:** 4.31.3n.   **prona ... metuebat:** this is very like Longus' description of Daphnis hanging over (κύψας Giangrande: κρύφα MSS) the sleeping Chloe (1.25.1–2), especially 'But I fear that by kissing her I shall wake her up.' Cf. also Prop. 1.3.11–17.   **in eum ... inhians:** Lucret. 1.36 (Mars gazing at Venus) *pascit amore auidos inhians in te, dea, uisus.* **efflictim** ironically picks up her own words at 5.6.7 and recalls her artless '*nec ipsi Cupidini comparo*'.

5.23.4 saucia mente: 4.32.4n.   **lucerna illa** 'that (wretched) lamp'; cf. 5.31.2 *Psychen illam* 'drat her'.   **siue ... siue ... siue:** A.'s hedging reflects the difficulty of making allegorical sense of this development: 5.28.1n.   **luminis** 'opening', 'spout': *OLD* s.v. 8b.

5.23.5 hem 'what!', expressing surprise and indignation. **amoris uile ministerium:** 5.22.2n.   **ignis totius dominum:** 'Cupidinem, qui tot ignibus hominum Deorumque pectora quotidie inflammat' (Floridus); perhaps also, as suggested by Grimal, a cosmogonical reference; for a comparison between Eros and the sun see Plut. *Amat.* 764b–d, and cf. perhaps Varro, *L.L.* 5.59, Cic. *N.D.* 2.57 (and Pease *ad loc.*), Fliedner 106 n. 60. *dominum*, the original reading of F, must be preferred to *deum*: *deus ignis* = 'god of fire' is not Latin, certainly not Apuleian Latin (Paratore 50–1).   **scilicet:** another authorial nudge (5.17.3n.) – 'when (as everybody knows) ...'   **cupitis:** 5.6.4n.   **primus inuenerit:** Ar. *Eccl.* 1–2 'O bright eye of wheel-turned lamp, best of shrewd inventions'. 'It was a widespread conviction in antiquity that all arts and artefacts must have been invented by somebody' (N–H on Hor. *C.* 1.3.12, q.v.). See esp. Leo (1912) 151–4 for examples in comedy and elegy, many relating to inventions both for the benefit and the bane of lovers.

5.23.6 uisaque detectae fidei colluuie 'seeing the filth of his uncovered trust', i.e. finding himself betrayed and contaminated. It is Cupid's identity rather than his trust which is disclosed, and *detectae* has been variously corrected (*defectae* Jahn, *deceptae* Helm), but the idea of revelation should not be lightly emended away.   **ex osculis et manibus:** a cliché of deathbed partings: Sen. *Dial.* 12.2.5 *in manibus et in osculis tuis mortuum funeraueras* (cf. ibid. 11.15.5 *in complexu et in osculis suis amisit*), Gell. 3.15.3 *in osculis atque in manibus filiorum animam efflauit*.

5.24.1 Plat. *Phaedr.* 248c 'When [the soul] is unable to follow [God] and fails to see, and through some misfortune grows heavy, being filled with forgetfulness and wickedness, it loses its wings and falls to earth.' Cf. Longus 2.7.1, where Philetas tells Daphnis and Chloe that 'Love is young and beautiful and winged; therefore he delights in youth and pursues beauty and gives wings to souls' (see Schönberger *ad loc.*). Cf. Walsh (1970) 206–7, Kenney (1990) 184–5. **appendix:** *appendix ... quasi ab alio pendens*, Non. p. 60 Lindsay; A. archly exploits the etymology, as also at 8.22.4 *se ... per altissimum* *puteum adpendicem paruulum trahens praecipitat.* **penduli comitatus extrema consequia (†)** 'a trailing attendance of dangling companionship', a very artificial expression even for A. – perhaps a military metaphor (Médan 353)? *consequia* is best taken as neuter plural, as at 10.18.3 (the only other instance of the word), jointly with *appendix miseranda* in apposition to the subject of the sentence. The description may, as suggested by Price (281), owe something to Ovid's picture of Scylla clinging to Minos' ship at *Met.* 8.142–4. It is a plausible speculation (Wagenvoort 383) that A. invented this aerial journey to get Psyche from the coast of Asia Minor, where her father's kingdom was, to the Peloponnese, where her sisters were evidently to be found (but cf. 5.26–27, 6.8.5nn.).

5.24.2 inuolauit ... adfatur: 5.2.1n.   **inuolauit proximam cupressum:** he perches in trees at Bion, fr. 13(10).3, Longus 2.6.1.

5.24.3–4 Cupid's deliberate disobedience of his mother's orders is now for the first time made explicit.

5.24.4 feci leuiter ...: an admission, not merely that he disobeyed his mother, but that in allowing himself to fall in love with Psyche he acted on the promptings of his mother as Venus II (cf. 4.30.5) and of his other (un-Platonic) self: see Kenney (1990) 185, Introd. p. 20. For *leuiter* cf. Ov. *Am.* 2.9.49 *tu leuis es multoque tuis uentosior alis*, *A.A.* 2.19 *et leuis est et habet geminas, quibus auolet, alas* and Hunter on Eubulus 41.5. The irresponsible use of his powerful weapons was one of the hallmarks of the Hellenistic, 'elegiac' Cupid as he first appeared in the story (4.30.4–31.3n.).   **praeclarus ille sagittarius etc.:** he is hoist with his own petard. For variants on this proverbial theme see Otto s. vv. *ars* 4, *gladius* 3, *laqueus* 1, *pinna* 4, *telum* 1; Häussler 136, 168, 176, 217. On Cupid in love cf. 5.6.10n. His words here recall those used by Callimachus of Acontius, fr. 70 Pfeiffer ἀλλ' ἀπὸ τόξου | αὐτὸς ὁ τοξευτὴς ἄρδιν ἔχων ἑτέρου 'but the archer himself, feeling the arrow-point from another's bow ...' With *praeclarus ille* here cf. 3.26.6 *praeclarus ille uector meus*, 5.9.1 *sorores egregiae*, 5.24.5 *illae ... consiliatrices egregiae*, a kind of irony of which A. is fond (Bernhard 239–40).   **coniugem meam feci** ~ 5.4.3 *uxorem sibi Psychen fecerat.*   **scilicet:** he knows the whole plot.   **amatores tuos oculos:** conceits involving lovers' eyes are frequent in elegy (Pichon

219), but to call his eyes her 'lovers' immediately after so styling himself (§3, cf. §2) is odd; Castiglioni's *tui* 'in love with you' is an easy correction.

5.24.5 identidem semper cauenda censebam 'I repeatedly warned you to be constantly on your guard', a thoroughly Apuleian pleonasm, but a more elegant example than that arrived at by construing both adverbs with *censebam*. Van der Vliet's transposition is attractive but not absolutely necessary.   **remonebam (*):** also at *CIL* v 8216.7 and (dubiously) *Il. Lat.* 151.   **consiliatrices:** (*).   **dabunt ... poenas:** see 5.26–27n.   **puniuero:** possibly emphasizing the certainty of their fate (4.30.3n.), but from Plautus onwards the future perfect is often used as a pure equivalent for the future simple: Bennett i 54–7, Blase 181–3, H–S 323. Cf. Callebat (1968) 502. **et cum termino sermonis etc.:** A.'s version of the epic *dixit/dixerat, et ...*; cf. e.g. Virg. *Aen.* 3.258 *dixit et in siluam pennis ablata refugit.* Cf. 6.21.1 *et cum dicto* and n.

Act III   Psyche Errans

5.25.1 quantum uisu poterat 'as far as her eyesight enabled her' (Purser). The sense with F's *uisi* 'to the extent that he could be seen' is strained. Michaelis's *prosequens* would require the transposition of *uisu*. **remigio plumae:** 6.15.5 *remigium dextra laeuaque porrigens*, Lucret. 6.743 *remigii oblitae pennarum*, Virg. *Aen.* 1.301 *remigio alarum*, 6.19 *remigium alarum*, al. The metaphor goes back to Aeschylus, *Ag.* 52; see Austin on Virg. *locc. cit.*   **fecerat alienum** 'had taken him from her'; cf. 8.8.9 *lancea mali Thrasylli me tibi fecit alienum*. The special sense 'physically separate' postulated by *OLD* s.v. 3c is uncalled-for. **praecipitem sese dedit:** Laevius 12–13 (p. 58 Morel) (Ino) *seseque in alta maria praecipem misit | inops et aegra sanitatis herois*, Virg. *Aen.* 9.815–16 *praeceps saltu sese omnibus armis | in flumen dedit* (but see next n.). Cf. 5.27.2n.

5.25.2 Psyche's attempted suicide (her second: 5.22.4n.) and the river's refusal to co-operate recall the story of Ilia (Rhea Silvia) at Ov. *Am.* 3.6.45–82 and *F.* 3.51–2 *amne iubet mergi geminos; scelus unda refugit, | in sicca pueri destituuntur humo.* Abortive suicide is a common theme in the Greek romances: Heliod. 2.2.1 and Maillon *ad loc.*,

Introd. p. 19.   mitis fluuius etc.: Virg. *Aen.* 9.817 (*fluuius*) *accepit uenientem et mollibus extulit undis.*   **scilicet** 'as my readers know': 5.17.3n.   **qui et ipsas aquas urere consueuit:** Ov. *Am.* 3.6.23-4 *flumina debebant iuuenes in amore iuuare:* | *flumina senserunt ipsa quid esset amor* − there follows a catalogue of amorous rivers ending with the story (cf. above) of Anio and Ilia. For the fire−water paradox cf. ibid. 25-6 *Inachus in Melie Bithynide pallidus isse* | *dicitur et gelidis incaluisse uadis*, 41-2, 83; Philostr. *Ep.* 11 'even water is set ablaze by love' (cit. Price 282).

5.25.3-6 Pan, so called (*Hom. Hymn* 19.47) 'because he delights the hearts of all', figures as the helper of lovers in Philetas' instruction of Daphnis and Chloe at Longus 2.7.6: 'I called on Pan to help me, since he had loved Pitys.' His intervention here may be seen as analogous to Prometheus' counselling of the wandering Io (Helm (1914) 200 = 220). His love for Echo is often represented as unsuccessful (Moschus, fr. 2, Longus 3.23, Anon. *A.P.* 9.825; see Hunter 52−7); in an epigram of Theaetetus Scholasticus (6th c. A.D.) he is called 'husband of Echo' (*A. Plan.* 233.1−2; cf. Archias, *A. Plan.* 154 (*GP* 3788−91)). See further Bömer on Ov. *Met.* 3.359. In Menander's *Dyscolus* it is he who makes Sostratus fall in love (43−4). He plays an important part in the erotic life of Arcadia: Theoc. 7.103−14, Virg. *E.* 10.26−30, Glaucus, *A.P.* 9.341 (*HE* 1819−24); cf. Borgeaud 115−35. A.'s description is full of pastoral reminiscences; cf. Heliod. 5.14.2−3 and Rattenbury *ad loc.*

5.25.3 iuxta supercilium amnis: Virg. *G.* 1.108−9 *ecce supercilio cliuosi tramitis undam* | *elicit.*   **complexus Echo etc.:** this is very close to the statuary group described by Callistratus (3rd/4th cent. A.D.) 1.5 with Pan 'rejoicing in the sound of the pipe with Echo in his arms'.   **uoculas ... reccinere:** Virg. *E.* 1.4−5 *lentus in umbra* | *formosam resonare doces Amaryllida siluas*; but *reccinere* of course exactly characterizes Echo: Ov. *Met.* 3.359−61 *usum* | *garrula non alium quam nunc habet oris habebat,* | *reddere de multis ut uerba nouissima posset.*   **omnimodas (*):** an adjectival back-formation from *omnimodis*, not uncommon after A.   **comam fluuii tondentes capellae:** Virg. *E.* 10.7 *tenera attondent simae uirgulta capellae.*

5.25.4 sauciam: 4.32.4n.   **utcumque ... non inscius:** clearly Pan has been 'planted'. Behind the scenes Providence (5.3.1n.) in the shape of Cupid is already at work, as it will continue to be during Psyche's various trials. Cf. 5.26.1 *numine salutari*.

5.25.5 si recte coniecto etc.: cf. for all this N−H on Hor. *C.* 1.13.5, Callim. *A.P.* 12.134 (*Epigr.* 43 Pf., *HE* 1103−8), Asclep. *A.P.* 12.135 (*HE* 894−7), Hor. Epod. 11.8−10, Prop. 1.9.5−8, 3.8.17−18, Ov. *A.A.* 1.733−8; cf. Heliod. 6.7.8 'A lover is quick to detect others in the same case' and Rattenbury *ad loc.*, P. G. Wodehouse, *Very good, Jeeves!* (Bertie Wooster speaking), 'But there is one department of life in which I am Hawkshaw the detective in person. I can recognize Love's Young Dream more quickly than any other bloke of my weight and age in the metropolis.'   **quod ... autumant:** Cic. *De div.* 2.12 *bene qui coniciet, uatem hunc perhibebo optimum*, translating a verse from an unknown Greek tragedy. The thought was proverbial: see Pease *ad loc.*, Otto s.v. *vates*. We are told by Apollodorus (1.4.1) that it was from Pan that Apollo learned the art of prophecy. Pan is heavily ironical: Psyche's symptoms are so clear that it does not need divination to tell what is wrong with her.   **ab isto titubante ... uestigio eqs.:** 10.2.6 *iam cetera salutis uultusque detrimenta et aegris et amantibus examussim conuenire nemo qui nesciat: pallor deformis, marcentes oculi, lassa genua, quies turbida et suspiritus cruciatus tarditate uehementior.* The archetype of all such inventories is Sappho's famous ode (fr. 31 L−P), imitated by Catullus (51). For pallor cf. also Theoc. 2.88, A.R. 3.297−8, Xen. *Eph.* 1.5.2, Catull. 64.100, Hor. *C.* 3.10.14, Prop. 1.5.21, 1.13.7, Ov. *A.A.* 1.729, al.; Pichon 224, Preston 49; and in the novelists Rohde (1914) 167 n. 2. For sighing Callim. *A.P.* 12.134 (*Epigr.* 43 Pfeiffer).1−2 (*HE* 1103−4), Hor. *Epod.* 11.10, Prop. 3.8.27, Ov. *Her.* 17.79; Pichon 272. For the language of the eyes Theoc. 1.38, Ov. *A.A.* 1.573 *oculis ... fatentibus ignem*; Pichon 219−20. For *marcentes* 'languid' 3.14.5 *oculos ... prona libidine marcidos*, Catull. 45.11 *dulcis pueri ebrios ocellos*, Quint. *I.O.* 11.3.76 (*oculi*) *natantes et quadam uoluptate suffusi*.

5.25.6 nec te rursus praecipitio ... perimas: precisely what she plans to do in her despair over her last mission (6.17.2). **precibusque ... promerere:** Pan's advice, emphasized by the alliteration of *p*, is pointed. Psyche has failed to recognize Cupid's godhead, and she must (re)deserve his favour. *deorum maximum* looks back to 5.22.7, *adolescentem delicatum luxuriosumque* to 4.30.4 (see nn. *ad*

locc.); both Cupids (Amor I and II) merge in Pan's synoptic view.
blandis obsequiis: both words suggest the compliances of the elegiac
lover: Prop. 1.8.39–40 *hanc ego non auro, non Indis flectere conchis,* | *sed
potui blandi carminis obsequio,* Tib. 1.4.40 *obsequio plurima uincet amor,* Ov.
A.A. 2.179–84, al.

5.26–27 'This introduction of the demise of the sisters on the one
hand lends an appropriate note of morality to the story, and on the
other has a symbolic import in the context of Psyche's pilgrimage.
The sisters represent the earthly attachments which are the cause of
her fall from grace, and which she must now slough off' (Walsh
(1970) 208). If this was A.'s intention, his manner of giving effect to it
is crude and melodramatic, calculated to gratify the (very human)
desire of the ordinary reader to see villains come to a sticky end. It no
doubt suited him also to eliminate the sisters promptly once they had
served their turn (cf. the deaths of Demaenete and Thermuthis in
Heliodorus, 1.14.3, 2.20.2). It is indeed plausible and neat that they
should overreach themselves and fall victim to the sort of credulity
that they had exploited in Psyche. That she, however, *simplex et animi
tenella*, should suddenly become both vindictive and crafty to this
degree is not (cf. Walsh ibid.). Admittedly A. has indicated that
Cupid is the real moving force behind all this (5.24.5), but there is
still an inconsistency in the portrayal of Psyche which he has not
attempted to mitigate, as he might easily have done by suggesting
that love or adversity had sharpened her wits, ideas which lay to his
hand both in Plato and in the elegiac tradition: *Symp.* 179a7–8, Ov.
Her. 20.25–6 *non ego* [Acontius] *natura nec sum tam callidus usu;* | *sollertem
tu me, crede, puella, facis* ..., 28 *ingeniosus Amor* (~ Callim. fr. 67.1–4
Pfeiffer), *A.A.* 2.43 *ingenium mala saepe mouent*; cf. Otto s.v. *paupertas* 1.
A similar disregard for consistency is evident in the geography:
whereas we are told more than once that the sisters had to take ship to
visit Psyche (5.12.3, 5.14.1, 5.21.2, 5.27.1), she reaches them on foot.
(To be scrupulously fair to A., we are not told how far her aerial
voyage had taken her; cf. 5.24.1, 6.8.5nn.) In itself the episode is well
contrived and spiritedly told (but see below, §§6–7n.).

5.26.1 aliquam multum 'a goodish amount', a favourite phrase of
A.'s; cf. 6.21.3 *aliquanta* and n., 4.30.4n. on *satis*.   **inscia:** this
simple correction of F's *inscio* is demanded by both sense and Latinity.

It is more pointed that Psyche should come unawares to her sister's home than that she (to whom all paths were perforce unknown) should come by an unknown path; and *inscius* is nowhere else reliably attested in the passive sense (*TLL* s.v. 1845.76–84; editors defend it by analogy with *nescius* (5.12.2n.) and *ignarus*). **unius** = *alterius*, answered eventually (5.27.4) by *alia*; cf. Caes. *B.G.* 1.1.1 *unam . . . aliam . . . tertiam* (hardly therefore either colloquial (Grimal) or late Latin (H–S 182)). Cf. 5.3.5n.

5.26.2 percontanti causas aduentus sui: she could hardly have expected Psyche, but in the light of their parting words (5.20.6) a less phlegmatic enquiry would have been in order. The detail accentuates A.'s failure to integrate the episode into his story.

5.26.4 aeque: sc. *mihi uobisque*.

5.26.5 dum . . . laborarem: the subjunctive with *dum* in strictly temporal clauses is colloquial and postclassical: *TLL* s.v. 2219.13ff. (the examples attributed to Virgil will not pass muster and many of the others are dubious). **copia . . . inopia:** the opposition is not infrequent from Plautus onwards (*TLL* s.v. *inopia* 1746.47–59); but A. is clearly recollecting the words of Ovid's Narcissus, *inopem me copia fecit* (*Met.* 3.466), for the point of the paradox is identical, an opportunity which is self-defeating, and A.'s phrase exactly describes Narcissus' frame of mind as depicted by Ovid. **scilicet:** if this is an ironical authorial judgement (5.17.3n.), A. appears to draw attention to a loose end in the narrative: 'you and I know it *wasn't* by chance . . .' – but why the lamp boils over and burns Cupid is never really made clear: Kenney (1990) 186–7.

5.26.6–7 Technical and specifically Roman terminology. *tuas res tibi habeto* was the regular formula of repudiation by a spouse (Gaius, *Dig.* 24.2.2) and *confarreatis nuptiis* refers to the most ancient and solemn form of marriage, virtually obsolete long before A.'s time. See Berger, s.vv. *Confarreatio*, *Divortium*; *OLD* s.vv. *diuerto* 1, *censeo* 6. Cf. 4.30.4–31.3, 5.28.7nn.

5.26.6 ferro et igne: a cliché (here used accurately) like English 'fire and sword': *OLD* s.v. *ferrum* 5c, Bömer on Ov. *Met.* 12.551.

5.26.7 praecipit . . . efflaret: 5.6.4n. The verb of a subordinate clause frequently behaves as if the main verb in the historic present were in fact preterite: H–S 551, Kenney on *Moret.* 17. Cf. 6.7.5 *continebatur*. Contrast 5.6.6n.   **eius:** *suae* might have been expected but cf. e.g. 6.16.4 *petit de te ... ei*, 6.18.4 *te rogabit ... ei*; this use of the oblique cases of *is* for *se/suus* is sometimes found in classical writers: H–S 175; on A. see Callebat (1968) 256. Kronenberg's *ocius* is tempting; cf. 5.20.6n.

5.27.1 necdum ... finierat, et ...: cf. 2.33.5 *uix finieram, et ilico me perducit* etc., al.; a variant of the common '*cum-inversum*' construction, with *et* for *cum*. See e.g. Williams on Virg. *Aen.* 5.858, Bömer on Ov. *Met.* 5.614, H–S 481–2. Koziol's conjecture is necessary; A. does not elsewhere omit *et* after the pluperfect.   **e re concinnato** 'improvised'; elsewhere in A. *e re* is found only in the phrase *e re nata* (5.8.4n.), which Augello (1977) 130 would restore here. Paratore (53–5) argues for *praeconcinnato* (the word is otherwise unattested) from a late MS. In classical Latin *e re esse* = 'to be of advantage': *OLD* s.v. 13b.   **quasi** 'on the ground (according to her) that': *OLD* s.v. 5a.

5.27.2 caeca spe 'with blind hope', ablative of cause.   **accipe me etc.:** Ov. *A.A.* 3.21–2 '*accipe me, Capaneu: cineres miscebimur*' inquit | *Iphias in medios desiluitque rogos.* The reminiscence is ironically pointed. Evadne was a devoted wife who immolated herself on her husband's pyre, the sister is *coniunx Cupidine (in)dign(issima).*   **se ... praecipitem dedit** ~ 5.25.1 *praecipitem sese dedit.*

5.27.3 nec ... uel saltem: 4.32.1n.   **saxa cautium** = *saxosas cautes* 'rocky crags', a variant on poetic pleonasms such as Virgil's *altas cautes proiectaque saxa* (*Aen.* 3.699) or Ovid's *rupes scopulosque aditque carentia saxa* (*Met.* 3.226). The grammatical form of the expression was possibly suggested by phrases of the type of *deuexa rupis* (4.35.4 and n.). For comparable pleonasms cf. below, §4 *uindictae ... poena*, §5 *mortis exitium.*   **proinde ut merebatur** ~ 5.11.1 *proinde ut merebantur.*   **laceratis uisceribus ... interiit:** one of the classic fates of those who failed to receive proper burial: Hom. *Il.* 1.4–5 'and it [the wrath of Apollo] made them the prey of dogs and all birds', 22.354, *Od.* 24.291–2, Aesch. *Suppl.* 800–1, Soph. *Aj.* 830 (see Jebb *ad loc.*), Eur. *Hec.* 1077–8, Lucret. 3.880 ... *corpus uti uolucres lacerent in morte feraeque*, Virg. *Aen.* 9.485–6 *heu terra ignota canibus data praeda*

Latinis | *alitibusque iaces*, Ov. *Her.* 11.83–4, etc. On the Virgilian echoes see Harrison 266–7.

5.27.4 nec ... tardauit 'was not slow in coming' (*tardo* intransitive: *OLD* s.v. 3). Traditionally divine justice, though sure, was slow: Eur. fr. 979 Nauck[2] 'Justice ... silently and with slow foot will come and · seize the wrongdoer whenever it shall happen' (cit. Plut. *De sera numinis vindicta* 549a), Hor. *C.* 3.2.31–2 *raro antecedentem scelestum* | *deseruit pede Poena claudo*, Tib. 1.9.4 *sera tamen tacitis Poena uenit pedibus*; Otto s.v. *deus* 11. A. wants the sisters out of the story.

5.27.5 fallacie germanitatis 'the deception of sisterhood', i.e. 'sisterly deception'. The examples of *germanitas* = 'brother' or 'sister' cited at *TLL* s.v. 1913.33–47 hardly justify taking the word here as simply = 'sister'. The abl. in *-e* of *fallacia* is attested nowhere else, and at 7.8.2 F transmits the usual *fallacia*; but such apparently arbitrary variations between 1st and 5th decl. forms occur elsewhere in *Met.* (e.g. 9.28.1 *blanditie*, 7.5.3 *crassitie*) and in other authors (cf. N–W I 560–9), and given A.'s masterful way with the language it is hazardous to normalize; cf. 5.6.10n.   **in ... nuptias aemula:** cf. 1.4.1 *in conuiuas aemulus*, 1.19.7 *argento uel uitro in colorem aemulus*.

5.28.1 at: this apodotic use of *at* following a *dum*-clause cannot be exactly paralleled (*TLL* s.v. 1007.13–15), but is supported by the analogous use of *et* at 7.26.4 *interim, dum puerum ... querebantur, et adueniens ecce rusticus ...*, itself apparently unique (*TLL* s.v. *et* 896.75–6), and it adds point: 'all this while Psyche was looking for Cupid, but he ...' It is, however, possible that A. wrote *interdum* (Colvius), rather than *interim, dum*.   **uulnere ... dolens:** cf. below, §3 *adustum ... graui uulneris dolore* and 4.30.4, 4.32.4nn. The tables are turned, the biter bit, the god of love is himself in love: 5.6.10, 5.24.4nn. For the theme in art of Cupid (Eros) burned see Schlam (1976) 16, 33. However, the implications of this *second* falling in love for the allegorical plot are unclear: Kenney (1990) 186–7.

5.28.2 auis peralba (*) illa gauia: for the probable identification of this bird as a tern see Arnott (1964) 261–2. Its role here as informer echoes the parts played by the raven and the crow in Ovid's story of Apollo and Coronis (*Met.* 2.531–632); the raven was originally white (ibid. 532–9). *illa* emphasizes *peralba* 'that (notably) white bird, the tern ...' 'No sea bird that the name *gauia* fits is entirely white from head to tail ... [but] the whiteness of a tern's plumage dazzles more brightly than that of gulls in full sunlight' (Arnott *loc. cit.*). *peralbus* otherwise only at *Grom.* p. 306.22 Lachmann.   **natat:** Virg. *Aen.* 6.15−16 (Daedalus) *praepetibus pennis ausus se credere caelo | insuetum per iter gelidas enauit ad Arctos* (see Austin *ad loc.*). At Lucan 5.554 *natanti* does not mean 'flying' (so *OLD* s.v. 2d, classifying it with this passage): see Housman *ad loc.*   **profundum gremium** 'the lowest depths' or 'a remote bay'; both words are ambiguous. *gremium* = 'bay' (cf. Gk κόλπος) is otherwise attested only in Pomponius Mela and Ennodius: *TLL* s.v. 2324.69−75 (this passage should be added). See next n.

5.28.3 ibi: perhaps in the sort of submarine grotto ('in ihrem Meerespalast', Reitzenstein 241) in which Cyrene received Aristaeus (Virg. *G.* 4.333−85; cf. Hom. *Il.* 18.35−64); but see previous n. **dubium salutis:** genitive of respect; cf. Ov. *Met.* 15.438 *dubio ... salutis* (where, however, the sense is 'doubtful of his safety'), *Tr.* 3.3.25 *dubius uitae*.

5.28.4 male audire 'had a bad name': *OLD* s.v. *audio* 5b.   **quod etc.:** the tern lapses into direct speech, but the subordinate verbs *secesseritis ... (§5) sint* remain in the subjunctive as giving the reasons attributed to the authors of the rumours.   **scortatu (‡) ... natatu** 'wivings ... divings' (Purser). *natatus* is previously attested only in Statius (*Ach.* 1.628, *Silv.* 1.3.73, 3.2.18).

5.28.5 The theme of nature in travail through the absence of a deity is most familiar in the myth of Ceres (Demeter); cf. *Hom. Hymn* 2 (Demeter).305−33 and Richardson *ad loc.*, Ov. *Am.* 3.10.29−36 (there with an erotic motivation, the love of the goddess for Iasius), *Met.* 5.481−6. The absence of love, the fundamental creative force, is even more catastrophic: Sen. *Phaedr.* 469−73 *excedat agedum rebus humanis Venus | quae supplet ac restituit exhaustum genus: | orbis iacebit squalido turpis situ, | uacuum sine ullis piscibus stabit mare, | alesque caelo derit et siluis fera* (and see Grimal *ad loc.*). A.'s list is the converse of what happens when Venus is present, as in Lucretius' great hymnic proem at *D.R.N.* 1.4−20; cf. *Hom. Hymn.* 5 (Aphrodite). 1−6, 69−74. A characteristically Ovidian note is struck by the words *incompta et* *agrestia et horrida*: cf. *Her.* 4.102 *si Venerem tollas, rustica silua tua est, Met.* 11.767–8 *non agreste tamen nec inexpugnabile amori* | *pectus habens* (cf. Bömer *ad loc.*), and for *uoluptas* as a civilizing influence the sub-Lucretian excursus at *A.A.* 2.473–80. Cf. 5.30.4 *rusticae squalentisque feminae*. The elaborate rhetorical structure of the paragraph lends an important emphasis: love, its presence, its absence, its quality, is what the story is about. See 6.24.4n., Kenney (1990) 187–8.   **enormis colluuies:** Jahn's correction of F's *gluuies* is supported by *colluuie* at 5.23.6; but both *illuuies* (Scioppius) and *eluuies* (Beroaldus) occur elsewhere in *Met.* and are equally possible. The strong emphasis on the sordid nature of sexual activity in the absence of (true) love is significant. The case for supposing that a genitival phrase balancing *squalentium foederum* has dropped out before *enormis colluuies* seems strong; Paratore's supplement *infimarum sordium* is very plausible.

5.28.6 illa: practically = 'the', cf. below, §8 *loquax illa . . . auis* and 5.7.1n.   **uerbosa et satis curiosa:** like the Ovidian informer-birds: *Met.* 2.535 *corue loquax*, 547–8 *garrula . . . cornix; curiosa* recalls Psyche (5.23.1 *satis . . . curiosa*); it can mean not only 'inquisitive', 'meddlesome' but also 'painstaking' – an appropriate term for the bird's elaborate verbal artifice (cf. above, §5n.): cf. Petronius' famous *Horatii curiosa felicitas* (118.5). For *satis* = 'very' see 4.30.4n.   **lacerans existimationem:** Suet. *Jul.* 75.5 *laceratam existimationem*.   **irata solidum** 'thoroughly furious': cf. 3.15.3 *formido solide*, 4.29.1n. This sense of *solidus* smacks of comedy: *OLD* s.vv. *solide* 1, *solidus* 2. *solidum* (‡) adverbial = *solide*.

5.28.7 puerum ingenuum et inuestem: comic exaggeration by an over-protective mother. The words can bear a technical sense (cf. 5.26.6–7n.) 'freeborn and a minor'; but applied to Cupid they are clearly coloured by Ovid's characterization of him at *Am.* 1.10.15–18 *et puer est et nudus Amor, sine sordibus annos* | *et nullas uestes, ut sit apertus, habet* etc. The motif of Love's nakedness is traditional: Mosch. 1.15 'wholly naked his body', Longus 2.4.1; the idea that it connotes innocence (cf. *OLD* s.v. *ingenuus* 3b) seems to be due to Ovid, but cf. Prop. 1.2.8 *nudus Amor formae non amat artificem*. One may detect here 'the oedipal love and possessive jealousy of a mother for her son' (Bettelheim 294), but the real point is perhaps more Platonic than Freudian: Venus (II) wants to keep Cupid a little boy (Amor II), but there is no question of his 'growing up' (Bettelheim ibid.); Amor I already *is* (and always has been).   **Nympharum ... Horarum ... Gratiarum:** cf. 5.32.2 *hinc Gratiae gratissimae, inde Horae pulcherrimae*, Hor. *C.* 1.4.5–7 *iam Cytherea choros ducit Venus imminente Luna | iunctaeque Nymphis Gratiae decentes | alterno terram quatiunt pede* and N–H *ad loc.*, Hom. *Hymn* 6 (Aphrodite).5–13, 3 (Apollo).194–6.   **populo ... numero ... choro ... ministerio:** Apuleian variation, at once exuberant and pointed: *numerus, chorus, ministerium*, each aptly characterizes.

5.28.8 puto puellam ... efflicte cupere: the sense is not in doubt, but the text is uncertain. The transmitted reading (printed here) gives the emphasis 'I think he loves a girl [sc. mortal?] – her name if I remember aright is Psyche', whereas one would expect 'I think it's a girl called Psyche that he loves'; and the omission of the subject of *cupere*, though not unexampled (H–S 362), is perhaps harsh. None of the various solutions proposed (see crit. n.) is free from objection.

5.28.9 succubam (*): also at 10.24.2, rare after A.   **incrementum** 'offshoot', 'sprig': in this sense previously only at Virg. *E.* 4.49 *magnum Iouis incrementum* (= *Cir.* 398), where the effect is grand and respectful – here very much the reverse. Cf. 5.12.2 *incrementulum* and n. In this and the following scene Venus sounds more like a matron in comedy or mime than an Olympian goddess – an anxious bourgeoise mother such as Herodas' Metrotime. We may also, however, as Dr Hunter has suggested, perhaps detect an echo of Hera's indignation on hearing of the accouchement of Leto (Callim. *Hymn* 4 (Delos).215–48); cf. 5.29.2n.   **cuius monstratu (*) ... cognosceret:** a final/consecutive relative (the distinction is sometimes harder to draw than the grammar-books allow). *cognosco* here has the nuance 'know sexually': *OLD* s.v. 5b.

5.29.1 quiritans: cf. 8.6.5, 8.18.1, Varro, *L.L.* 6.68 *quiritare dicitur is qui Quiritium fidem clamans implorat* – 'makes a public outcry'.   **properiter emergit ... thalamum petit:** presumably somewhere on Olympus. This abrupt and unceremonious transit of Venus contrasts strikingly with the state visit of 6.6, as does her equally abrupt return (5.31.7) with the marine cortège of 4.31. *properiter* for classical *propere* is found in the Republican dramatists Accius and Pacuvius, then not

until A. and his contemporary Septimius Serenus (p. 146 Morel).
aureum: 'golden' Venus (5.14.5n.) naturally has a golden bedroom;
like her chariot (6.6.1) it was made for her by her husband Vulcan
(Hephaestus): A.R. 3.36–8. The homes and belongings of the
Olympians are generally of gold.

5.29.2 natalibus nostris: 'our (family) origins' or 'my birth';
ironically ambiguous, in view of the gory details of the latter (4.28.4,
6.6.4nn.).   **ut ... calcares:** A.R. 3.93–4 'he pays no attention
to me [Aphrodite], always provoking and scorning me', *Cir.* 133–4
malus ille puer, quem nec sua flectere mater | iratum potuit. The *ut*-clause is
(ironically) consecutive: 'so virtuous (forsooth), that you ...' For
calcares cf. Callim. *Hymn* 4.227 οἳ σεῖο πέδον πατέουσιν ἐφετμήν
'who trample your commands underfoot' (5.28.9n.).

5.29.3 hoc aetatis 'of your age', 'at your time of life', cf. 10.8.3 *quod
aetatis sum* 'at my age', *Apol.* 98 (p. 108. 24 Helm) *puer hoc aeui*; idiomatic,
like *id aetatis* and similar expression (H–S 47); cf. 6.12.2 *istud horae*,
Callebat (1968) 191.

5.29.4 utique praesumis 'no doubt you take it for granted'; *utique*
virtually = *nimirum*. The word should probably be pronounced *utĭque*
(Ter. Maur. 592, *GLK* vi 342) rather than *utīque* (Lachmann on
Lucret. 4.638, *OLD* s.v.). Terentianus was writing in and on metre,
and though the spelling *uteique* occurs in inscriptions, 'inscriptional
writing with *ei* is poor evidence for long *i*, since there is much archaizing
in this respect' (Professor W. S. Allen, *per litteras*).   **nugo (†):**
only here and at 5.30.4.   **et inamabilis:** an adjective as the third
member of a tricolon (Bernhard 70) is awkward and there is much
to be said for Rohde's deletion of *et*.   **te solum generosum** 'the
only (member of the family) able to reproduce'. In this context the
etymology of *generosus* (~ *genus*, *genero*) must be felt; for the active
sense 'productive' (= *fertilis*) cf. Virg. *Aen.* 10.174 *insula inexhaustis
Chalybum generosa metallis* and Servius *ad loc.* 'hoc est πολύγονος', Ov.
Met. 15.710 *generosos palmite colles* and Bömer *ad loc.*, Macrob. *Sat.*
7.5.26 *herbarum quibus Creta generosa est.* Cf. *TLL* s.v. 1802.30–3; but it
explains the expression here as '*fere i.q. genuinum, legitimum filium*' (ibid.
1800.13–14). So Purser (after Norden) 'that there is no other prince
except yourself'.

5.29.5 uelim ... scias: 5.6.4n.   **genituram:** sc. *me esse.*   **non ad hos usus:** Virg. *Aen.* 4.647 *non hos quaesitum munus in usus,* Ov. *Met.* 5.111 *non hos adhibendus ad usus* and Bömer *ad loc.* The *magni dei propitia tela* are in Venus' eyes 'gear' (*supellectilem*) to be held and used at her pleasure. So Aphrodite had threatened to break Eros' bow and arrows in Apollonius (3.95–9); cf. 5.30.5n.

5.29.6 patris tui: whoever that was; Cupid (Eros) had more than one genealogy (*LIMC* III 1.850–1, 952–3); Venus' husband was Vulcan (Hephaestus). Cf. 5.30.1, 6.22.3nn. The hint of a Roman legal reference in *bona paterna* and *materna* accentuates the comic-bourgeois tone of the episode; cf. 6.4.4–5n. She represents her adulterous liaison (as it is usually described) with Mars as a legitimate remarriage: cf. 5.30.1n. on *uitricum.*

5.30.1 male ... inductus 'misguided', 'badly brought up': *OLD* s.v. 8b, *TLL* s.v. 1236.77ff. (*) in this sense.   **acutas manus habes** 'you are quarrelsome', a literal (mis)rendering of Greek ὀξύχειρ 'quick with the hands', but also referring to the deadly sharpness of his arrows. See next n.   **pulsasti ... parricida ... percussisti:** he wounds her with his arrows (cf. Mosch. 1.21), but the words also convey that he is a parent-batterer, what the Greeks called a πατραλοίας, a sense of *parricida* ignored by Latin lexicographers. **denudas** 'strip' – he is also a λωποδύτης, a clothes-stealer, a footpad – and 'leave defenceless', i.e. by making her fall in love. Venus was usually depicted naked in art.   **uitricum:** Mars; calling him Cupid's stepfather was evidently a private joke of Ovid's (*Am.* 1.2.24, 2.9.48, *Rem.* 27), not taken up by any other writer before A.

5.30.2 quidni? 'Of course!', i.e. what else would you expect?   **in angorem mei paelicatus** 'to cause distress (consisting) of my having a rival', i.e. to vex me (and oblige him) by providing him with mistresses. Cf. 8.22.3 *dolore paelicatus uxor ... instricta.* Mars' mythological amours were many and various. Since Venus is herself Mars' mistress, this is highly ironical.   **faxo ... paeniteat:** she echoes the words of her original threat against Psyche: 4.30.3 and n.   **sentias acidas et amaras** 'find it to be bitter'; the adjectives are predicative. A Graecism modelled on the similar use of πικρός? Cf. Hunter on Eubulus 120.6.

5.30.3 sed nunc ... quid agam? etc.: this string of agitated questions recalls and burlesques the laments of abandoned heroines such as Ariadne and Dido (cf. 6.5.3n.); cf. Enn. *Androm.* 81–3 Jocelyn *quid petam praesidi aut exequar? ... quo accedam? quo applicem?*, Medea 217 Jocelyn *quo nunc me uortam? quod iter incipiam ingredi?*, Catull. 64.177–73 *nam quo me referam?* etc., Virg. *Aen.* 4.534 *en quid ago?* etc. (see Austin *ad loc.*). The phrase *quo me conferam?* was in fact a cliché (*TLL* s.v. *confero* 182.77–80) originating in a famous outburst of Gaius Gracchus quoted by Cicero at *De or.* 3.214 *quo me miser conferam?* etc.   **inrisui habita** 'treated as a laughing-stock', predicative dative: *OLD* s.v. *habeo* 24e. Cf. A.R. 3.102 (Aphrodite to Hera and Athene) 'others laugh at my troubles'.   **stelionem** 'twister', lit. 'lizard' (gecko): Plin. *N.H.* 30.89 *nullum animal fraudulentius inuidere homini tradunt, inde stelionum nomine in maledictum translato* – as at Petron. 50.5 (Trimalchio speaking) *Hannibal, homo uafer et magnus stelio.* The term *stellionatus* is a regular one in Roman law for underhand dealing: Berger s.v. An abrupt descent from paratragedy to colloquialism (Callebat (1968) 75).   **ab inimica mea Sobrietate:** Ov. *Am.* 1.2.31–2 (the Triumph of Cupid) *Mens Bona ducetur manibus post terga retortis* | *et Pudor et castris quidquid Amoris obest.* The idea of an alliance between Venus and Sobriety, mutually exclusive forces, recalls Ceres' appeal to *Fames* in Ovid's story of Erysichthon: cf. esp. *Met.* 8.814–15 *dicta Fames Cereris, quamuis contraria semper* | *illius est operi, peragit* etc. Nothing in fact comes of it. For other such abstract figures cf. 6.8.5, 6.9.2nn.

5.30.4 rusticae squalentisque feminae: on the (Ovidian) connexion between love and *cultus* cf. 5.28.5n. *rusticus* and *rusticitas* are Ovid's favourite words for lack of amatory *savoir-faire*: *OLD* s.vv. 7, 3. **nec tamen ... spernendum est:** an echo of Virgil's Juno, *Aen.* 7.310–12 *quodsi mea numina non sunt* | *magna satis, dubitem haud equidem implorare quod usquam est* etc.

5.30.5 explicet ... dearmet ... enodet ... deflammet (‡): the diction is recherché, *EXplicet ... Enodet* balanced by *DEarmet ... DEflammet*; the last word clearly coined by A. to pick up the almost equally rare (Livy 4.10.7) *dearmo. explicet* = 'undo', i.e. strip off him: *TLL* s.v. 1729.12–23. These threats again recall those of Aphrodite in Apollonius (3.95–9), and in Lucian 79 (*Dial. deor.*).19 (11).1; cf. 5.29.5, 6.22.1nn.

5.30.6 quas in meo gremio nectarei fontis infeci 'which in my own bosom I have impregnated from the source of nectar', i.e. which she had groomed (?) with milk from her own breasts, an odd idea. For the Graecizing genitive of origin with *inficio* (cf. *TLL* s.v. 1411.40–1) cf. 5.9.3n. Price (290) acutely suggested a hypallage (= enallage: 4.29.2n.), thus construing the phrase as = *mei gremii nectareo fonte*, but though double enallage is a characteristic Ovidian ploy his Apuleian parallel (6.6.1 *terrenis remediis inquisitionis abnuens*) is not very close. Cornelissen's addition of *in* is necessary; the word frequently disappeared in copying by haplography with following *m*. For *nectar* of milk cf. Ov. *Met.* 15.117, Mart. 13.47.1, but here the word is perhaps to be understood literally. 'Cupid is strangely silent, as if to underplay the incongruity of his resumed Alexandrian role' (Walsh (1970) 209). It is in fact resumed, not so much *by*, as *for* him: see nn. on next chapter.   **praetotonderit (*):** otherwise attested only in the fifth-century medical writer Cassius Felix.

5.31.1 sic effata foras sese proripit: with *se* for *sese*, two-thirds of a good hexameter; Price (209) compared Andromache's wild exit from her house at Hom. *Il.* 22.460 ὡς φαμένη μεγάροιο διέσσυτο μαινάδι ἴση. On *sic effata* see 4.31.4n.   **stomachata biles Venerias** 'angry with Venerean rage', i.e. as only Venus can be; cf. 4.29.5n., and for the rage of jealousy Prop. 4.8.55 *quantum femina saeuit*, Ov. *A.A.* 2.379 *in ferrum flammasque ruit. biles V.* is cognate accusative: Müller 51, H–S 38–9. The plural may be an allusion to the fact that doctors distinguished more than one kind of bile (Callebat (1968) 248) – i.e. she is as angry as is medically possible, or perhaps more so – but only *atra bilis* was associated with rage, and it seems more likely that the pl. is merely rhetorical.   **continantur ... quaesiere:** 5.2.1n.   **uultu tumido** 'with swelling face', descriptive ablative. **quaesiere:** a natural dramatic touch; cf. Ar. *Lys.* 6–8 'Lysistrata, why in such a taking? Don't scowl, my dear, knitted brows don't become you', and Henderson *ad loc.*   **uenustatem micantium oculorum:** Amm. 25.4.22 (the Emperor Julian) *uenustate oculorum micantium flagrans.*   **coerceret** 'repressed', 'confined', i.e. spoiled their appearance by scowling.

5.31.2 isto is dative, as at 6.17.3; the form is almost confined to *Met.* (six instances): *TLL* s.v. 496.34–8.   **uolentiam (*):** a rare word (restored here by Markland; cf. Solinus 36.2, where Salmasius similarly corrected *uiolentiam*), found at 11.6.2, Fronto, *Epp.* p. 137 Naber (*s.v.l.*), and a handful of mostly Christian texts.   **scilicet:** their motives, as emerges, are not quite so altruistic; cf. 5.17.3n. **Psychen . . . requirite:** the conceit of the soul as a runaway is exploited by Callimachus, *A.P.* 12.73 (*Epigr.* 41 Pfeiffer, *HE* 1057−62) and Meleager, *A.P.* 12.80 (4082−7); but it is likely that Moschus' 'Love the Runaway' (Mosch. 1) suggested it to A. here; cf. 6.8.2−3, 6.4.5nn. Venus' claim to Psyche as her slave reflects both the philosophical commonplace that men are the slaves of their passions (see e.g. Cic. *Parad. Stoic.* 35, 40−1, Hor. *Sat.* 2.7, esp. 83−8, D.L. 6.66 (Diogenes)) and the literary *seruitium amoris*, the enslavement of the lover to the beloved (see e.g. Men. *Mis.* fr. 2 Sandbach, Pichon 262; and cf. 5.25.6, 6.1.2nn.). By losing Cupid, Love in its higher, Platonic–Isiac guise (Amor I), Psyche has automatically passed under the dominion of Venus (identified by her words and actions as Aphrodite Pandemos), Love in its lower, earthly guise (Venus II). See Kenney (1990) 190. **non dicendi filii mei:** generally taken = 'not to be spoken of as my son', for which see 5.12.6 *quas . . . sorores appellare non licet*; but 'my unspeakable son' (Purser) is supported by the evidence, for what it is worth, of the glossaries: cf. ἄλεκτος *infandus indicendus indictus*, cit. *TLL* s.v. *indicendus.* Cf. also Aphrodite to Eros at A.R. 3.129 ἄφατον κακόν 'unspeakable plague'. However, *dicenda* (P. Faber) is worth considering, as producing a syntactical structure to balance the preceding *domus meae famosa fabula.*

5.31.3−7 In the Apollonian scene which A. evidently had in mind Hera (Juno) had put in a plea for Eros (3.106−10). A.'s goddesses dispense conventional wisdom as women of the world: youth must have its fling. In point of fact, like everybody else on Olympus (4.33.2.7, 8nn.), they are terrified of Cupid's irresistible and (as they see him) irresponsible power.

5.31.3 quae gesta sunt: 5.9.5n.   **quoque** 'even', with *perdere*; cf. Kenney on Lucret. 3.470 (*Addenda*, p. 250). Cf. below, §4 *iam quot sit annorum* 'how old he now is'.

5.31.4 puellae lepidae libenter adrisit: cf. 5.24.4 *feci leuiter*. Their language trivializes the matter.   **portat:** *portas* (van der Vliet) is tempting; but would not A. have written *ipsa portas*? For the point made by *portat* cf. Lucian 79 (*Dial. deor.*).6(2).1 (Zeus speaking) 'Do you think that because you are beardless and your hair isn't yet white you can claim to be treated as a child?' In the oldest version of his genealogy Eros was older than Aphrodite: Hes. *Theog.* 120 and West *ad loc.*

5.31.5 This plea for forbearance is reminiscent of Micio's relaxed attitude to the goings-on of his nephew and adopted son Aeschinus in Terence's *Adelphi* (50–76).   **tuas artes tuasque delicias:** *tuas* is maliciously ambiguous. As goddess of love Venus presided *ex officio* over all amatory activity, but her own affairs were notorious: *fabula ... toto notissima caelo* is Ovid's description of the episode when she and Mars were surprised by Vulcan *in flagrante delicto* (*A.A.* 2.561–92). No wonder she flounces off in a huff.

5.31.6 populis: 4.34.5n.   **amores amare:** Lucret. 4.1134 *surgit amari aliquid quod in ipsis floribus* [i.e. *in ipso amore*] *angat*, Plaut. *Cist.* 68 *eho an amare occipere amarum est, opsecro?*, Virg. *E.* 3.109–10 *quisquis amores | aut metuet dulcis aut experietur amaros.*   **uitiorum muliebrium publicam ... officinam** 'the public manufactory of female frailties' (Purser); this is open mockery. Robertson ingeniously rewrites *cum Amoris amores amare coerceas et tuae domui uitiorum* etc. For A.'s liking for this kind of word-play see Callebat (1968) 470–3 and cf. 6.8.3 *sauia suauia*, 6.13.2n.   **concito gradu pelago uiam capessit:** she returns as unceremoniously as she came (5.29.1n.). *pelago* is dative of direction: H–S 100–1.

VI

6.1.1 interea: 4.32.1n.   **mariti uestigationibus (*) intenta et quanto magis inquieta animi, tanto ...:** van der Vliet's supplement, though it cannot be regarded as certain, provides both a construction for *uestigationibus* (since *inquieta* can hardly do double duty with this word and with *animi*) and a complement for the following *tanto cupidior*. For *u. intenta* cf. 5.28.1 *quaestioni Cupidinis intenta.* Robertson's correction of *animo* to *animi* restores the usual construction: cf. e.g. 6.2.2 *furens animi* and 4.32.4n., Callebat (1968) 489.   **iratum licet =** *quamuis iratum*: *OLD* s.v. *licet* 4c, 5.1.6n.   **blanditiis lenire ... precibus propitiare:** an important antithesis; see 5.6.9, 5.13.3–6, 5.22.7, 5.25.6nn.

6.1.2 prospecto templo quodam: temples and shrines were as much a feature of the ancient landscape as the parish church or the wayside crucifix in our own time, and frequently figured in art: Helbig nos. 1555ff., Rostowzew 82–7 and index (183) s.v. 'Tempel', Grimal (1986) 1 246 and n. 38. Cf. 6.3.3n.   **unde ... scio an ...?** 'Perhaps', 'probably', a variant on *haud scio an*; cf. 1.15.4, 10.26.2, *OLD* s.v. *an* 8. **dominus** 'lord and master'; as a lover's endearment the word seems to be peculiar to Ovid (*Am.* 3.7.11, *A.A.* 1.314, *Met.* 9.466); but cf. Fragm. Grenf. 27 Powell κύριε, μή μ' ἀφῇις ἀποκεκλειμένην, Mart. 10.68.5 κύριέ μου, μέλι μου, ψυχή μου. In two of the Greek romances (Ach. Tat. 5.26.7, Xen. *Eph.* 2.4.5, 5.14.2) girls address their lovers as δεσπότης ψυχῆς τῆς ἐμῆς 'lord of my soul'. In later antiquity, however, the phrase (with its Latin calque *dominus pectoris mei*) is used as an epistolary formula: Bruggisser 232 and *passim*. Cf. 5.31.2n.

6.1.3–4 Cf. Helbig 1555, describing a landscape with 'a circular temple with Corinthian columns ... on the threshold in a *vannus mystica* all kinds of cult-apparatus'; and the offerings listed by Longus in his description of the grotto of the Nymphs in which Chloe is found (1.4.3).

6.1.3 celsioribus 'pretty high': 5.20.6n.   **puluinari** 'shrine'; the word was corrupted to *puluinaribus* under the influence of *celsioribus*. For this sense of *puluinar* (not noticed by *OLD*) cf. Augustus, *Res gestae* 2.19.4.4 (ναόν in the Greek version), Serv. on Virg. *G.* 3.532 *puluinaria pro templis ponimus, cum sint proprie lectuli, qui sterni in templis plerisque consuerunt* (sc. to display images of the gods).   **in corona:** the *spicea corona* was Ceres' symbol: Hor. *C.S.* 29–30, Tib. 1.1.15–16, Ov. *Met.* 2.28 and Bömer *ad loc.*   **et spicas hordei uidet:** for the repetition of *uidet* cf. 5.1.2, though the parallel is not exact, any more than with those cited by Augello (1977) 137; the whole phrase has the air of an afterthought. See crit. n.

6.1.4 cuncta passim iacentia etc.: Ov. *Met.* 11.35–6 *uacuosque iacent dispersa per agros | sarculaque rastrique graues longique ligones.*   **ut solet** 'as usual', impersonal: *OLD* s.v. 4.

6.1.5 discretim (*): *TLL* s.v. *discerno* 1308.57–71. For A.'s fondness for adverbs in -*im* see Reitzenstein 131–2, comparing him in this respect with Sisenna; and in *Cupid & Psyche* cf. e.g. 6.10.1 *aceruatim*,

5.4.6, 6.8.4 *certatim*, 4.30.4, 4.33.5, al. *confestim*, 5.6.7, 5.23.3 *efflictim*, 6.10.7 *granatim* (‡), 5.20.4 *paullulatim* (†), 6.10.6 *separatim*, 5.5.6 *ubertim*.

6.2.1 Ceres alma ∼ 11.2.1 (Lucius to Isis) *siue Ceres alma* ... The epithet traditionally attaches to Venus (4.30.1n.); Isis, 'who reveals herself to Lucius as *deorum dearumque facies uniformis*, includes among her aspects both Ceres and Juno (XI 5)' (Schlam (1976) 27). Cf. 6.4.1–3n.   **longum exclamat:** for the adverbial accusative of *longus* used of vociferation cf. Juv. 6.64–5 *longum* | ... *et miserabile gannit*, *OLD* s.v. *longum* 4, *TLL* s.v. *longus* 1643.62–72.   **ain ...?** = *aisne?* 'you don't say?', 'oh dear'.

6.2.2 tuum uestigium ... requirit ∼ 5.5.3 *tuum* ... *uestigium requirentes*.   **furens animi:** 4.32.4n.

6.2.3 pedes eius aduoluta: as Callirhoe embraces the feet of (the statue of) Aphrodite (Chariton 2.2.7); for her repeated prayers to the goddess cf. Molinié, Index s.v. Ἀφροδίτη. It is only now that Psyche learns it is Venus she has to propitiate. Cf. 11.24.7 (cit. 6.4.4n.).   **humumque uerrens etc.:** Livy 3.7.8 *stratae passim matres crinibus templa uerrentes ueniam irarum caelestium finemque pesti exposcunt* (see Ogilvie *ad loc.*), 26.9.7; Appel 203.   **multiiugis precibus:** this and her prayer to Juno are far too elaborate and learned for poor simple Psyche; this is Lucius–Apuleius speaking (cf. 6.4.1–3, 6.5.4nn., Introd. p. 33). *multiiugus* is a favourite word of A.'s: Hijmans al. 105.

6.2.4 per ego te etc.: 4.31.1n.   **per tacita secreta cistarum:** a reference to the festival of the Thesmophoria: Callim. *Hymn* 6 (Demeter).3 'As the holy basket returns you shall watch from the ground, you who are uninitiated'; 'the κάλαθος contains ritual objects, which the βέβαλοι are forbidden to see' (Hopkinson, ed. p. 42). Cf. 11.11.2 *cista secretorum capax penitus celans operta magnificae religionis* (sc. of Isis)   **famulorum ... curricula:** on Ceres' dragon-chariot see Frazer and Bömer on Ov. *F.* 4.497. The snake figured in the chthonic aspects of her cult.

6.2.5 glebae Siculae sulcamina: Sicily was the scene of the rape of Proserpine (see below) and proverbial for its fertility.   **sulcamina** (‡) ... **inluminarum** (‡) ... **demeacula** (‡) ... **remeacula** (‡): words evidently coined by A. to impart sonority and balance. The 'poetic' plurals add to the effect. Psyche does not explicitly compare her own wanderings to Ceres' in search of Proserpine, but *demeacula ... remeacula* foreshadow her own descent to and return from Hell. **currum rapacem et terram tenacem** 'the clasping car and the grasping ground' (Purser). The story of the rape of Ceres' daughter Proserpina (Persephone) by Dis (Hades, Pluto), her imprisonment in the Underworld, and her return to earth for part of the year is told at length in the Homeric Hymn to Demeter (2). However, it is Ovid's version (*Met.* 5.341–571) that A. has in mind, for in that Dis is shot by Cupid at Venus' instigation (365–84; cf. 4.33.2.7n.). Ceres indeed has good reason to be wary of offending this pair.   **cetera quae silentio tegit etc.:** cf. above, §4 *tacita secreta cistarum.* Only initiates were supposed to know what happened in the Eleusinian Mysteries. Their central feature was a scene of revelation, in which light (cf. *luminosarum ... inuentionum*) succeeded darkness (cf. *inluminarum ... nuptiarum*); see Richardson, ed. *Hom. Hymn Dem.* pp. 26–7.   **Psyches animae:** 5.6.5n.

6.2.6 patere ... delitescam: 5.6.4n.   **uires ... fessae ... leniantur** '(until) my fatigue ... is assuaged'; *uires fessae = fatigatio.* More straightforward Latin is yielded by *leuentur* (Rohde) or *leuigentur* (in A. only at 4.1.4 as a *v.l.*, but cf. *TLL* s.v. 2 *leuigo* 1199.41).

6.3.1–2 The language of Ceres' rebuff signals a deliberately bathetic descent to the level (once more) of bourgeois comedy. Venus is *bona femina*, a relative and crony who must not be offended. The idea that one god should not meddle in the province of another is enunciated as a law by Euripides' Artemis (*Hipp.* 1328–30); cf. Ov. *Met.* 3.336–7 *neque enim licet irrita cuiquam | facta dei fecisse deo,* 14.784–5 *rescindere numquam | dis licet acta deum, Am.* 1.1.5–12. Ceres and Juno (6.4.4–5) take a rather lower ground.   **foedus antiquum amicitiae:** with a metonymical glance at the proverbial association of food (and drink) with love: Ter. *Eun.* 732 *sine Cerere et Libero friget Venus,* cf. Pease on Cic. *N.D.* 2.60, Otto s.v. *Venus.*

6.3.2 fueris: For the usual *sis*; cf. 5.7.1n.   **optimi consule** 'take in good part', lit. 'regard as in the sphere of good', genitive of the rubric; cf. 8.9.7 *boni ergo et optimi consules,* H–S 71–2, *OLD* s.v. *consulo* 5. Cf. 1.5.1, 11.18.3 *aequi bonique facio* (*OLD* s.v. *aequus* 6b) and 4.30.4n.

6.3.3 subsitae (‡) 'placed below'; *subditae* (Salmasius) is paralleled by 4.35.4 *uallis subditae*. The details and the contrast with the siting of Ceres' temple reflect a preoccupation with the picturesque; cf. 6.1.2, 6.14.2–3nn., Pavlovskis 7 n. 22, Grimal (1969) 301–49, Leach 197–306. For the woodland setting cf. Virg. *Aen.* 1.441–9 (also a shrine to Juno), 7.172, Ov. *Met.* 10.686–8 *templa, deum matri quae quondam clarus Echion | fecerat ex uoto, nemorosis abdita* [n.b.] *siluis | transibant,* 11.359–60 and Bömer *ad loc. sublucidam* (*) may have been suggested by *sublucent* in Ovid's description of the epiphany of Corinna (*Am.* 1.5.3–6). Cf. also Plaut. *Rud.* 255 *uideo decorum dis locum uiderier.* **adire ... ueniam:** Lucret. 5.1229 *non diuum pacem uotis adit* and Costa *ad loc.*; the commentators on Lucretius quote only this passage as a parallel for the brachylogy *adire* (*deum/templum*: *OLD* s.v. *adeo*[1] 9) (*ut*) *pacem/ueniam* (*petas*). Cf. Plaut. *Rud.* 257 *quisquis est deu', ueneror ut nos ex hac aerumna eximat.*

6.3.4 lacinias ... suffixas: Ov. *Met.* 8.744–5 *uittae mediam* [*quercum*] *memoresque tabellae | sertaque cingebant, uoti argumenta potentum, F.* 3.267–8 *licia dependent longas uelantia saepes, | et posita est meritae multa tabella deae* (Bömer *ad locc.*). The use of strips of cloth (*OLD* s.v. *lacinia* 2a) as ex-votos is widespread: see e.g. Frazer II (edn 3, 1911) 16, 32, 42, Doughty I 497, Hogarth (1910) 112 = (1925) 198. Embroidered inscriptions, however, do not appear to be otherwise attested. **cum gratia facti** 'with thanks for her action'; cf. Virg. *Aen.* 4.539 *ueteris stat gratia facti,* 7.232, Ov. *Met.* 2.693–4 *neu gratia facto | nulla rependatur,* Manil. 2.618 *nec longa est gratia facti.* **genu nixa ... adprecatur:** Plaut. *Rud.* 694–5 *tibi auscultamus et, Venus alma, ambae te opsecramus, | aram amplexantes hanc tuam lacrumantes, genibus nixae* (cf. above, §3nn.); cf. Appel 208. **amplexans:** this was evidently the original reading of F; A. nowhere else uses *amplexor,* but cf. Plaut. *loc. cit.* (previous n.). **detersis ante lacrimis:** 11.24.7 (Lucius before praying to Isis) *prouolutus ... ante conspectum deae et facie mea diu detersis uestigiis eius, lacrimis obortis* etc.

6.4.1–3 The form of this prayer, with its list of alternatives, reflects actual usage: Callim. *Hymn* 5.60–5 and Bulloch *ad loc.*, Norden (1923) 144–6, Appel 75–8, 114–15. Psyche's appeal to Juno as goddess of childbirth (§3) is especially appropriate.

6.4.1 magni Iouis germana et coniuga (*): an epic-style formula: Virg. *Aen.* 10.607 *o germana mihi atque eadem gratissima coniunx*, 1.46–7 *quae diuum incedo regina Iouisque | et soror et coniunx*, Ov. *Met.* 3.265–6 *si sum regina Iouisque | et soror et coniunx* (Bömer *ad loc.*), 13.574; the model was Homer's κασιγνήτην ἄλοχόν τε (*Il.* 16.432, 18.356; *Hom. Hym.* 5.40, 12.3). **quae sola etc.:** cf. Paus. 7.4.4; the birthplaces of gods and heroes were often a subject of contention and rival claims. Cf. below, §2n. **celsae Carthaginis:** according to Virgil (*Aen.* 1.15–16) preferred by her to Samos. *Iuno Caelestis* was the Carthaginian Tanit, represented riding on a lion, in Roman guise: see Ov. *F.* 6.45–6 and Bömer *ad loc.*

6.4.2 iam: A. artfully associates the chronology of Juno's life – child, young girl, wife and mother – with the chief places of her cult. Argos also claimed to be her birthplace (Strabo 9.2.36); her shrine there, the Heraeum, was a major tourist attraction (Pausanias 2.17). **nuptam Tonantis:** Ov. *Met.* 2.466, *F.* 6.33 *matrona Tonantis*. The temple of Jupiter Tonans was dedicated by Augustus in 22 B.C. (Bömer on *F.* 2.69–70); Ovid appears to have introduced *Tonans* as a synonym for Jupiter to the poetic vocabulary. **reginam dearum:** this is a possible interpretation of the original reading of F (see crit. n.), and Ovid, whom A. may have had in mind here (cf. preceding n.), has Juno exclaim *cur igitur regina uocor princepsque dearum?* (*F.* 6.37). Her usual title as Jupiter's consort is *regina deorum* 'queen of heaven'.

6.4.3 oriens ... occidens: i.e. the whole world over, a traditional 'polar' formulation: cf. e.g. Hor. *C.* 4.15.14–16, Prop. 2.3.43–4, Ov. *Am.* 1.15.29, *A.A.* 3.537, *Met.* 1.338, 354, 2.190, 5.445, al. *F.* 5.557–8 (Bömer *ad loc.*), Sen. *Phaedr.* 285–6, al. **Zygiam (‡)** 'Yoker', a Greek rendering of her Latin title *Iuno Iuga/Iugalis*; cf. 4.33.4 *tibiae zygiae* and n. For the idea of marriage or love as a yoke cf. Hor. *C.* 1.33.10–12 *Veneri, cui placet impares | formas atque animos sub iuga aenea | saeuo mittere cum ioco* and N–H *ad loc.*; Pichon 177, Preston 41. There is no obvious reason for A.'s choice of the Greek word, except that he liked the sound of it. **Lucinam:** more usually identified with Diana, but Juno Lucina is mentioned by Varro, *L.L.* 5.49–50. **meis extremis casibus** ~ 1.2.4 (Lucius to Isis) *tu meis iam nunc extremis aerumnis subsiste.* **Sospita:** the title under which she was worshipped at Lanuvium in Latium, a specifically Roman reference.

in 'by', as at 2.2.5 *grauis in annis*; classical Latin would use *ab* or plain abl.: *TLL* s.v. 793.27–38, H–S 126, Callebat (1968) 224.   **quod sciam** 'to my knowledge': 5.13.1n.

6.4.4–5 Like Ceres (6.3.1–2n.) Juno replies prosaically to this highly-charged supplication: she must keep on the right side of her daughter-in-law, and in any case her hands are tied by the law. (For the possible bearing of this point on the dating of *Met.* see Walsh (1970) 250; *contra* Summers 379–82.) However, she refrains from turning Psyche in, as she had been asked to do (5.31.2).

6.4.4 nutum ... accommodare: i.e. *adnuere*, the word commonly used of favourable answers to prayer: *OLD* s.v. 3. Cf. Virg. *Aen.* 9.106, 10.115 (Jupiter) *adnuit et totum nutu tremefecit Olympum.*   **nurus meae:** Venus was married to her son Vulcan.   **praestare me** 'behave', 'act': *OLD* s.v. *praesto*[2] 7. If the text is correct, *me* does double duty as object of both *sinit* and *praestare* (amphibole: Bell 293–303). Critics supply *opem* (Cornelissen) or *praesidium* (van der Vliet) before *praestare* as its object.

6.4.5 legibus etc.: cf. 5.29.6n. She picks up Venus' words at 5.31.2 *illam fugitiuam uolaticam* (see n.).

6.5.1 Fortunae naufragio: Fortune is often represented with nautical attributes (N–H on Hor. *C.* 1.35.6).   **quiens:** present participle of *queo*, attested only in A. (N–W III 626; the references to Ovid are erroneous).

6.5.2 nec ... quidem: 5.5.5n.   **potuerunt:** in such causal relative clauses classical Latin prefers the subjunctive, but the 'rule' is not rigid: K–S II 292–3, Bennett I 137–8. A., for instance, uses the regular construction at 6.9.6 *inepta ego quae ... dicam*, the indicative at 6.20.6 *inepta ego ... quae nec tantillum quidem ... delibo.*

6.5.3 quorsum ... effugiam?: the classic plea of the abandoned heroine: Xen. *Eph.* 3.8.7, cf. 5.30.3n. *quorsum* (Mercier) seems a more apposite interpretation of the ambiguous reading of F than *quo rursum* (cf. Paratore 63).   **quin ... animum?** = 6.26.7, Lucius to himself almost immediately after the end of the story. Cf. also Catullus to himself, 76.11 *quin tu animo offirmas?*, Ovid's Iphis to herself, *Met.* 9.745 *quin animum firmas?*   **uel** 'even though'.

6.5.4 qui scis: for the indicative restored by Philomathes' correction cf. 6.1.2 *unde . . . scio?* The proper idiomatic sense of *qui scias?* is 'how can *one* know?'; in this context of Psyche's soliloquy a direct, not a generalizing question is called for. For *qui* = 'how' see *OLD* s.v. *qui²* 1a.   **principium ... meditabatur** 'started to rehearse her exordium'; cf. 6.2.3n.

6.6 On her earlier visit to Olympus Venus had not stood on the order of her going (5.29.1). She now makes a state entry. Formally the scene is a counterpart to the marine cortège at 4.31.4–7; it also conveys hints of the epiphany of Isis in Book xi (see below, §§3, 4nn.). Venus first resumes her Lucretian *persona* (4.30.1) only to shed it no less abruptly on completing her mission (§4, 6.7.3nn.).

6.6.1 inquisitionis: genitive of definition.   **abnuens** 'saying no to' (i.e. giving up), with dative (*TLL* s.v. 113.72–5), as analogy with *adnuo* suggests, rather than ablative (*OLD* s.v. 8).   **construi** 'to be prepared'; *construo* is sometimes used 'latiore sensu' (*TLL* s.v. 547.68–78), as at Catull. 64.304 *large multiplici constructae sunt dape mensae* (= *exstructae*), A. *Met.* 10.32.2 *Horae ... scitissimum construxerant chorum* (= *instruxerant*). Here, however, the literal sense 'put together' best fits the context. Both A. and Ovid (see below) recall the scene in the *Iliad* in which Hera and Athene harness a chariot to attack Ares; but whereas Ovid merely enumerates the components of the vehicle, A. describes its *assembly*, as in Homer it was assembled by Hebe (*Il.* 5.722–31). Purser rightly kept and defended *construi* against Oudendorp's *instrui*, but cited a less cogent Homeric parallel, the assembly of Priam's cart, a different kind of conveyance and a different context (*Il.* 24.266–74). That Homer preserved a memory of actual practice is shown by the Mycenaean palace records: see Ventris–Chadwick 361–75.   **quem ... Vulcanus ... poliuerat eqs.:** cf. Ovid's description of the chariot of the Sun, *Met.* 2.105–10 *ad altos | deducit iuuenem Vulcania munera currus. | aureus axis erat, temo aureus, aurea summae | curuatura rotae, radiorum argenteus ordo; | per iuga chrysolithi positaeque ex ordine gemmae | clara repercusso reddebant lumina Phoebo.* A.'s emphasis on the quality of the workmanship recalls Ovid's comment on the doors of the palace of the Sun, also made by Vulcan, *materiam superabat opus, Met.* 2.5.   **ipsius auri damno pretiosum:** Plin. *N.H.* 33.140 *interradimus alia* [sc. kinds of plate], *ut quam plurimum lima* *perdiderit.* In sense *ipsius* refers to *damno* (enallage: 4.29.2n.): 'la perte même de l'or' (Vallette).

6.6.2 columbae: doves were Venus' birds, favoured as lovers' gifts (Bömer on Ov. *Met.* 13.833). Cf. Ov. *Am.* 1.2.23 (to Cupid) *maternas iunge columbas*, *Met.* 14.597 (Venus) *perque leues auras iunctis inuecta columbis* etc. and Bömer *ad loc.*   **picta** 'nuancés' Vallette, in an attempt to save A.'s face, since we have just been told that they were white. The varying sheen of pigeons' plumage was frequently remarked; cf. 2.9.2 (*capillus*) *nunc coruina nigredine caerulus columbarum colli flosculos aemulatur.* However, scrutiny of the pair of white doves currently (1988) frequenting Peterhouse justifies the suspicion that A. is being careless.   **iugum gemmeum:** Ov. *Met.* 2.109 (cit. above, §1n.).

6.6.3 lasciuiunt passeres: sparrows were traditionally accounted lecherous: Plin. *N.H.* 10.107 *columbae et turtures octonis annis uiuunt, contra passeri minimum uitae, cui salacitas par*; cf. 10.22.3 (cit. 5.13.5n.), Plaut. *Cas.* 138 *meu' pullus passer, mea columba, mi lepus.* In Sappho's famous ode it is they who draw Aphrodite's car, fr. 1.9–12 L–P, and at Xen. *Eph.* 1.8.2 they are ridden by Erotes. In art it is usually the Erotes (Cupids) who draw her: *LIMC* ɪɪ 1.117–18 (Aphrodite 1189–1208), ɪɪɪ 1.918 (Eros 805–7), 1026 (Amor/Cupido) 597–8. Cf. 4.31.4–7n. **suaue ... pronuntiant** ~ 11.7.4 ... *ut canorae etiam auiculae prolectatae uerno uapore concentus suaues adsonarent* (the prelude to the procession of Isis). Here the detail also picks up and varies the fanfares of the Tritons at 4.31.6–7 (see n.). On *suaue* adverbial see 5.1.1n.

6.6.4 cedunt nubes et Caelus filiae panditur etc.: Lucret. 1.6–7 *te, dea, te fugiunt uenti, te nubila caeli | aduentumque tuum.* The word *cedunt* = both 'make way for' (i.e. *decedunt*) and 'part' (i.e. *discedunt*); the use of the simple for the compound verb is a hallmark of high poetic style (H–S 298–300). There is here another hint (4.28.4n.) of the story of Venus' birth from the sea fertilized by the severed genitals of Uranus (οὐρανός = *caelum*); this was the version canonized by Hesiod (*Theog.* 188–200); cf. Cic. *N.D.* 3.59 and Pease *ad loc.* Cf. 10.31.2 (*deae*) *corpus candidum, quod caelo demeat, amictus caerulus, quod mari remeat.* A. must have written *Caelus*, the old Latin form: cf. Enn. *Ann.* 23–4 Skutsch *Saturno | quem Caelus genuit* and Skutsch *ad loc.* After the neuter became the accepted literary usage the *lèse-majesté* of referring to a god in that gender (Serv. on Virg. *Aen.* 5.801) was generally avoided by the use of the oblique cases: *TLL Onom.* II s.v. *Caelus*. Cf. 6.7.3n. **Aether:** father of Caelus: Cic. *N.D.* 3.44 and Pease *ad loc.*   **nec obuias ... canora familia:** Lucret. 1.12–13 *aeriae primum uolucres te, diua, tuumque | significant initum perculsae corda tua ui,* and cf. 11.7.4 (cit. above, §3n.). This is an appropriate conclusion to the portrayal of the 'Lucretian' Venus; Bintz's transposition ('fort. recte' Robertson) is obtuse.

6.7.1 dei uocalis: he was the herald of the gods, now to be impressed as town-crier.   **necessariam** 'essential', but perhaps also 'brotherly': *OLD* s.v. 6.

6.7.2 nec rennuit Iouis caerulum supercilium: an almost literal rendering of Hom. *Il.* 1.528 ἦ καὶ κυανέηισιν ἐπ᾽ ὀφρύσι νεῦσε Κρονίων 'the son of Kronos spoke and nodded with dark [lit. dark-blue] eyebrows'. Appeals to Jupiter (Zeus) are a stock feature of Homeric and Virgilian epic; here we think of Venus' outbursts at *Aen.* 1.229–53 and 10.17–62, but her demand turns out to be amusingly modest.   **caelo demeat:** 'comes back to earth' but also 'descends from Uranus'; the ambiguity slily signals her transformation from Venus (I) Caelestis (Urania) back to Venus (II) Vulgaris (Pandemos); cf. Kenney (1990) 192 and next n., 10.31.2 (cit. 6.6.4n.). A. shares a liking for *demeo* ((*) but cf. Fronto, *Epp.* p. 66.12 Naber) with Martianus Capella (*TLL* s.v.). He wastes no time on the return trip; cf. below, §5 fin.

6.7.3 frater Arcadi: Mercury was born on Mt Cyllene in Arcadia. Venus' greeting presupposes another (and more producible) genealogy in which she is daughter of Zeus (Jupiter) and Dione: Hom. *Il.* 5.370–1, Cic. *N.D.* 3.59 and Pease *ad loc.* On leaving Olympus she drops her Lucretian *persona* to become a (literary) Olympian. A. adroitly juggles (preceding n.) with the two Aphrodites distinguished by Pausanias in Plato's *Symposium*: 'Of course there are two goddesses. One, the elder, is the motherless daughter of Uranus, whom we call Heavenly (Οὐρανίαν); the younger is the child of Zeus and Dione, whom we call Vulgar (Πάνδημον)', *Symp.* 180d; cf. Dover *ad loc.* See Introd. pp. 19–20.   **scis ... fecisse:** 'Mercurius quippe

dolis et furtis praeest, sine quibus vix geruntur Veneris negotia'
(Floridus). As Ovid had emphasized, a lover must cultivate the gift of
the gab (*A.A.* 1.459–69), and Mercury was an accomplished liar as
well as a thief (N–H on Hor. *C.* 1.10.7). For his association with
Venus see Hor. *C.* 1.30.8 and N–H *ad loc.*   **ancillam:** 5.31.2n.

6.7.4 fac ... matures: 5.6.4n.   **qui** 'whereby' (*OLD* s.v. *qui*² 3);
for its use after a plural antecedent see Munro on Lucret. 5.233,
H–S 557, Callebat (1968) 493. Cf. 6.5.4 *qui scis ...?*   **ignorantiae:**
not in general a valid defence in Roman law, but exceptions might be
allowed: Berger s.v. *Ignorantia iuris.*

6.7.5 haec: Price's correction (301) restores an Apuleian formula:
2.17.4, 2.24.8; cf. 2.8.1 *haec dicens.*   **libellum** 'placard', 'handbill':
OLD s.v. 4.   **continebatur:** 5.26.7n.   **facessit:** Scioppius' correction of F's *secessit* is required by Apuleian usage. All Venus' actions
have been described in the historic present, and A. normally uses the
present for such exits (Paratore 63); cf. 5.31.7 *pelago uiam capessit,*
6.11.2 *cubitum facessit.*

Act IV Psyche patiens

6.8.1 per omnium ora populorum ~ 5.28.4 *per cunctorum ora
populorum*; the god and the message are identified, cf. *OLD* s.v. *os* 3d.
A. is playing both on the (Stoic) identification of Mercury (Hermes)
with the divine logos and on etymological speculation: *Mercurius quasi
medius currens dicitur appellatus, quod sermo currat inter homines medius*
(Varro, *Antiqu. rer. diu.* fr. 250 Cardauns). See Marangoni 58–60.

6.8.2–3 Mercury's proclamation recalls and is evidently modelled
on Mosch. 1.1–5 'Cypris was calling loudly after her son Eros:
"Whoever has seen Eros at large in the street, he is my runaway.
There will be a reward for any informer: a kiss from Cypris. And if
you bring him back, no mere kiss [lit. no naked kiss] but something
more awaits you".' For the town-crier motif cf. also Meleager, *A.P.*
5.177 (*HE* 4190–9).

6.8.2 si quis ... poterit: Petron. 97.2 (a proclamation by a *praeco*) *si
quis eum reddere aut commonstrare uoluerit, accipiet nummos mille.*   **retro
metas Murtias:** the shrine of the goddess Murcia was incorporated in

the Circus Maximus, which was a well-known haunt of prostitutes. A. was evidently aware of the tradition connecting her with *Venus Murtea* (*myrtea*): Varro, *L.L.* 5.154, Plin. *N.H.* 15.121, Ogilvie on Livy 1.33.5. *retro* (*) as a preposition.   **praedicatorem** 'crier', cf. §1 *praedicationis*; here first for the usual *praeco*; *TLL* s.v. *praedicator* 549.3–9. Cf. 2.21.5 *praedicabat, si qui mortuum seruare uellet, de pretio liceretur.*

6.8.3 accepturus '(in which case) he will receive'; a free use of the future participle on the Greek model which became common from the Augustan period onwards: Westman 13–14. Cf. 4.30.2n. **indiciuae nomine** 'by way of reward'; *OLD* s.v. *nomen* 24. *indiciua* is a rare word, usually corrupted in MSS; for the spelling see *TLL* s.v., Haupt III 443–4.   **septem sauia suauia etc.:** Ov. *Am.* 2.5.23–4 *improba tum uero iungentes oscula uidi* | (*illa mihi lingua nexa fuisse liquet*), 57–8 *tota labellis* | *lingua tua est nostris, nostra recepta tuis,* 3.7.9 *osculaque inseruit cupida luctantia lingua,* Ach. Tat. 2.37.8. This reduces Venus to the level of Photis: 2.10.5 *iam patentis oris inhalatu cinnameo et occursantis linguae inlisu nectareo* etc. (cf. ibid. §1 *mellitissimum ... sauium*). Cf. 5.31.6, 6.7.3nn. It may be significant that the number seven is also that of Lucius' ritual immersions before his invocation of Isis, *quod eum numerum praecipue religionibus aptissimum diuinus ille Pythagoras prodidit* (11.1.4), Isis who is also Venus Caelestis (cf. Bernhard 118). **longe:** 5.11.3n.

6.8.4 Psyches: 5.6.9n.

6.8.5 Psyche gives herself up. 'Ce point de rencontre est le véritable centre de gravité des *Métamorphoses*, il constitue le moment du passage entre le malheur et la rédemption, car l'acceptation de la catharsis ouvre le chemin du salut ... jusqu'à cet instant précis, le conte n'avait qu'une valeur récapitulative par rapport a l'histoire de Lucius; à partir de maintenant, il va prendre un sens préfiguratif' (Fry 154 n. 59, 155); cf. Introd. p. 15. This is well observed; but it is Venus II, not Venus–Isis, who prescribes Psyche's ordeals – another loose end in the allegory (Kenney (1990) 187, 178).   **fores ... dominae:** where is this house of Venus? Evidently within easy reach of Taenarum; for the geographical problems of the story see 5.24.1, 5.26–27nn.   **famulitione:** *famulitio* (†) is attested only here and at 2.2.3, whereas *famulitium* (*) occurs both elsewhere in A. and fairly commonly in other authors (*TLL* s.vv.). Roaldus's correction may therefore well be right, but it is hazardous to seek to confine A.'s exuberance.   **Consuetudo:** on these personified abstractions cf. 5.30.3, 6.9.2nn. For the role of habit in love cf. 5.9.6 *procedente consue-tudine et adfectione roborata*, 8.2.7 *quidni, cum flamma saeui Amoris parua quidem primo uapore delectet, sed fomentis consuetudinis exaestuans immodicis ardoribus amburat homines?*, Lucret. 4.1283 *consuetudo concinnat amorem*, Ov. *A.A.* 2.345 *fac tibi consuescat: nil adsuetudine maius*, Rem. 503 *intrat amor mentes usu, dediscitur usu*, Chariton 5.9.9, Ach. Tat. 1.9.5 'the quickest way to win her is always to be with her'. The word can in fact = 'love', 'intercourse', 'marriage': *OLD* s.v. 5b, *TLL* s.v. 561.46–75; cf. 5.4.5n. Here, however, her function appears to be to accustom Psyche to the *pains* of love; cf. below, §7.

6.8.6 pro 'as one might expect from': *OLD* s.v. *pro*[1] 16b.

6.8.7 sed bene, quod ... = 3.25.3, 10.14.7; cf. Ov. *A.A.* 1.141 *et bene, quod* ... (see Hollis *ad loc.*), 2.605 *o bene, quod* ...; *TLL* s.v. *bonus* 2122.84–2123.5.   **meas ... manus incidisti:** *in meas* would be an easy correction (5.30.6n.), but *incido* is not uncommon as a transitive verb; in A. in the same sense as here at 2.13.2, 2.14.1 (*TLL* s.v. 1 *incido* 905.67–906.26, Callebat (1968) 184). Cf. 6.14.3n.   **inter Orci cancros ... haesisti:** i.e. you are as good as dead already; cf. 3.9.8 *iam in peculio Proserpinae et Orci familia numeratus*. The word *cancros* however is puzzling. If Orcus can have jaws (7.7.4 *mediis Orci faucibus ... euasi*) and hands (7.24.1 *mediis Orci manibus extractus*), there is no reason why he should not have claws; but *cancer*, though it is once glossed *forceps*, nowhere else has that meaning. However, the parallel-ism *manus incidisti* ~ *inter cancros haesisti* suggests that this, rather than the tame 'barriers' (*OLD* s.v. *cancer*[2]) is the sense. Obviously Consuetudo wants to make Psyche's flesh creep.   **datura:** 4.30.2n.

6.9.1 latissimum: 10.16.1 *risu ... latissimo*. F's *laetissimum* is far too restrained for Venus in her present mood. As her stock epithet in Homer is φιλομμειδής 'laughter-loving' (but cf. Hes. *Theog.* 200 and West, ed. p. 88), the phrase is clearly ironical. Cf. 6.13.2 *subridens amarum*. Devotees of E. F. Benson will remember his Miss Mapp, who was at her most formidable when her smile was widest. However, this is not one of the classic symptoms as listed by e.g. Ov. *A.A.* 3.503–4, Sen. *De ira* 2.35.3–6.   **furenter:** the phrase *furenter irasci* is used by Cicero (*Att.* 6.1.12), but the word is excessively rare, and F's *frequenter*

should not be dismissed out of hand as too banal to be what A. wrote
(Paratore 65–6).   **ascalpens (‡) aurem:** 'The gesture of nervous
irritability' (Purser); cf. Heliod. 2.8.1, where Chariclea prefaces a
sarcastic question by 'scratching her cheek under the ear.'

6.9.2 interuisere: infinitive of purpose; it is not infrequent, usually
after a verb of motion, in old and colloquial Latin, relatively rare in
classical poetry, increasingly common in post-classical prose: Bennett
1 418–19, H–S 344–5.   **Sollicitudo atque Tristities:** the tri-
bulations of the lover have always been proverbial: e.g. Plaut. *Merc.*
24–31 *sed amori accedunt etiam haec quae dixi minus:* | *insomnia aerumna error
terror et fuga* etc. (cf. Preston 11), Lucret. 4.1141–4, Ov. *Her.* 1.12 *res
est solliciti plena timoris amor*; cf. 4.33.1.4n., Lier 17–18, 22–3. Here,
however, in the context of punishment and expiation, these grim
personifications are more reminiscent of the symbolic figures who
camp on the doorstep of Virgil's Hell: *Aen.* 6.273–4 *uestibulum ante
ipsum primisque in faucibus Orci* [cf. 6.8.7n.] | *Luctus et ultrices posuere
cubilia Curae* etc., cf. Ov. *Met.* 4.484–5. Cf. 10.24.1 *saeua Riualitas.* Cf.
also the sufferings of heroines in the Greek romances, e.g. Leucippe
(Ach. Tat. 5.17.3–7): Hoevels 185 n. 118. For the theme of the
tormented Psyche in art cf. Schlam (1976) 14–15, 33.

6.9.3 flagellis afflictam: for whipping as part of the ritual of
initiation into mystery cults see Burkert 96, 102, 104 and the famous
wall-painting in the Villa of the Mysteries at Pompeii (cf. Jeanmaire
35–48 = 318–33).

6.9.4 Venus' indignation is fuelled by Psyche's pregnancy as is
Juno's by those of Callisto and Semele: Ov. *Met.* 2.471–2 *'scilicet*
[n.b.] *hoc etiam restabat, adultera' dixit* | *'ut fecunda fores'*, 3.268 *'concipit! id
deerat.'*   **commouet** 'seeks to move', conative present: Blase 112,
H–S 316, Bömer on Ov. *Met.* 5.77, 10.187–8.   **praeclara ...
faciat:** Virg. *Aen.* 1.75 *pulchra faciat te prole parentem.*

6.9.5 uilis ancillae: 5.31.2n. In the eyes of the world Psyche is a
king's daughter. Cf. Tac. *Ann.* 13.13.1 *Agrippina ... nurum ancillam ...
muliebriter fremere.*   **audiet** = *uocabitur*: 5.16.4n.

6.9.6 quanquam 'but': *OLD* s.v. 3c.   **inepta ego quae ...** ~
6.20.6, Cic. *Att.* 4.15.6 *ego ineptus qui scripserim*; cf. *TLL* s.v. *ineptus*

1301.34–9.   **impares enim nuptiae etc.:** more contemporary legalism. She takes a proper bourgeois exception to informalities which, though not actually illegal, might in certain circumstances invalidate a marriage. There may well be a sarcastic allusion to the charges brought against A. himself in respect of his own marriage *in uilla* to Pudentilla: *Apol.* 67, 88 (pp. 75.26–76, 1.97.9–16 Helm) and Butler–Owen *ad locc*. Venus' feeling that a country wedding was a dubious hugger-mugger affair is shared by Chaereas, the hero of Chariton's novel (3.2.7–8). Jupiter is made to pick up these words at 6.23.4.   **patre non consentiente:** if Cupid was indeed *ingenuus et inuestis* in the technical sense (5.28.7n.), this was a real objection. As his parentage was notoriously a matter of debate (5.29.6n.) we may suspect an authorial joke at Venus' expense.   **perferre** 'carry to term', a sense from the language of farming: *OLD* s.v. 4.

6.10.1 his editis etc.: Ov. *Met.* 2.476–7 (Juno and Callisto) *dixit et aduersam prensis a fronte capillis* | *strauit humi pronam*. Venus behaves exactly like the kind of Roman mistress described unflatteringly by Ovid (*A.A.* 3.239–42), Juvenal (6.487–93) and Martial (2.66). **grumulum:** only here and at Plin. *N.H.* 19.112; like *grumus* a non-literary word (Kenney on *Moret.* 46).

6.10.2 enim 'Now!', explaining both what she has just done and what she is going to say next.   **sedulo ministerio ... promereri** ~ 5.25.6 *blandis obsequiis promerere*.

6.10.3 passiuam (*) 'random', from *passus* (*pando*); common after A. in ecclesiastical Latin.   **approbato mihi** 'offer for my approval', 'show up': *TLL* s.v. 313.3–37.

6.10.4 tantorum = *tot*: *OLD* s.v. 5; cf. 5.9.5n.   **silens obstupescit:** Virg. *Aen.* 11.120 *illi obstipuere silentes*.

6.10.5 formicula: (*), but cf. *TLL* s.v. *formica* 1091.22–3; not uncommon in later ecclesiastical Latin.   **illa:** 5.7.1n.   **certa** 'knowing', 'understanding'; cf. 4.12.5 *iam certus erroris*, 9.18.2 *certus ... fragilitatis humanae fidei*, *OLD* s.v. 12.   **contubernalis magni dei:** cf. below, §6 *Amoris uxori ... periclitanti*. This is the first overt hint (cf. 5.25.4n.) that the power of Cupid is somehow behind the help received by Psyche. Cf. 6.12.1, 6.15.2 and Venus' reactions at 6.11.2, 6.13.3.

6.10.6 Terrae omniparentis ... alumnae: Virg. *Aen.* 6.595 *Terrae omniparentis alumnum.* The idea of the intervention of the ants may well have been suggested to A. by the famous simile at *Aen.* 4.402–7.

6.10.7 sepedum (‡) 'six-footed'. **populorum:** 4.29.4n. **undae:** in addition to the passages cited at *OLD* s.v. 5 cf. the graphic simile at Virg. *Aen.* 2.496–9. **singulae granatim** (‡) **... digerunt** ~ §3 *singulis ... granis rite dispositis.*

6.11.1 fraglans balsama: cf. 2.8.6 *cinnama fraglans et balsama rorans.* For the use of perfume at weddings cf. Hunter on Eubulus 100, 102. For the cognate accusatives cf. 5.31.1n.; for such accusatives with *olere* et sim. see Müller 45–6, 82. On the spelling of *fraglo* see 4.31.3n. **rosis:** the rose was, then as now, associated with love and pleasure: N–H on Hor. *C.* 1.5.1, Ach. Tat. 2.1.3 Ἀφροδίτην προξενεῖ 'Aphrodite's go-between'. In *Met.* it is bound up with the fate of Lucius, who needed to eat roses to regain his human shape.

6.11.3 Enforced separation is a recurrent, indeed a fundamental, theme in Greek and Latin love-poetry and in one way or another the leitmotiv of the Greek novels: Preston 25–6, Copley *passim.* When the separated lovers are beneath the same roof the situation is especially piquant: Ov. *Her.* 16.213–18, Chariton 5.2.4, 6.2.11, Longus 3.9.5, Ach. Tat. 4.1. A. introduces the theme very casually, not really exploiting the paradox that Psyche's hope of finding Cupid in his mother's house (6.5.4, cf. 6.9.2) is realized in this frustrating way. If there is a hint of the theme of enforced chastity as a requirement of religious initiation (Walsh (1970) 213 n. 3), it likewise is not exploited. **unici** gives good sense, accentuating the severity of his confinement, and the word contributes its mite to the strongly emphatic alliteration of *c* in the sentence. Of the emendations proposed, Heinsius' *inuii* is the best; cf. his escape through the window at 6.21.2. **sua cupita** 'his inamorata'; cf. 3.21.1 *ad suum cupitum*, 9.18.3 *ni ... cupito potiatur* (*cupita* Price), *Schol. Ter.* p. 112.19 Schlee *Omphalae cupitae suae.* For the neuter plural = 'one's desire' cf. 5.6.4 *cupitis* and n.

6.11.4 Aurora commodum inequitante: cf. 3.1.1 *commodum ... Aurora ... caelum inequitabat*, which led Wernicke to add *caelum* here before *inequitante.* A variation on an epic cliché (cf. 5.5.1n.): Kenney on *Moret.* 1–2, Pease and Austin on Virg. *Aen.* 4.6–7. For others cf.

e.g. 2.1.1, 7.1.1, 9.22.5 (Bernhard 215–16, Westerbrink 65–6);
Heliodorus' *Aethiopica* opens with just such an elegant periphrasis.
fluuio praeterluenti (‡) ripisque longis 'along the banks of the
river that washes them as it passes', a striking example of hendiadys
(4.33.2.8n.). *praeterluo* is otherwise found only in Glossaries, and the
sense 'wash in passing' is perhaps strained, hence the easy correction
praeterfluenti (Colvius). *longis* means 'the length of', 'all along'; this
predicative sense is more familiar with *latus*, as at e.g. Virg. *G.* 4.522
latos . . . per agros 'far and wide over the countryside'.

6.11.5–6 Psyche's second trial seems to have been suggested to A.
by his reading in epic. The golden wool recalls the Golden Fleece
retrieved by the Argonauts, and the monstrous sheep with their
poisonous bites (6.12.3) may owe something to its dragon guardian,
uncis | dentibus horrendus, Ov. *Met.* 7.150–1. (It is at least an interesting
coincidence that in Apollonius the dragon's roar was re-echoed by
'the long banks of the river and the vast wood', ἀμφὶ δὲ μακραί |
ἠιόνες ποταμοῖο καὶ ἄσπετον ἴαχεν ἄλσος, A.R. 4.129–30 ∼ §4; cf.
also the sleepless serpents in the next trial, 6.14.4.) However, the
closest analogy for the episode is to be found in the scene in the
Odyssey in which Menelaus captures Proteus as advised by Idothea
(4.363ff.) and in Virgil's adaptation in the story of Aristaeus in the
Georgics (4.387ff.):

    (*a*) In each case the hero/heroine is at his/her wits' end.

    (*b*) Saving counsel comes (in Psyche's case indirectly) from a
divine source.

    (*c*) The stratagem recommended is to lie in ambush while a flock
composes itself to rest in or after the heat of midday.

See also 6.12.3n.

6.11.5 frutices: van der Vliet's correction (after Lütjohann) of F's
gurgites is the minimum change necessary to restore sense, but many
other improvements to the text have been suggested (Capponi
610–11), and what A. actually wrote remains uncertain. See next n.
auri uero decore: Robertson's plausible correction; again, what A.
actually wrote we cannot tell.   **florentes:** 5.12.1n.

6.11.6 afferas censeo 'I recommend you to bring', a surprisingly
urbane phrase in the mouth of Venus, but Eng. 'suggest' can carry a
similarly threatening nuance. For the omission of *ut* see 5.6.4n.

6.12.1 non ... illa 'not indeed'; for this emphatic use of *ille* cf. e.g. Virg. *Aen.* 9.478–80 *agmina cursu | prima petit, non illa uirum, non illa pericli | telorumque memor*, Austin on *Aen.* 1.3, 6.593, *OLD* s.v. 17c, *TLL* s.v. 352.14–15, 353.24–38.   **non ... functura sed ... habitura** 'not as expecting to perform, but meaning to die': 6.8.3n. Her third attempt at suicide (5.25.2n.).   **praecipitio fluuialis rupis** (lit.) 'by a leap of the river-rock', i.e. from a rock on the bank, a use of the genitive difficult to parallel precisely but essentially possessive: the leap belongs to the rock, is the rock's.   **musicae suauis nutricula:** the story of the invention of the panpipes is told by Ovid (*Met.* 1.689–712), Achilles Tatius (8.6.7–10) and Longus (2.34). **diuinitus inspirata:** sc. by Cupid: 6.10.5n.   **uaticinatur:** a rare word in poetry (not in Virg. or Hor.) but a favourite of Ovid's. It may be pure chance that two rather mannered hexameter endings can be heard in *dīuīnĭtŭs īnspīrātă* (spondeiazon) and *sīc uātĭcĭnātŭr hărūndō*. **harundo uiridis:** this talkative reed may have been suggested to A. by the story of Midas at Ov. *Met.* 11.190–3 (cf. Helm (1914) 203 = 224); cf. *leni crepitu dulcis aurae* ∼ 192 *leni ... motus ab austro*. The only reference to the story outside Ovid is at Dioscorides, *A.P.* 5.56.7–8 (*HE* 1469–70). However, the connexion with Pan (see above) may also be significant (Hoevels 189–90).

6.12.2 neque ... polluas nec ... feras: 5.5.3n.   **istud horae** 'at this moment': cf. 1.15.5 *illud horae* and 5.29.3n.

6.12.3 fraglantia: 4.31.3n.   **efferari:** Colvius' correction suits these ovine monsters better than F's colourless *efferri* 'are carried away'; cf. Petron. 94.9 *in rabiem efferatus*. The word is rare: 5.1.4n. **non nunquam** 'often'; the double negative commonly intensifies. **uenenatis morsibus:** a reference to rabies? The same words are used at 9.2.3 of a rabid dog; and cf. *truci rabie*, Plin. *N.H.* 8.152 *rabies canum sirio ardente homini pestifera*. The idea of these savage sheep may have been suggested to A. by the man-eating mares of Diomedes, the object of Hercules' eighth Labour (Apollod. 2.5.8) and later referred to by Lucius (7.16.5); but no direct parallel is forthcoming.

6.12.4 sed dum meridies etc.: Hom. *Od.* 4.400–1 'When the sun has reached mid-heaven, then the old man of the sea emerges from the water ...', Virg. *G.* 4.401–2 *... medios cum sol accenderit aestus, |*

cum sitiunt herbae et pecori iam gratior umbra est . . . ; see 6.11.5–6n. Flocks normally rested in the midday heat: Varro, *R.R.* 2.2.11, Virg. *G.* 3.327–30.   **spiritus fluuialis:** Hom. *Od.* 5.469 αὔρη δ' ἐκ ποταμοῦ ψυχρὴ πνέει ἠῶθι πρό 'the breeze blows cold off the river early in the morning', Calp. Sic. 4.4 *leuat . . . diem uicini spiritus amnis* (cf. Korzeniewski *ad loc.*).   **abscondere:** intransitive as at 8.5.1 (v.l. *abscondimur*) and in the Vulgate, Ps. 55.7 (< Greek κατακρύψουσιν): *TLL* s.v. 157.64–9, LSJ s.v. κατακρύπτω II. But cf. Paratore 71–2, arguing for *latenter ⟨te⟩ abscondere* (ς).

6.12.5 cum primum . . . laxauerint oues animum: cf. 8.15.8 *cum et ipso lumine dirarum bestiarum* [wolves] *repigratur impetus . . .* **furia:** in the sense of 'passion' the singular is found in literature only here, at 10.24.5 and at *A.L.* 294.5 Riese² = 289.5 S–B: *TLL* s.v. 1616.73–1617.14.

6.13.1 simplex: the reed's laudable frankness contrasts with Psyche's (culpable) *simplicitas.*   **suam:** Psyche's; *suus* need not refer to the subject of the sentence: K–S 1 600–2, H–S 175.   **nec . . . paenitendo . . . indiligenter . . . cessauit:** *nec* modifies all three words, which are all explicitly or implicitly negative: Psyche had no reason to repent of listening to the reed's advice, did not neglect it, and lost no time in following it (cf. 6.12.3 *non nunquam* and n.). The translator is forced to paraphrase. The text yielded by Robertson's *indiligenter* seems marginally more satisfactory than with Petschenig's *impaenitendo*, though this is an Apuleian word (11.28.4; otherwise unattested in Pagan Latin).   **auscultatu:** (*).   **cessauit . . . reportat:** 5.2.1n.   **furatrina:** (*).   **auri mollitie** 'soft gold'; cf. Lucret. 1.492 *rigor auri* and Munro and Bailey *ad loc.*, Virg. *G.* 1.143 *ferri rigor.* For A.'s use of qualifying genitive for adjective cf. Bernhard 97.

6.13.2 secundi . . . secundum 'But the danger in this her second task did not . . . second Psyche's hopes' (Purser); cf. 5.31.6n. **subridens amarum:** Amm. 21.9.8 *cui amarum Iulianus subridens . . .* (cf. *TLL* s.v. *amarus* 1823.37–41), 6.16.2 *renidens exitiabile,* 10.32.1 *Venus . . . dulce subridens,* Hor. *C.* 3.27.67 *perfidum ridens Venus;* 5.1.1n. **inquit:** either *incipit* (Stoll; cf. 5.26.2) or *infit* (Robertson; cf. 5.5.1n.) would give more usual Latin: cf. *TLL* s.v. *inquam* 1795.80–1.

6.13.3 nec: sc. on this occasion either; with *huius quoque* following the
connective is strictly speaking superfluous. *nec* cannot here = *ne ...
quidem*, as suggested by Grimal. **auctor adulterinus:** an
ambiguous and ironical reference to Cupid's machinations behind the
scenes (6.10.5n.). Venus' words can mean both (i) 'I know who is the
licentious agent behind this deed too' (so *OLD* s.v. *adulterinus* 3a),
recalling her unflattering characterization at 5.29.3, 5.30.3; and (ii)
'It does not escape me (that) the doer of this deed too is not the real
one' (a Graecism = οὐ λανθάνει με νόθος ὢν ὁ δράσας?), with
adulterinus used in its commoner sense of 'false', 'spurious' (so *TLL* s.v.
882.13–14).

6.13.4 Stygias ... paludes et ... Cocyti fluenta: this recalls Virgil's
Cocyti stagna alta uides Stygiamque paludem and *rauca fluenta*, *Aen.* 6.323,
327; cf. 2.29.3 *me post Lethaea pocula iam Stygiis paludibus innatantem.*
A's *mise-en-scène*, however, is clearly inspired by the traditional
identification of the infernal Styx (4.33.2.8n.) with the Arcadian river
of that name: Paus. 8.17.6 'Not far from these ruins [of Nonacris] is a
high crag: I have never seen a rock face so high; the water falls sheer
down it, and this is the stream that the Greeks call Styx' (tr. Levi; cf.
West on Hes. *Theog.* 778–9). On Arcadian features in the landscape
of Psyche's wanderings and adventures see Herrmann 18–21.

6.13.5 de summi fontis penita scaturrigine ... defer urnula:
Hes. *Theog.* 782–7 (When any of the gods is suspected of lying) 'then
Zeus sends Iris to bring back from afar in a golden pitcher the great
oath of the gods, (that is) the famous cold water which flows down the
steep and lofty rock'. It is not clear what Venus wants with a lie-
detector (for the dire consequences of perjury by Styx see Hes. *Theog.*
793–804 and West *ad loc.*); there may be an ironical allusion to the
proverbial worthlessness of lover's oaths (Lier 47–51). The idea that
in the 'original Psyche-story it was ... the water of the fountain of
life' that she was sent to fetch (Rohde (1898) 390 n. 1 = (1925) 575
n. 151; cf. Hoevels 191), developed elaborately by Bieler 336–46, is
refuted by Wright (J. R. G.) 282–4; cf. Fehling 20 and n. 41. Cf.
Introd. pp. 18, 25. **hauritum** = *haustum*: the form is peculiar to A.
(also at 2.15.6, 3.24.2). **crustallo dedolatum uasculum:** 'Iris is
sent out with a jug, just as a Greek girl would be sent for water ...
Because these are gods, the jug is of gold' (West on Hes. *Theog.* 784,

cit. above). A.'s choice of crystal reflects contemporary Roman fashion: 2.19.2 *hic uitrum fabre sigillatum, ibi crustallum inpunctum* etc., *OLD* s.vv. *crystallinum, crystallinus, crystallum.*

6.14.1 illa studiose gradum celerans: Virg. *Aen.* 4.641 *illa gradum studio celerabat anili.* Some of Virgil's MSS offer and some editors print *celebrabat,* and here the first hand of F may have read *celebrans* before correction (see critical n.). *celebro* = 'move rapidly' cannot be convincingly paralleled, but A. may have read *celebrabat* in his copy of the *Aeneid* and imitated what he took to be a Virgilian usage. Cf. however 2.6.4 *celero uestigium.* **tumulum:** a necessary correction of F's *cumulum,* which is nowhere else used literally = 'summit'. **certe uel illic inuentura …** 'sure to find there at least …'; Beroaldus' correction restores a characteristic use of the future participle (6.8.3n.). *uel* 'at least', 'if only': *OLD* s.v. 6. Her fourth suicide-attempt/intention (5.25.2n.). **appulit** 'came to'; the nearest parallel to this use of *appello* of travel by land and with a direct object cited by *TLL* s.v. 276.52–3 is Jul. Val. 1.42 *transmisso mari Persas ueluti hostes appellere.* Cf. 5.5.3n.

6.14.2–3 A. is fond of *ecphraseis* (4.31.4–7, 5.1nn.) of scenery; a particularly elaborate example, introduced with a self-conscious flourish, is the description of the robbers' lair at 4.6 (see Hijmans al. *ad loc.*). On the two passages as exx. of the *locus horridus,* antitype of the idyllic *locus amoenus* (5.1n.) see Schiesaro, esp. 219–22. In both the details suggest that he had in mind the natural or artificial cascades to be found in many Roman gardens and often depicted in mural art: see Grimal (1969) 293–9, (1986) I 243 and n. 26 and cf. 6.3.3n. Cf. Ovid's description of the grotto in which *simulauerat artem | ingenio natura suo, Met.* 3.158–9 and Bömer *ad loc.,* and Lucius' reference to *ars aemula naturae* at 2.4.7.

6.14.2 salebritate: (‡).

6.14.3 conuallem … incidebant: 6.8.7n.; for *incido* + accusative in this literal sense see *TLL* s.v. 1 *incido* 897.70–2.

6.14.4 These sleepless serpents recall the dragons that guarded the Golden Fleece (6.11.5–6n.) or the Apples of the Hesperides (Helm (1914) 203 = 224), *poma … ab insomni concustodita dracone,* Ov. *Met.*

9.190 and Bömer *ad loc.*   **proserpunt ecce:** Walter's correction of
F's *et* produces a readable text very economically but is not therefore
necessarily what A. wrote. Most edd. postulate the loss of a word
before *et*; an alternative approach is to keep *et* and read *saeuiunt* before
(Purser) or instead of (Frassinetti 125) *saeui*.   **inconiuae:** (*).
in perpetuam lucem ... excubantibus 'on the alert for perpetual
seeing', 'wakeful in unceasing vision' (Purser), rather than 'per-
pétuellement ouvertes à la lumière' (Vallette); for *lux* used of the
eyesight see *OLD* s.v. 8. For final/consecutive *in* in *Met.* cf. Callebat
(1968) 227–8.

6.14.5 ipsae semet: for the usual *semet ipsae*; *semet* is not very
common in A. (some ten instances), but there is no call to emend.

6.14.6 impossibilitate: (*) but common after A.   **praesenti ...
aberat:** Donatus on Ter. *Andr.* 24 *'adeste' non ut absentibus dicit, quippe
qui corporibus praesto erant, sed 'intenti estote'*; cf. *TLL* s.v. *absum* 209.1–5.

6.15.1 nec 'but': 4.32.1n.   **Prouidentiae bonae:** 5.3.1n.
graues 'august', 'authoritative' (*OLD* s.v. 13) rather than 'serious'.
animae: 5.6.9n.   **illa** 'the famous', 'that very'. The grammatical
gender of *aquila* is here, as usual, feminine, but he is a male bird
(below, §6 *innoxius*). Cf. 8.4.4, 5.5–6 *aper immanis atque inuisitatus* etc.
... bestiam ... illa.   **propansis:** (†) but *propessi* conjectured at
Acc. *Trag.* 255 Ribbeck[3].

6.15.2 pocillatorem: (†) apart from Glosses.   **deique numen
... percolens** ~ 5.25.6 *Cupidinem deorum maximum percole*. Cupid's off-
stage role is now made explicit. The story of the abduction of
Ganymede was so familiar that A. does not need to name him: see e.g.
Bömer on Ov. *Met.* 10.155–61. Cupid's participation in the rape is
attested in art: Helbig nos. 154–5, 157, *LIMC* IV 1.156–7 (Ganymedes
10, 27, 49), 159–62 (84–5, 96 (Eros guiding the eagle), 104, 107, 138,
140 (E. riding the eagle), 165), 165 (243).   **Diales uias** 'Jove's
pathways' (Purser); cf. 8.8.4 *uelut ... ipso Diali fulmine percussa* 'as if
smitten with Jove's thunderbolt'. There is no need to postulate a
special sense 'aerial', 'heavenly' (*OLD*).

6.15.3 alioquin et imparts an emphasis not unlike that of Greek
ἄλλως τε καί; Psyche is naive in general and inexperienced in this

sort of situation in particular. Cf. 5.22.1n.   **truculenti** 'dangerous';
cf. Hes. *Theog.* 792 'it flows out from the rock, a great trouble to the
gods' (μέγα πῆμα θεοῖσιν), Paus. 8.18.4 'its water is death to men
and to all animals'.

6.15.4 uel fando 'if only by report': 6.14.1n., *OLD* s.v. *for* 1b, Pease
on Cic. *N.D.* 1.82. On this 'impersonal' use of the gerund see Austin
on Virg. *Aen.* 2.81. Cf. 5.21.3n.   **cĕdo** 'give', imperative: *OLD* s.v.
cedo^2.

6.15.5 adrepta complexaque: sc. *urnula*; none of the various corrections of F's text is superior to Leo's, but it cannot be regarded as
certain. *complexa* is passive: *OLD* s.v. *complector* headn.   **libratisque
pinnarum nutantium molibus** 'balancing the vastness of his
swaying wings', a vivid word-picture of the hovering motion of a huge
bird. *nuto* in this sense is found elsewhere only at Catull. 66.53
impellens nutantibus aera pennis; *moles* of wings (the unusual plural
heightens the effect) only here (*TLL* s.v. 1345.12–13). The aspect of
the perfect participle is, as often, contemporaneous: Kenney on
Lucret. 3.171.   **genas saeuientium dentium** 'the jaws with their
ferocious teeth', descriptive genitive.   **trisulca uibramina (*)**
'three-forked flickerings'; Virg. *Aen.* 2.475 (= *G.* 3.439) *linguis micat ore
trisulcis* and Austin *ad loc. uibramen* otherwise only at Fulg. *Aet. mund.*
p. 148. 8 Helm and in Glosses.   **remigium ... porrigens** 'extending his oarage now to the left, now to the right', i.e. banking
between the hazards, another vivid phrase. On *remigium* see 5.25.1n.

6.15.6 innoxius: sc. while the going was good.   **paulo facilior:**
merely a little easier, presumably because (*Hesiodo teste*) the only
accredited messenger was Iris; but Venus' name would at least put
the snakes off their stroke.

6.16.2 flagitia 'outrages', 'shameful treatment', an extension of the
usual sense of 'shameful conduct'; cf. 1.6.2 *quae facies? quod flagitium?*
'What have they done to you?' 'Disgrace' is too mild for what Venus
would intend. There is no parallel for the sense apparently demanded
by the context and assumed by commentators, 'punishments'.
ridens exitiabile ~ 6.13.2 *subridens amarum* and n.   **malefica: (*)**
subst. = 'witch'; only here in A.

6.16.3–20.6 The last and most elaborate of Psyche's trials exploits a well-worn literary theme, the Catabasis or Descent to the Underworld, familiar from Homer (*Od.* 11, esp. 568–635), Aristophanes (*Frogs*), Virgil (*G.* 4.467–84, *Aen.* 6.268–899), Ovid (*Met.* 4.432–80) and the p̄s.-Virgilian *Culex* (214ff.). It is Virgil above all to whom A. is indebted. This episode too has been explained as derived from the 'water of life' theme (6.13.5n.): Hoevels 201–2.

6.16.4–5 This deceitful description of the mission allows A. an opportunity for witty by-play. Venus is usually the lender, not the borrower, in such transactions, as when she lends Hera her cestus (Hom̄. *Il.* 14.197–223) or when Athene makes Penelope especially beautiful (*Od.* 18.190–4); it is clearly to this latter passage that A. is indebted for the idea of beauty as a salve or chrism (Fehling 20): 'immortal beauty such as that with which Cytherea is anointed whenever she dances with the Graces'. Translation of this last motif into a visit to the theatre introduces another contemporary allusion.

6.16.4 petit ... mittas: 5.6.4n.   **ei:** 5.26.7n.

6.16.5 haud immaturius 'pretty quickly': cf. 2.18.3 *caue regrediare cena maturius*, 5.20.6n.   **theatrum deorum:** Venus' wish to look her best suggests that 'theatre' rather than 'assembly' (6.23.1n.) is meant. A.'s Olympus, like Ovid's (*Met.* 1.168–76), is an urban sort of place.

6.17.1 ultro 'actually', 'even': *OLD* s.v. 3a. Cf. *Apol.* 91 (p. 101.5 Helm) *formam mulieris et aetatem ipsi ultro improbauerunt.*

6.17.2 pergit ad quampiam turrim: the idea that jumping off a tower is the most convenient route to Hades can only have been suggested to A. by Heracles' sarcastic advice to Dionysus in Aristophanes' *Frogs.* (But cf. Hor. *Epod.* 17.70, Tib. 2.6.39–40, cit. Herrmann 22.) Cf. esp. *recte atque pulcherrime* ~ *Ran.* 127 (ἀτραπὸν) ταχεῖαν καὶ κατάντη 'a fast downhill road', *suis pedibus* ~ 128 ὡς ὄντος γε μὴ βαδιστικοῦ 'as I'm no great walker' (Dietze 141, Helm (1914) 204 = 225). That the tower should assume the role of cicerone taken previously by Circe, Heracles and the Sibyl is a piece of gratuitous pleasantry; cf. the quasi-apology at 6.20.1. Whereas ants, reed and eagle, living things, can plausibly respond to the power of Cupid, impressionable and communicative masonry is a different matter.   **sese   datura   praecipitem:**   her   fifth   attempt

(5.25.2n.).   **pulcherrime** 'neatly', 'elegantly', ironical: *OLD* s.v. *pulchre* 2c.

6.17.3 isto: 5.31.2n.

6.18.1 Lacedaemo ... Taenarum: Taenarus, now Cape Matapan, the southernmost point of the Peloponnese. The identification was traditional (Apollod 2.5.12, N–H on Hor. *C.* 1.34.10); Pausanias (3.25.5) notes sceptically that 'no road leads underground through the cave'. On the geographical implications for A.'s conduct of the story cf. 6.8.5n.

6.18.2 spiraculum Ditis ... monstratur: Virg. *G.* 4.467 *Taenarias ... fauces, alta ostia Ditis*, *Aen.* 7.568–9 *hic specus horrendum et saeui spiracula Ditis | monstrantur.* 'This description is virtually a mosaic of Virgilian phrases' (Walsh (1970) 57); cf. Wright (J. R. G.) 280–1. **inuium** 'forbidden', lit. 'pathless', sc. for the living; cf. Virg. *Aen.* 6.154–5 *sic demum lucos Stygis et regna inuia uiuis | aspicies.*   **canale derecto:** the *uia decliuis* and *adcliuis trames* of Ovid's descriptions, *Met.* 4.432, 7.410, 10.53; cf. Virg. *Aen.* 6.126 *facilis descensus Auerno.* For *canalis* = 'beaten track' cf. 9.11.3 *incurua spatia flexuosi canalis* (of a donkey-mill); cf. *TLL* s.v. 225.63–75 – apparently a colloquial usage.

6.18.3 hactenus 'thus', sc. as now; cf. 3.20.4 *omnibus abiectis amiculis hactenus denique intecti atque nudati* 'and so at last completely naked': *TLL* s.v. *hic* 2752.17–21. Robertson, however (on 3.20.4), where see also van der Paardt, understands it as = *prorsus.*   **offas polentae mulso concretas:** the traditional 'sop for Cerberus' (6.19.3–4); cf. Virg. *Aen.* 6.420–1 *melle soporatam et medicatis frugibus offam | obicit.* **duas ... stipes:** the return fare (6.18.7, 6.19.6); cf. Ar. *Ran.* 140 (and Stanford *ad loc.*), 270. It was usual to put a coin in the mouth of the dead: Callim. fr. 278 Pfeiffer, Juv. 3.267 *nec habet quem porrigat ore trientem.* Psyche is not dead but needs to have both hands free for the sops.

6.18.4 The three encounters designed by Venus to entrap Psyche (6.19.1) sound like ritual ordeals: cf. 5.5.3n. They have no real parallels in classical literature or myth (but see below, §8n.), and analogies in folktale are not very close: see Arnott (1962). Walsh (1970) 222–3 detects a parallel between the lame donkey and his driver and the donkey in the procession of Isis *pinnis adglutinatis* *adambulantem seni debili* (11.8.4), but the significance of the latter is itself far from clear (cf. Vallette *ad loc.*). Other references to lameness in the novel (Lucius: 3.27.6, 4.4.2, 6.26.1, 8, 6.30.4; a groom: 9.27.1; an initiate seen in a dream: 11.27.5) do not seem particularly relevant. For compulsory silence as a feature of mystery religions and religious ceremonies see Richardson on *Hom. Hymn* 2 (Demeter).478–9. See also below, §8, 6.19.1nn.   **rogabit ... porrigas:** 5.6.4n.   **ei:** 5.26.7n.; cf. below, §8 *eum.*

6.18.5 flumen mortuorum: Styx.   **praefectus ... portorium:** Charon is characterized in contemporary *officialese* as a harbour-master collecting tolls; Virgil, followed by Ovid, had styled him *portitor* (*G.* 4.502, *Aen.* 6.298, 326; *Met.* 10.73). Cf. below, §6 *exactor* and n.   **sic** 'thus (and only thus)', i.e. on these terms, when payment has been made: *OLD* s.v. 8a. Cf. below, §7 *sic tamen ut ...* and n.   **ad ripam ulteriorem:** Virg. *Aen.* 6.314 *ripae ulterioris amore.*   **sutili cumba:** Virg. *Aen.* 6.413–14 *cumba | sutilis.*

6.18.6 et inter mortuos auaritia uiuit: Ar. *Ran.* 141–2 'What power two obols have the world over! How did they get down there?' Cf. next n.   **Ditis exactor tantus deus:** Robertson's brilliant correction continues the parody of official language (above, §5n.). *Dis* was derived from *diues*; cf. Cic. *N.D.* 2.66 *Diti patri ... qui diues ut apud Graecos* Πλούτων (~ πλοῦτος 'wealth'). A. humorously implies a mundane commercial source for Dis's (Pluto's) fabled riches; the usual explanation is that of Cicero (*loc. cit.*), *quia et recidunt omnia in terras et oriuntur a terris* (cf. Pease *ad loc.*). *Ditis portitor* (Gronovius) is less pointed, but receives support from Virgil, who thrice (*G.* 4.502, *Aen.* 6.298, 326) so refers to Charon. For *deus* cf. Virg. *Aen.* 6.304 *cruda deo uiridisque senectus, CIL* VIII 8992 *deo Charoni Iulius Anabus uotum soluit.* At Cic. *N.D.* 3.43 Cotta is made to repudiate Charon's claims to divinity (cf. Pease *ad loc.*). For the Underworld and its gods as greedy cf. Virg. *G.* 2.492 *strepitumque Acherontis auari*, Stat. *Theb.* 4.474, Tarrant on Sen. *Ag.* 752.

6.18.7 squalido: Virg. *Aen.* 6.299 *terribili squalore Charon* etc. **dabis:** fut. for imperative, precisely as in English; common from Plautus onwards.   **sic tamen ut ...** 'but (only) on condition that ...'; she must not put down her *offae.*

6.18.8 This 'temptation' was evidently suggested by the episode in which the dead Palinurus begs Aeneas for a lift across the Styx and is refused as ineligible because unburied (Virg. *Aen.* 6.337–83); the word *pietate* recalls Aeneas' leading quality.   **pigrum fluentum:** cf. 6.13.4 *Stygias ... paludes*, Virg. *Aen.* 6.296 *turbidus ... caeno ... gurges*, 107 *tenebrosa palus*, 323 *Stygiam ... paludem*, Ar. *Ran.* 145–6 'a mass of muck and ever-flowing sewage'.   **eum:** 5.26.7n.

6.19.1 As a general rule it was prudent to heed such appeals, as such old women had a habit of turning out to be goddesses in disguise: Hom. *Il.* 3.383–420 (Aphrodite and Helen), *Hom. Hymn* 2 (Demeter).98–303 (Demeter and Celeus: Richardson on 101), Callim. *Hymn* 6.42–65 (Demeter and Erysichthon), A.R. 3.66–75 (Hera and Jason: Vian–Delage *ad loc.*), Virg. *Aen.* 7.415–57 (Allecto and Turnus), Ov. *Met.* 6.26–44 (Athene and Arachne), *F.* 4.507–62 (Ceres and Celeus). Cf. Arnott (1962) 243, who notes that in Scandinavian myth the heroine is normally instructed to help in such circumstances; Hoevels 206, pointing out that in fairytales helpfulness is universally the order of the day.   **orabunt ... accommodes:** 5.6.4n.

6.19.2 polentacium (‡) damnum 'barley-meal loss'; cf. *polentarius* at Plaut. *Curc.* 295. For such replacements of the genitive by an adjective cf. e.g. 5.8.4 *coniugale ... praeceptum*, 6.20.3 *Veneriam legationem*, 5.21.5n.

6.19.3 canis ... teriugo (*) ... capite: Virg. *Aen.* 6.417–18 *Cerberus haec ingens latratu regna trifauci | personat aduerso recubans immanis in antro.* A. gives him the usual number of heads (cf. Frazer on Apollod. 2.5.12, N–H on Hor. *C.* 2.13.34) but achieves originality by using a very rare word for 'triple', otherwise found only at Auson. 18.4.11, p. 226 Peiper and the anon. *Carmen de figuris* 145.   **oblatrans ... territando:** Virg. *Aen.* 6.400–1 *licet ingens ianitor antro | aeternum latrans exsanguis terreat umbras.*   **atra atria:** A. was evidently aware of the current etymology of *atrium* from *ater*: *TLL*, Ernout–Meillet s.v. *atrium.*   **uacuam Ditis domum:** cf. Virg. *Aen.* 6.269 *perque domos Ditis uacuas et inania regna.*

6.19.4 offrenatum: elsewhere only at Plaut. *Capt.* 755 and *Apol.* 77 (p. 86.14–15 Helm).   **unius offulae praeda** 'by the reward (consisting) of one cake', defining genitive. Cf. 6.20.2 *offulae cibo.*

6.19.5 panem sordidum ~ 6.11.2 *frusto cibarii panis*. This and the warning against accepting a seat seem to have more to do with the idea of suffering as the price of salvation than that of a trap to keep Psyche in the Underworld, though that idea naturally comes to mind with mention of Proserpine.   **esto** 'eat', imperative of *ĕdo*.

6.19.6 recalcans ... uestigia = 9.11.3. *recolo* is not attested in this sense (*OLD* s.v. 1 should be corrected).   **caelestium siderum ... chorum:** for the stars as a 'heavenly choir' cf. A. *De mundo* 1 (p. 137.17 Thomas), 30 (p. 165.15), *De deo Socr.* 2 (p. 8.4). The Latin poets (Tib. 2.1.88, Manil. 2.118) took the conceit over from the Greek (Eur. *El.* 467, Diggle on Eur. *Phaeth.* 66).   **redies** = *redibis* (as at 3.25.3): such forms, rare in the classical period, became common in biblical and church Latin: N–W III 326–8, Murgatroyd on Tib. 1.4.27.

6.19.7 This and the sequel recall the story of Pandora's 'box' (West on Hes. *W. & D.* 94), but the transmitted version of the Pandora legend nowhere explicitly mentions a ban on opening the receptacle. (For this idea cf. the story of Erichthonius: Apollod. 3.14.6, Ov. *Met.* 2.552–61.) In the context the Orpheus legend is perhaps a more likely influence (6.20.5n.). Nor does Isis' *cista secretorum* (11.11.2), *pace* Walsh (1970) 223, offer a really convincing parallel; cf. 6.18.4n. However, whatever the source of the motif, the point of the prohibition lies in the reference to *diuina formonsitas*: cf. 5.3.4 ... *meos explorare uultus, quos ... non uidebis si uideris*. This second test of her obedience she also fails.   **curiosius temptare thensaurum:** it is anybody's guess which of several possible verbs has fallen out and whether it preceded or followed *curiosius*; see crit. n.

6.20.1 turris illa prospicua (‡): an arch aside to the reader; cf. 6.17.2n. For *prospicuus* 'foreseeing' cf. 1.21.8, 11.18.3 *prospicue* 'providently'; attestations of the word in other (late Christian) sources are extremely dubious.

6.20.1–4 A.'s rapid and elegant paraphrase of the tower's instructions as Psyche enacts them follows the conventions of post-Homeric narrative. In the *Iliad* and the *Odyssey* such passages are usually repeated verbatim with the minimum of necessary change. Cf. Introd. pp. 37–8.

6.20.1–2 nec morata ... penetrat: three main verbs and seven participles, six of them in the abl. absolute, articulate this fast-moving sentence; cf. §§3–4 following, Introd. p. 34 n. 153.

6.20.1 sumptisque: A. does not care to hold up the action by telling us how or where.

6.20.2 offulae cibo ~ 6.19.4 *offulae praeda* and n.

6.20.3 nec ... uel: 5.19.2n.

6.20.4 longe uegetior 'with a much more lively step' – ironical in view of what is to follow.

6.20.5 mentem capitur: 1.13.1 *tremore uiscera quatior*, Lucret. 1.13 *perculsae corda tua ui*, Virg. *Aen.* 3.47 *mentem formidine pressus*. For this accusative of respect cf. e.g. Williams on *Aen.* 5.135, K–S 1 291, H–S 36–7.   **temeraria curiositate:** in succumbing to this, her be-setting weakness, on the very last stage of her mission, Psyche resembles Orpheus: Virg. *G.* 4.485, 488, 491–3 *iamque pedem referens casus euaserat omnis | ... | cum subita incautum dementia cepit amantem | ... | immemor heu! uictusque animi respexit: ibi omnis | effusus labor atque immitis rupta tyranni | foedera.*

6.20.6 inepta ego ... quae: 6.9.6n.   **nec ... quidem:** 5.5.5n. **delibo:** 6.5.2n.   **uel sic ... placitura:** 6.8.3, 6.14.1nn.

6.21.1 et cum dicto: like *nec mora, cum* (5.6.1n.) a favourite phrase of A.'s (apparently his own invention), though this is the only instance in *Cupid & Psyche* (Bernhard 50: 18 in all *Met.*). Cf. 5.24.5n.   **nec quicquam ... rerum** 'nothing at all', on the analogy of the common (colloquial) *quid rerum? = quid?*; see Bömer on Ov. *Met.* 12.62, Callebat (1968) 190.   **infernus somnus ac uere Stygius:** i.e. death. Cf. 11.23.7 (Lucius on his Isiac initiation) *accessi confinium mortis et calcato Proserpinae limine per omnia uectus elementa remeaui.* For apparent death as a motif in the novel cf. Xen. *Eph.* 3.6–7, Chariton 1.6–10, *Hist. Apoll. Reg. Tyr.* 25–6, al. (Hoevels 213 n. 209). Here, however, Psyche's condition can only be a metaphor for the spiritual death of the soul that is wholly given over to the wrong kind of love, and from this plight only Love in its higher guise can rescue it; cf. Plut. *Amat.* 764–5, Walsh (1981) 29–30, Kenney (1990) 193–4.   **coperculo**

reuelatus 'uncovered by (the removal of) the lid'; the expression is slightly strained (cf. *OLD* s.v. *reuelo* 1a), but more pointed than Jahn's colourless *releuatus* 'relieved of its covering'. *reuelo* occurs some eight times in *Met.*, *releuo* not at all.   **soporis nebula** ~ 2.30.3 *iniecta somni nebula.*

6.21.2 A. has created an impasse which only a *deus ex machina* can resolve. Cupid (Eros) as an emblem of salvation is attested in art (Schlam (1976) 26–7); but here the motivation is specifically Platonic (see preceding n.). The manner of his re-entry into the plot is somewhat reminiscent of the 'with one bound our hero was free' of the older style of penny dreadful. In intervening to save a soul whose only claim to salvation is desperate need (rather than merit acquired through suffering or good works) he is like Isis rescuing Lucius in Book XI. However, his escape from his room via the window is in the best tradition of elegiac intrigue: Prop. 4.7.16 *mea nocturnis trita fenestra dolis*, Ov. *A.A.* 2.245–6 *at tu per praeceps tecto delabere aperto,* | *det quoque furtiuas alta fenestra uias*, 3.605, 644, *F.* 6.577–8; cf. the vase-paintings of scenes from phlyax-plays (Trenkner 129–30, Trendall–Webster 143).   **solidata:** for *solido* as a medical term cf. Cels. 8.4.17, 8.6.1.

Act V Psyche felix

6.21.3 aliquanta '(quite) some', i.e. a good deal; cf. 1.24.5 *aliquantum multum*, 5.26.1n.   **longe uelocius** 'very fast': 5.20.6n.   **detersoque ... recondito** ~ 1 *crassa ... nebula.*   **innoxio punctulo:** for once his arrow is not harmful. Why that should be so in this instance is not spelled out; the implication must be that Psyche is now awakened to a true perception of Love (cf. 6.21.1n.). There is a curious parallel to this scene at Stat. *Silv.* 2.3.26–30, where Diana alerts a sleeping nymph to danger by touching her with (the blunt end of) an arrow; but it is not easy (*pace* Reitzenstein 158) to see any connexion.

6.21.4 perieras: sc. had I not appeared; cf. Hor. *C.* 2.17.27–9 *me truncus illapsus cerebro* | *sustulerat* [had as good as done for me] *nisi Faunus ictum* | *dextra leuasset* and N–H *ad loc.*   **sed interim etc.:** Cupid becomes curt and official: *prouincia* = 'duty', 'official mission'. *uidero* = 'I'll see to it' is colloquial (Callebat (1968) 502); cf. 5.10.3n.

amator leuis 'her fickle lover', the first and most obvious sense, with an allusion to 5.24.4 *feci leuiter*; Cupid now reverts to his initial role of wanton irresponsible boy (see 6.22–24n.). But *leuis* can also be construed (i) as acc. pl. with *pinnas* (cf. e.g. Ov. *Am.* 3.5.21, *Met.* 2.581, al.; *TLL* s.v. 1203.43ff.) or (ii) predicatively with *se dedit* = 'nimbly'. These ambiguities must be deliberate: see Kenney (1990) 194.   **in pinnas se dedit:** on the analogy of *se in pedes dare* (Plaut. *Capt.* 121): *OLD* s.v. *do*[1] 19b. Cf. 5.25.1 *praecipitem sese dedit*, 5.27.2 *se . . . praecipitem dedit*.

6.22–24 For the last scene of the story, laid on a traditional literary Olympus, Cupid is once more figured as the wayward godling of epigram, elegy, and Apollonian epic. This is not only awkward on the purely technical plane; it obscures the application of the story to the novel as a whole, for the allegory, to be effective, ought to end with an emphasis on the idea of love as a high and ennobling force. Cf. 6.22.1n., Introd. pp. 20, 25–6, Kenney (1990) 194–5.

6.22.1 interea: 4.32.1n.   **amore nimio peresus:** Virg. *Aen.* 6.442 . . . *quos durus amor crudeli tabe peredit*. With no more interval than that implied by the foregoing *interea* Cupid is transformed from powerful rescuer to an ailing and apprehensive child. By commonsense standards this is implausible: what cause has he now to fear his mother's *repentina sobrietas* if he is strong enough to escape and exercise his powers? Robertson's *sociam Sobrietatem* does not confront this difficulty. The figure of the chastened Eros (Cupid) is familiar in literature and art: *A. Plan.* 195–9, Schlam (1976) 15–17, *LIMC* III 1.884–5 (Eros 417–26), 966–9 (Amor/Cupid 64–87).   **aegra facie:** sc. with love: Ov. *A.A.* 1.729–38 and Hollis *ad loc.*, Pichon 81 s.v. *aeger*. The love-god himself betrays the tell-tale symptoms.   **ad armillum redit** 'reverted to type', lit. returned to the winejar (Otto s.v. *anus* 4), an unflattering equivalent of the more urbane *ad ingenium redire* (Ter. *Ad.* 71, *Hec.* 113); cf. 9.29.1 *ad armillum reuertit et ad familiares feminarum artes accenditur* etc. The implication can only be that Cupid's behaviour in the interval has been out of character. In the sense that it is not this Cupid (Amor II) but Love in his higher (Platonic–Isiac) guise (Amor I) who has been actively controlling events this is strictly true, but by his choice of phrase A. seems to go out of his way to draw attention to the switch of identities. Cf. 6.7.2n. on *caelo demeat*, Kenney (1990) 194–5.

6.22.2 prehensa ... buccula etc.: A.R. 3.149–50 'She pulled his face (ἐπειρύσσασα παρειάς) to hers and kissed him' (cf. 4.31.4n.), Suet. *Galba* 4.1 *constat Augustum puero adhuc ... apprehensa buccula dixisse* etc., Serv. on *Aen.* 1.256 OSCVLA LIBAVIT ... *id est, contigit, scilicet ut nos solemus cum blandimentis quibusdam sinistram maxillam contingere liberorum ac deinde ad os nostrum dextram referre.*   **consauiat (†):** read *consauiatur*? The word is deponent at 2.13.5, its only other occurrence in Latin, and *sauior* is always deponent in A.: 2.10.3, 4.31.4, 10.22.1.

6.22.3 domine fili 'dear boy'; Cupid's parentage was much debated (5.29.6n.) but his many attributed fathers did not generally include Jupiter (cf. Pease on Cic. *N.D.* 3.60); see however Eur. *Hipp.* 534 and Barrett *ad loc.* For *filius* used without reference to fatherhood cf. 9.27.4 *fili* 'my boy', Fronto, *Amic.* 2.7, p. 181 v.d. Hout (192 Naber) (to a former pupil) *haue mi domine fili carissime*: *OLD* s.v. 3. For this affectionate use of *dominus* see *TLL* s.v. 1925.75–8, (in epitaphs) 1926.43–52. **concessu deum decretum:** Cic. *Tim.* 52 *philosophiam ... quo bono nullum praestantius neque datum est mortalium generi deorum concessu atque munere neque dabitur.*   **pectus ... quo ... disponuntur:** the breast rather than the head was thought of as the seat of the will and the intellect as well as of the emotions: Munro on Lucret. 3.140, *OLD* s.v. *pectus* 3a, 6. This summary of Jupiter's sway owes more to contemporary philosophy than to traditional mythology, in which the fundamental workings of the universe are governed by Fate. Cf. A. *Plat.* 1.11 (p. 95. 8–10 Thomas) *unus et solus summus ille, ultramundanus, incorporeus, quem patrem et architectum huius diuini orbis superius ostendimus.*   **terrenae libidinis ... casibus** 'incidents of earth(l)y lust', characterizing genitive.

6.22.4 contraque leges etc.: cf. 4.30.4–31.3n. On the *lex Iulia de adulteriis* see Berger s.v. It was passed in 18 B.C. and was of fundamental importance: 'Augustus for the first time made adultery by a woman, and condonation of it by her husband, a crime' (Crook 106). Cf. e.g. Juv. 2.37 (the cry of an ostensibly stern moralist) *ubi nunc lex Iulia dormis?*, Stat. *Silv.* 5.2.102 (*cum*) *castum uibraret Iulia fulmen.* **disciplinamque publicam** ~ 4.30.4.   **in serpentes etc.:** every transformation in this list of Jupiter's disguises except one is found (with others) in the description of Arachne's tapestry at Ov. *Met.* 6.103–14, which A. clearly had in mind. The exception (*feras*) occurs in the tale of Apollo's delinquencies, ibid. 123–4 *ut ... terga leonis | gesserit.* Zeus similarly reproaches Eros at Lucian 79 (*Dial. deor.*).6(2).1. The words *sordide reformando* may glance at Lucius' transformation, also the result of *terrena libido.*

6.22.5 inter istas meas manus creueris: cf. 6.23.2. This is not otherwise attested, but Jupiter needs a pretext for coming the heavy father.   **aemulos tuos cauere:** Ov. *Am.* 1.4.45–6 *multa miser timeo, quia feci multa proterue,* | *exemplique metu torqueor ipse mei,* 2.19.34 *ei mihi, ne monitis torquear ipse meis.*   **ac si qua nunc . . . :** this stipulation of a *quid pro quo* (to be read as an aside?) effectively deflates the preceding pomposities. Jupiter, like Cupid, *ad armillum redit.*

6.23 The Council of the Gods is a stock feature of epic from Homer onwards. The theme had been burlesqued in Latin by Lucilius, who seems to have set the fashion of making the gods follow the procedures of the Roman Senate (Coffey 43), Seneca in the *Apocolocyntosis,* and Ovid in the *Metamorphoses* (1.167–76). In Greek it was exploited satirically by Lucian in the *Concilium Deorum* and *Icaromenippus* and by the Emperor Julian in his *Caesares.* On possible Hellenistic models see Coffey 175.

6.23.1 sic fatus: an epic cliché: *TLL* s.v. *for* 1030.47–51, and cf. 5.5.1n.   **si qui:** for the more usual *si quis;* possibly colloquial, but A.'s usage, if the MSS are true to it, is not consistent (6.7.4, 6.8.2 *si quis;* both, however, before vowels): Löfstedt II 78–96, esp. 94, Callebat (1968) 289–90.   **in poenam ... conuentum iri** 'would be sued for a fine': *OLD* s.v. *conuenio* 2b. *nummum = sestertium;* this short form of the genitive plural is usual in words denoting weights and measures (N–W I 166–72, Sommer 349). Fines for non-attendance at meetings of the Senate had been increased by Augustus (Dio Cass. 54.18.3, 55.3.2; cf. Gell. 14.7.10).   **caelesti theatro:** cf. 6.16.5n. From the late Hellenistic period on Greek assemblies were commonly held in theatres: cf. Lucius' spoof trial at 3.2.6–9, Chariton 3.4.4, 8.7.1, Heliod. 4.19.5 and Rattenbury *ad loc.,* Juv. 10.128 and Mayor *ad loc.*   **pro sede sublimi:** Ov. *Met.* 1.178 *celsior ipse loco.* For *pro =* 'on' (a seat of honour) see *OLD* s.v. *pro*[1] 2a.

6.23.2 dei conscripti Musarum albo: a parody of official terminology. Senators were addressed as *patres conscripti* (as are the gods in Sen. *Apoc.*), and the Muses, daughters of Mnemosyne (Memory), are the natural custodians of the Olympian equivalent of the *album senatorium*, the roll of the House. Cf. Lucian 21 (*Jup. Trag.*).15 ὦ ἄνδρες θεοί. **adolescentem ... scitis:** a variant of the colloquial proleptic 'I know thee who thou art' construction (H–S 471–2, Bennett II 222–4), but with an indirect statement instead of the usual indirect question or *ut/ne/dum*-clause. For *quod* + subjunctive in indirect statement instead of the classical accusative + infinitive cf. e.g. 4.1.3 and Hijmans al. 24, 4.5.6, etc.; H–S 576–7. **alumnatus sim:** (*).

6.23.3 nuptialibus pedicis: [Plut.] *De educ. puer.* 13e 'Care should be taken to yoke (καταζεῦξαι) in marriage those under the sway of pleasures and resistant to reproof, for that is the safest bond (δεσμός) for young men'; Ach. Tat. 1.8.1 'Marriage! ... What have you done to be put in fetters?' Cf. Juv. 6.43 *stulta maritali iam porrigit ora capistro* and Kipling's 'terrible thorn-bit of marriage'. For the image cf. also *OLD* s.v. *catena* 4a, Pichon 102. 'Nous sommes au dénouement d'une comédie bourgeoise' (Grimal). **teneat, possideat:** it is tempting to add *habeat* with Brantz to complete the full formula, as at e.g. Plin. *Ep.* 1.16.1 *teneat habeat possideat*. **amoribus** 'his beloved': for this concrete use of the plural see *OLD* s.v. 1c.

6.23.4 et ad Venerem etc.: this looks back to Jupiter's reassurances at the beginning of the *Aeneid*, esp. *parce metu ... manent immota tuorum | fata tibi,* 1.257–8 ~ *nec prosapiae tantae tuae ... metuas.* **prosapiae ... statuque:** datt. with *metuas* 'fear for'. The form of the dat. in -*u* for -*ui* is used freely by poets for metrical convenience; it is relatively uncommon in prose (N–W I 542–6). **de** 'on account of': 5.19.3n. **nuptias non impares sed legitimas:** 6.9.6n. **iam faxo:** Jupiter takes up the words of and cancels Venus' threats at 4.30.3, 5.30.2. **iure ciuili congruas:** *iure,* if correct (*iuri* Jahn), is dative on the analogy of *iure dicundo* et sim.: N–W I 298–9, *TLL* s.v. 1 *ius* 679.2–6. This recalls Chariton's assurance that his story ends in 'legitimate loves and lawful marriages', ἔρωτες δίκαιοι ... καὶ νόμιμοι γάμοι (8.1.4), and the formal terms in which Hydaspes pronounces Theagenes and Chariclea man and wife, Heliod. 10.40.2.

6.23.5 per Mercurium: in his traditional role of Psychopompos, conductor of souls to the Underworld – here, however, to Heaven. **ambrosiae poculo:** cf. 5.22.5n. For ambrosia as a drink cf. Anaxandrides *ap.* Athen. 2.39A (II 160 Kock) 'I [Ganymede? Hunter, *Eubulus* p. 109] eat nectar, chewing it well, and drink ambrosia.' For its use to confer immortality cf. Ov. *Met.* 14.605–7 (Venus and Adonis) *genetrix diuino corpus odore | unxit et ambrosia cum dulci nectare mixta | contigit os fecitque deum.* (But nectar is drunk at 6.24.2.)   **immortalis esto, nec ...:** equivalent to a causal clause: 'now that you are (to be) immortal, Cupid will never leave you'.

6.24 'The opera ends amidst general rejoicing.' A divine banquet is another epic theme: Hom. *Il.* 1.601–11. The details of this one are closely paralleled at Lucian 24 (*Icarom.*).27–8.

6.24.1 nec mora, cum ...: 5.6.1n.   **summum torum:** cf. 7.9.1 *in summo puluinari locatus*; A. may have had in mind a *sigma* (5.3.2n.) rather than the traditional Roman arrangement of three tables, in which the order of precedence was *medius, summus, imus.* The construction *accumbo* + accusative (cf. 5.6.1n.) is an old Latin one revived by A.: *TLL* s.v. 340.26–9, 79–81.   **gremio suo complexus:** traditionally Roman women sat at table while their menfolk reclined, but the rule might be breached by the time of Cicero (*Fam.* 9.26.2 and Shackleton Bailey *ad loc.*) and was clearly a dead letter in Augustan society (Ov. *Am.* 1.4 *passim*). Cf. Juv. 2.119–20 *ingens | cena sedet, gremio iacuit noua nupta mariti.* In this respect Milo, Lucius' host at Hypata, was old-fashioned (1.22.7, Vallette *ad loc.*) – perhaps an accurate reflection of provincial conservatism?   **toti** 'all': 4.32.4n.

6.24.2 nectaris: no ancient reader needed to have this explained; the 'glossema putidissimum' (Price 322) *quod uinum deorum est* was rightly expelled by Wouwere. It was ingeniously defended by Oudendorp as an aside by the narratrix, *temulenta anicula* (6.25.1); but, unlike A.'s, her *persona* nowhere else intrudes into the story. See Introd. p. 22.   **pocillator (†):** Ganymede; cf. 6.15.2n.   **Liber:** Bacchus (Dionysus).   **ministrabat:** sc. *se*; cf. Virg. *Aen.* 8.180–1 *onerantque canistris | dona laboratae Cereris Bacchumque ministrant*, Eur. *Bacch.* 284 'He [Dionysus], being a god, is poured out to the gods', Ov. *A.A.* 1.231–2 and Hollis *ad loc.*, Lucian 24 (*Icarom.*).27 'Demeter provided bread,

Dionysus wine'. Bacchus offered much scope to the poets for meto-
nymical diversions; cf. next n.   **Vulcanus cenam coquebat:** A.
exploits the common metonymy by which the god = fire (*OLD* s.v. 2);
cf. *Moret.* 51 *dum ... suas peragit Vulcanus Vestaque partes*, i.e. while the
bread was baking.

6.24.3 Horae ... Gratiae: 5.28.7n.   **Musae ... Apollo:** Hom.
Il. 1.603-4 'and the gods enjoyed Apollo's lyre and the sweet singing
of the Muses'; cf. *Hom. Hymn* 3 (Apollo). 184-206.   **superingressa
(*)** 'making her entry on cue'; the word is found elsewhere
only (3 instances) in late Christian texts. Purser well compares the
ballet at 10.31.1 *super has introcessit alia ... designans Venerem*. Scaliger's
ingenious *suppari gressu* is disqualified by sense: *suppar* = 'almost/
approximately equal'.   **formonsa:** probably nominative singular
feminine used predicatively rather than adverbial accusative plural
neuter (5.9.1n.).   **aut tibias:** some connective is necessary, though
between *aut* (Oudendorp), *et* (Hildebrand) and *-ue* (Heinsius) the
choice verges on the arbitrary. Robertson reads ... *canerent, tibias
inflaret* (ζ) *Saturus, et Paniscus ad fistulam diceret* (ζ), but this lacks concinnity,
and the rustic *fistula* suits Saturus better than the *tibia*.   **Saturus
... Paniscus:** Cic. *N.D.* 3.43 *si Nymphae* [sc. *deae sunt*], *Panisci etiam et
Satyri?* On Panisci, little Pans, see Pease on Cic. *De div.* 1. 23. This
pastoral note recalls the wedding of Daphnis and Chloe, who set up
altars to Shepherd Eros and Soldier Pan (Longus 4.39.2; Hunter
36-7), but is in any case appropriate: *Per. Ven.* 76-7 *rura fecundat
uoluptas, rura Venerem sentiunt:* | *ipse Amor, puer Dionae, rure natus dicitur*;
cf. Tib. 2.1.67-8 *ipse quoque inter agros interque armenta Cupido* | *natus et
indomitas dicitur inter equas.* If the spelling of *Saturus* is A.'s own it may
reflect awareness of learned speculation connecting Satyrs and satire
(*satura*): see Diomedes, *GLK* 1 485 and cf. Wiseman 5 n. 39.

6.24.4 conuenit in manum: the technical phrase for the passing of
a wife from her father's power to her husband's: Berger s.v. *Manus*.
Voluptatem: A. springs a surprise. We have been led to believe that
the child would be a son (5.11.6, 5.12.5). In the immediate context of
a story designed to take Charite's mind off her troubles this cheerful
note provides an appropriate ending. With the birth of this divine
child there is restored to the world the (true) *uoluptas* in love of which
it was deprived by the secession of Venus and Cupid (5.28.5n.). In

the larger context of the *Metamorphoses* as a whole we recall that the first chapter of Book I ends *lector intende: laetaberis* and that the last words of Book XI are *gaudens obibam*. We also recall that Lucius, who heard and has just repeated the tale, is in the resumed action of the novel in danger of his life (6.26) because of his own surrender to *seruiles uoluptates* (11.15.1), and that he finally experiences *inexplicabilis uoluptas* in contemplating the image of Isis (11.24.5; cf. Walsh (1970) 192 and n. 5). We also recall that, though Voluptas has some claim to divinity in her own right (Pease on Cic. *N.D.* 2.61; cf. Hoevels 227 n. 24), she had been by Lucretius, who we have seen was in A.'s mind as he wrote, identified with Venus herself in the first line of the *De rerum natura*: *Aeneadum genetrix, hominum diuumque uoluptas* (cf. Kenney (1977) 13 and n. 26, Schlam (1976) 38–40). These and other ambiguities reflect those of the *Metamorphoses* as a whole; they do not justify the conclusion of Penwill (59) that 'we are not dealing with a *redemption* but a *fall*'. Cf. Kenney (1990) 196, Introd. p. 11.

Addendum

5.2.2 A. may be recalling Tibullus on the Golden Age: *tum, quibus adspirabat Amor, praebebat aperte | mitis in umbrosa gaudia ualle Venus. | nullus erat custos, nulla exclusura dolentes | ianua ...* (2.3.71–4).

WORKS CITED BY SHORT TITLE

Standard commentaries referred to by the name of the commentator (e.g. 'Bömer on Ov. *Met.* 1.466') are not included in this list.

Adams, J. N. (1982). *The Latin sexual vocabulary*. London.

Ahl, F. M. (1976). *Lucan. An introduction*. Ithaca and London.

Amat, J. (1972). 'Sur quelques aspects de l'esthétique baroque dans les *Métamorphoses* d'Apulée', *R.E.A.* 74: 107–52.

Anderson, G. (1982). *Eros Sophistes. Ancient novelists at play*. (American Classical Studies 9.) Chico, Calif.

Appel, G. (1909). *De Romanorum precationibus*. Giessen, repr. New York 1975.

Arndt, W. F. and Gingrich, F. W. (1957). *A Greek–English lexicon of the New Testament and other early Christian literature*. Chicago and Cambridge.

Arnott, W. G. (1962). 'Ocnus, with reference to a passage of Apuleius and to a black-figure lekythos in Palermo', *C. & M.* 23: 233–47.

    (1964). 'Notes on *gauia* and *mergus* in Latin authors', *C.Q.* 14: 249–62.

Augello, G. (1977). *Studi Apuleiani. Problemi di testo e loci vexati delle Metamorfosi*. Palermo.

    (1977–9). 'Nota apuleiana', *Annali del Liceo classico G. Garibaldi di Palermo* 14–16: 175–80.

Balme, M. G. and Morwood, J. H. W. (1976). *Cupid and Psyche. An adaptation from the Golden Ass of Apuleius*. Oxford.

Bell, A. J. (1923). *The Latin dual & poetic diction. Studies in numbers and figures*. London.

Bennett, C. E. (1910, 1914). *Syntax of early Latin*. I *The verb*; II *The cases*. Boston.

Berger, A. (1953). *Encyclopedic dictionary of Roman Law*. (*Trans. Amer. Philosophical Soc.* N.S. 43, 2.) Philadelphia.

Bernhard, M. (1927). *Der Stil des Apuleius von Madaura. Ein Beitrag zur Stilistik des Spätlateins*. (Tübinger Beiträge zur Altertumswissenschaft 2.) Stuttgart, repr. Amsterdam 1965.

Bettelheim, B. (1976). *The uses of enchantment. The meaning and importance of fairy tales*. London.

Bieler, L. (1933). 'Psyches dritte und vierte Arbeit bei Apuleius', *Archiv für Religionsgeschichte* 30: 242–70 = Binder–Merkelbach 334–69.

Binder, G. and Merkelbach, R. (edd.) (1968). *Amor und Psyche*. (Wege der Forschung 126.) Darmstadt.

Blase, H. (1903). *Tempora und Modi*, in (ed.) G. Landgraf, *Historische Grammatik der lateinischen Sprache*. III *Syntax des einfachen Satzes*. Leipzig.

Borgeaud, P. (1979). *Recherches sur le dieu Pan*. (Bibl. Helvetica Romana 17.) Geneva.

Bréguet, Esther. (1960). 'In una parce duobus', *Hommages Herrmann* (Coll. Latomus 44) 205–14. Brussels.

Brock, M. Dorothy. (1911). *Studies in Fronto and his age*. (Girton College Studies 5.) Cambridge.

Brotherton, Blanche. (1934). 'The introduction of characters by name in the *Metamorphoses* of Apuleius', *C.P.* 29: 36–52.

Bruggisser, P. (1989). 'L'appellation δεσπότης μου τῆς ψυχῆς dans la lettre P. Strasb. III 286', *M.H.* 46: 231–6.

Burkert, W. (1987). *Ancient mystery cults*. Cambridge, Mass. and London.

Butler, H. E. and Owen, A. S. (edd.) (1914). *Apulei Apologia sive Pro se de magia liber*. Oxford.

Calboli, G. (1968). 'Un ennianismo di Apuleio', *Athenaeum* 46: 72–9.

Callebat, L. (1964). 'L'archaïsme dans les *Métamorphoses* d'Apulée', *R.E.L.* 42: 346–61.

(1968). *Sermo cotidianus dans les Métamorphoses d'Apulée*. (Publ. de la Fac. des lettres et sc. hum. de l'Univ. de Caen 13.) Caen.

(1978). 'La prose des *Métamorphoses*: genèse et spécificité', in Hijmans–van der Paardt 167–87.

Camps, W. A. (1969). *An introduction to Virgil's Aeneid*. Oxford.

Capponi, F. (1987). 'Cruces Apuleiane', *Latomus* 46: 603–12.

Coffey, M. (1976). *Roman satire*. London, 2nd edn 1989.

Coleman, R. (ed.) (1977). *Vergil Eclogues*. Cambridge.

Copley, F. O. (1956). '*Exclusus amator*'. *A study in Latin love poetry*. (A.P.A. Philological Monographs 17.) Madison.

Crook, J. A. (1967). *Law and life of Rome*. London.

Curtius, E. R. (1953). *European literature and the Latin middle ages*, tr. W. R. Trask. London.

Dalmeyda, G. (ed.) (1926). *Xénophon d'Ephèse. Les Ephésiaques*. Paris.

Dietrich, B. C. (1966). 'The golden art of Apuleius', *G. & R.* 13: 189–206.

Dietze, J. (1900). 'Zum Märchen von Amor und Psyche', *Philol.* 59: 136–47.

Doughty, C. M. (1936). *Travels in Arabia Deserta*. New edn introd. T. E. Lawrence. 2 vols. London.

Dowden, K. (1979). Review of Fehling, *C.R.* 29: 314.

(1980). 'Eleven notes on the text of Apuleius' *Metamorphoses*', *C.Q.* 30: 218–26.

(1982a). 'Apuleius and the art of narration', *C.Q.* 32: 419–35.

(1982b). 'Psyche on the rock', *Latomus* 41: 336–52.

Dragonetti, Mariapina. (1981). 'Uso dei tempi e degli aspetti verbali a fini stilistici nella favola di Amore e Psiche di Apuleio', *Aevum* 55: 69–79.

Eliade, M. (1973). 'Myth in the nineteenth and twentieth centuries', in Wiener III 307–16.

Ernout, A. and Meillet, A. (1959, 1960). *Dictionnaire étymologique de la langue latine*. 4th edn 2 vols. Paris.

Fedeli, P. (1972). *Il carme 61 di Catullo*. (Seges 16.) Friburg.

Fehling, D. (1977). *Amor und Psyche: Die Schöpfung des Apuleius und ihre Einwirkung auf das Märchen, eine Kritik der romantischen Märchentheorie*. (Akad. d. Wiss. und d. Literatur: Abh. d. Geistes- und Sozialwissensch. Kl. 1977, nr. 9.) Wiesbaden.

Ferrari, G. R. F. (1987). *Listening to the cicadas. A study of Plato's 'Phaedrus'*. Cambridge.

Fick, N. (1969). 'Du palais d'Eros à la robe olympienne de Lucius', *R.E.L.* 47: 378–96.

Fletcher, A. (1973). 'Allegory in literary history', in Wiener I 41–8.

Fliedner, H. (1974). *Amor und Cupido. Untersuchungen über den römischen Liebesgott*. (Beiträge zur klass. Philol. 53.) Meisenheim am Glan.

Fowler, A. (1970). *Triumphal forms. Structural patterns in Elizabethan poetry*. Cambridge.

Fowler, D. (1987). 'Vergil on killing virgins', in (edd.) M. Whitby al. *Homo Viator. Classical essays for John Bramble*. Bristol.

Fraenkel, E. (1957). *Horace*. Oxford.

Frassinetti, P. (1960). '*Cruces* Apuleiane (Metamorfosi)', *Athenaeum* 38: 118–31.

Frazer, J. G. (1930–6). *The Golden Bough. A study in magic and religion.* 3rd edn 12 vols. London.

Fredouille, J.-C. (ed.) (1975). *Apulei Metamorphoseon Liber XI.* Paris.

Friedländer, L. (1921). 'Das Märchen von Amor und Psyche', in *Darstellungen aus der Sittengeschichte Roms* IV (9./10. Auflage, Leipzig) 104–21 = Binder–Merkelbach 16–43.

Fry, G. (1984). 'Philosophie et mystique de la destinée. Etude du thème de la Fortune dans les *Métamorphoses* d'Apulée', *Quad. Urb. di cultura classica* 47: 137–70.

Gargantini, Luisa. (1963). 'Ricerche intorno alla formazione dei temi nominali nelle metamorfosi di Apuleio', *Rend. Ist. Lombardo*, Classe di Lett. e Sc. Morali e Storiche 97: 33–43.

Gianotti, G. F. (1986). *'Romanzo' e ideologia. Studi sulle 'Metamorfosi' di Apuleio.* (Forme materiali e ideologie del mondo antico 26.) Naples.

Graur, A. (1969). '*Quidam* chez Apulée', in (ed.) J. Bibauw, *Hommages M. Renard* (Coll. Latomus 101–3) I 378–82.

Graves, R. (1950). *The Transformations of Lucius otherwise known as the Golden Ass by Lucius Apuleius.* Harmondsworth.

Grimal, P. (ed.) (1963). *Apulei Metamorphoseis* IV, 28 – V, 24. Paris, 2nd edn 1976.

    (1969). *Les jardins romains.* 2nd edn Paris.

    (1986). *Rome, la littérature et l'histoire.* (Coll. de l'Ecole Française de Rome 93.) 2 vols. Rome.

Guthrie, W. K. C. (1975). *A history of Greek philosophy.* IV *Plato. The man and his dialogues: earlier period.* Cambridge.

Gwynn Griffiths, J. (1975). *Apuleius of Madauros. The Isis-Book (Metamorphoses, Book XI).* Leiden.

    (1978). 'Isis in the *Metamorphoses* of Apuleius', in Hijmans–van der Paardt 141–66.

Hägg, T. (1983). *The novel in antiquity.* 2nd (English) edn Oxford.

Haight, Elizabeth H. (1927). *Apuleius and his influence.* New York, repr. 1963.

Harrauer, Christine. (1983). 'Lector, intende, laetaberis', *W.S.* N.F. 17: 126–36.

Harrison, S. J. (1988). 'Three notes on Apuleius', *C.Q.* 38: 265–7.

Haupt, M. (1875, 1876, 1876). *Opuscula.* 3 vols. Leipzig.

Häussler, R. (1968). *Nachträge zu A. Otto* ... [q.v.]. Darmstadt.

Heine, R. (1978). 'Picaresque novel versus allegory', in Hijmans–van der Paardt 25–42.

Heiserman, A. (1977). *The novel before the novel. Essays and discussions about the beginnings of prose fiction in the West.* Chicago and London.

Helbig, W. (1868). *Wandgemälde der von Vesuv verschütterten Städte Campaniens.* Leipzig.

Heller, S. (1983). 'Apuleius, Platonic dualism, and eleven', *A.J.P.* 104: 321–39.

Helm, R. (1913). *Apulei Platonici Madaurensis Metamorphoseon Libri XI.* 2nd edn Leipzig. (3rd edn 1931, repr. w. *addenda* 1968.)

(1914). 'Das "Märchen" von Amor und Psyche', *Neue Jahrb. für das klass. Altertum* 33: 170–209 = Binder–Merkelbach 175–234.

Helm, R. (1957). '*Ceterum* bei Apuleius', *W.S.* 70: 131–47.

Herescu, N. I. (1960). *La poésie latine. Etude des structures phoniques.* Paris.

Herrmann, L. (1952). 'Légendes locales et thèmes littéraires dans le conte de Psyché', *Ant. Class.* 21: 13–27.

Hijmans, B. L. (1978). 'Significant names and their function in Apuleius' *Metamorphoses*', in Hijmans–van der Paardt 107–22.

Hijmans, B. L. al. (1977). *Apuleius Madaurensis Metamorphoses Book IV 1–27* ed. B. L. Hijmans, R. Th. van der Paardt, E. R. Smits, R. E. H. Westendorp Boerma, A. G. Westerbrink. Groningen.

Hijmans, B. L. and van der Paardt, R. Th. (edd.) (1978). *Aspects of Apuleius' Golden Ass.* Groningen.

Hinds, S. (1987). 'Generalising about Ovid', *Ramus* 16: 4–31.

Hoevels, F. E. (1979). *Märchen und Magie in den Metamorphosen des Apuleius von Madaura.* (Studies in Classical Antiquity 1.) Amsterdam.

Hogarth, D. G. (1910). *Accidents of an antiquary's life.* London.

(1925). *The wandering scholar.* London.

Hooker, W. (1955). 'Apuleius's "Cupid and Psyche" as a Platonic myth', *The Bucknell Review* 5, 3: 24–38.

Hopwood, K. (1989). 'Bandits, elites and rural order', in (ed.) A. Wallace-Hadrill, *Patronage in ancient society.* London and New York.

Horsfall, N. M. (1982). 'Allecto and *natura*. A pattern of allusion in Apuleius', *L.C.M.* 7: 41.

Hunter, R. L. (1983). *A study of 'Daphnis & Chloe'.* Cambridge.

Jeanmaire, H. (1930). 'Le conte d'Amour et de Psyché', *Bull. de l'Inst. Français de sociologie* 1: 29–48 = Binder–Merkelbach 313–33.

Kajanto, I. (1961). *Ovid's conception of Fate.* (Annales Univ. Turkuensis Ser. B 80.) Turku.

(1981). 'Fortuna', *ANRW* II 17.1: 502–58.

Kenney, E. J. (1970). 'Doctus Lucretius', *Mnem.* 4, 23: 366–92 = (ed.) C. J. Classen, *Probleme der Lukrezforschung* (Hildesheim 1986) 237–65.

(ed.) (1971). *Lucretius De Rerum Natura Book III.* Cambridge, corr. repr. 1984.

(1973). 'The style of the *Metamorphoses*', in (ed.) J. W. Binns, *Ovid* 116–53. London.

(1977). *Lucretius.* (Greece & Rome New Surveys in the Classics 11.) Oxford.

(ed.) (1984). *The Ploughman's Lunch. Moretum: a poem ascribed to Virgil.* Bristol.

(1986). *Ovid, Metamorphoses* tr. A. D. Melville with introd. and notes by E. J. Kenney. Oxford, publ. in 'World's Classics' 1987.

(1990). 'Psyche and her mysterious husband', in (ed.) D. A. Russell, *Antonine literature* 175–98. Oxford.

Knox, P. E. (1986). *Ovid's 'Metamorphoses' and the traditions of Augustan poetry.* (Cambridge Philological Society Suppl. vol. 11.) Cambridge.

Labhardt, A. (1960). '*Curiositas.* Notes sur l'histoire d'un mot et d'une notion', *M.H.* 17: 206–24.

Lancel, S. (1987). 'Y a-t-il une *Africitas?*', *R.E.L.* 63: 161–82.

Lausdei, C. (1983). 'Alcune note alle *Metamorfosi* di Apuleio', *Prometheus* 9: 232–42.

Leach, Eleanor W. (1988). *The rhetoric of space. Literary and artistic representations of landscape in Republican and Augustan Rome.* Princeton, N.J.

Leo, F. (1912). *Plautinische Forschungen zur Kritik und Geschichte der Komödie.* 2. Auflage. Berlin, repr. Darmstadt 1966.

(1913). *Geschichte der römischen Literatur.* 1 *Die archaische Literatur.* [All pubd.] Berlin, repr. 1967.

Lier, B. (1914). *Ad topica carminum amatoriorum symbolae.* Progr. Stettin, repr. New York and London 1978.

Lilja, Saara (1965). *The Roman elegists' attitude to women.* (Annales Acad. Scient. Fennicae 135, 1.) Helsinki.

Lindsay, W. M. (1907). *Syntax of Plautus.* Oxford, repr. New York 1936.

Löfstedt, E. (1942, 1933). *Syntactica. Studien und Beiträge zur historischen*

Syntax des Lateins. I *Über einige Grundfragen der lateinischen Nominal-syntax.* 2nd edn. II *Syntaktisch-stilistische Gesichtspunkte und Probleme,* repr. 1956. Lund.

MacKay, L. A. (1965). 'The sin of the Golden Ass', *Arion* 4: 474–80.

Mantero, Teresa (1973). *Amore e Psiche. Struttura di una 'fiaba di magia'.* Genoa.

Marangoni, C. (1985). 'Un *lusus* etimologico sul nome di Mercurio (Apul. *met.* 6, 8)', *Atene e Roma* 30: 52–65.

Marshall, P. K. (1983). 'Apuleius. *Apologia, Metamorphoses, Florida*', in (ed.) L. D. Reynolds, *Texts and transmission. A survey of the Latin classics* 15–16. Oxford.

Mason, H. J. (1978). 'Fabula Graecanica: Apuleius and his Greek sources', in Hijmans–van der Paardt 1–15.

  (1983). 'The distinction of Lucius in Apuleius' *Metamorphoses*', *Phoenix* 37: 135–43.

Médan, P. (1925). *La latinité d'Apulée dans les Métamorphoses. Etude de grammaire et de stylistique.* Paris.

Mellet, Sylvie (1987). 'Présent de narration et parfait dans le conte de Psyché', *R.E.L.* 63: 148–60.

Meo, C. de (1983). *Lingue techniche del Latino.* (Testi e manuali per l'insegnamento universitario del Latino 16.) Bologna.

Merkelbach, R. (1958). 'Eros und Psyche', *Philol.* 102: 103–16 = Binder–Merkelbach 392–407.

Millar, F. (1981). 'The world of the Golden Ass', *J.R.S.* 101: 63–75.

Molinié, G. (ed.) (1979). *Chariton, Le roman de Chairéas et Callirhoé.* Paris.

Moore, J. L. (1891). 'Servius on the tropes and figures of Virgil', *A.J.P.* 12: 157–92, 267–92.

Müller, C.F.W. (1908). *Syntax des Nominativs und Akkusativs im Lateinischen. Hist. Gr. d. lat. Sprache* [see under Blase], Supplement. Leipzig and Berlin.

Murgatroyd, P. (1975). '*Militia amoris* and the Roman elegists', *Latomus* 34: 59–79.

Nethercut, W. R. (1968). 'Apuleius' literary art. Resonance and depth in the *Metamorphoses*', *C.J.* 64: 110–19.

Nettleship, H. (1892). 'Notes on Latin lexicography', *J.P.* 20: 175–84.

Norden, E. (1915). *Die antike Kunstprosa vom VI. Jahrhundert v. Chr. bis in die Zeit der Renaissance.* 3rd edn Berlin, repr. 1958.

(1923). *Agnostos Theos. Untersuchungen zur Formengeschichte religiöser Rede.* 3rd edn Leipzig and Berlin, repr. Stuttgart 1956.

Otto, A. (1890). *Die Sprichwörter und sprichwortlichen Redensarten der Römer.* Leipzig.

Palmer, L. R. (1954). *The Latin language.* London.

Paratore, E. (ed.) (1948). *Apulei Metamorphoseon Libri IV–VI (La favola di Amore e Psiche).* (Bibl. di studi superiori 1.) Florence.

Parke, H. W. and Wormell, D. E. W. (1956). *The Delphic Oracle.* 2 vols. Oxford.

Pasoli, E. (1966). 'De Apulei testimonio ad vocum Venus, veneror, venia originem et significationem pertinenti', *Latinitas* 14: 192–204.

Pasquali, G. (1981). *Preistoria della poesia romana.* New edn introd. S. Timpanaro. Florence.

Pavlovskis, Zoja (1973). *Man in an artificial landscape. The marvels of civilization in Imperial Roman literature.* (Mnemosyne Suppl. 25.) Leiden.

Penwill, J. L. (1975). 'Slavish pleasures and thoughtless curiosity: fall and redemption in Apuleius' *Metamorphoses*', *Ramus* 4: 49–82.

Perry, B. E. (1967). *The ancient romances. A literary-historical account of their origins.* (Sather Classical Lectures 37.) Berkeley and Los Angeles.

Pichon, R. (1902). *De sermone amatorio apud Latinos elegiarum scriptores.* Paris [*Index verborum amatoriorum* = pp. 75–303 repr. Hildesheim 1966.]

Platnauer, M. (1951). *Latin elegiac verse. A study of the metrical usages of Tibullus, Propertius & Ovid.* Cambridge.

Preston, K. (1916). *Studies in the diction of the Sermo Amatorius in Roman Comedy.* Chicago, repr. New York and London 1978.

Price, J. (ed.) (1635). *L. Apuleii Madaurensis Metamorphoseos Libri XI.* Paris. [References in this edn are to the edition pubd at Gouda 1650.]

Purser, L. C. (ed.) (1910). *The story of Cupid and Psyche as related by Apuleius.* London, repr. New Rochelle 1983.

Raby, F. J. E. (1957). *A history of secular Latin poetry in the Middle Ages.* 2nd edn 2 vols. Oxford.

Rambaux, C. (1985). *Trois analyses de l'Amour. Catulle: Poésies. Ovide: les Amours. Apulée: le conte de Psyché.* Paris.

Reitzenstein, R. (1912). *Das Märchen von Amor und Psyche bei Apuleius.* Leipzig = Binder–Merkelbach 87–158.

Robertson, D. S. (ed.) and Vallette, P. (trans.) (1940, 1946, 1945). *Apulée. Les Métamorphoses.* 3 vols. Paris.

Roccavini, Anna M. (1979). 'La nozione di fortuna nelle Metamorfosi', in A. Pennacini al., *Apuleio, letterato, filosofo, mago* 167–77. Bologna.

Rohde, E. (1898). *Psyche. Seelenkult und Unsterblichkeitsglaube der Griechen.* 2nd edn Freiburg i. B., Leipzig, Tübingen, repr. Darmstadt 1961. Eng. tr. W. B. Hills, London and New York 1925, repr. New York 1966.

——— (1914). *Der griechische Roman und seine Vorläufer.* 3rd edn Leipzig, repr. introd. K. Kerényi Darmstadt 1960.

Rostowzew, M. (1911). 'Die hellenistisch-römische Architektur-landschaft', *Mitt. d. kaiserl. deutschen Archaeologischen Inst. Röm. Abteilung* 26: 1–185.

Russell, D. A. and Winterbottom, M. (1972). *Ancient literary criticism. The principal texts in a new translation.* Oxford.

Sandy, G. N. (1972). 'Knowledge and curiosity in Apuleius' *Metamorphoses*', *Latomus* 31: 179–83.

——— (1972–3). 'Foreshadowing and suspense in Apuleius' *Metamorphoses*', *C.J.* 68: 232–5.

——— (1978). 'Book 11: ballast or anchor?', in Hijmans–van der Paardt 123–40.

Schanz, M., Hosius, C. and Krüger, G. (1922). *Geschichte der römischen Literatur zum Gesetzgebungswerk des Kaisers Justinian.* 3. Teil *Die Zeit von Hadrian 117 bis auf Constantin 324.* 3rd edn Munich.

Schiesaro, A. (1985). 'Il "locus horridus" nelle "Metamorfosi" di Apuleio', *Maia* N.S. 37: 211–23.

Schissel, O. (1941). 'Die Ethopoiie der Psyche bei Apuleius Met. IV 34', *Hermes* 76: 106–11.

Schlam, C. C. (1968). 'The curiosity of the Golden Ass', *C.J.* 64: 120–5.

——— (1976). *Cupid and Psyche. Apuleius and the monuments.* University Park, Pa.

Schönbeck, G. (1962). *Der Locus Amoenus von Homer bis Horaz.* Heidelberg.

Scobie, A. (1969). *Aspects of the ancient romance and its heritage. Essays on*

Apuleius, Petronius and the Greek Romances. Meisenheim am Glan.

(1973). *More essays on the ancient romance and its heritage.* Meisenheim am Glan.

(1975). *Apuleius' Metamorphoses I: a commentary.* Meisenheim am Glan.

(1978a). 'The structure of Apuleius' *Metamorphoses*', in Hijmans–van der Paardt 43–61.

(1978b). 'The influence of Apuleius' *Metamorphoses* in Renaissance Italy and Spain', in Hijmans–van der Paardt 211–30.

Scotti, Mariateresa (1982). 'Il proemio delle *Metamorfosi* tra Ovidio ed Apuleio', *G.I.F.* 34: 43–65.

Seaford, R. A. S. (1987). 'The tragic wedding', *J.R.S.* 107: 106–30.

Shackleton Bailey, D. R. (1988). 'On Apuleius' *Metamorphoses*', *R.M.* 131: 167–77.

Skutsch, O. (1963) 'The structure of the Propertian *Monobiblos*', *C.P.* 58: 238–9.

(1985). *The 'Annals' of Q. Ennius.* Oxford, corr. repr. 1986.

Smet, R. de (1987). 'The erotic adventures of Lucius and Photis in Apuleius' *Metamorphoses*', *Latomus* 46: 613–23.

Smith, W. S. (1972). 'The narrative voice in Apuleius' *Metamorphoses*', *T.A.P.A.* 103: 513–34.

Sommer, F. (1948). *Handbuch der lateinischen Laut- und Formenlehre.* Heidelberg.

Spies, A. (1930). *Militat omnis amans. Ein Beitrag zur Bildersprache der antiken Erotik.* Tübingen, repr. New York and London 1978.

Stabryła, L. S. (1973). 'The functions of the tale of Cupid and Psyche in the structure of the Metamorphoses of Apuleius', *Eos* 61: 261–72.

Summers, R. G. (1973). 'A note on the date of *The Golden Ass*', *A.J.P.* 94: 375–83.

Swahn, J.-Ö. (1955). *The tale of Cupid and Psyche.* Lund.

Szepessy, T. (1972). 'The story of the girl who died on the day of her wedding', *A. Ant. Hung.* 20: 341–57.

Tatum, J. (1969). 'The tales in Apuleius' *Metamorphoses*', *T.A.P.A.* 100: 487–527.

(1972). 'Apuleius and metamorphosis', *A.J.P.* 93: 306–13.

(1979). *Apuleius and 'The Golden Ass'.* Ithaca and London.

(1982). 'Apuleius', in (ed.) T. J. Luce, *Ancient writers. Greece and*

Rome II 1099–1116. New York.

Traina, A. (1975). *Poeti latini (e neolatini). Note e saggi filologici*. Bologna.

Trendall, A. D. and Webster, T. B. L. (1971). *Illustrations of Greek drama*. London.

Trenkner, Sophie (1958). *The Greek Novella in the classical period*. Cambridge.

Vallette, see under Robertson–Vallette.

van der Paardt, R. Th. (1978). 'Various aspects of narrative technique in Apuleius' *Metamorphoses*', in (edd.) Hijmans–van der Paardt 75–94.

van Thiel, H. (1971). *Der Eselsroman*. (Zetemata 54, 1 & 2.) 2 vols. Munich.

Ventris, M. and Chadwick, J. (1973). *Documents in Mycenaean Greek*. 2nd edn Cambridge.

Wagenvoort, H. (1953/4). 'Apuleius' Sprookje van Amor en Psyche', *Jaarboek d. konink. Nederl. Akad. van Wetensch*. 243–52 = Binder–Merkelbach 382–91.

Walsh, P. G. (1970). *The Roman novel*. Cambridge.

    (1974). Review of van Thiel, *C.R.* 24: 215–18.

    (1978) 'Petronius and Apuleius', in Hijmans–van der Paardt 17–24.

    (1981). 'Apuleius and Plutarch', in (edd.) H. J. Blumenthal and R. A. Markus, *Neoplatonism and early Christian thought. Essays in honour of A. H. Armstrong* 20–32. London.

Webster, T. B. L. (1964). *Hellenistic poetry and art*. London.

Westerbrink, A. G. (1978). 'Some parodies in Apuleius' *Metamorphoses*', in Hijmans–van der Paardt 63–73.

Westman, R. (1961). *Das Futurpartizip als Ausdrucksmittel bei Seneca*. (Soc. Scient. Fennica Comm. Human. Litt. 27. 3.) Helsinki–Helsingfors.

Whittaker, T. (1923). *Macrobius or philosophy, science and letters in the year 400*. Cambridge.

Wiener, P. P. (ed.) (1973). *Dictionary of the history of ideas*. 4 vols. New York.

Wilkinson, L. P. (1963). *Golden Latin artistry*. Cambridge.

Winkler, J. J. (1985). *Auctor & Actor. A narratological reading of Apuleius's* Golden Ass. Berkeley, Los Angeles and London.

Wiseman, T. P. (1988). 'Satyrs in Rome? The background to Horace's *Ars Poetica*', *J.R.S.* 78: 1–13.

Wlosok, Antonie (1969). 'Zur Einheit der Metamorphosen des Apuleius', *Philol.* 113: 68–84.

Wright, Constance S. (1973). ' "No art at all": a note on the prooemium of Apuleius' *Metamorphoses*', *C.P.* 68: 217–19.

Wright, J. R. G. (1971). 'Folk-tale and literary technique in *Cupid and Psyche*', *C.Q.* 21: 273–84.

INDEXES

References are to lemmata in the Commentary.

1 Latin words

abscondo (intrans.), 6.12.4
adulo (for *adulor*), 5.14.1
alienus, 5.25.1
alioquin, 5.22.1, 6.15.3
aliquam (= 'a lot'), 5.26.1
aliquantus (= 'a lot'), 6.21.3
alius (=*alter*), 5.3.5
almus (in active sense), 4.30.1; (as epithet of Venus and Ceres), 6.2.1
altrinsecus (as prep. + genit.), 5.2.1
aquila (gender and sex of), 6.15.1
at (apodotic), 5.28.1
atque (emphatic), 5.4.5; (unelided in verse), 4.33.1.4

bene, quod . . ., 6.8.7

Caelum/-us, 6.6.4
certus (+ genit.), 6.10.5
ciuitas, 4.28.1
complector (-*exus* passive), 6.15.5
consauio(r), 6.22.2
construo, 6.6.1
cuius (adj.), 5.15.3
cum (after *nec mora*), 5.6.1, 6.24.1
curiositas, 5.6.6

denique (= 'indeed'), 4.28.3; (= 'thus'), 5.8.3, 5.9.1
dominus, 6.1.2, 6.22.3
domuitio, 4.35.2
dum (= 'by . . .'), 5.6.4; (+ subj. in temporal clause), 5.26.5

en, 4.30.1
e re nata (et sim.), 5.8.4, 5.27.1
et (= *etiam*), 5.23.1; ('explicative'), 4.33.2.8; (for *cum* in 'inverse'

construction), 5.27.1; (= 'for instance'), 5.9.3

facio (+ *se* = 'betake oneself'), 5.2.1
fallacia (-*e* abl.), 5.27.5
faxo (= *fecero*), 4.30.3
filius, 6.22.3
flagitium, 6.16.2
flagro, fragro (orthography of), 4.31.3
floreo, 5.12.1, 6.11.5
formonse, 5.22.2
formonsitas etc. (orthography of), 4.28.3
furia (sing.), 6.12.5

gentes (sing. in sense), 4.32.4
genus (in *id genus* et sim.), 5.1.3

hactenus, 6.18.3
hauritus (= *haustus*), 6.13.5
hercules (exclam.), 5.9.6

iam (= δέ), 5.1.5
ille, 5.4.6, 5.11.1, 5.15.1, 5.22.2, 5.23.4, 5.24.4, 5.28.2, 5.28.6, 6.10.5, 6.15.1; (emphatic), 6.12.1; (= def. article), 5.7.1, 5.7.5; (not distinguished from *iste*), 4.34.6
-im (adverbs in), 6.1.5
in (final-consecutive), 6.14.4; (instrumental), 5.13.5
Iouis (nom. = *Iuppiter*), 4.33.2.7
ipse (emphatic), 4.35.4, 5.1.1
is (for *se, suus*), 5.26.7, 6.16.4, 6.18.4, 6.18.8
iste (not distinguished from *ille*), 4.34.6; (not = def. article), 5.5.3; *isto* (dat.), 5.31.2, 6.17.3

238

ius (*iure* dat.), 6.23.4

labes, 5.8.5
lamentor, 4.33.3
licet (w. abl. abs.), 5.1.6; (= *quamuis*), 6.1.1
locus (collective pl.), 5.2.1
longe (as prep. + genit.), 5.9.3; (= 'very'), 5.11.3, 6.8.3

mi (for *mea* voc.), 5.16.3
Milesia (sc. *fabula*), 4.32.6
mutor (in middle sense), 5.22.1

namque (postponed), 5.19.3
ne . . . neue . . . nec, 5.6.6
nec (adversative), 4.32.1, 6.15.1; (connective), 5.13.5; (elliptical), 6.13.3; (= *ne . . . quidem*), 5.3.5, 5.6.2, 5.9.4, 5.10.7, 5.11.5, 5.13.5, 5.14.1
nec . . . ac ne . . . quidem, 4.28.2; cf. 4.29.3, 5.10.7
nec . . . nec (w. subj. for *ne . . . neue*), 5.5.3, 6.12.2
nec . . . quidem (= *ne . . . quidem*), 5.5.5, 6.5.2, 6.20.6
nec . . . saltem (= *ne . . . quidem*), 4.32.1; cf. 5.27.3, 6.13.2
nec . . . uel, 5.19.2, 6.20.3
nedum (w. *ut*), 5.10.8
nescius (passive), 5.12.2
neue (rarity of in *Met.*), 5.6.6
nullus (emphatic), 4.32.2

paeniteo (personal), 5.6.3, 5.22.2
parricida (= πατραλοίας), 5.30.1
persono (pf. forms of), 5.12.4
populi (sing. in sense), 4.29.4, 5.10.8, 5.31.6, 6.10.7
Psyche (genit. of), 5.6.9, 5.13.4, 6.2.5, 6.8.4
puluinar (sing. = 'shrine'), 6.1.3

quantus (pl. = *quot*), 5.9.5
-que . . . et, 5.15.1

qui (for *quis* in condit. clause), 6.23.1
qui (abl. = 'how'), 6.5.4; (= 'whereby' w. pl. antecedent), 6.7.4
quidam (in weakened sense = *aliquis*, 'a'), 5.3.3, 5.8.4, 6.1.2, 6.16.2
quidem . . . uerum (= μὲν . . . δέ), 5.19.1
quod (= *quoad*), 5.13.1
quod (w. subj. in indirect speech), 6.23.2

redies (= *redibis*), 6.19.6
refluus, 4.31.4

satis, 4.30.4, 5.8.3, 5.23.1, 5.28.6
scilicet, 5.17.3, 5.23.5, 5.24.4, 5.25.2, 5.26.5, 5.31.2, 6.1.5; cf. p. 23 n. 105
se(se) (in reciprocal sense), 5.7.5, 5.9.1, 5.16.1
sic (in wishes or prayers), 5.13.3; (= 'on that condition'), 6.18.5, 6.18.7
solet (impersonal), 6.1.4
solidum (adv. = 'thoroughly'), 5.28.6
subaudio, 5.19.2
sui (for *suus*), 5.3.1
susurrus (heteroclite), 5.6.10
suus (not referring to subject of sentence), 6.13.1
suus sibi, 4.32.1, 5.1.6

tantus (pl. = *tot*), 6.10.4
tenebra (sing.), 5.20.4
totus (pl. = 'all'), 4.32.4, 5.1.6, 5.11.1, 6.2.2, 6.24.1

-ue (= 'and'), 5.8.3
uel, 6.5.3, 6.14.1, 6.15.4, 6.20.6
uel . . . uel (for *aut . . . aut*), 5.11.5, 5.12.6, 5.16.3
uidero/-is/-it, 5.10.3, 6.21.4
uindico (w. *in* + accus.), 4.31.2
unde (+ genit.), 5.15.3
unde scio an? (= *haud scio an*), 6.1.2
unus (= *alter*), 5.26.1
utique (prosody of), 5.29.4

2 General

ablative
  absolute w. *licet*, 5.1.6
  adnominal, 4.28.1
  causal/instrumental, 4.28.2,
    5.12.1, 5.12.2, 5.15.4, 5.21.3,
    5.27.2
  descriptive/qualifying, 4.28.1,
    4.30.4, 5.16.2
  locative, 5.4.4
  of origin (w. *prouenio*), 5.13.3
accusative
  adnominal ('retained'), 4.35.2
  adverbial, 4.29.1, 5.1.1, 5.9.1,
    5.21.3, 5.22.6, 6.2.1, 6.6.3,
    6.13.2, 6.16.2, 6.24.3
  internal/cognate, 4.28.4, 5.9.7,
    5.31.1, 6.11.1
  of respect, 5.15.1, 5.17.3, 5.22.1,
    6.20.5
  in phrases of type *id genus* = indecl.
    adj., 5.1.3
  w. verbs: *accedo*, 5.4.1; *accumbo*,
    6.24.1; *accubo*, 5.6.1; *adsum*,
    5.5.3; *affero*, 5.3.5; *appello*,
    6.14.1; *fungor*, 5.13.2; *grauor*,
    5.10.5; *incido*, 6.8.7, 6.14.3;
    inuolo, 5.24.2; *peruolo*, 5.17.1;
    suadeo, 5.6.6, 5.11.4
Ammianus, 5.7.2, 5.10.3, 5.31.1
amphibole, 6.4.4
Andromeda, 4.32.2, 4.33, 4.34.1,
    4.35.4
Apollonius, 4.30.4–31.3, 4.31.4,
    5.29.5, 5.30.5, 5.31.3–7,
    6.11.5–6, 6.22.2
Apuleius (authorial references to),
    4.32.6, 6.9.6
Arcadia, 5.25.3–6, 6.13.4
Aristophanes, 6.17.2

brachylogy, 6.3.3

Callimachus, 4.28.3, 4.29.2–3,
    4.29.4, 4.32.5, 4.33.4, 5.24.4,
    5.26–27, 6.24.4

colloquialisms, 4.31.2, 4.32.1, 4.33.3,
    5.2.1, 5.9.5, 5.11.5, 5.26.1,
    5.30.3, 6.4.3, 6.9.2, 6.10.1,
    6.18.2, 6.21.1, 6.21.4, 6.23.1
comparative (w. positive or
    superlative force), 5.20.6, 6.1.3,
    6.16.5, 6.21.3
'compendious comparison', 5.13.3
concord
  pl. verb w. sing. subject, 4.29.3
  sing. verb w. compound subject,
    5.22.7
  qui = 'whereby' w. pl. antecedent,
    6.7.4
Corippus, 5.1.6
Cupid
  dual nature of (cf. pp. 19–20): as
    'Amor I'', 5.3.1, 5.6.3, 5.6.9,
    5.11.4, 6.21.2; power of working
    through agents etc., 5.22.2,
    5.22.4, 5.22.5, 5.25.2, 5.25.4,
    6.10.5, 6.12.1, 6.15.2, 6.17.1; as
    'Amor II'', 4.30.4–31.3, 5.28.7,
    5.29.5, 5.30.1, 5.30.6, 6.20–24,
    6.22.1, 6.22.4; identities
    blended, 4.33, 5.22.5–7, 5.25.6,
    6.21.4, contrasted, 5.24.4; *see also*
    Venus
  as primeval/cosmogonical power,
    5.23.5, 5.31.4
  in love, 5.6.10, 5.24.4, 5.28.1
  name, plays on, 5.6.7, 5.14.5,
    5.23.3
  parentage, 5.29.6, 6.9.6, 6.22.3
  punished, 6.22.1

dative
  adnominal, 5.13.1
  form in -*u*, 4.31.7, 6.23.4
  of motion towards, 5.31.6
  predicative, 5.30.3
  w. verbs: *abnuo*, 6.6.1; *metuo*, 6.23.4;
    nascor, 4.34.6; *subnato*, 4.31.7
declension, heteroclite, 5.6.10, 5.27.5
diminutives, 5.18.4, 5.22.6

'do' for 'allow to be done' et sim., 5.8.4, 5.16.2

ecphrasis, 4.31.4–7, 5.1, 5.22.5–7, 6.14.2–3
ellipse
  of subject of verb in indirect speech, 5.18.1, 5.28.8, 5.29.5
  of verb to be, 4.32.3, 5.18.1, 5.29.5
  see also paratactic constructions
enallage, 4.29.2, 5.30.6, 6.6.1
Ennius, 4.32.4, 4.33.3, 6.6.4
epicisms, 4.31.4, 4.35.1, 5.5.1, 5.9.1, 5.20.5, 5.24.5, 5.31.1, 6.4.1, 6.7.2, 6.11.4, 6.23.1
Europa, 4.31.4–7, 4.35.4

Fate, 5.22.1; see also Fortune, Prouidentia
Fortune, 5.5.2, 5.9.2, 5.22.1, 6.5.1

Ganymede, 6.15.2, 6.24.2
genitive
  defining, 4.30.2, 5.14.1, 6.3.2, 6.6.1, 6.19.4, 6.20.2
  descriptive/characterizing, 6.15.5, 6.22.3
  of origin, 5.30.6
  partitive, 4.35.4, 5.6.5
  periphrastic, 6.21.1
  possessive, 6.12.1
  of respect, 4.32.4, 5.2.3, 5.2.4, 5.4.4, 5.17.2, 5.18.2, 5.18.4, 5.21.3, 5.22.1, 5.22.4, 5.28.3, 6.1.1, 6.2.2
  for adj., 5.8.4, 5.21.5, 6.1.1, 6.19.2, 6.20.3
  w. altrinsecus, 5.2.1; certus, 6.10.5; longe, 5.9.3; unde, 5.15.3
  in phrases of type hoc aetatis, 5.29.3, 6.12.2
gerund, 5.21.3, 6.15.4
Graecisms, 4.30.3, 4.34.4, 5.2.1, 5.8.4, 5.9.3, 5.19.2, 5.30.2, 5.30.6, 6.13.3; cf. 5.30.1

Hellenistic epigram, 4.33.4, 5.25.5, 5.31.2
hendiadys, 4.33.2.8, 6.11.4
Homer, 4.31.4–7, 5.1, 5.1.3, 5.22.2, 5.31.1, 6.4.1, 6.6.1, 6.7.2, 6.11.5–6, 6.12.4, 6.16.4–5, 6.24

imagery
  death: as bridal, 4.33.4; as sleep, 6.21.1
  girl as statue, 4.32.2
  marriage: as fetters, 6.23.3; as yoke, 6.4.3
  military, 5.11.3, 5.14.3, 5.19.5, 5.21.5, 5.24.1
  wounds of love, 4.30.4, 4.31.1, 4.32.4, 5.23.4, 5.25.4, 5.28.1
imperative
  'future' form, 5.6.3
  fut. simple used for, 6.18.7
indicative, see mood
indirect statement
  w. quod + subj., 6.23.2
  modulation from into direct, 5.28.4
infinitive of purpose, 6.9.2

'locus amoenus', 5.1; 'locus horridus', 6.14.2–3
Longus, 5.1, 5.23.3, 5.24.1, 6.1.3–4
Lucian, 5.30.5, 5.31.4, 6.22.4, 6.23, 6.24
Lucretius, 4.30, 4.30.1, 6.3.3, 6.6, 6.6.4, 6.24.4

Manilius, 4.33.1.2
Mercury
  associated w. Venus, 6.7.3
  identified w. logos, 6.8.1
  Psychopompos, 6.23.5
metonymy, 6.3.1–2, 6.24.2
mood
  indicative: in causal relative clause, 6.5.2, 6.20.6; in deliberative question, 4.34.6, 5.6.2, 5.16.1; in indirect question, 5.9.5, 5.11.3, 5.31.3; in past unreal condition, 6.21.4

subjunctive: generalizing (*scires*),
  5.1.3; giving attributed reason,
  5.28.4; limiting/restrictive (w.
  quoad), 5.13.1, 6.4.3; w. *dum* in
  temporal clause, 5.26.5; w. *ut*
  after *summa est*, 5.11.4
Moschus, 4.31.4–7, 5.31.2, 6.8.2–3

negative, double for emphasis,
  6.12.3, 6.13.1
negative nuance in positive question,
  5.11.3
neuter
  of adj. used adverbially: sing.,
    4.29.1, 5.1.1, 5.21.3, 5.28.6,
    6.2.1, 6.6.3, 6.13.2; pl., 5.9.1,
    5.22.6
  pl. in phrases of type *deuexa rupis*,
    4.35.4; cf. 5.27.3
  cupita n. pl. = 'the beloved', 5.6.4,
    5.23.5
number
  plural: *barbae* = 'beard', 4.31.6;
    chori = 'a choir', 5.15.2; *copiosi* =
    'numerous', 4.28.3, 5.3.3; *gentes*
    = 'people', 4.32.4; *loci* =
    'locality', 5.2.1; *populi* =
    'people', 4.29.4, 5.10.8, 5.31.6,
    6.10.7 (cf. *ceruices*, 5.22.5);
    'poetic', 5.17.3, 6.2.5;
    'rhetorical', 5.31.1
  singular: *articulus* = 'hand', 5.23.2;
    digitus = 'fingers', 4.28.3

Orpheus, 6.20.5
Ovid, 4.28.3, 4.29.3, 4.29.4, 4.30,
  4.30.1, 4.34.3, 5.1, 5.1.3, 5.2.2,
  5.6.9, 5.7.1, 5.10.3, 5.10.6,
  5.12.6, 5.13.1, 5.14.3, 5.16.4,
  5.17.3, 5.20.2, 5.20.3, 5.21.3–4,
  5.22.2, 5.22.7, 5.23.2–3, 5.24.1,
  5.25.2, 5.26.5, 5.27.2, 5.28.2,
  5.28.5, 5.28.7, 5.30.1, 5.30.3,
  5.30.4, 6.1.2, 6.2.5, 6.3.3, 6.4.2,
  6.6.1, 6.8.7, 6.9.4, 6.12.1,
  6.14.2–3, 6.16.5, 6.18.2, 6.22.4

oxymoron, 4.31.1, 5.1.6, 5.12.2,
  5.23.3

Pan, 5.25.3–6, 6.24.3
Pandora, 6.19.7
paratactic constructions, 4.30.3,
  5.6.4, 5.6.8, 5.13.2, 5.26.7,
  5.29.5, 5.30.2, 6.2.6, 6.7.4,
  6.11.6, 6.16.4, 6.18.4, 6.19.1
participles
  articulating sentence, 4.35.4,
    6.20.1–2
  future, 4.30.2, 6.8.3, 6.8.7, 6.12.1,
    6.14.1, 6.17.2, 6.20.6
  perfect: for acc. + inf., 4.34.4;
    contemporaneous in aspect,
    6.15.5
  passive, impersonal, 4.29.4, 4.33.3,
    4.35.1, 5.15.2
Petronius, 5.2.1
Plato, 5.1, 5.6.3, 5.12.6, 5.24.1,
  5.26–27, 5.28.7
pleonasm, 4.31.4, 4.33.4, 5.3.5,
  5.11.5, 5.24.5, 5.27.3
positive for superlative w. *quam*,
  5.16.5, 5.20.5
predicative expressions, 4.32.1,
  5.30.2, 6.11.4, 6.21.4, 6.24.3
prolepsis ('I know thee who thou
  art'), 6.23.2
Prouidentia, 5.3.1, 5.19.4, 6.15.1; *see
  also* Fate, Fortune
Psyche
  characterized: as tragic heroine,
    4.34.3–6, 6.5.3; as (implausibly)
    cunning and vindictive, 5.26–27,
    learned and eloquent, 6.2.3
  fails test of obedience, 5.3.4, 6.19.7
  name: first introduced, 4.30.5;
    played on, 4.34.3, 5.6.7, 5.6.9,
    5.7.6, 5.13.4, 5.31.2, 6.2.5,
    6.15.1
  spiritual death of, 6.21.1
  suicide intended or attempted,
    5.22.4, 5.25.2, 6.12.1, 6.14.1,
    6.17.2

tormented, 6.9.2

relative clauses
  causal, 6.5.2, 6.9.6, 6.20.6
  final-consecutive, 5.28.9
repetition, pointless, 5.10.1, 6.1.3
Roman references, 4.30.4–31.3,
  4.33.5, 5.26.6–7, 5.28.7, 5.29.6,
  6.4.3, 6.4.4–5, 6.4.4, 6.7.4,
  6.8.2, 6.9.6, 6.13.5, 6.16.4–5,
  6.16.5, 6.18.5, 6.18.6, 6.22.3,
  6.22.4, 6.23.1, 6.23.2, 6.23.3,
  6.23.4, 6.24.1, 6.24.4

Sappho, 4.31.1, 4.33.1.4, 5.25.5, 6.6.3
simple for compound verb, 6.6.4
Sirens, Platonic connotations of,
  5.12.6
subjunctive, see mood

Tacitus, 4.29.1
tenses
  future simple for imperative,
    6.18.7
  fut. pf., 4.30.3, 5.10.3, 5.24.5,
    6.21.4; for pres., 6.3.2
  imperfect, 4.34.4, 5.19.1
  pf.: 'gnomic', 5.4.5; part w.
    contemporaneous aspect, 6.15.5
  plupf., 5.4.3, 5.19.1, 6.21.4;
    'double', 5.7.1
  present, conative, 6.9.4
  sequence of, 5.6.6, 5.26.7, 6.7.5
  variation of in narrative, 4.29.1,
    5.2.1, 5.7.1, 5.23.1, 5.24.2,
    5.31.1, 6.7.5, 6.13.1

Venus
  burlesqued, 5.28.9, 5.30.3
  dual nature of (cf. pp. 19–20): as
  'Venus I', 4.31.4–7, 6.6, 6.6.4,
    6.7.2; as 'Venus II', 4.30.4–
    31.3, 5.28.7, 6.7.2, 6.8.3;
    identities blended, 4.30; see also
    Cupid
  identified with Fortune, 5.5.2
  parentage, 4.28.4, 5.29.2, 6.6.4,
    6.7.2, 6.7.3
Virgil, 4.30, 4.30.1, 4.30.4–31.3,
  4.30.5, 4.31.1, 4.31.4–7, 4.34.4,
  5.6.9, 5.8.5, 5.12.6, 5.13.3,
  5.13.6, 5.17.3, 5.19.5, 5.27.3,
  5.28.9, 5.30.4, 6.10.6, 6.11.5–6,
  6.12.4, 6.13.4, 6.14.1, 6.16.3–
  20.6, 6.18.2, 6.18.6, 6.18.8,
  6.23.4
Voluptas, 6.24.4

word-order
  chiasmus, 5.15.3
  framing, 5.20.2–5
  hyperbaton, 4.31.1, 5.31.3, 6.2.4
  namque postponed, 5.19.3
word-play, verbal ambiguity,
  etymology, 4.28.3, 4.28.4,
  4.31.4, 4.31.6, 4.31.7, 4.33
  passim, 4.34.5, 5.2.2, 5.3.5, 5.4.3,
  5.4.5, 5.5.4, 5.6.3, 5.6.7, 5.6.9,
  5.7.6, 5.9.7, 5.10.1, 5.11.4,
  5.12.2, 5.12.3, 5.13.4, 5.13.5,
  5.14.1, 5.16.5, 5.18.1, 5.19.4,
  5.19.5, 5.22.5, 5.23.3, 5.24.1,
  5.28.2, 5.29.2, 5.29.4, 5.30.1,
  5.31.2, 5.31.6, 6.2.5, 6.7.1, 6.7.2,
  6.8.1, 6.8.2, 6.8.5, 6.13.2, 6.13.3,
  6.15.1, 6.18.6, 6.19.3, 6.21.4,
  6.24.3

Zephyrus, 4.35.4
zeugma, 5.8.1, 5.12.4